Llewellyn's
Rid

"*Llewellyn's Complete Book of the Rider-Waite-Smith Tarot* is the most researched, authoritative text ever written on the world's most famous tarot deck. Sasha Graham has delivered a true masterpiece—and a book that every tarot buff or Rider-Waite-Smith lover will devour and refer to again and again. An instant classic you'll want on your bookshelf!"

Theresa Reed, author of *The Tarot Coloring Book*

"*Llewellyn's Complete Book of the Rider-Waite-Smith Tarot* is to date my favorite work about my favorite tarot deck…It consolidates the tarot's connections to the Hermetic Qabalah, numerology, astrology, and Golden Dawn mysticism in an easy-to-digest format. A new milestone in the written body of works on the Rider-Waite-Smith has been set. Graham delivers magnificently, blending the exoteric and esoteric with seamless rigor."

Benebell Wen, author of *Holistic Tarot*

"With *Llewellyn's Complete Book of the Rider-Waite-Smith Tarot*, Sasha Graham dives deep into the well of enchantment to offer up a perfectly balanced trinity of history, wisdom, and inspiration. This may be the ultimate book about the world's most famous tarot deck, for everything you ever imagined wanting to know about the Rider-Waite-Smith is here: from the story of its collaborative creation and esoteric roots and symbolism, to an insightful compendium of practical use and magical methodology. A thoughtfully written and virtuosic masterwork from a tarotist at the top of her powers."

Kris Waldherr, creator of *The Goddess Tarot*

"A teacher's greatest joy is when a student becomes a master. Sasha Graham has done just that, and we couldn't be more proud. Her latest book, *Llewellyn's Complete Book of the Rider-Waite-Smith Tarot,* is a beautifully organized, insightful, and thorough guide. But unlike some 'research' books, it's a delightful page-turner, filled with little-known anecdotes, artwork, and Sasha's magical storytelling. There's much to discover here, whether you have decades of experience or are just embarking on your tarot journey!"

Ruth Ann and Wald Amberstone, directors of the Tarot
School and coauthors of *Secret Language of Tarot*

"Ms. Graham certainly entertains us along the way with Waite's understandings of each of the 78 cards, RWS's variations from previous tarot decks, Pixie's fascinating body of work and artistic colleagues, and even the yoga equivalent for each of the cards. I was very pleased with the depth and haiku titles of 78 unique spreads based on the symbology of each of the cards. This is a must-have resource book for a deep understanding of the Rider-Waite structure, intention, and art organized within the Kabbalistic Tree of Life."

Nancy Antenucci, author of *Psychic Tarot: Using
Your Natural Psychic Abilities to Read the Cards*

"Sasha Graham's *Complete Book of the Rider-Waite-Smith Tarot* is a tour de force. It is equal parts historical whodunit, symbolical tarot encyclopedia, and ultimate tarot guide. Sasha Graham weaves the fascinating tale of Pamela Colman Smith, Arthur Edward Waite, and Stuart Kaplan's creation of the best-selling tarot deck of all time…This is a definitive exploration in the intent, purpose, and possibilities of the Rider-Waite-Smith Tarot."

Susan Wands, author of *Magician and Fool*

LLEWELLYN'S

COMPLETE BOOK OF THE

RIDER-WAITE-SMITH TAROT

ABOUT THE AUTHOR

Sasha Graham teaches tarot classes and produces tarot events at New York City's premier cultural institutions, including the Metropolitan Museum of Art. She has appeared on film, television, radio, and in the *New York Times,* and she hosts *The Enchanted Kitchen,* a tarot-inspired cooking show. She splits her time between New York City and the Catskills.

Visit her online at sashagraham.com.

Other titles by Sasha Graham:

365 Tarot Spells

365 Tarot Spreads

Tarot Diva

Editor and Author:

Tarot Fundamentals

Tarot Experience

Tarot Compendium

Tarot Decks:

Haunted House Tarot

Dark Wood Tarot

LLEWELLYN'S

······· COMPLETE BOOK OF THE ·······
RIDER-WAITE-SMITH TAROT

A Journey Through the History, Meaning,
and Use of the World's Most Famous Deck

Foreword by Stuart R. Kaplan

SASHA GRAHAM

LLEWELLYN PUBLICATIONS
Woodbury, Minnesota

FIRST EDITION
Fourth Printing, 2021

Book design by Rebecca Zins
Cover design by Shira Atakpu
Rider-Waite Tarot Deck®, also known as the Rider Tarot and the Waite Tarot,
reproduced by permission of U.S. Games Systems, Inc., Stamford, CT 06902 USA.
Copyright ©1971 by U.S. Games Systems, Inc. Further reproduction prohibited.
The Rider-Waite Tarot Deck® is a registered trademark of U.S. Games Systems, Inc.

For a complete list of image credits, see page 475

Llewellyn Publications is a registered trademark of Llewellyn Worldwide Ltd.

Library of Congress Cataloging-in-Publication Data
Names: Graham, Sasha, author.
Title: Llewellyn's complete book of the Rider-Waite-Smith tarot : a journey
  through the history, meaning, and use of the world's most famous deck /
  foreword by Stuart R. Kaplan ; Sasha Graham.
Description: first edition. | Woodbury : Llewellyn Worldwide, Ltd., 2018. |
  Includes bibliographical references and index.
Identifiers: LCCN 2018031414 (print) | LCCN 2018032645 (ebook) | ISBN
  9780738755366 (ebook) | ISBN 9780738753195 (alk. paper)
Subjects: LCSH: Tarot.
Classification: LCC BF1879.T2 (ebook) | LCC BF1879.T2 G6567 2018 (print) |
  DDC 133.3/2424—dc23
LC record available at https://lccn.loc.gov/2018031414

Llewellyn Publications
A Division of Llewellyn Worldwide Ltd.
2143 Wooddale Drive
Woodbury, MN 55125-2989

www.llewellyn.com

Printed in the United States of America

To those traversing mystery, magic, and enchantment, even when
it's not warm, fuzzy, and sprinkled with fairy dust,
this book is for you.

To those diving deep, reading between lines, and
asking questions of consequence,
this is for you.

To those basking in shadows with
card, cup, and candle,
this is for you.

To my beautiful Isabella,

as always,

this book

is for

you.

PERHAPS YOU USE your physical eyes too much
and only see the mask. Find eyes within,
look for the door into the unknown country.

PAMELA COLMAN SMITH

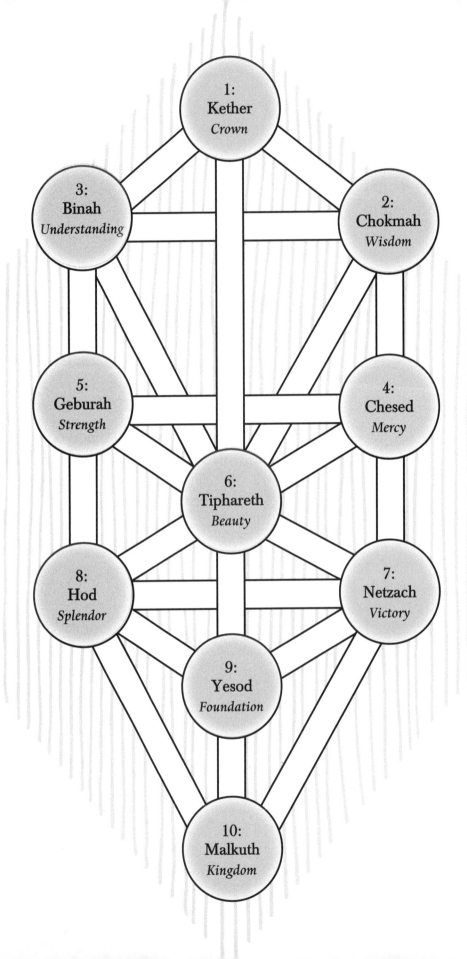

CONTENTS

FOREWORD

There are countless ways to understand tarot. Some people view tarot cards as an unbound storybook containing seventy-eight pages changing with each card shuffle. Other tarot users focus on the social and historical background of the cards and the allegorical symbols that appear on the cards. Whether your interest in tarot centers on meditation, inspiration, or guidance, Sasha Graham reveals new interpretations of the symbolic images drawn by Pamela Colman Smith.

Although Pamela Colman Smith and Sasha Graham live a century apart in time, some of their interests are strikingly parallel. Pamela was active in the theater, a storyteller, and an author. Sasha too is active in the theater, a storyteller, and an author. Each of them entertains the public in unique ways. Pamela dressed herself in colorful scarves and frocks, lit oil lanterns, and entertained with her Jamaican folk tales. Sasha dresses in sequins and silks, lights candles, and entertains by reading tarot at glittering Manhattan parties and events. Pamela and Sasha leave a legacy of books, Pamela with multiple illustrated and authored volumes such as *The Book of Friendly Giants* and *The Annancy Stories*. Sasha has authored three books on tarot: *Tarot Diva*, *365 Tarot Spreads*, and *365 Tarot Spells*, and she has contributed to several additional tarot titles.

I first met Sasha in 2012 at a booksellers trade show in New York City. There was an immediate connection between us. We both had symbolic birthdays: Sasha was born on Halloween, and I was born on April Fools' Day. At age seventeen Sasha longed for a deeper cultural life and fled from her family's country home to New York City, where she would enroll at Hunter College. At age eighteen I fled from New York City to Paris, France, and enrolled at the Sorbonne. She appeared in a variety of off-Broadway theaters and became a B-movie star, playing roles as a vampire, a werewolf, and an alien. After receiving a degree in literature and comparative religion, Sasha forged a career in the metaphysics of tarot. Our mutual interest in the Rider-Waite tarot is a special bond that all tarot believers share with each other.

My first encounter with tarot was in my mid-thirties when I traveled to the Nuremberg Toy Fair. I came across the Swiss 1JJ tarot deck at a printer's exhibition booth. My direction for tarot was to publish the cards by U.S. Games Systems and to make them readily available. Thereafter, I secured the rights to the Rider-Waite tarot deck, which is now the most popular tarot deck, enjoyed by millions of people.

· · · · · · ·

Sasha's first encounter with a tarot deck was at twelve years of age. She always had an interest in the unexplained, and she was drawn to the yellow Rider-Waite box that she saw in a store. The mysterious card images inside the box intrigued her. After studying the tarot, Sasha became proficient in reading the cards and has enjoyed a loyal following for many years. She delights in finding innovative ways to incorporate tarot into modern life.

This book is quite unique in a marketplace selling hundreds of books about the Rider-Waite tarot deck. Sasha gathers the complexity and history of Pamela's deck and presents it to the reader in an entertaining and understandable way. Pamela reached beyond the veil to reveal hidden worlds with her brushes and inks; Sasha does the same with her language and research. Sasha takes up Pamela's role as storyteller and crafts a text that is grounded in practical tarot information yet reveals the divine nature of the creative minds that created it.

The book often reads like a novel, and other times we feel we are in the hands of a mystic. Sasha's research moves us to the original source of the deck. She returns us to Pamela and Waite's original intentions repeatedly. Using her knowledge of the Kabbalah and the Tree of Life, Sasha Graham presents a down-to-earth approach to understanding the Rider-Waite tarot deck in a fresh and lively manner. Each card is described in detail as it relates to the branches of the Tree of Life.

The result is a text as rich, complex, and entertaining as the tarot deck itself. This book is indispensable for the tarot lover. It is a rare text that can be read for learning and pleasure. Sasha, in her undeniably creative way, finishes her beautiful book with seventy-eight spreads. Each spread is based on one of Pamela's cards so the reader may get to the good work of reading their cards and putting their newfound knowledge to use.

After Pamela finished creating the Rider-Waite tarot deck, she never again referred to the cards. Instead, for Sasha and for me, the Rider-Waite tarot deck opened new opportunities that altered our future careers.

Pamela would be surprised to learn that her cards today enjoy a worldwide popularity. Readers of this book will view the Rider-Waite tarot deck from a new perspective. They will come away with a greater appreciation for the depth of the Rider-Waite tarot thanks to Sasha's insights and research.

Stuart R. Kaplan
STAMFORD, CT

TIMELINE

Tarot has no certifiable "beginning" or start date of invention or use as an art object or gaming or divination tool.

c. 1440—Tarot decks are commissioned by wealthy families. In Italy common tarot is played as a game in Renaissance courts and as a game of chance in taverns.

1650—Marseille Tarot, an iconographic model, spreads across Europe.

1770—Tarot's first divinatory book, *A Way to Entertain Yourself with a Deck of Cards* by Etteilla, is published in France.

1855—Tarot's first connection to Hebrew letters and the Tree of Life is made by Éliphas Lévi in his book *Dogma and Ritual of High Magic*.

1857—Arthur Edward Waite is born in Brooklyn, New York.

1858—Waite's father, Charles Waite, a Merchant Marine, dies on September 29. Waite's sister is born three days later.

1859—Waite's English mother, Emma Lovell, brings the family home to England.

1863—Waite's mother leaves the Church of England and converts the family to Roman Catholicism on October 8.

1874—Waite's sister dies at age 15.

1876—Waite begins a correspondence with English poet Robert Browning regarding poetry and publishing advice.

1877—Waite's first book, *Ode to Astronomy*, is published.

1878—Pamela Colman Smith is born in London to American parents.

1878—At age 20, Waite publishes his first story in *The Idler*. It is "Tom Trueheart," a work of fiction in the style of penny dreadfuls. Waite embraces Spiritualism.

1881—Waite discovers Éliphas Lévi's canon of work connecting the tarot to the Tree of Life.

· · · · · · ·

1888—*The Tarot: Its Occult Significance, Use in Fortune-Telling and Method of Play* by S. L. MacGregor Mathers is published in England.

1888—The Hermetic Order of the Golden Dawn is established in England.

1888—Waite's daughter, Sybil, is born October 22.

1889—Pamela and family move to Jamaica.

1889—*Tarot of the Bohemians* by Papus is published in France, expanding on Lévi's Tarot/Kabbalah connections.

1891—Arthur Waite and his wife, Ada, are initiated into the Hermetic Order of the Golden Dawn. Waite calls the organization "the House of Hidden Stairs."

1893—Pamela moves to New York and enrolls at Brooklyn's Pratt Institute. She studies under Arthur Wesley Dow. She declares "teaching or illustration" as her career goal.

1896—Pamela's mother, Corrine Colman, dies in Jamaica.

1897—Pamela leaves the Pratt Institute the same year Bram Stoker publishes *Dracula* in England.

1899—Pamela's father brings her to London and arranges an interview with Bram Stoker, who works as manager of the Lyceum Theater. Pamela is hired to illustrate a souvenir brochure for an upcoming Lyceum Theater American tour.

1899—Pamela joins Lyceum Theater's American tour as a designer and background player.

1899—Pamela's father dies and she returns to England with the Lyceum Theater, her newly adopted theatrical family.

1899—Waite purchases a home at 31 South Ealing Road, London.

1900—Pamela begins work with various London theaters.

1901—Pamela establishes a residence in London and holds bohemian open house evenings.

1901—Pamela's friend W. B. Yeats, poet and playwright, introduces her to the Golden Dawn.

1901—Waite becomes a Freemason, initiated into Runymede Lodge in Buckinghamshire.

1902—Waite joins the Pen and Pencil, a literary club. He and literary friend Arthur Machen create a small literary club called "the Sodality of the Shadows," where members are initiated with a drunken twenty-two-stage ritual based on Hebrew letters.

· · · · · ·

1903—Waite founds his version of the Golden Dawn, the Independent and Rectified Order R.R. ae A. C.

1903—Pamela launches her own private press magazine, *The Green Sheaf.*

1905—A monthly occult magazine, *The Occult Review*, begins publication. Waite will write, edit, and contribute for the next twenty years.

1907—At the National Arts Club, NYC, Pamela presents a recital of folk stories from Jamaica and reads Old English ballads and poems by W. B. Yeats.

1908—Pamela exhibits 72 pieces at Arthur Stieglitz's Photo Secession Gallery in New York City, January 5–15. Pamela is the first non-photographic artist to be shown at "291."

1909—Pamela exhibits a second show at Arthur Stieglitz's Photo Secession Gallery in New York City.

1909—The Rider-Waite Deck is published by William Rider and Sons of London.

1911—Pamela illustrates Bram Stoker's novel *Lair of the White Worm.*

1911—Pamela converts to Catholicism.

1912—Pamela has a show at the Berlin Photographic Company in New York City.

1915—Waite leaves the Golden Dawn and brings ten former members to create the Fellowship of the Rosy Cross. Magical, pagan, and Egyptian references are removed while the order focuses on Rosicrucian and Christian symbolism.

1917—Pamela illustrates *The Way of the Cross*, a deck of thirty cards with French verses.

1919—Waite leaves London and moves to the Kent coast.

1924—Waite's wife, Ada, dies.

1932—Stuart Kaplan is born on April Fool's Day.

1933—Waite marries Mary Broadbent Schofield.

1942—Arthur Waite dies at age 90. His grave is at Bishopsbourne.

1951—Pamela Colman Smith dies at age 73.

1951—Stuart Kaplan moves to Paris.

1968—Stuart Kaplan forms U.S. Games Systems, Inc.

1968—Stuart Kaplan discovers the Swiss 1JJ Tarot at a German toy fair and negotiates the rights and distribution into the United States.

1970—Stuart Kaplan writes and publishes *Tarot Cards for Fun and Fortune Telling.*

• • • • • • •

Timeline

1971—The Rider Tarot Deck is published by U.S. Games Systems, Inc.

1972—Stuart Kaplan writes and publishes *The Tarot Classic*.

1975—The Delaware Art Museum and the Princeton University Art Museum present a show: *To All Believers—The Art of Pamela Colman Smith*.

1977—McMaster University Art Gallery presents *Pamela Colman Smith: An Exhibition of Her Work* in association with the tenth annual seminar of the Canadian Association for Irish Studies.

INTRODUCTION

Welcome to *Llewellyn's Complete Book of the Rider-Waite-Smith Tarot*. The RWS deck (as I will refer to it through the book) is the most used, shuffled, and read tarot deck of all time. This guide is an attempt to understand exactly what its creators, Arthur Edward Waite and Pamela Colman Smith, were doing when they made it over one hundred years ago. What was their intention? What were they trying to accomplish? Why did they think it was important to create a tarot deck? Illustrator Pamela Colman Smith and author Arthur Edward Waite are my main sources of information for this book. We will return to their words and ideas again and again.

Moving past the initial reasons as to why Pamela and Waite created the deck are more evocative questions. What does tarot mean for you? How can you use tarot? How does tarot help you understand the world? What does tarot represent? Why do people come to tarot? What lies beneath the cards' images? What does tarot teach us? Where can tarot bring us? What does tarot reveal? How does tarot evolve?

The chapters in this book align with the Kabbalistic Tree of Life. The Tree of Life is a mystical representation of how reality takes shape and form in the material world. Occultists call the material world's unfolding or emerging process the Journey of Emergence. In this book we will work our way down through the tree and the tarot to understand how the RWS deck emerged. The tree will give context and history. The deck's magical underlying principles will unfold before you. The book culminates in grounded instructions on how to use the cards. Seventy-eight tarot spreads are included, each one based on a specific tarot card.

Occultists are explorers by nature. They venture into realms of sacred imagination, scout inner landscapes, and walk between worlds. Occultists use symbol, ritual, and ancient knowledge to traverse into magic, mysticism, and the meaning of life and death. Once the occultist witnesses the journey of emergence via the tree, they find themselves in the middle of the material world. The only option is to turn around and work their way back up. They go up the tree ready to greet divinity on its own terms. This is called the Journey of Return. Initiates, occultists, and seers travel their path alone. Their experiences are as different as the people who have them. I do hope you make an attempt to reach the summit. Treasures, gifts, and uncanny possibilities await.

Tarot's gift is that *all* cultural and spiritual or nonspiritual beliefs, ideas, and dogmas may be placed on top of it. *Llewellyn's Complete Book of the Rider-Waite-Smith Tarot* does not preach, proselytize, or promote any particular worldview. Arthur Waite, author of the deck, was a Christian mystic. Although he was a practicing occultist, he was raised in a Catholic household. Catholicism informed his spiritual life even as it intertwined with alchemy, Freemasonry, and magic. As such, the RWS deck contains multiple Christian allegories, as does his accompanying text.

Wherever you find the word "Divine" or "God," feel free to insert your own meaning: Goddess, God, Zeus, Buddha, Yahweh, Allah, Pan, Puck, Ryan Gosling, Elmer Fudd, Chocolate Cake, or Nothingness—whatever you like; whatever makes sense to you. You can use this book with any deck of cards. Tarot decks are like people: it's what's inside that counts. The inner landscape of tarot is where its meat and bones lie. That's the juicy stuff you'll want to get to. And this book brings you straight to the main course. It doesn't matter if you don't use the RWS deck or if it is not your favorite deck. The RWS's impact is so great, the deck you are using is likely a derivative of it. The archetypes inside tarot remain the same, regardless of what the cards look like.

Pamela Colman Smith is referred to as "Pamela" throughout the book. Arthur Waite is commonly referred to as "Waite" by cartomancers and tarotists. I have stuck with this tradition. Pamela is also known as "Pixie" in the tarot world. This is due to the affinity we all have for her remarkable illustrations. Pamela's images have found a permanent residency inside the psyche of tarotists. We find a comfortable, intimate, and familiar relationship with her images. They offer solace and understanding. Pamela offers a sacred space for us to work out our issues and even test our psychic and intuitive abilities.

Research for this book was done in conjunction with the New York Public Library, specifically the Berg Collection, the Art and Architecture Division, and the General Research Division. U.S. Games Systems, Inc., and Stuart Kaplan gifted me immense guidance, as did the work, research, and support of Mary Greer. Practical tarot matters stemmed from my years of professional tarot education reading and writing in New York City.

Tarot is a doorway or one might say seventy-eight gates. It is a threshold into other planes of existence. Anything can act as a portal: people, art, architecture, nature, etc. Tarot is a logical tool because it is described as magical, mysterious, and powerful. These words are associated with the deck, and people project these associations to the cards, thus echoing the power of words. Tarot operates on a symbolic level. It moves past linguistics. Like love and compassion, tarot's symbolism—all symbolism—speaks directly to the soul. The most profound knowledge in the world is usually felt and seen rather than articulated. Conversations around tarot and the supernatural induce words like intense, knowing, and uncanny. You'll laugh the day you realize

· · · · · · ·

every word anyone has ever used to describe the tarot—words like magical, mysterious, and powerful—also describes you. You hold the magic and the knowledge; tarot simply reflects it.

It was my absolute pleasure to make this book for you. I hope you find it useful in your journey. You will likely discover surprising personal insights as you unravel the story and structure of the RWS deck. Tarot has a funny way of doing that. We think we are reading for others, and we wind up reading for ourselves. We think we are asking about the future, and the cards point us toward our past and inform our present. We encounter the unexpected, the uncanny, every time we turn a card. This is what makes tarot exciting every time we sit down to read.

So take my hand. Let's venture into the Rider-Waite-Smith deck together. I promise you'll enjoy it. And when we reach the threshold where you continue forth without me, venture wisely. Let the torchlight of authenticity and grace light your way. Shed light where others find darkness. Use your guts, intuitions, and cards to propel you. You will discover the magic you were searching for was inside you all along. Welcome home.

Believing in you always,

Sasha Graham
NEW YORK CITY, 2017

· · · · · ·

Clone decks follow Pamela's symbolism closely. Here are three versions of the Hermit: the RWS deck (below left), the Steampunk Tarot by Barbara Moore and Aly Fell (above), and the Shadowscapes Tarot by Barbara Moore and Stephanie Pui-Mun Law (below right).

IX

THE HERMIT.

IX. The Hermit

Kether (Crown)

The Big Picture Show

. . . .

Kether—Crown—Ace

The RWS deck is the best-selling tarot deck in the world to date. The RWS deck is referenced in literature and used in all forms of media, including film and television. It is often a beginning reader's first deck. History, evolution, and circumstance created an extraordinary device that people use for fortunetelling, self-knowledge, and art. Tarot decks with new themes are created by the hundreds, maybe thousands, each year. New decks with differing themes are usually called RWS clones. Clone decks' illustrations are derivative of Pamela's RWS illustrations. A clone deck's Eight of Swords will likely have a bound and blindfolded female figure evocative of the image Pamela drew for the RWS deck.

The RWS deck is an enigma. It is a complex tarot deck filled with esoteric symbols and secret meanings, yet the illustrations are surprisingly simple. A beginner can use the deck as easily and deftly as a professional. The deck is a perfect artifact of the year of its creation, 1909, yet remains shockingly modern and perfectly usable over a hundred years later. The RWS deck is a Modernist art object as important and impactful as Picasso's *Les Demoiselles d'Avignon* or Edward Munch's *The Scream*, also painted in 1909, yet the RWS deck does not haunt history by hanging on the wall of a museum. Anyone in the world can buy, borrow, or own a copy. The RWS deck is tucked into backpacks, wrapped in silks, consecrated on alters, stored in college dormitories, and stocked in bookstores around the world.

The esoteric structure behind the RWS deck is simple yet extremely complex. It is as simple and complex as all the world's spiritual traditions. Spiritual knowledge, dogma, and teachings can usually be reduced to a small number of basic truths, or tenets essential to each particular system, yet it can take a lifetime of understanding and study to authentically adapt and

. . . .

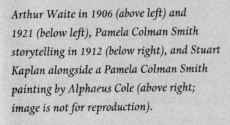

Arthur Waite in 1906 (above left) and 1921 (below left), Pamela Colman Smith storytelling in 1912 (below right), and Stuart Kaplan alongside a Pamela Colman Smith painting by Alphaeus Cole (above right; image is not for reproduction).

incorporate such systems into life. A person who approaches the unfolding of a system slowly and with an open mind finds that esoteric and spiritual structure becomes a path instead of a means to an end. The same is true of tarot and the RWS deck.

Tarot decks existed long before the cards were connected to esoteric or spiritual systems. Hundreds of years transpired before occultists realized they could connect Hebraic letters and the Tree of Life structure to tarot. The numerical structure of a tarot deck and the four suits of tarot make the connections possible. The major arcana, the twenty-two cards separating tarot from an ordinary deck of cards, also represent sacred and profane allegories of life.

The number three and the concept of a trinity or triad is useful in grasping the significance, emergence, and usage of the RWS deck. A triangle contains three specific points. The concept of three echoes in all facets of RWS usage, its history and its application. Keep the idea of a simple triangle in your mind's eye as you continue reading. Using the concept of three, we can examine why tarot works, where it comes from, and how the RWS deck became the world's most infamous tarot.

· ·

RWS Creators

Pamela Colman Smith—Arthur Waite—Stuart Kaplan

Illustrator—Author—Businessman

Pamela Colman Smith (illustrator), Arthur Waite (author), and Stuart Kaplan (author and businessman) are three people directly responsible for the Rider-Waite-Smith deck and its worldwide success. Pamela was a bohemian illustrator, highly gifted colorist, storyteller, folklorist, performer, stage designer, costume designer, and author. Arthur Waite was an occult mystic and prolific author of dozens of books on esoteric subjects. Pamela and Waite both belonged to the most famous and revered magical secret society in the world, the Hermetic Order of the Golden Dawn. Waite hired Pamela to illustrate his "rectified" tarot deck.

The Golden Dawn's monumental impact is still felt today though it existed for only a brief period at the turn of the twentieth century. The Golden Dawn is considered one of the greatest influences of Western magical tradition and subsequently modern New Age thought. The organization studied and experimented in all areas of magic and the paranormal in a systematic and purposeful way. The Golden Dawn used tarot as a way to visualize, understand, and execute their magical workings, which were deeply grounded in symbolic work. It attracted artists and intellectuals alike, including W. B. Yeats, Florence Farr, Bram Stoker, and Aleister Crowley. The society was prone to wild internal disputes. Purposeful magic is a source of intense power.

· · · · · · ·

Wielded in irresponsible and egocentric ways, power is bound to create disagreements and squabbles between members and leaders. Waite formed his own offshoot of the group in 1903. He brought Pamela with him.

Waite had a personal and idealized vision of his own tarot deck. Pamela was the perfect candidate to illustrate a deck to Waite's specifications. Tarot was required study for all Golden Dawn members, and she was well versed in the group's esoteric secrets. Pamela was a rising star in the art world outside of the Golden Dawn. Personal letters and articles show Pamela was highly gifted, hungry for work, and eager for money. Waite enjoyed a close working relationship with the Rider Publishing Company. Rider published a regular stream of occult literature, including early works of Waite's and an array of horror fiction, including works by Bram Stoker. They published the deck under a title combining their own and Waite's name: the Rider-Waite tarot.

The original Rider-Waite tarot and its accompanying book, *The Pictorial Key to the Tarot,* was published in 1909 to very little fanfare. The RWS deck kicked around for decades and through two world wars. The Rider-Waite and a few other tarot decks lingered in the back of dusty bookstores and hidden occult shops. Stuart Kaplan, a Wall Street businessman and author with a deep passion for research, wrote a book called *Tarot Cards for Fun and Fortune Telling* in 1970. The fate of the RWS deck took a rapid turn at this point. Stuart couldn't keep his book in stock. It flew off the shelves, and after printing 700,000 copies, he knew he was onto something. He followed the advice of Don Weiser and licensed a little-known Rider-Waite tarot deck. It would go on to sell millions of copies, becoming the most beloved tarot of all time.

. . . .

Creators' Talents

Creativity—Occultism—Business Acumen

Each party brought a particular and unique quality to the table, paving the way for the deck's success. Pamela was a creative genius who crafted thousands of art pieces during her career. Artists are mystics who make invisible worlds visible to the public through their works. Pamela was known for her otherworldly visions and vivid use of color. Pamela's theater background profoundly influenced the RWS deck. Each card appears like a scene from a play. She created androgynous figures, perfect for the projection of issues, questions, and concerns from readers. Pamela's body of work reveals a world of castles, rising mountains, and evocative oceans. Pamela's mix of playful and theatrical, deeply grounded in symbolic reference, made for the perfect tarot deck. It speaks today as brightly as it did over a hundred years ago.

. . . .

Pamela's illustration for The Book of Friendly Giants *reveals a landscape indicative of her tarot deck. It is full of billowing clouds, open sea, rolling hills, and tiny clusters of towns and towers.*

Waite published forty-six books and edited, translated, or introduced forty others in the course of his life. His tomes, as per the style of the day, are heavily worded and challenging to read. Additionally, Waite published *The Pictorial Key* after taking a vow never to reveal Golden Dawn secrets, so his vision is coded into his writing, making it doubly hard to ingest. Through Waite's writing and research and through his exploration of the tarot and subsequent rectification, he created a deck grounded in profoundly spiritual structure. Raised as a Catholic, his education could not be cast aside but was incorporated into his works, so many of the RWS deck's images feel familiar to the Western Anglo-Saxon person looking at the cards. His descriptions, words, and cards evoke an experiential spiritual experience akin to an initiation. The deeper the reader moves, the more they uncover. Waite imagined and experienced the lessons of the RWS deck, and Pamela brought the vision to life.

Stuart Kaplan is a driven businessman and passionate writer/researcher. He set out to make his mark on the world through research and commerce. Like a detective, Stuart sought to discover something the public would devour. He successfully uncovered an interest in tarot, fed the public's desire, and proceeded to publish an anthology of tarot books and make the RWS deck available to the world. His singular focus, stellar instincts, and Ivy League education combined with a righteous work ethic ensured his success. He elevated himself out of the Bronx and created a multimillion-dollar company. U.S. Games Systems, Inc., distributes new tarot and oracle decks and books each year alongside the RWS deck. He is also the world's premier collector of Pamela Colman Smith art objects.

· · · · · · ·

. . . .

RWS Uniqueness

Illustrated Minors—Gender Ambiguity—Esoteric Symbolism

Hundreds of tarot decks predated and postdated the RWS deck. What makes the RWS different? What makes it so darn special? Three variables set this deck apart from all other decks created at the time. The biggest difference is the minor arcana of the RWS is fully illustrated, which was the first time this had occurred since the Sola Busca deck (Italy, circa 1491). Every other tarot deck, with the exception of the Sola Busca, had fifty-six minor cards like traditional playing cards. No images, just symbols and numbers. Once Pamela illustrated the minor arcana with scenes, the RWS deck's colorful and evocative visuals became easily readable. Pamela used the Sola Busca illustrations for inspiration. They happened to be on display at the British Museum at the same time she was commissioned to create the deck.

Pamela's tarot figures are infused with gender ambiguity. Many characters appear to be both masculine and feminine. The characters are soft, open, and inviting. Her characters' abstract expressions can be colored by anyone's experience. Additionally, Pamela's theatrical costume design experience came in handy. The characters are dressed in Shakespearean clothing that feels timeless and evocative. The clothing is faintly ceremonial yet grounded in Elizabethan realism. The costuming is true to its time period yet abstract enough for anyone to encounter it. It acts like Waite's underlying mysticism, grounded in the truth of experience and available for anyone to consume. Ultimately, any experience can easily be projected onto the cards.

Pamela and Waite encoded clever Western esoteric symbolism into the cards. Astrology and mythology, Christian and Hebraic symbols fill the images. Symbols rich with meaning can be unraveled and explored to provide new discoveries. The cards can be aligned with multiple schools of study. The esoteric symbols merge seamlessly with Pamela's clothing and theatrical setting. It is as if a great performance unfolds before our eyes. Infinite possibility exists.

. . . .

Triple Threat Threefold Examination

Hindsight—Insight—Foresight

Past—Present—Future

Fate—Fortune—Destiny

Tarot has always involved the examination of the forces at play in our lives (except when it was used for gaming in ancient Italy and France). Ancient tarot was predictive. Modern tarot leans toward empowerment. It puts power squarely in the reader's hands. Tarot, no matter whose

. . . .

hands it is in and how it is used, has always been tied to a threefold quality inherent to everyone's life. What was once fate, fortune, and destiny became past, present, and future and has evolved to hindsight, insight, and foresight.

Hindsight is the ability to look at past events to gain clarity. Hindsight makes our lessons and mistakes worth learning so we don't repeat them in the future. We glean understanding from an event after it has unfolded. This equates to the "past" space in a past/present/future spread. A "past" card is flipped to express an event that has already unfolded. It also aligns with fate. Fate is the situation, life circumstance, and family we were born into.

Insight is understanding the context of the circumstances surrounding and enveloping you. Insight is the ability to peer directly into the present moment and see the root of any issue at hand. Grasping the root allows you to sustain it or pull it free. Insight provides a grounded place from which to make decisions. Insight provides self-knowledge and knowing who you are. It aligns with the "present" space of a past/present/future spread. This card suggests what is happening in the present moment. It aligns with fortune, which reflects what a person has going for them in the present moment. Fortune is all the gifts, talents, and sensitivities each and every one of us is born with.

Foresight is having a sense of what has the highest probability of happening based on past and present events. Colleges use foresight to shape their admission policies. They believe examining the past and present habits and achievements of students will give them the highest degree of foresight into the future achievements of their students. Personal foresight allows you to make good and sound decisions based on the information in front of you. This aligns with the "future" section of a past/present/future spread and describes potential future events. Destiny is how an individual makes use of their fate and fortune.

. . . .

Tarot's Usage

Divination—Self-Knowledge/Empowerment—Creative Arts

Divination is the cross-cultural act of using any variety of objects or means—sticks, stones, or bones, etc.—to foretell future events. Early tarot was used for trick-taking card games in the rowdy taverns of Europe. Tarrochi was a game of chance. It offered gamblers an opportunity to play the odds, perhaps even altering their personal destiny. Tarot, with its twenty-two illustrated major arcana and numerical structure, was a no-brainer for fortunetelling and divination aficionados. The card's major arcana illustrations create easy-to-read narratives. Cards have always been a metaphor for life, whether under the auspices of gaming or fortunetelling.

Tarot predates Europe's first printing press. The deck is older than printed and bound books. Offering lessons and allegories in place of words, the major arcana's images likely spoke to a

. . . .

largely illiterate public. Historical documentation of card divination is not well recorded. The practice was passed generationally, orally, or it sprang up intuitively. It usually occurred behind closed doors. Modern tarot divination exists at every level of western society. Tarotists are hired as entertainment for parties and events. College students cluster and giggle around tarot in dorm rooms. Wise old grannies read tarot on Formica tabletops. Metaphysical shops across the county offer tarot in addition to other modalities like astrology, Reiki, and angel readings. Storefront gypsies entice customers with glowing neon signs and sparkling crystal balls. Tarot readers work online via email, video, or even phone texts. Newcomers often purchase a tarot deck in hopes of divining their own future. Tarot use often switches from a fortunetelling device to self-knowledge and empowerment as it is incorporated into daily life.

Tarot becomes a contemplative practice for readers who look at the cards and toss aside conventional fortunetelling questions such as "When will I be rich?" Instead, they ask introspective questions: "What do I need to know?" "What gift does this challenge bring?" "What can I do to obtain the outcome I desire?" These questions place the reader in the driver's seat of their life. They may ask philosophical questions such as "What is my life's purpose?" or "What is the nature of God?" Self-knowledge and empowerment blossom when symbol and archetype are blended with psychology, offering a deeper human experience of tarot. The deeper experience of tarot fosters a richer experience of life. Tarot is an excellent visual aid and powerful tool for spellcasting. Tarot is used as a portal into guided meditations. It brings us into the inner recesses of the psyche or outward into the elemental world.

Tarot's creative use is infinite. Writers and authors pull cards for plot points, character traits, and writing prompts. Painters and visual artists use tarot archetypes for creating single or unified sets of original work. Tarot crafts and goodies are sold online and at fairs and festivals. Movies, literature, and all forms of media pull from the tarot when it suits them, often from the RWS deck. Tarot images inspire tattoo and skin art. Companies borrow tarot images to suit their advertising needs when wishing to appear mystical, trendy, or edgy.

Tarot is more popular today than it has ever been. Tarot use will continue to unfold, evolve, and move to the outer reaches of human creativity and innovation. What new and exciting ways do you use tarot? How do you incorporate the cards into your life? You move tarot forward with every spread and spell. Each time you enter a card via contemplation, you tread into an unfolding world of dazzling possibility.

· · · · · · ·

. . . .

Western Esoteric Pillars

Kabbalah—Astrology—Numerology

Nineteenth-century European occultists studied medieval grimoires on alchemy, magic, and mysticism in the great libraries of Europe. Tarot already existed independently and apart from all esoteric studies. Occultists realized they could place tarot's perfect structure on top of their work, integrating it with their systems. Joseph Campbell described the "Hero's Journey" as a similar narrative reaching across all myth, religion, and storytelling. Tarot, too, contains this narrative. It aligns perfectly with metaphysical systems used to describe the nature of reality and man's relation to the Divine. Imagine the occultists' delight when they discovered the systems they worked with could be quantified with this mysterious deck of cards.

Kabbalah is an ancient Hebraic mystical system. The Kabbalistic Tree of Life is a visual representation of the divine manifestation of life on earth. The tree contains an all-knowing, all-loving, divine source at its top. This source filters down through the tree's branches until it manifests at the bottom, on the earthly realm. Rabbinical scholars created Kabbalah, and it was later adapted by other mystical schools of thought. The Tree of Life contains a numerical structure of the nature of divinity. The Tree of Life links linguistic, astrological, and numerical associations. It aligns with tarot's structure. Tarot's major arcana connects to the tree's paths; tarot's four suits connect to the tree's four worlds.

Astrology is the ancient practice of looking skyward and observing the motions and positions of celestial bodies to explain and express an individual's psychology and the human condition and predict future events. Astrology, like tarot, can be used for prediction or empowerment or both. Astrology slices the firmament into twelve segments, thus creating the twelve signs of the zodiac. The Golden Dawn tweaked their tarot and made minor adjustments so their astrology would fit on top of the deck with near-perfect symmetry. Once the Golden Dawn had unified the two systems, each tarot card assumed additional astrological richness, meaning, and symbolism.

Numerology is a practice using mathematical principles to define the nature of the material and spiritual world. Humans organize the world by counting, organizing, and detecting patterns. Childhood's earliest lessons include counting and numbers—hours in a day, days in a week, etc. The nature of reality can be measured numerically. It is possible to discover meaningful patterns and cycles and glean personal empowerment and information. Tarotists can use numerology to gaze through the veil of the material world and into otherworldly realms of sacred imagination. Once patterns are detected, meanings can be placed behind the patterns. Tarot reading always displays numerical information via card numbers. Like a poker game, repeating suits and numbers are important in tarot. Tarot's numerical structure makes it infinitely adaptable.

. . . .

. . . .

Tarot's Psychic Trinity

Conscious—Subconscious—Possibility

The human mind can be understood in a threefold manner. The threefold nature of the mind includes the conscious, subconscious, and possibility. The conscious mind consists of present thought patterns, which are the thoughts you are aware of. We all experience inner dialogue in the conscious mind. Right now, my present consciousness is entering your consciousness. You read the words of this book, which were written in the past, yet the writing of these words occurred in my present. You, mysterious reader, loom in my future. The words you read are at the forefront of your conscious mind this very moment. The magic of this book has brought our consciousnesses together. We are having a dialogue though we are miles apart in time and space.

The conscious mind is what the individual is aware of at any given time. It is revealed through speech. The subconscious mind reflects possibilities rumbling around like a subway beneath the surface area of your mind. The subconscious is a darker, murkier place where deep desires, repressed feelings, and forgotten events exist. Events unprocessed by the conscious mind reside in the subconscious alongside memories. Memories of memories are stored here. The subconscious is also the breeding ground of creativity and renewal. It acts like the rich, fecund earth of the mind, from which all things are born.

Human possibility exists outside, above and beyond the conscious and subconscious mind. Possibility is everything an individual is capable of doing, experiencing, and embracing. Human possibility knows no bounds and is inescapable. It always exists. All spectrums of human behavior exist inside and alongside possibility. Possibility is the space between thoughts. It is the silence between sound. Possibility is the space between stars and solar systems. It is the space inside the atoms that make your body. Tarot can be used to activate the threefold presence of the human mind.

Tarot opens an active dialogue between the conscious and subconscious mind through symbols. The subconscious recognizes and responds to symbols in the same way the physical body intuitively responds to any sensorial input like music, taste, or beauty. A meaningful song will transport you back fifteen years in a flash, like childhood comfort foods or the whiff of a particular fragrance. The memories exist side by side between the physical body and the subconscious. Useful memories and associations are put away like toys in a chest until they are needed. It is often easier to identify an underlying problem or issue using symbols. Tarot symbols and images communicate directly to the subconscious.

. . . . . .

Possibilities become meaningful reality because tarot induces questions. The cards inspire advice, action, and direction. Problems are taken out of the head and spread as cards on the table before the reader. A personal bird's-eye view unfolds. Issues are examined. Root issues are identified. Action steps are encouraged. Personal impulses, hunches, and instincts are validated. The act of forming tarot questions paves the way for mindfulness. It leads the psyche in new directions. The brain is like a computer trying to find the quickest route from A to B. The subconscious is made conscious. What is conscious is acted upon and moved into the real world. New possibilities appear. The ripple effect of inner and outer events unfolds.

. . . .
Tarot Activation
Art—Storytelling—Lesson

Tarot, whether for divination or empowerment, works via a threefold synthesis. The card's artwork, first and foremost, provides a framework and image, no matter the deck. It holds true even if the card is selected electronically. Pictures and images appear, cards are flipped like sections of a graphic novel. Numerous symbols, actions, and activities are interpreted by the reader. The power of tarot stems purely from the reader's interpretation and not from the cards, as many people assume.

The narrative of a story is crafted after the art images are ingested. The human mind is ensconced in storytelling structure. Storytelling is how we organize ourself and our placement in the world. Someone asks us how our day went, and we respond with the story of our day. Someone inquires as to how we grew up, and we respond with the story of our childhood. We place ourselves in the leading role of events and circumstances all day long. We weave stories about ourselves in our own head, telling ourselves what we are worth, what we deserve, and how situations should go. We can look to the cards and allow them to describe elements of our story or give us advice. Often it leaps out at the reader. The resulting story can be formulated in a variety of ways. The reader creates the framework for the story by phrasing questions or intentions around the card or tarot spread.

The story told by the cards results in confirmation, a lesson, or advice. Subsequent action is usually taken. Information is devoured like a child's bedtime story, even if the reader reads for themselves alone. Insight is gleaned. The world is examined from a different perspective. Possibilities are entertained and weighed. The individual walks away from the cards with a takeaway from the experience. An exchange of energy occurs, and the subtle body changes.

. . . . . .

· ·

Tarot Reader's Triad
Physical Body—Cards/Client—Higher Self

Tarot readers activate a threefold process each time they read the cards. The energetic exchange is familiar to artists, writers, poets, actors, photographers, musicians, dancers, etc. This process is often taken for granted. Readers need to be aware and open to examine how they engage with the cards. The triad process involves three distinct sensibilities, which can be refined and honed with time and practice.

The reader activates the physical body when preparing to read the cards. Ritualized behavior puts the body on alert. Readers will light candles, ignite incense, burn sage, or drink tea or coffee. Light meditations or energy work may be performed to cleanse and open the body and invite insight and inspiration. Alternatively, grounding work or protective energetic shields may be placed for readers who read for the public. Prayers, blessings, or consecrations may be uttered. Touching, feeling, and listening to the cards as they shuffle is a simple and effective activation. Consider the way you prepare for a reading. Every person contains subtle differences. Each body is unique. Consider the physical and spiritual ways your body can prepare for a reading. This helps you to cultivate and understand what you are doing energetically. This can be considered the warm-up.

Attention moves away from the body once the cards and client are engaged. Conversations are had and questions posed; if readers read for themselves, they have the conversation with themselves and perhaps write down questions and notes. The cards are shuffled and laid out according to the reader's choosing. The images wash over the senses of the reader. Information hits the reader in any number of ways according to the reader's sensitivity. The reader looks to see what is before them like the moment a painter turns their attention to the subject.

The higher self, inspiration, muse, spirit, or (insert your preferred name) is activated for information and the resulting narrative. This is the sacred imagination and creative mind space. This space is opened and experienced in a million different ways by different people. It is as unique as each person's kiss. Doing so, the reader accesses insight, story, guidance, and inspiration for the reading and the conclusions. It is the same energetic process used by poet/imagination/paper and dancer/music/stage. This triad is at the heart of creative work and is a three-part participatory act.

· · · · · · ·

. . . .

Tarot's Traditional Publishing Trinity

Author—Illustrator—Publishing House

Tarot publishing usually contains a three-part process between author, illustrator, and publisher. People who purchase, play, or read the cards rarely think about how the cards were created. Authors conceive of ideas and themes for decks and sell their ideas to a publisher. Conversely, publishers conceive of decks and seek authors to flesh the idea out. Tarot themes are wildly imaginative, from cats to vampires, from historical decks to futuristic decks. A tarot theme can be any imaginable subject. Once the tarot deck idea is outlined by the author, each card is described and written out in detail. An artist is sought to illustrate the cards and bring the writer's (or publisher's) vision to life.

The search for an illustrator begins once an author's proposal is approved by a publishing house or once the publisher finds a theme they would like to create. Finding the right artist is time consuming and not as easy as one might guess. Conversely, artists often find themselves drawn to tarot as a theme. The illustrator may innovate a deck themselves and sell it to a publisher. Designing a seventy-eight-card deck is time consuming. It involves many approvals and revisions between author, artist, and publisher.

Once the deck is complete, accompanying text is written. This could be a little white pamphlet or a full-sized companion book to the deck. Variations to the publishing trinity exist. Artists often conceive of decks on their own; self-published decks are readily available, yet the triad of author, illustrator, and publisher is common. This is the process employed in the original creation of the RWS deck between Waite as author, Smith as illustrator, and Rider as the publisher.

. . . . . .

Chokmah (Wisdom)
A Deeper Look

Tarot is linear and logical in structure and suit. Its numerical ordering contains the capacity to extend in all directions at once. This is the reason tarot can be used for fortunetelling or spiritual exploration both exclusively or simultaneously. It is why tarot works well for psychological analysis or artistic inspiration. Tarot's path and usage zigzags and takes peculiar, strange turns through history. Upon its publication in 1909, the RWS deck appeared quietly, with little fanfare. How did this particular pack of cards sell millions of copies decades after its initial appearance? How did the RWS deck beguile users, foster a cultural tarot explosion, and become the number-one tarot deck in the world?

The RWS deck is a result of three particular talents and personalities. Their paths crossed at different points in history. The story and success of the RWS deck teaches an evocative lesson regarding personal talents or life's purpose for anyone who approaches the cards. It is impossible to predict and sometimes even destructive to idealize what a future life of success, happiness, and fulfillment will look like. "The universe works in mysterious ways," so the saying goes. This sentiment was never more true than with the historical evolution of the RWS deck.

The dots of our lives connect in ways we can scarcely comprehend. Outcomes and possibilities often unfold in unimaginable ways. It's better to do our best in the moment and release personal attachment to any particular outcome. Trust. Let mysterious forces take care of the details for us while we focus on the work at hand. This notion is not random flagrancy toward the future, nor is it a recipe for irresponsibility. Strive to do the best work possible and trust it will work itself out. Examine your past; you'll see this element at play and know it to be true.

The story of the three people responsible for the RWS deck reminds us of this lesson. Each one of them answered a specific personal calling. Each one of them showed up daily and worked hard. Each one of them has secured a place for themselves in history. They speak to us, informing us through their work, dedication, and perseverance, as they are living inside the

· · · · · · ·

RWS deck. They remind us to stay true to our inner stirrings, to trust our unique voice, and to focus on the task at hand.

. . . .

British Museum, London, 1909

The woman lurks like a minotaur in a labyrinth. She inhabits a maze of bookshelves before an exhibition of cards. The satisfying scratch of graphite moving across creamy white paper fills her ears. Form and gesture flow through her and onto the sketchbook. She allows the images, cards, and photographs to pass through her consciousness like gossamer ghosts through walls. Librarians flicker around her like shadowy angels, scanning, referencing, organizing. The shelves, heavy with medieval tomes, grimoires, and celestial astrology, surround her diminutive figure. She pays no mind to the intimidating stacks or the overbearing language stuffed inside the ancient books. Her name is Pamela Colman Smith, but to her wide circle of friends and acquaintances she is Pixie.

The name Pixie was bestowed upon Pamela's head like a glittering tiara by England's most celebrated actress, Ellen Terry, the Judi Dench of her day. The name Pixie is selected because it aligns with Pamela's fairy qualities. Fairies inhabit unknown and magical realms, as does Pamela. One might say Pixie Pamela was born into unknown landscapes, where she thrives to this very day. Journalist Irwin MacDonald describes Pamela's gifts in an article about her artwork:

> We all share the hidden life, but only the few have the power to express it or make it visible. Great poets, artists and musicians have it, and children are so close to it that they try sometimes to make the grown folk see and understand what is so real to them. But they have not the power…(Pamela's) pictures are wholly symbolic, not in the conventional sense, but as the natural expression of one who puts thought and feeling into symbolic forms rather than into tones or words.[1]

Pamela had a supernatural knack for making the unseen seen and the unknown malleable. Like a free-formed sprite, she traveled extensively in her formative years. "She took her first sea voyage when she was three months old, and since then has crossed the ocean twenty-five times"[2] claims an article about Pamela written when she was only twenty-two years old.

Pamela the Pixie lives with a foot in each world, both in a literal and a figurative sense. She was born in London to American parents and raised in parallel universes. Half of her

---

1   MacDonald, "The Fairy Faith and Pictured Music of Pamela Colman Smith," 27, 28.
2   "Representative Women Illustrators," 527.

. . . .

childhood was spent on the sensual, balmy Caribbean island of Jamaica and the other half in clamoring, clattering Brooklyn, New York. Kingston, Jamaica, provided long, languid, colorful days. Tangerine sunrises in violet-blue waters and a local community of spiritual folk magic saturated her impressionable mind. Pamela's caretaker came in the form of a beloved, devoted nanny who nurtured Pamela with maternal love, storytelling and island mythology: "Everywhere since her babyhood days, a quaint old Negro mammy has accompanied her."[3] Pamela devoured tales of island peoples, wild creatures, and folklore. Her art and tarot are saturated with the mountains and oceans of the Jamaican landscape. MacDonald describes how Pamela's childhood affected her art while describing her published collection of Jamaican fairy tales:

> She listened to many tales and legends of the unseen world, told by witch-like old women in the firelight,—because in Jamaica no one dares to speak of such things in the broad light of day,—and she made a collection of them…[4]

Brooklyn offered intellectual stimulation in opposition to languid island life. Pamela learned to funnel her imagination out of her mind's eye and onto the canvas at Pratt Institute's school of art as a teenager. Her roommate describes her to the *Brooklyn Eagle* newspaper: "Pamela liked to sleep until noon and then design and draw under artificial light."[5] Pamela dresses as electrically as she paints. She was known to wear "bizarre and barbaric colors."[6] The colors she wore matched the jars of pigment and paint in her art studio.

Pamela left the Pratt Institute and found employment at London's famous Lyceum Theater. Author Bram Stoker was the Lyceum's business manager. Pamela's father arranged a meeting between Pamela and the towering six foot two *Dracula* author. Stoker was immediately charmed by Pamela and her obvious talent. He hired her. Pamela joined the Lyceum, traveling with them on an American tour. She worked as a background player, painting stage sets and designing programs and stage costumes. Pamela's father died during the tour, and Pamela returned to England with the theater company, who would become like an adoptive family.

Pamela and Stoker shared a close relationship. Bram Stoker, in addition to his business duties, wrote and created lusciously detailed Lyceum programs sold to patrons and attendees of the theater. Theatrical programs, called "Souvaneers" in 1900, were an excellent secondary source of revenue for the theater, just as they are today. Broadway shows and concerts often erect stands selling merchandise, T-shirts, and programs of the show. The same was true for the Lyceum. Photography was an expensive young art form and complicated to

3 "Witchery in London Drawing Rooms."
4 MacDonald, 32.
5 "Witchery in London Drawing Rooms."
6 Ibid.

· · · · · ·

print. Artistic illustrations peppered the program pages with scenes from the plays, intimate moments between actors and full-color costume representations. Pamela filled the programs with vibrant play illustrations and portraits of the charismatic actors who performed at the Lyceum. Bram Stoker wrote the text. The two collaborated long after Pamela left the Lyceum, when Stoker hired Pamela to illustrate his book *Lair of the White Worm*, which had its cinematic adaptation in 1988.

Stoker, godfather of vampire literature, published *Dracula* in 1897, two years before meeting Pamela. *Dracula* was well received by critics, but neither it nor its author would become iconic until the novel was adapted into film versions later in the century. Bram Stoker never lived to see the success of his book or realize his fame. Ironically, the sketches Pamela currently works on will follow in *Dracula's* fate. She has been commissioned to create a tarot deck. Her deck's illustrations, like *Dracula*, will sell millions upon million of copies. It will become the gold standard to which thousands of new tarot decks will pattern themselves. Pamela will never know this.

Pamela pauses her sketching to rearrange her shaft of silken skirts of deep cerulean fabric folding over her short legs. Twenty-three original engravings and fifty-five photographs are spread before her. Suns, moons, stars, and odd figures fill the Italian cards. It is the Sola Busca tarot deck. She's come for inspiration for the deck she is crafting for her colleague Arthur Waite. They have decided to create something unique and extra special in their cards. Usually a tarot deck only illustrates the major arcana, but Pamela is going to illustrate every single card. She's come to see the Sola Busca deck, the only other deck to illustrate the minors, for ideas. She is delighted to see it on display at the British Museum.

Her eyes flash across a figure bent over an armful of swords. Her work is made quick, flipping her sketchbook as impression after impression is made. She snaps the sketchbook shut, secures it inside a brown leather case, and makes her way out to the rotunda. Pixie Pamela moves through a golden beam of sunlight streaming through the oculus eye in the ceiling of the British Museum's reading room. The vast treasury of holdings inside the British Museum is open only by special request to guests. Library card holders including Virginia Woolf, Sir Arthur Conan Doyle, and H. G. Wells are a few who are granted access. She's glad to have finished enough sketches to complete the deck. She moves with urgency, a look of satisfaction across her intense face. Existing photographs reveal Pamela's physical features to be unique. Her face carries a shapeshifting quality, remaining true to her fairy calling. It is near impossible to identify her cultural heritage. Born to American parents in London, she looks to be of Asian and African descent. She is childlike and womanly, vulnerable yet closed. Letters reveal she is quick to anger. Her poetry reveals a stunning vulnerability. Her opinions of art and love for the-

The British Library's domed reading room, 1859.

ater remained strong and true till the end of her life, as evidenced in articles she wrote about stage design, production, and creativity.

London's clash and clamor greets her ears as she exits the museum. She makes her way past the clip-clopping of horses pulling Victoria carriages to London's Chelsea district, her home. Night falls quickly as she clinks the gate behind her. English rose and cindery smoke fill the air as she enters her chambers. She strikes a match, and lamplight flickers across her forest-green walls. Her eyes twinkle like a mischievous fairy as she moves through her chambers. It looks more like a curiosity shop than an apartment. Brass candlesticks glimmer from a grand piano. Heavy crystal ashtrays spill over with the remnants of last night's guests. Loose leaf music sheets are scattered like leaves on the floor. Miniature china toys line the shelves. Heavy artifacts, books, and portfolios act like weights holding down pieces of her room, as if to keep reality from slipping away.

• • • • • •

Chapter Two

She moves through the parlor and into her studio in the back, where she tosses her leather case and sketchbook. Dozens of bottled inks hold the fanatical colors she employs on her illustrations. Gardner Tell describes her workspace:

> If you should enjoy the great privilege of a peep into her studio—a great room joyously free from the commonplaces that have come to make one studio generally representative of every other one, a room where art is living rather than imprisoned—you will see over in a corner by the window a little table quite quivering with curious bottles, saucers of pigment, vivid inks, Chinese whites, blacks, and indigoes, while one little corner of it is a veritable chemical emporium. Before this material panegyric of paint the clever artist sits, and dipping a Japanese brush in this place or that, fixes her inimitable creations deftly and definitely and without affectation or pottering.[7]

Her growing artistic reputation is built not only on her unique vision but on her vibrant choices of color. Her studio is as eccentric and varied as her talents. She holds the esteem of being the first non-photographic artist to exhibit at Arthur Stieglitz's Photo Secession Gallery in New York. Stieglitz, a famed photographer in his own right, introduces Europe's avant-garde artists to the New York City art scene. Pamela will soon pen a letter to Stieglitz saying, "I've just finished a big job for very little cash," referring to her tarot deck.[8]

For someone as young as Pamela to show at the Stieglitz gallery is a coup d'état. Pamela enjoys a second show at the Photo Secession gallery and includes illustrations from the tarot deck she is currently working on. Stieglitz's wife and muse is American painter Georgia O'Keeffe, renowned for her lush feminist Southwestern paintings. Decades from this moment, O'Keeffe will posthumously donate remaining unsold Pamela paintings to Yale University's Beinecke Rare Book and Manuscript Library. Tell describes Pamela's talent and use of vibrant color:

> The colored drawings cannot be appreciated through the interpretation of black and white, and their exquisite brilliancy, reached a manner that would startle any plodding artist or technician, can scarcely be described by words.[9]

Tell is on point with his description. One can't believe the worlds Pamela unleashes though her work until you are looking with your own eyes at the colors and shapes she creates. The RWS deck is a mere suggestion of Pamela's talent.

7   Tell, "Cleverness, Art and an Artist," 139.
8   Pamela Colman Smith, handwritten letter to Arthur Stieglitz, November 19, 1909.
9   Tell, "Cleverness, Art and an Artist," 139.

Literary giant W. B. Yeats, who introduced Pamela to the Golden Dawn, as seen by Pamela Colman Smith in Dublin, 1901.

Pamela throws her doors open on various evenings to host bohemian house parties. Artists, poets, and writers typical of the day attend in droves. She carries a special fondness for actors due to her formative years working for the Lyceum Theater. Pamela engages in deep friendships with renowned artists through the years. In addition to her friendship and working relationship with Bram Stoker, she was a close confidant and friend of William Butler Yeats. Yeats introduced Pamela to the Hermetic Order of the Golden Dawn. She was symbolically adopted by actress Ellen Terry after her father passed. Ellen Terry was one of the most famous actresses in England; imagine Meryl Streep taking you under her wing. Pamela and Edith Craig, Ellen's daughter, were like sisters.

> She traveled with Sir Henry Irving and Ellen Terry, playing small parts and having the greatest time ever, when she was in her middle teens, and for years lived with Ellen Terry and her daughter, Edith Craig. You can imagine what years they were—busy years of painting and sketching, designing stage costumes, illustrating pirate songs, writing and telling fairy-stories, doing countless interesting things, and doing them all amazing well![10]

10   R. R. G., "Pamela Colman Smith, She Believes in Fairies," 320.

• • • • • • •

Pamela dresses in colorful costumes and performs her Jamaican folktales for party guests. The *Brooklyn Eagle* describes her as "a whimsical tale teller" who "has all of London on their feet." She turns her storytelling talent into a paying profession and is hired out as party entertainment. Pamela makes an appearance at Mark Twain's New Year's Eve party and a journalist describes her as "an exotic young woman with melting dark eyes and a sweet crooning voice."[11] She was so charming, the journalist states that he "and all his (Mark Twain's) distinguished company of guests forgot time, space and the everyday world of commonplace reality."[12] Pamela places her rich experience of Jamaica into her folk stories. She even uses her voice:

> In the weird dialect of the Jamaican Negroes—a sort of cockney English with Spanish coloring, a rhythmic rising inflection at the end of each sentence that must have come directly from the voodoo worshipers of the African jungle—she told fairy folk tales...[13]

Pamela's theatrical presentations do not end with her presentation of folk tales. She additionally

> varies her unique programs of entertainment by singing old English ballads and songs in a sixteenth-century costume, also by "lilting" such modern Irish poets as W. B. Yeats' "Dream of the Wandering Angus" in the manner of ye ancient bards and troubadours.[14]

Pamela devotes herself, above all, to story. To her story, she will be true.

> I tell the same stories to the Russian, Jewish and Italian children at the east side settlement schools that I do in the literary salons and at the National Arts Club, and they seem to go equally well though the comments are different.[15]

Pamela employs methods expressing her narrative differently depending on her audience:

> When I tell the Jamaica stories to very young children I illustrate them with dolls, which I make myself—saw them out of wood with a fret-saw, then paint them and stick on feathers and beads, Jamaica mammy style. These are to little kiddies what book illustrations are to grown-ups. But the real, universal world-old way is to tell the stories orally, and put the illustrations in as you go along, by sign language, facial expression, gesture and all that sort of thing.[16]

---

11   "Made Veteran Humorist Laugh."
12   Ibid.
13   Ibid.
14   Ibid.
15   Ibid.
16   Ibid.

Photograph of Pamela's personal toy theater from
**Brush and Pencil: An Illustrated Magazine of
the Arts of Today,** *volume 6, issue 3, page 153.*

Pamela's theatrical passion, work, and knowledge held immense value when she designed the tarot deck. Each card appears like a scene on a stage. The reader is free to project themselves onto the cards like the audience in a play or film. Pamela creates a mysterious series of cards inside her deck. Waite never mentions these thirteen cards; however, I call them "stage cards." Stage cards are examined in detail on page 370. They appear to be derived from Pamela's toy theater.

The toy theater concept was introduced in England circa 1810. Pamela created a miniature and portable theater at her home in London. Her miniature theater is a lifelong passion; as the *Brooklyn Eagle* reports, "One of the earliest stories that is told of her is the pastime of her childhood of making little theaters, of writing plays and of managing puppets."[17] The catalogue of the posthumous Pamela Colman Smith show "To All Believers" expresses the direct result the toy theater had on the RWS deck: "The simplified renderings of her figures, the dark outlines, and the bright colors were all reminiscent of the theatrical sheets. The oriental character of many of her drawings must have been fostered in part by her enthusiasm for miniature dramas as well as Dow's emphasis on Japanese art." The theatrical sheets with their "wild forests, frowning fortresses, extravagant castles, mountain torrents, haunted glens, and picturesque huts" probably also influenced the choice of landscape elements she later incorporated into her paintings and tarot card designs.

17   "Witchery in London Drawing Rooms."

All the scenery and decorations in the theater were created by Pamela. Inside her toy theater she performed ballads of forgotten lore. A writer for *Brush and Pencil* states

> I have never seen a more gorgeous presentation on any stage. The knights and ladies of the buskin are first drawn on stiff paper and colored, then cut and made to lead upright lives with a bit of glue and proper manipulation. Oh, that some of our modern playwrights might come here for a lesson in dramatic construction or that the scenic artists of to-day did not feel that they could not learn a thing or two! Here a professional stage costumer might well gasp envious; and you should see the procession of over three hundred figures called forth…It is marvelous, and when you come away you feel that art is a tangible thing after all, tangible because it had been brought before you in an enjoyable way; and in the sanctity of your own chamber when you look over your possession of some of Pamela Colman Smith's prints…you will feel that you have something beautiful and enjoyable; therefore something which must be art.[18]

Compare the RWS images to this description; what she created for her miniature theater and her tarot deck are practically interchangeable.

Pamela is described by critics as having synesthesia. The modern definition of synesthesia, the root of which means "joined condition," is when a single sensory condition is perceived by a second sense. Synesthesiatics possess senses that cross in a number of ways. Colors provoke a taste. For example, the color blue tastes like cotton candy. Smells induce sound; for instance, the scent of apple pie evokes a Vivaldi concerto. The crossing of senses occurs every time the color is seen or the flavor is smelled. It happens involuntarily. It is believed that human babies contain completely connected senses. As babies mature, the senses separate. Sight becomes clear, taste becomes distinct, and tactile touch is developed. However, individuals with synesthesia maintain some crossover connections.

She is described by Melinda Boyd Parson as having synesthesia, yet Pamela's synesthesia is a technique employed for painting, not an inborn crossing of the senses. Pamela uses music to open visions within her. She paints these visions. This is different than the medical definition of synesthesia. Pamela uses it as a modern art technique.

> One of the earliest artists to incorporate direct visual interpretations of specific musical compositions into her paintings. Not conscious representations but spontaneous representations of the same emotions which had inspired the composers. Color, line and form were intended to correspond with sound…the compositional elements functioned as concrete symbols of their idealogical equivalents in the spiritual realm.[19]

---

18   *Brush and Pencil*, volume VI, 1900.

19   Melinda Boyd Parsons, *To All Believers—The Art of Pamela Colman Smith* (Delaware Art Museum, 1975).

· · · · · · ·

This version of synesthesia differs from the involuntary kind. Synesthesia is a condition people are born with. Pamela was listening to specific concertos and painting what came to mind as she worked.

Pamela's synesthesia technique was learned at the Pratt Institute under the tutelage of Arthur Wesley Dow. Much of her work depicted imagery spontaneously brought to her mind while listening to music by the likes of Beethoven, Bach, and Schumann: "what I see when I hear music-thoughts loosened and set free from the spell of sound," as she wrote in a 1908 article.[20]

Pamela continues painting pieces inspired by music. Pamela says,

> Why, sometimes a single concert gives me as many as 25 or 30 ideas, and I have to put them all down on paper before I can rest. I am handicapped, I know, by deficient technique. But then there are times when the idea is the thing and the technique is forgotten. One art is not enough—the others must be ransacked.[21]

Tarot images spring from archetypes. Archetypes reflect ideas and concepts evident in human consciousness. Pamela reaches right into the world of archetypes and pulls them out so we can recognize them. Art critic Irwin MacDonald reports on her circle of friends and her ability to reach inside the human subconscious:

> Again environment played its part, for she was the friend and close associate of the group of poets and playwrights who are restoring Celtic literature and tradition to the world. On the Continent, her friends were Maeterlinck, Debussy and others who were endeavoring, each in his own way, to pierce the veil that hid the subjective world. Pamela Colman Smith had not the great creative power of these men, but it soon became evident that she has something quite as rare—the power to see clearly the invisible realm of which they all dreamed. She entered it or shut it out at will, but when music opened the gates everything became clear to her inner vision. She learned to distinguish the elementals of the earth, air, fire and water, the gnomes, goblins, wraiths, leprechauns, pixies, salamanders and peoples of the sea.[22]

Pamela finishes the RWS deck and continues making art and storytelling. She hustles for work, opens a drawing shop, and remains busy and industrious. Though she is considered one of the most promising artists of her generation, fame and money remain elusive. By 1911, Pamela converts to Catholicism. She eventually leaves London and moves to the country to enjoy a quieter life, like so many of the bohemians around her who scattered into Europe's countryside after their heyday in London and Paris. There is no record of romantic entanglements and not

---

20   Garrett Caples, *Retrievals* (Wave Books, 2014).
21   "Made Veteran Humorist Laugh."
22   MacDonald, "The Fairy Faith and Pictured Music of Pamela Colman Smith."

much is heard from Pamela after she leaves London. An inheritance allows her to open up a retreat for Catholic priests.

Asked by the *Delineator* magazine what she would call herself and her many talents, she answers, "Why, I suppose I am an expressionist. I try to express myself in the best possible way."[23] Pamela was an artist, designer, storyteller, and woman of innumerable talents. She led a rich life during a riveting historical time period. She traveled extensively and shared relationships with some of the most famous artists and occultists the world has ever seen. Her tarot deck was one item—one commission, a single cohesive piece of art—amongst the thousands of works, stories, illustrations, and paintings she created. A single common thread wove through all she created. It was strung through her collections of myth, illustrations of children's books, portraits of famous actors, and her private press magazine. The thread is her dedication to story: sacred, perfect story.

W. B. Yeats once said of Pamela,

> Our Father Time and Mother Space have said to you, as they say to none but excellent artists; You are so good a child that we need not trouble about you. We are as contented as if you were a sod of grass. Our of your croon comes into the silence or across the voices, like a bird's chuckle among the leaves outside the window. One forgets civilization in the very act of 5 o'clock tea.[24]

People often lament the sadness of Pamela dying without recognition for her tarot deck, yet she created an object that brings joy, comfort, and guidance to untold numbers of people. It is utterly beautiful and profound that Pamela Colman Smith, a true storyteller at heart, created the very instrument that millions of people would use to tell their stories with. It is Pamela's tarot we bring out on dark nights for intimate conversations. When we read her cards, we light lanterns and candles and fill the air with hushed sighs, just as she did when regaling a rapt audience with her Jamaican folktales. She whispers to our imagination as we look to her images with glee. Pamela is smiling over our shoulders every time we shuffle the cards. It is just what she did when mysteries unveiled themselves through her work. Pamela remains a gateway between worlds in death, as she did in life. Her work continues to inspire magic, enchantment, and contemporary artists, one card at a time. It is an electrifying legacy. This writer and tarot reader thinks that is exactly what Pixie would have desired.

---

23   R. R. G., "Pamela Colman Smith, She Believes in Fairies," 320.

24   "Made Veteran Humorist Laugh."

• • • • • • •

. . . .
31 South Ealing Road, London, 1909

Sodden leaves fill the street while raindrops pepper the windows like tiny stones on a damp Tuesday night. A mustached man writes prose across clean white sheets while sequestered inside a cozy office. The words tumble out of him and across the page like a fountain of language. A separate part of his consciousness, the active observing part of his own mind, realizes he is not alone as he authors this work. A third hand works through him, feeding him knowledge and insight. At times he feels this presence, like a pouring of morning light through a clean and clear window. His hands can barely keep up. "There is no such thing as a common life," he writes.

> The convention under which we regard it is alone common. The key of the great mysteries lies hidden in all things round us, but the perplexities of the convention hinder us from finding it. The gift of understanding is within us, and we might read the world's language if we dared, but the inherited averseness of all the centuries to a first-hand experience of things sets an effectual check on the attempt. The inclination of the axis of the soul places us outside the direct line of vision; that inclination can be rectified, and the operation may not be essentially difficult, but it calls for a peculiar courage.[25]

Arthur Waite stands from his writing desk and rubs his eyes. The hearth cradles a crackling woody fire that bravely fights off the damp air and fills the room with rosy warmth. He feels renewed, filled with a sense of purpose, satisfied, as he always feels when his writing goes well. His solace is the written word. His act of writing is a form of devotion itself and is an exploration in its own right. It is the place where he finds perfect expression of thought and emotion. *I see it all so clearly*, he thinks to himself. *Why is it so hard for others to see the obvious?*

His eyes beam with pride over a pine shelf holding nine of his published books. "More to come," he thinks with delight, "more to come." He glances to a small yet important manuscript. It is his tenth book, *The Pictorial Key to the Tarot*. His deadline from the Rider Publishing Company looms. He is anxious for the last illustrations to be finished. There's a small chance he will see his artist this evening, but he doesn't cling to much hope. Pamela is erratic in her attendance of his meetings. Waite knows erraticism is the hallmark of many artists. He recognizes at once that Pamela adores the ritualistic aspect of his group's work, but she has little care for the intellectual side. He believes her brilliant talent and unique abilities make up for what she lacks in discipline as a neophyte in his society.

He bids his daughter Sybil a good evening and moves toward his wife. "Good night, Lucasta," he whispers to her. She barely glances up from her needlework. Lucasta is her pet name, yet

---

25   Waite, *Collected Poems, Volume 1.*

she all but ignores him. He exits the house and enters the rain carrying a familiar annoyance. *She does not respect my great work*, he thinks to himself. *She looks at me with the eyes of my jealous colleagues. My work binds me to the highest source*, he thinks. *Of course they are frustrated when they find themselves immune to my level of understanding. I lay it all out; still they fail to see it. To grasp it. It frustrates them and makes them feel small. What can I do but stand as an example? I must lead the way with thoughts and actions*, he thinks as he moves through the mist, becoming a shadow beneath the flickering torchlight.

He arrives at his destination and snaps the door shut behind him. He shakes the water from his top hat and trench and hangs it up. A circle of people have gathered in the room beyond, and he makes his way toward them. The room smells of tobacco and wool. Any passerby may believe this to be a social or church group. It is not. These artists and intellectuals are bound by metaphysical purposes. Arthur Waite has created an offshoot of the Hermetic Order of the Golden Dawn in this group. They are intent on furthering the exploration of occult and spiritual study. He makes his apologies for being late and takes a seat. Their secret work begins.

The hallmark of highly creative people is often borne in the wounds they endure early on in life. Arthur Waite was born in the fall of 1857 on October 2 in Brooklyn, New York. He was an illegitimate child whose father was a seafaring adventurer. Charles Waite, an American Merchant Marine, died at sea when Arthur was less than a year old. Waite's mother, Emma Lovell, came from a wealthy English family. She returned to London with Waite and his little sister, Frederika, after his father's death. His mother's wealthy family shunned the trio, and they were forced to live in poverty.

Waite's fascination with the nature of mystery and hidden worlds began in childhood with the love of penny dreadfuls. Penny dreadfuls were serialized magazines telling fantastical horror stories and were wildly popular during Waite's youth. Waite devoured hair-raising tales like candy even though his mother strictly forbade him to read them. As a path of darkness often leads to light, Waite began writing fiction and poetry. His first published story was "Tom Trueheart," appearing in the *Idler* in 1878.

Waite had a strict Catholic upbringing, which served as the spiritual springboard for all his subsequent work. Waite's beloved sister, Frederika, died when he was seventeen. Her passing led him down a path of psychical research. Waite examined and studied paranormal events and psychic phenomena while trying to make sense of the loss of his sister. The Spiritualist movement claimed to prove life after death through communication with the spirit world. Waite devoured their teachings.

Waite's occult research led him to the British Museum. The British Museum was a hotbed of research and intellectualism at the turn of the century. Waite discovered a vast collection of alchemical, astrological, hermetic, and magical grimoires in the reading room. Waite was on

· · · · · ·

his way to becoming a prolific occult author due to his significant relationship with the Rider and Co. Publishing House. Rider and Co. would eventually publish twenty of Waite's books, and he was a regular contributor to the *Occult Review* magazine.

He met Samuel MacGregor Mathers, co-founder of the Golden Dawn, in 1883 at the British Museum's reading room. Mathers describes them both as "haunting the British Museum, trying many paths of search, and having been introduced." Waite already belonged to many fraternal organizations, and in January 1891 Waite became the ninety-ninth member initiated into the Hermetic Order of the Golden Dawn.

Golden Dawn's infighting commenced. Secret groups forged secret groups within its ranks. Secluded rituals were being performed, and excluded members struggled to ascertain their power and ideas within the group. W. B. Yeats published a pamphlet advocating against secret sects within the group. He believed the subversive groups were committing an irresponsible and dangerous act by meeting separately. Disarray continued as the group fractured. Arthur Waite split from the group, forming his own. He brought Pamela Colman Smith along with him. It was during this time period that he and Pamela undertook the work of creating Waite's rectified tarot, which was to become the RWS deck.

> Waite, however, was dissatisfied with both traditional tarot cards and the designs devised by the order by Westcott and Mathers; with the founding of the Independent and Rectified Rite, the tarot designs were jettisoned in company with the old rituals and he determined to create a wholly new pack.[26]

Waite, though he writes in a formal, scholarly, often condescending tone, admits that anyone, anywhere, can place the meaning they like upon the tarot. In *Shadows and Thought* he says,

> We have to recognize, in a word, that there is no public canon of authority in the interpretation of Tarot Symbolism. The field is open therefore; it is indeed so open that any one of my readers is free to produce an entirely new explanation, making no appeal to past experiments; but the adventure will be at his or her own risk and peril as to whether they can make it work and thus produce a harmony of interpretation throughout.[27]

Waite combines the traditional fortunetelling meanings with his own veiled experience of the tarot as a picture book of his occult work while allowing anyone the room to place their own definitions on the cards.

---

26   Gilbert, *A. E. Waite.*

27   Waite, *Shadows of Light and Thought*, 194.

· · · · · · ·

He calls Pamela "a most imaginative and abnormally psychic artist."[28] Waite's great area of concern is in regard to the major arcana and the esoteric journey they describe. He describes in his memoir how he "spoon fed" the imagery of the Fool, High Priestess, and Hanged Man to Pamela. The minor arcana seems to have been an afterthought. Many of his descriptions do not even match the images on the cards, leading to the popular assumption that he gave Pamela free rein in designing the minors.

Waite went on publishing numerous books after the RWS deck. The Rare Manuscript Division at the New York Public Library reveals that at age 75, Waite attempted to sell a large collection of his original manuscripts, some unpublished, for 3,500 pounds through bookseller John Jeffery. Waite lived another ten years before his death in 1942. Author Kenneth Rexroth described Waite as "an odd fish in an odder barrel." He is, however, respected as a renowned occult author who was the first to "attempt a systematic study of the history of Western occultism"[29]—no easy task. Biographer R. A. Gilbert marvels, pointing out of Waite that

> against all expectation he found a unique path to the direct experience of God. All mystics turn within, but Waite was alone in grasping what he found and bringing it back so that all mankind could understand its nature and be offered a means of attaining it.[30]

Waite bridged the literary chasm between ancient occult grimoires and present-day New Age authors. Waite is mostly remembered for his rectified tarot deck. Like Pamela, he never lived to see its massive success.

East Thirty-Second Street, New York City, 1974

The sweaty taxi driver chews into his cigar and lays heavily on his horn. The sound misses its target but curls up and through a window three stories above. A tall gentleman hangs up the phone, rubs his chin, and stares ahead, oblivious to the honking. This boy from the Bronx is all grown up. Manhattan is separated from the Bronx by a thin stretch of the Harlem River, but it may as well be as wide as the Atlantic Ocean. Stuart Kaplan is president of a coal mine, a juvenile furniture company, and many other sectors. His Wall Street power broker's phone bears a constant ring. His secretary informs him a second call waits on the other line. Ignoring her voice, he looks at the note he's just scribbled on a piece of paper. Its a note from a conversation he's just had with Donald Weiser of Weiser Books. It says, "Contact Hutchinson Publishing regarding the Rider-Waite deck. Do something with it."

28 Ibid.
29 Waite, *The Holy Kabbalah*.
30 Gilbert, *A. E. Waite*.

His office is not far from Grand Central Station, the bustling behemoth of daily commuters hopping trains and escaping the madness and sleaze of midtown to the safety of suburban Connecticut. Unlike many of his contemporaries, he is not content to slurp down whiskeys and chase secretaries, nor does he join the daily Metro-North marching commute of briefcases ending at manicured lawns, tennis wives, and prep school children. A greater calling tugs at the heart beating beneath his Brooks Brothers tie. He knows there is a mission he is here to fulfill. He's been put on earth to pioneer something. Writing and researching are his first loves. That's exactly what he plans to do.

Stuart's divorced working-class parents sent him to a new private school in the deep woods of New Hampshire. Their intention was to get him away from stickball and the streets. His class was small, the location remote, far from girls, noise, and the hustling city streets he grew up on. He was among the first graduating class, along with classmate F. Lee Bailey. Bailey was the famed Patty Hearst lawyer who was involved in the Boston Strangler case and who overturned a murder case, inspiring the movie *The Fugitive*. Bailey gained further notoriety on the O. J. Simpson trial defense team. Bailey went off to Harvard while Stuart rebelled against higher education. He followed Hemingway's footsteps and moved to Paris to become a writer.

The year was 1951. Stuart was eighteen years old. Paris's ancient cobblestone streets echo with history. The magic of meandering stone streets reminds the traveler of kernels of deep recovered truth. Forgotten knowledge fills the body, as if heard and felt for the first time. It is like music notes drifting from a cafe window of a long-forgotten song whose every lyric you recall. It is seen with perfect clarity. Stuart began to understand the breadth of his parents' prep school gift.

While living in Paris, he enjoyed long weekends in London. He swapped French life for English during June, July, and August of 1951. In September of the very same year a woman lay dying a five-hour drive from London. At eighteen years old, Stuart had no clue that the woman dying on the second floor of a cottage in Bude, a mere half-day's drive away, was Pixie—Pamela Colman Smith. At eighteen, he had no idea that he would resurrect her legacy, which had turned dormant after she exited London for a quiet life in the country. She had departed the bohemian life, tired, as many artists and members of the Lost Generation were. Stuart had no idea that he would return to England in the future, knocking on doors, following clues, and asking anyone anything they knew about Pamela Colman Smith and her artwork. Pamela took her last breath on September 18, 1951.

Stuart traveled to the deserts of Algiers for the New Year holiday two months later, oblivious of Pamela's passing. He was at a crossroads. What next? The yellow desert's wild landscape allowed his mind to reach natural conclusions about the direction he needed to take. He applied by cable to two schools, Dartmouth and Wharton. Dartmouth said no. Wharton said yes. Stuart packed his bags and headed to school in Pennsylvania. He graduated from Wharton,

• • • • • • •

joined the army, and upon release moved into a small studio on Forty-Second Street and Lexington Avenue with his wife. He managed his Wall Street duties while looking for something he might pioneer. He wrote and published an expansive sourcebook called *Mining, Minerals, and Geosciences*. He was ready to write another if the public demanded.

Stuart was perusing a German toy fair when he stumbled across a 1JJ Swiss tarot deck. The tarot images captured his imagination, and he thought the public might like it too. He secured the rights to the deck and ordered a small printing. Henry Levy, a buyer for New York City's tony Fifth Avenue bookshop Brentano's, suggested Stuart write a book about how to use a deck of tarot cards. Ironically, Brentano's downtown Union Square location once sold copies of Pamela Colman Smith's self-published magazine, the *Green Sheath*. Stuart followed Levy's advice and wrote *Tarot for Fun and Fortune Telling*. After twenty printings and 700,000 copies sold, he realized he was onto something. He went on to publish four more books about tarot, cumulatively selling over a million copies.

Stuart went to England and signed a contract for the RWS deck after Weiser suggested he look into it. Stuart had been balancing his publishing with Wall Street for ten years. Stuart took the plunge with a mortgage and four children. He left Wall Street and moved his company, U.S. Games, Inc., to Stamford, Connecticut, near his home and family. Twenty-five dedicated employees work there to this day. The facility acquires, prints, and ships decks, books, and oracle cards. U.S. Games's buzzing offices create new products each year and is a family affair, employing family members and loyal employees. Stuart even built a luscious outdoor dog run for employees' dogs, landscaped with fruit trees.

Stuart is a collector and researcher by nature. When asked what he likes to collect, he replies, "What I don't have," with a smile. He has amassed the largest private Pamela Colman Smith collection in the world. Pamela was a prolific artist, her tarot deck being one small piece in an enormous career spanning years. An oil painting of Pamela hangs above Stuart's desk. It is his most prized acquisition and the single Pamela object he says he would rescue from a burning building. Arthur Waite, Alister Crowley, and the Golden Dawn esotericists never resonated for Stuart. For him, Pamela is the pure source. Everything begins and ends with Pamela's art. Stuart plans to keep the Pamela collection intact and to someday donate it to a library or museum where her legacy will live on.

Stuart is often found at U.S. Games seven days a week, researching, writing, and working. He sees no separation between work and home. Stuart has always stuck to a simple recipe for success. His advice is simple, and it will ensure progress no matter how it is used. It can be applied to a personal life, creativity, or a passion. He advises people to move forward and never allow themselves to get bogged down in minor details, saying, "It's better to do something and get it wrong than not do it at all."

· · · · · · ·

. . . .

The Lesson

These three people are the exclusive reason the RWS deck is the most beloved deck of all time. Their lessons are valuable to each and every soul who shuffles cards to seek answers to life's most important questions. Pamela, Waite, and Stuart all focused on their passions and abilities. They did not conceive of an end plan or know exactly what it would look like. They trusted in their gifts and followed their instincts. Each knew they held special talents. Each knew they would impact the world. Not one of them realized it would be through tarot.

Pamela wrote about "a big job for little money." Waite had no idea out of his forty-plus books that his smallest tome, *The Pictorial Key,* and his rectified tarot would arrest the world's imagination and become a best seller. Stuart claims he would have happily continued writing about minerals and gems if that was where the market had carried him.

These three figures are a lesson for anyone who asks the tarot, "What should I be doing with my life?" Their lives and stories are the answer to this question. The lesson from each of them remains the same. Stay in the moment. Focus on the task at hand. Work hard at what you like and what you are talented at. Do not anticipate the outcome. Rid yourself of any preconceived ideas and notions. Make room for the unimaginable.

Who ever would have believed that seventy-eight cards would affect the lives of millions of people? Who would have thought tarot would become a legitimate career, enabling female entrepreneurs to create holistic start-up businesses? Who could have imagined the world's literary giants from T. S. Eliot to Italo Calvino and fashion powerhouses from Dolce and Gabana to Karl Lagerfeld would look to tarot for inspiration? Who could have foreseen ancient tarot cards becoming an important contemporary holistic tool?

Tarot existed before the RWS deck. It will continue to evolve after it. The RWS deck's popularity, availability, and charm reflect the biggest milestone in tarot's evolution to date. Stuart Kaplan says, "Tarot is the ultimate book. Every time the deck is shuffled, new stories are formed and possibilities appear." Stuart's favorite card is the Fool; its image is his company's logo. The RWS deck specifically moved the Fool to the front of the pack. Stuart's birthday is April 1, April Fool's Day. The signs were there all along.

Signs surround us at all times. It is up to us to decipher them. If we are good detectives, if we read the omens and patterns of our life, if we listen to internal whispers, we will cultivate our special gifts and unique talents. We will figure out the mystery of why we are here. Once we embrace the mystery, we can jump inside. The work and play begins as we experiment inside the infinity of it. We realize that uncovering our whole self to the world is the greatest gift of all.

. . . . . .

Binah (Understanding)
The Golden Dawn

What would you consider the most important human invention of all time? What makes life easiest for you? The wheel, the light bulb? The internet, the hairdryer? All inventions, from electricity to computers, have their raw materials already in existence. People figured out how to piece the invention together. From the telephone to the refrigerator, inventions were waiting for the human mind to connect the dots and put them to use. Indispensable future inventions, new technologies, medicines, cures, things we can't imagine in the present moment—all their base materials exist in the present. We simply haven't figured out how to put it together yet.

Early people used water and fire for basics. As cultures grew more complex, they refined the use of essentials. A simple campfire was prized for its ability to heat the body and transform hunted meat into savory meals. Through centuries of evolution, people transmuted fire into the energy to power steam ships and trains. Water, initially used for drinking, bathing, and washing, became hydropower and irrigation sources for complex farming. Water is now crafted into backyard lagoons, swimming pools, and water parks. The same process occurred with the tarot deck. Tarot existed for hundreds of years. Europeans used the cards for gaming and fortunetelling, while elite royal families commissioned tarot decks as art objects. It wasn't until the nineteenth century that tarot's usage would be altered forever as occultists discovered a brand-new way to use the cards.

Occult fascination was brewing in Europe at a fevered pace during the nineteenth century. Egyptian treasures were plundered and brought back to Europe on a daily basis. The public's interest in Spiritualism, table tipping, séances, fairy lore, and fantasy was at an all-time high. The British Museum's reading room was a hotbed of esoteric study. The museum's massive dome housed page after page of ancient manuscripts. Medieval grimoires written by history's greatest magicians, alchemists, and astrologers such as Queen Elizabeth's John Dee filled the shelves. These rare, dusty books and pamphlets were a physical source of great research in a pre-internet world. Occultists pored over these works during reading room hours. Intellectuals, writers, and researchers met each other and formed friendships and bonds that took them out of the museum and into local pubs and social clubs.

The Hermetic Order of the Golden Dawn was an enterprising group of occultists who would create a secret society the likes of which the world had never known. The Golden Dawn formed in London's deep shadows. They set off to embrace the outer limits of human consciousness. The club allowed women to join, breaking with the patriarchal tradition of the day. These men and women practiced ceremonial magic, induced out-of-body experiences, astral traveled, studied Jewish mysticism, and made contact with divine entities and spirits. They practiced divination and scrying, and they studied alchemy. The focal point of their work was the active working up and down of the Kabbalistic Tree of Life. It incorporated Enochian magic, shamanic journeying, and cartomancy. Tarot operated as a visual workbook for the Golden Dawn. Each of the esoteric practices they worked behind shuttered doors linked perfectly to tarot's structure. Tarot continued a perfectly crafted archetypal framework through which they would view, understand, and approach the mysterious operations they undertook. The tarot already existed in its original form. The Golden Dawn reinvented what could be accomplished with the deck and made minor readjustments to the deck as needed. They altered the trajectory of tarot forever.

. . . .

Masonic Structure

The Golden Dawn's structural forefather is Freemasonry. Freemasonry and tarot's common denominator is a perfectly designed structure. Freemasonry's elegant organization was a core reason the Golden Dawn existed with ease. Freemasonry provided a workable structure for the group to organize itself, while tarot provided a workable tool to support and examine all esoteric and occult arts. The Golden Dawn peeled away the Masonic symbolism and replaced it with magical symbolism.

Tarot does not contain all occult arts, nor was the Golden Dawn a Masonic organization. Each system was used as a blueprint. The Golden Dawn's core contingency was a group of artistic, imaginative, and fiercely intellectual people. They approached their work with the utmost seriousness. Their experiments and explorations required discipline and structure. Tarot and Freemasonry provided the dual pillars that would enhance their profound influence on the Western magical tradition. The Golden Dawn's effects are still felt in modern New Age practices, magical circles, and power of attraction principles.

. . . .

Freemasonry is a secret society. It contains two specific and separate groups, operative and speculative. Operative masons are the stoneworkers, architects, and builders. These workers organized themselves into trade guilds in feudal Europe. They used secret signs and rituals to safeguard their profession. Masons held highly specialized skills. They were able to move freely through a society full of serfs and peasants. Masons traveled to where the work was. They often spent years constructing grand cathedrals, chapels, and castles.

Masons are in the business of creating sacred space. As builders of holy places and houses of divine presence, it wasn't surprising the group moved toward spiritual pursuits. They used principles of science and logic and aligned them with spiritual enlightenment. Freemasonry evolved past trade unions and into social clubs engaging in a spiritual practice. The Grand Architect became a metaphor for god. The builder became a metaphor for a man who crafts his life though actions, choices, and deeds.

Speculative Masons are Masonic organizations whose members are not actually builders and stoneworkers. Drive through any sizable American town and you'll notice a local Freemason lodge. They are usually marked with a Masonic square and compass with a "G" in the center. The "G" stands for Grand Architect. The square and compass, a symbolic circle and cube, contain multiple spiritual lessons. They additionally correlate to the Empress and Emperor cards of the tarot deck. Speculative Masonry spread like wildfire in pre-twentieth-century Europe and America. Members used them as fashionable social clubs. Speculative Masons created a path of moral and spiritual development based on preexisting Masonic rituals. Famous Masons include American founding fathers George Washington, Benjamin Franklin, and Alexander Hamilton. Masonic imagery and symbols appear on US currency, most pointedly the pyramid with the all-seeing eye on the American dollar bill.

Initiation served an essential quality of Masonic operation. It played a key role in the Golden Dawn, and it operates in modern tarot usage. Initiation serves the same purpose in any fraternal organization, from indigenous tribes to Greek mystery schools to fraternities. Initiation is a global and cross-cultural practice. The spiritual lessons of these groups were more than stories and parables in a book. They are not taught or orated. It was essential that the lessons be experienced by the practitioner. The individual meets the experience at a personal level, through their unique viewpoint. The process is immersive.

A boy on the threshold of adulthood can't understand what it means to fend for his life until he actually does it. He is trained, given survival tools, and sent on a multi-day adventure into the wild. His experience occurs alone. He quests to find himself. He returns and is declared a man. Each of us must meet life on our own terms and experience certain key moments for ourselves. We don't know what it means to fall in love until lightning strikes our heart and we tremble in passion's wake. A woman can anticipate and imagine childbirth yet never

. . . .

know what contractions feel like until she experiences them. Tarot is initiatory because our experience colors the card's meanings. Events unfold as each card is encountered. Each of us brings our own unique experience to the cards. Our past/present/future experiences can be held against the cards for further understanding.

Tribal initiations are extreme, external, and physical in nature. Masonic and mystery initiations seek to transform via symbol. It is an interior transformation. The initiate is blindfolded. The blindfold represents darkness and the former life of the initiate. The initiate moves through an ordeal. Down is up and up is down. The ego breaks and the soul is reborn. The blindfold is removed. The initiate sees the world with a new set of eyes. The initiate is accepted by the tribe and recognized as one of their own. The same system is used in fraternities and sororities on college campuses.

Freemasonry and occultism gained momentum among buttoned-down Victorian societies who held strict moral and ethical codes. Their behavior reflects a universal human desire for archetypal, primal experience. Victorians sought the tribal experience inside the parameters of their "proper" and colonialist culture. They embraced the initiatory experience, an essential step for the mystical and magical practitioner, inside their lodges. The Worshipful Grandmaster would rattle chains, make strange noises, and create an intense sensory experience for his blindfolded initiate, all the while dressed in a three-piece suit decorated with medals and medallions. The initiatory experience, rooted in indigenous cultures, played out in Masonic halls across Europe and the United States. The fact that millions of European and American men participated in such rituals, even if its aims were social rather than spiritual, is a startling and interesting commentary on human nature's primal desires.

Masonic grades marked the Mason as he rose to higher levels. The Golden Dawn used these grades, but instead of applying Masonic ideals, they placed occult and magical philosophy inside their systems. The Masonic framework gave them structure. They filled the structure with their own unique blend of magic and mystery. The Masonic structure gave the Golden Dawn the building blocks for their magical organization.

. . . .

Tarot Structure

Once the Golden Dawn had an organizational structure for members to adhere to, it was time to organize their work. French occultist Éliphas Lévi predated the Golden Dawn. He inspired Golden Dawn magicians with a stroke of sheer genius. Lévi was the first person to place tarot at the center of occult science. He considered astrology, alchemy, and Kabbalah to be actual sciences worth study, examination, and experimentation. He famously stated, "To practice magic is to be a quack; to know magic is to be a sage." He means that once an individual understands the true nature of magic and divinity, there is no need to practice spells or incantations. To know true magic is to understand you are infused with magic and energy at every level. Once Lévi placed tarot at the center of all occult sciences, it altered tarot's usage forever. Lévi believed tarot was "the most perfect instrument of divination." He believed it was a symbolic synthesis of all earthly and supernatural knowledge. Every magical system could be placed within the context of tarot due to tarot's sublime structure. It fit together perfectly.

1888: Golden Dawn's Creation and the Triad of Secret Chiefs

The Secret Chiefs were a trio of enterprising gentleman who plotted and planned the formation of the Golden Dawn. Doctor William Wynn Westcott was a "Coroner of the Crown," a London doctor. His day job was examining corpses to determine the cause of death. Westcott conducted inquests for twenty years and published numerous works on the nature of pharmacology, suicide causation and prevention, and the effects of alcoholism on the body. Occult study captivated Westcott's imagination. This large, grandfatherly looking fellow would go on to publish dozens of books, articles, and lectures on vast occult subjects. Westcott called on his friend and colleague William K. Woodman, a forensic pathologist. He asked Woodman to join him in creating the Golden Dawn, a society to study occult and magical practice. Westcott envisioned his group to be highly secretive, select, and intensely productive. Woodman, a passionate gardener, agreed. Woodman died in 1891, three years after the formation of the Golden Dawn.

The third Secret Chief was Samuel MacGregor Mathers, a handsome English chap with intense eyes. He was fluent in multiple languages, including Latin, Greek, French, and Gaelic. He translated numerous works of occult literature throughout his life. He penned many of the Golden Dawn rituals and took over as head of the organization when Woodman passed away. Mathers's wife, Moina, was the first member to be initiated into the Golden Dawn. Moina was an extraordinary visual artist, psychic medium, and Egyptologist who played a significant role in the group. Mathers wrote the highly influential *Book T*, which was circulated among Golden Dawn members. The *Book T* creates a perfectly workable system aligning tarot with the Kabbalah. Mathers says of his work, "The result of these has been to show me how absolutely correct the symbolism of the *Book T* is, and how exactly it represents the Occult Forces of the Universe." The *Book T* bore direct impact on the creation of the RWS deck. The *Book T* was obviously referenced many times by both Pamela and Waite while creating their rectified tarot.

. . . .

Cipher Manuscripts

The Golden Dawn needed a fascinating, entrancing origin story to draw members into its ranks. After all, every religion and organization worth its salt contains an essential creation story. The Mormon Joseph Smith discovered angelic plates in the woods. L. Ron Hubbard, the science-fiction author, created an extraterrestrial Scientology origin story. Christianity contains a virgin birth and a god who is murdered and reborn as the savior of all humankind. The Secret Chiefs wanted a juicy story, and they wasted no time creating one.

The Cipher Manuscripts became the center of the Golden Dawn's origin story. Westcott claimed he'd come into possession of a number of secret manuscripts. They were written in code. Two versions of his acquisition exist. The first version claims Westcott found the manuscripts in old book stalls. The second version says he inherited them amongst a series of papers from a friend. Either way, Westcott, a self-proclaimed expert on occult matters, deciphered the sixty folios.

The documents contained a collection of Masonic-type rituals that could be used by both men and woman. These magical rituals aligned with the elements of earth, air, fire, and water. The papers were written in English with Hebrew letters. They held diagrams, contained numerous tarot cards, and included typical subjects of esoteric study. It contained a perfectly workable system of how to progress through a series of esoteric knowledge. The systems were Masonic in structure. They allowed the occultist to work like a Mason progressing through higher and higher grades. The story details of the Cipher Manuscripts' acquisition never matched up. The Secret Chiefs likely invented the story. The documents gave their organization an ancient lineage and thrilled its members. The Golden Dawn was off and running. Members were invited and admitted. Once their status as neophyte, the first level of the order, was secured, dues were paid and their work began. Membership included lessons and rituals in all areas of occult work.

The Golden Dawn's work was grounded in study and scholarship. Written and oral exams were administered. Members would advance through ten grades aligning with the Kabbalistic Tree of Life. Three orders aligned with the three triads of the Tree of Life. Basic symbols, the Hebrew alphabet, and astrological information were memorized. Once an initiate moved into the Second Order, they were allowed to practice magic and create rituals for themselves. Golden Dawn magic took place in the spiritual plane. The spiritual plane could be understood by the layperson as the creative imagination. It is the subtle space entered into during a guided meditation. Spirits were evoked, ritual items infused with energy, psychic protective circles cast. All of this work was done specifically and coordinated carefully. The three orders and ten grades matched up to the ten Sephiroth on the Tree of Life, which also aligned with tarot.

. . . . . .

. . . .

Golden Dawn Membership

The Golden Dawn attracted an intellectual and artistic membership. Women and men participated. Numerous romantic liaisons ensued, entanglements occurred, and married couples joined the group. Nobel laureate playwright George Bernard Shaw was a member. His lover Florence Farr became a member in 1890. Irish literary giant, poet, and playwright W. B. Yeats was an extremely active Golden Dawn member. His muse, the aristocratic Maude Gonne, actress, suffragette, and Irish revolutionary, was a member of the group too. She refused to marry Yeats and famously said of Yeats's proclaimed unhappiness, "Oh yes, you are, because you make beautiful poetry out of what you call your unhappiness and are happy in that. Marriage would be such a dull affair. Poets should never marry. The world should thank me for not marrying you."

Dark master Aleister Crowley, a divisive member of the Golden Dawn, was initiated in 1898. He was dubbed "the wickedest man in the world" by the British press. He delighted in controversy and called himself "the Great Beast 666." Crowley went on to create his own magical societies, including a salacious temple called the Sicilian Abbey and the Thelema religion. This subversive magician practiced all manner of dark, chaos, and sex magic. Crowley exalted the idea of a Scarlett Woman, a high priestess and sexual partner. Crowley sold tickets to his public ceremonial magic performances. He was a serious mountaineer who co-led the first British expedition to K2, the second-highest mountain in the world. He was an occult writer, and he created the Thoth tarot deck, illustrated by Lady Frieda Harris. His deck was profoundly influenced by the Golden Dawn's tarot associations. Arthur Waite and Crowley often butted heads during their time together in the Golden Dawn.

The Golden Dawn contained an intense power structure. Where power exists, people will vie for it. Magic is power. True magic empowers anyone and everyone due to its infinite nature. Like love, individuals can't hoard magic all to themselves, yet it is the nature of any organization, from governments to parent-teacher associations, to experience power struggles within its ranks. Individuals always think they know best, crave the top of the perceived food chain, or believe they understand the work better than anyone else. The Hermetic Order of the Golden Dawn was no exception. Members fought, broke rules, disagreed, and formed numerous factions. Ultimately, the Golden Dawn could not maintain itself. It disbanded, yet they had the single biggest impact on Western occultism. It left behind dozens of rituals, instructions, and research materials for future occultists. Today, Golden Dawn systems are performed and operated around the globe.

. . . . . .

. . . .

Waite and Smith's
Golden Dawn–Influenced Deck

Arthur Waite created his own faction of the Golden Dawn after schisms divided the group. Pamela Colman Smith was among the members joining him. It was during this time that Pamela and Waite created the RWS tarot. Golden Dawn members took an oath of silence regarding their occult work. Waite was faced with the challenge of preserving the esoteric secrets of the Golden Dawn when he commissioned the deck and wrote the accompanying book. To keep his secrets, Waite printed the fortunetelling points of the cards. He coded the Golden Dawn occult secrets in vague language. By coding his work and paying heed to traditional fortunetelling definitions, Waite proved an excellent point. He inadvertently made the case for why tarot is universally adaptable. *The Pictorial Key* reflects how tarot can be used for fortunetelling or great spiritual insight.

Waite described the major arcana in a section titled "The Doctrine Behind the Veil." The veil he speaks of is what separates the material and spiritual worlds. Waite tells us,

> The Tarot embodies symbolical presentations of universal ideas, behind which lie all the implicits of the human mind, and it is in this sense that they contain secret doctrine, which is the realization by the few of truths embedded in the consciousness of all, though they have not passed into express recognition by ordinary men.

His sentiment expresses that tarot contains a secret truth that is embedded in everyone, yet few people recognize and understand it. The secret truth, for Waite, securely rests in the major arcana cards, and he speaks of the "higher intentions" of these cards, meaning the spiritual journey of the cards. He acknowledges this with an ultimate tease, saying,

> There is a Secret Tradition concerning the Tarot, as well as a Secret Doctrine contained therein; I have followed some part of it without exceeding the limits which are drawn about matters of this kind and belong to the laws of honor.

Waite hints at the esoteric meanings without ever fully explaining them. He discusses "inner symbolism," meaning the symbols are meant to evoke meaning inside the reader and awaken truths lying dormant in our consciousness.

Waite calls the court cards "the bridge between the Greater and Lesser Arcana." Waite gives little detail and explanation to the minor arcana cards. He admits they relate to the "divinatory meanings." He tells his reader that they "have been drawn by many sources." This reflects the various influences that Pamela used to illustrate the minors. Waite's great concern and focus is the major arcana. A few of Waite's descriptions of the minors do not match Pamela's illustra-

. . . .

tions. Waite claims all the minor arcana cards, with the exception of the aces, are designed for the benefit of divination:

> In the rectified Tarot which illustrates the present handbook, all numbered cards of the Lesser Arcana—the Aces only excepted—are furnished with figures or pictures to illustrate—but without exhausting—the divinatory meanings attached thereto.

Regardless, Pamela Colman Smith was well versed in Golden Dawn theory and couldn't help but include occult symbolism even in the cards designed to display divinatory meanings. For Pamela Colman Smith, all imagination was a shared landscape. It is clear there is no separation for her between the minor and major, all cards being of the same imaginary universe.

Waite admits that the cards offer hints of the occult treasure that lay beyond. He tells the reader what to do when they encounter cards loaded with occult symbolism, such as the Ten of Pentacles: "When the pictures in the present case go beyond the conventional meanings, they should be taken as hints of possible developments along the same lines." He claims the minor arcana will help the intuition uncover occult truth:

> The mere numerical powers and bare words of the meanings are insufficient by themselves; but the pictures are like doors which open into unexpected chambers, or like a turn in the open road with a wide prospect beyond.

His words here are beautiful, elegant, and perfectly describe a deck whose pictures keep opening into unexpected chambers over a hundred years after they were drawn.

The deck was originally titled the Rider-Waite Deck. The title combined Waite's name with that of his publisher, William Rider. Tarotists felt the title of the deck overlooked Pamela's impact and underscored the importance of her illustrations. Later editions of the deck changed the name to the Rider-Waite-Smith deck to honor Pamela's contribution.

• • • • • • •

Chesed (Mercy)
Kabbalistic Tree of Life

It is essential to understand the Tree of Life if you are to deeply recognize the symbolism of the RWS deck. There is no way around it. Thankfully, knowing how the Tree of Life relates to tarot will blow your mind. It is worth grasping Tree of Life basics, even if you do not intend to become a practicing Kabbalist. It will add depth to your tarot reading and bring the RWS deck to life before your eyes. Dozens of RWS cards are imbued with the tree's symbolism. The tree is a fascinating esoteric system combining language, numbers, and graphics aligning perfectly with the structure of the tarot deck. In a sense, if you study the tree, you study tarot, and vice versa. The tree can sometimes feel overwhelming and intimidating. This chapter will provide a quick overview on a deep metaphysical system. We'll have some fun while we're exploring it.

The Golden Dawn knew structure was essential for their organization's success. They used Masonic structure to organize their rituals and degree systems. They infused tarot and the Kabbalistic Tree of Life's structure into their metaphysical workings. Tarot was connected to the Tree of Life by Éliphas Lévi. The Tree of Life has no "official" connection to tarot. Occultists simply realized the systems blended seamlessly.

The tree expresses divine nature as it appears, manifests, and seeps through reality into everyday life and the material world. Ancient Kabbalists were pre-medieval Jewish holy men who meditated and worked with Talmudic works and Hebrew scripture to understand the nature of divinity. Literally translated, *Kabbalah* means "to receive," and it can be spelled many different ways, including Kabalah, Cabala, and Qabala. Any spelling is valid. Over the years, other faiths, including Christianity, placed Tree of Life symbolism in the context of their spiritual stories. The Golden Dawn occultists and the Western traditions that sprang up from the Golden Dawn's work would go on to do the same thing. Waite explains it perfectly in his book *The Doctrine and Literature of the Kabalah*:

The true student of occultism believes in the existence of a knowledge—which in effect is occult science—handed down from remote ages, and that it concerns, broadly speaking, the way of union between man and God.[31]

The best way to explain the Tree of Life, which can feel weighty and confusing due to its philosophical nature and complex Hebrew alphabet and language, is to place it in the simplest possible terms. Indulge me: let's go time traveling. Let's head back—not to foggy London, not to ancient holy men in dark medieval times, but to the flashy, colorful, and hilarious 1980s. We are heading to the mall. If you wore deep blue Jordache denim, feathered your hair, and popped your puberty hormones around the time MTV debuted, you recall gaming arcades. If you weren't around in the '80s, you've probably seen arcades in movies and TV shows.

Gaming arcades were a major teen hangout found in most American malls and bowling alleys in the 1980s. They were dark rooms filled with kids and electrified with hot pink and lemon yellow neon. Flashing electronic games and snacks lured teenagers inside. Digital sound effects popped and zoomed from games like Pac-Man, Centipede, and Space Invaders. The arcade's wall-to-wall carpeting was usually soaked with soda stains and sneaker grease. Speakers blasted Pat Benatar, Journey, and Madonna through smoky cigarette air.

Video games glowed at the front of the arcade while old-school '70s pinball machines, a dying breed of game, were pushed to the back. Pinball machines had different themes. The themes took inspiration from popular TV shows like *CHiPS* or *Dukes of Hazzard* or movies like *Star Wars* or *Jaws*. The game itself remained the same no matter what theme the machine took: two flippers, three or four shining silver balls, and glowing bumpers set to ricocheting the ball anytime it hit.

The arcade will help us understand the Kabbalistic Tree of Life. Now that you have the scene in mind, take my hand. Let's move through the arcade and check out this room in back. We'll step through this door, and now I'm closing the door. It's pitch-black inside, totally dark, but bear with me. The darkness has something to show you. In fact, this darkness is *everything*. It is nothing, or *no thing*. You can't see your hand in front of your face. This is the state of not-being that theoretically exists before the appearance of the Tree of Life.

Cross-cultural religious and spiritual creation stories usually include a time of nothingness prior to the beginning of god/human time. This is due to the linear nature of the human mind. Humans tend to think in beginning, middle, and end terms because our life, our days, and our experience of most things contains a beginning, middle, and end. We apply this structure to all our narratives, including our creation stories. Inside this state of darkness the divine presence usually makes its first appearance. As a reminder, I'm using the word "divine," but you can

---

31   *The Doctrine and Literature of the Kabalah*, 37.

· · · · · · ·

insert any meaning you want: God, aliens, Buddha, Jesus, Zeus, David Lee Roth, whatever you like. I am not here to preach specifics or dogma. I am simply showing you how this really cool Tree of Life machine works and how it applies to tarot. Are you with me so far?

Here we are in the inky darkness. We can't even hear the arcade music anymore. It's like we are cut off from the world. *No thing*. Blackness falling like a curtain. A glowing light pierces the dark. This singular light appears in the center of the room, bright white but not blinding. It is warm and pulsating and you feel yourself drawn to it. The glowing circle has the word Kether (Crown) written above it. You move toward the light, intrigued and relieved to find something to look at. You bump into something cold and metallic. It hits you at your waist and hipbone. As you feel it with your hands, you realize you are standing against a giant pinball machine. The glowing light is a bumper beneath the glass of the game.

The circle, the light in the dark, is divine presence. The word Kether is its Hebrew name. The word Crown is its English translation because the word Kether means crown. It aligns with your crown chakra. The light looks like the eyeball of a god opening up. However, this circle is more than an eyeball looking at you and me. The circle is like a funnel or a waterfall. Divinity pours out like a fountain. This space allows Divinity to unfold its consciousness in this particular place and in this particular context. The material world, the human idea of darkness, gives a "thing" a context in which to exist; otherwise the thing or divine presence would be invisible. Divine consciousness appears just as you appeared when your consciousness unfolded.

A giant electric sign appears with an electric buzz and flash across the top board of the pinball machine. It says "Sepher Yetzirah (Book of Creation)." Sepher Yetzirah is the theme of this pinball machine. In real life, the Sepher Yetzirah is the title of an ancient Hebrew text created circa 200 CE. Sepher Yetzirah is the Hebrew title; it is also called the Book of Creation. The book explains how the Tree of Life operates. William Westcott, a founding secret chief of the Golden Dawn, wrote a translation of the Sepher Yetzirah in 1887 that was used as a primary text for the group.

The Sepher Yetzirah is a simple and concise manual explaining how divinity manifests in the world. How can an event as monumental as divine presence appearing be so simple? Think about it for a moment. The essence of all dogmatic and religious principles usually boils down to a few essential concepts. How people integrate, understand, and work with these concepts is where massive texts and years of study, work, and contemplation begin.

The nature of religious and mystical texts echo the occultist's statement "as above, so below." What is complex is actually simple, and what is simple is complex. Cool, isn't it? It is just like us. We appear simple to an outside observer. Most of us usually come with one head, two arms, and two legs, yet the deeper you look into us, the more complex we become. Each of us is as unique as a snowflake, imprinted with personal memories, experiences, talents, preferences,

· · · · · · ·

and emotional makeups. Spiritual dogma reflects the humans who craft it. Therefore, spiritual dogma, like humans, is both simple and complex.

Back to our pinball machine—I promise you'll be playing in no time, and I brought plenty of quarters. Don't be shocked or offended that I am taking ancient rabbinical, mystic, esoteric studies and reducing them to a pinball game. This is a starting point. Tarot is complicated enough without throwing Hebraic mysticism on top of it. Here is the Tree of Life in simple terms. You can pursue a deeper practice on your own.

The game is currently dark below the glass, except for the Kether (Crown) circle. It's glowing away, like Divinity is apt to do. I plug the game into an outlet to show you the nine other circles, called Sephiroth (singular Sephira). Bells clang and lights flash as the entire pinball machine springs to life. Ten glowing bumper circles appear, including Kether. The glowing yellow circles are emanations on the Tree of Life. Each one has a different name, a different function, and a different number, one through ten. Kether (Crown), at the top of the game, is the highest, holiest, most sacred Sephira you will ever encounter. Everything begins and ends here. It is important to keep in mind that the energy of the tree moves down toward the material world, the same way a silver pinball moves down between bumpers or glowing circles until it slips through the flippers and back into the game.

Kether (Crown) is the highest point of the tree and is connected to pure divine energy. The Kabbalistic tree is upside down compared to our earthly trees. Because the Tree of Life is divine in nature, it is rooted in the highest spiritual place "above." Our earthly trees grow their roots at the base in soft soil and gather nutrients from the ground. Earthly trees reach upward like steeples, temples, and holy architecture pointing upward toward the divine nature above us. The Tree of Life takes its nutrients from the Divine. The Tree of Life sprouts opposite to earth—it grows, spirals, and reaches down toward us. As above, so below.

The entire tree funnels into a single lone Sephira circle. It stands alone at the bottom and is numbered ten and called Malkuth (Kingdom). This is where you stand leaning against the corner of the pinball machine. Malkuth represents everything in the material world. It aligns with your root chakra. This is the place our bodies live, love, and exist in. It is the physical world around us. Every other Sephira exists in the invisible spiritual world. They are unseen by normal human eyes. Divinity pours out of Kether and moves through each Sephira until it emerges in the material world inside Malkuth.

It may feel counterintuitive or uncomfortable to know most of the Tree of Life is invisible to the human eye. At first, it can feel like a lot to swallow until we consider the tarot deck. The tarot, too, is mostly invisible to the human eye. It is made up of the major arcana and the four suits of the minor arcana. The four suits represents emotions and feelings (cups), thoughts and calculations (swords), passion and spirituality (wands), objects and people (pentacles), and archetypes (majors). We observe emotions in others and in ourselves, but we can't hold them. We think thoughts and see others making calculations, but you can't smell a thought. Our bodies experience and express passion, but passion itself is tasteless. Even pure archetypes of the major arcana are impossible to find in their entirety in daily life. There are only fourteen cards in the tarot deck that you can see, feel, touch, smell, and taste with your bodily senses, and that's the suit of the material world: pentacles.

Tarot and the Tree of Life reflect life's unseen qualities. Our experience of life occurs inside our minds and inside the individual's experience. Our consciousness springs from deep inside us, our body and our mind. Life is experienced through personal perception. It is completely subjective. One person sees a glass half empty while another sees the glass half full. Once we know, understand, and integrate this truth, we have the opportunity to become powerful beings. We dictate our experience of life. Life does not define us. Technology is clever at tricking us into thinking we are having an authentic experience when we are not. To become grounded in the self, walk or move through nature. It will put you in touch with you. Nature, like tarot, will open doors of perception you didn't realize existed if you pay attention closely.

The Sefer Yetzirah explains two Kabbalistic concepts intimately connected to tarot. The ten glowing circles on the tree called Sephiroth and the twenty-two letters of the Hebrew alphabet. Can you see the connection between the Sephiroth and tarot? If you figured out there are ten cards in each suit of the minor arcana, excluding the court cards, I'm running to the snack bar to buy you a cherry slushy. Esotericists connect the ten Sephiroth to the ten cards of the minor arcana.

Did you realize the twenty-two Hebrew letters match up to the twenty-two major arcana cards? I'm treating you to an order of french fries with extra ketchup. The Sephiroth reflect and direct divine awareness. They are arranged like glowing circle bumpers on a pinball machine. The Sephiroth are connected by paths. Each path is like the straight line a silver pinball takes as it shoots through the game. The paths on the Tree of Life reflect energy moving from one Sephiroth to the next. All the Sephiroth are connected. It's just like the veins in your body. Instead of pumping blood, the Sephiroth and its paths pump divine energy. All this circulatory energy winds up on earth in Malkuth (Kingdom). The paths are straight and specific.

I'm going to show you how they work by releasing a ball into the pinball machine. Ready? Pop in your quarter. A silver ball appears with a slew of ringing bells. You pull back and release the spring and send the ball to the top of the game. The ball moves in straight lines between the first and second Sephiroth. This is the Fool's path. It moves between the first and second Sephiroth, Kether and Chokmah, back and forth. Here is the Magician's path between the first and third Sephiroth, Kether and Binah. As I said, there are twenty-two paths on the tree. There are twenty-two major arcana cards. Each path is connected to a major card, but guess what?

• • • • • • •

There are also twenty-two letters in the Hebrew alphabet. Each path connects to a card and to a Hebrew letter.

Observe the Sephiroth's pattern. The tree is constructed in a trio of triads. The three triangles funnel down into the tenth Sephira, Malkuth (Kingdom). The top triad is important, especially in regard to the tarot deck. The top triad is called the supernal triad. The word supernal means celestial or heavenly. Triad, as you know, means three. This celestial trio relates to all divine trinities found in religions across the world. It coincides with the trinity of Father, Son, and Holy Spirit. It relates to the Wiccan Maiden, Mother, and Crone. The Tree of Life's supernal triad contains Crown, Wisdom, and Understanding. Keep your eyes peeled—you'll see many graphic representations of the supernal triad and larger versions of the tree inside the RWS deck.

Ancient scholars considered the Hebrew language to be infused with divine energy. The letters of the alphabet help divine energy manifest in the world. This concept holds true of any language that sculpts, shapes, and informs the nature of reality. Remember when your mom told you that your words count? According to the Tree of Life, words really do matter. Each letter holds an additional meaning or metaphor inside the letter itself.

Here's a cheat sheet for the Hebrew letters, tarot associations, and letter meanings:

Aleph	The Fool	Ox
Beth	The Magician	House
Gimel	High Priestess	Camel
Daleth	The Empress	Door
Heh	The Emperor	Window
Vau	Hierophant	Nail
Zain	The Lovers	Sword
Cheth	The Chariot	Field/Fence
Teth	Strength	Serpent
Yod	Hermit	Hand
Kaph	Wheel of Fortune	Palm
Lamed	Justice	Teach
Mem	Hanged Man	Water
Nun	Death	Fish

Samekh	Temperance	Peg
Ayin	The Devil	Eye
Peh	The Tower	Mouth
Tzaddi	The Star	Fishhook
Qoph	The Moon	Back of the Head
Resh	The Sun	Face
Shin	Judgement	Tooth
Tau	The World	Signature

. . . .

Numerology and the Tree of Life

Each Sephiroth contains a number, one through ten. Align the Sephiroth numbers to their corresponding tarot numbers to bring rich and deep meaning to the cards. Look and see how they enhance the meaning of each card:

One: CROWN / KETHER (TAROT'S ACES)

The Godhead appears. Perfect wholeness. One is the spark. Beginning. Something out of nothing. Consciousness. Possibility exists. Options become available. The blank page contains a mark, a spot. A figure appears on the horizon. It is one. It is you. It is awareness. It is a thing. It is the most sacred act of manifestation. It is the Primal Force. It is the root of all thought. It is ultimate creativity. In *The Doctrine and Literature of the Kabalah,* Waite tells us that

> Kether contains all things, is it the egg in which reposes the germ of the universe, to borrow the symbolism of another system. In particular it contains the remaining Sephiroth, which are the sum of all things.

The Tree of Life grows exactly like an earthbound tree except it springs from above. It is a reflection of what is found on earth; as such, it is opposite to earth. Imagine a tall green tree in your backyard or local park. Imagine a giant hand appearing out of a cloud like a tarot ace. It holds a huge mirror over the tree. The reflection of the tree is oppositional to how the tree grows on earth. This is exactly how the Tree of Life grows. Its roots are at the highest point of the universe. It grows down and points toward the earth. This is why the root of the tree is located at the top and called Crown. This is why the root of the tree is called Kether and translates into the word "crown." One single thing.

- Body part: crown of head

. . . .

Two: WISDOM / CHOKMAH (TAROT'S TWOS)

Energetic duality reflects the churning engine of life. Force and energy is expansion with no end until there is two. Rather than radiating into infinity, energy now has something specific to react to. Yin and yang appear. Dark and light. Sun and moon. Day and night. The recognition of oneself and a mirror. The definition of the "other." The masculine and feminine. Mother to child. Lover to lover. Dancer and stage. Writer and page. Bees and flowers. Two white towers. Reflection. In *The Doctrine and Literature of the Kabalah,* Waite reminds us that "Chokmah is described in the 'Book of Formation' as the Breath of the Spirit of God."

The High Priestess is numbered two, and she is drawn in the RWS deck as the card through which tarot's water flows. Water moving through the tarot deck is an apt metaphor for emotional compassion and love. It also reflects the nature of energy in motion, a here and there. It is ultimate intuition and ultimate paradox. A paradox is a concept feeling counterintuitive. A paradox is seemingly contradictory, yet it sees and feels true. The number two is the wellspring of complexity allowing diametric opposition. Can a single thing, being, or consciousness hold duality? Is it possible to hold two oppositional things equally? Yes, it is possible, and this remarkable intelligence is why Chokmah translates to the word "wisdom." Two is duality.

- Body part: right side of the head

Three: UNDERSTANDING / BINAH (TAROT'S THREES)

Triplicity is the ultimate creative act. The pairing results in a third. Two react to each other and a third appears. A result springs from the duo. The soul responds to the Divine, causing the Divine to respond in ecstatic manifestation. This is the ultimate act of creativity found in the trinity, the most powerful shape and form in the universe. In *The Doctrine and Literature of the Kabalah,* Waite tells us that "Binah, Intelligence or Understanding, is…the highest Sephiroth with which man can establish correspondence."

It is beauty but also elements of the mind. Archetypal patterns are formulated here. The ability to communicate is born. Pattern and structure appear. A blueprint has emerged, and it makes logical analytical sense. All creative acts make sense in their context. The third element is often the integration and combination of the first two points, and this is why Binah translates to "understanding." You can understand something when you see yourself in it. In the number three dual elements combine equally, and understanding is born. Three is creativity.

- Body part: left side of the head

Four: Mercy / Chesed (Tarot's Fours)

The number four fosters stability. Maturity is achieved. A groundwork and foundation is laid. Structure endures, and systems are placed. A house is built. A book is outlined. The plan is hatched. The recipe's ingredients are gathered. The spell is plotted. Structural components line up. This is where spiritual essence moves toward manifestation. In *The Doctrine and Literature of the Kabalah*, Waite tells us that "it expresses the eternal love and compassion, connecting with life and vitality."

Devotion explodes from this Sephira like a parent's love for their child. Deep compassion is born. Kindness is fostered. Forgiveness is offered. The empathetic qualities inside of a four's structure is why Chesed translates into the word "mercy." The material world and its blueprint is now a distinct possibility. A map is there. The plans have emerged. The future is foreshadowed. Four grounds the world.

- Body part: right arm

Five: Strength / Geburah (Tarot's Fives)

Force must be applied in order for the material world to materialize. This effort and energy is found in the place of Geburah. Challenge is confronted. Unexpected outcomes complicate the matter. Stakes rise. Old patterns return to haunt. Wounds rip open and bleed. Past meets present as new formulations occur. True evolution requires moving past old boundaries. In *The Doctrine and Literature of the Kabalah*, Waite tells us Geburah signifies "Judgment, Justice, Judicial Power, known also as *Pachad*, or Fear."

Limits must be placed on expansion in order for enduring possibility to emerge. This is how the Emperor reacts to the Empress's creativity. By imposing limits, boundaries, and parameters, her creativity is actualized. It becomes real. This is why material limitations exist inside the material world. Without these limitations, the earth itself cannot exist. Emperor-like limitations are like gravity keeping the world together. Without gravity we would detach from the earth. Once a habit is formed, it is simple to maintain because natural energy supports repetition. Bread must be kneaded, nails hammered, and bedtimes enforced. Repetition becomes easier after the original effort. Tarot is grounded in repetition, matching the cycles of the solar system and the known universe. Material expansion and limitations come through discipline and specific applied energy. This is why Geburah translates into "strength." Five challenges everything.

- Body part: left arm

Six: Beauty / Tiphareth (Tarot's Sixes)

Six is the heart center. This is the place of love. It is the place of giving. It is heart consciousness and divine compassion. Vulnerability is developed here because it has experienced the pain of loss and separation in the previous numbers. Six is the divine space of meditation bringing us back to our essential self. It is the gap and silence allowing the individual to reach straight into the godhead. Sixes are the notes between the music. The subtext of a poem. The unspoken truth. The place of listening. It is learning from another person just by being in their presence. The harmony felt when attention is placed on beauty and love. By extension, the individual becomes beauty and love. Six is the place of deep humor because laughter is a spiritual opening. In *The Doctrine and Literature of the Kabalah*, Waite tells us that "the sixth Sephira… summarizes the Divine goodness; it is the heart of the pillar of benignity."

Structure and form make their way to the material world and a sense of aesthetic sensitivity is fostered. Appreciation for the complexity and variety of the world to come fills the soul. Evocative fall foliage stops you in your tracks during an October stroll. Time stops as you witness a searing orange sunset. Newborn babies swaddled in white cotton inspire a compassion and sensitivity you didn't know you had. A stranger steps up out of the background to help you. Forgiveness is cultivated toward the one who wounded you. You discover compassion toward yourself in thoughts and actions. This compassion spreads to the world around you. Love is fully expressed. You become a healing force in the world. Kindness is given freely, with no reservations, no strings, and no expectations. This is why Tiphareth translates into the word "beauty." Six is love.

- Body part: heart

Seven: Victory / Netzach (Tarot's Sevens)

Spiritual experience expands as the tree spirals downward like a DNA helix reaching toward earthly realms. Mystery and divinity take shape and merge as the material world. The world of form and shape is approached. Strangeness occurs as separation from the godhead elongates. Spiritual landscapes take form, each unique to the energy traversing it. The creative mind takes over out of sheer necessity. Solutions are arrived at. Creativity and spirituality intertwine at Netzach, mingling inside the same landscape. Knowledge occurs in progress of the work. Inside this knowledge dwells perseverance in adversity. Manifestation is neither easy nor comfortable in its nature. Boundaries are constantly pushed to gain ground. Growth requires expansion. In *The Doctrine and Literature of the Kabalah*, Waite tells us, "Divine goodness itself looks forth upon all creatures, and all the worlds are in fulness and completeness. This Sephira is also termed Eternity."

Find comfort in the expansion to exercise freedom and growth without internal resistance. Embrace discomfort and do not be fooled by it. Make discomfort your friend and cohort. Do not run away from the fine edge, the creative edge, where you find yourself dangling over an ocean of possibility. Instead, move into it. You may feel discomfort in a creative project, moving deeper into a pose in yoga class, or inside the fear of a new life situation. Baby steps; a little at a time. If you push too hard, damage may ensue. Take it easy, yet take it steady. If you do, you will push personal barriers and break new ground every day of your life. Discomfort and strangeness, once embraced, become the mystery taking shape. They create new possibility and unimagined outcomes. This is why Netzach translates into the word "victory." Seven is the uncanny.

- Body part: right leg

Eight: SPLENDOR/HOD (TAROT'S EIGHTS)

Eight is flow. The lemniscate. It is the place where all things add up. The energetic duality of two operates at a full-throttle flow. Work is completed, yet more is to come. Eight is the place of beauty, of refinement, of shining examples. Here is the window glancing down upon the material world. The molecular world is glimpsed in kaleidoscopic splendor. Work happens quickly; it is gaining speed. This is where ideas fly at the creators who will make them a reality. Ideas, stories, inventions, and possibilities come to the world from every direction. They are begging to be turned into reality. What is tugging at your heartstrings? What do you feel compelled to make and create in your life?

In *The Doctrine and Literature of the Kabalah*, Waite tells us, "It is the place of praise, the place of wars and victories, and of the treasury of benefits." This is pure, perfect archetype about to be made real in the material world. The cookies are about to come from the oven. The baby's head is crowning. The artist sees the painting take shape before her. A poem advances toward the poet. Lyrics take aim at the songwriter. The equation and solution enter the mathematician's mind. This is the place where shining invisible things with a consciousness of their own are about to be made manifest in the world of form and shape. This is why Hod translates into the world "splendor." Eight is arrival.

- Body part: left leg

Nine: Foundation/Yesod (Tarot's Nines)

Nine is the filter. Like a coffee grinder or a kitchen sieve, this is the space where everything is ground down and processed through the tree and into the material world. Nine is like a funnel. Matter becomes real, moving from the unseen through the veil into the seen world. Character and personality take shape in this space. Awareness of all possibility takes hold. Understanding is flush, ripe and running through the human body. The individual fills their skin. Blood pumps, features are defined, breath is exchanged. Hidden aspirations become crystal clear and apparent. Desire rushes to the surface. Heady moments of anticipation.

In *The Doctrine and Literature of the Kabalah*, Waite tells us that "it is the storehouse of all forces, the seat of life and vitality, and the nourishment of all the worlds." The baby's body moves through the mother's birth canal. The writer flurries words. Snowflakes shower across fields. Wind gathers its speed across the mountain peaks. Lovers recognize one another. Feelings are put into words. Words translate into actions. Action causes a physical result. Results change reality. There is no going back. Something is about to exist. This is why Yesod translates into "foundation." Nine is threshold.

- Body parts: genitals and anus

Ten: Kingdom/Malkuth (Tarot's Tens)

The ten is the complete manifestation in the material world. Completion. Success. Finality. Existence is real. It is done. It cannot be undone. This is the place of assumed possession. Objects and people can be seen, felt, and touched. This is the place where we spy what we want. Blueprints take shape. Results emerge. The individual stands in flesh and bone. Every form of perception is seen by its respective viewer. Colors dance, light reflects, waters lap. Green leaves shutter with cool breezes, volcanoes spew molten lava, roses bloom. Life, as we understand it, begins.

In *The Doctrine and Literature of the Kabalah*, Waite tells us that "it is the final manifestation, emanation, or development of the Divine Nature taking place in the Divine World." The earth and physical reality exists in Malkuth, or Kingdom. This is the place where you can find everything in the world. This world is a reflection and manifestation of the Divinity above who casts infinite realities through infinite trees. An individual never knows what they might uncover once they begin to experiment with the metaphysics of the material world because each of us is built with different sensitivities. Kingdom is the party we all attend and the dance floor we all slink across. It is the home we inhabit. It is what we see, feel, touch, taste, and integrate. Ten is the material world.

- Body parts: feet

Tree of Life Secret and
Kundalini Connection

Arthur Waite's work with the Tree of Life did not stop once the tree manifested results in the material world. Once the tree is understood, one discovers the nature of the self in relation to the universe around them. These new eyes discover mystery at every turn. The mysterious is imbued in everything surrounding it. Every part, parcel, and piece of life is alive with energy, consciousness, and divinity. This mystery is examined and ultimately it leads us back up the tree, path by path, Sephira after Sephira, into infinite metaphysical journeys. The occultist travels the Tree on their own. They move through each Sephira until they rise to the highest point on the tree, the crown. Here they gaze directly into the eyes of the Divine.

Symbolically, this aligns with the Kundalini yogi who encourages life-force energy to rise from the root chakra to the crown chakra. It is the same process explored via two distinctly different cultural systems. Each achieves the same result: enlightenment and shifting perceptions of the universe and one's place inside it. Christianity places the snake or serpent as a symbol of temptation, while yogis use the snake as a symbol of coiled energy at the base of the spine. This energy travels upward and enlightens the yogi as it activates every part of the body in a form of energetic resurrection.

Pillars

Can you make out three vertical pillars on the Tree of Life? The left Sephiroth line up to form the tree's left pillar. The left side is masculine. The right three Sephiroth line up to make the right pillar. The right side is feminine. The center pillar is gender fluid, infused with both masculine and feminine qualities. It is an integrative center force. The middle pillar leads directly from divine awareness in the Crown to manifestation in the number in Kingdom. The RWS deck makes extensive use of the three pillars of the tree as a spiritual reminder. The High Priestess, the Hierophant, and Justice embody a physical center between two pillars. Their bodies become the center pillar sitting between two pillars, male and female. Pamela fills the deck and finds graphic balance for many of her cards using the three pillars. Pamela places many tarot characters between two mountains, trees, or towers, and in doing so she makes additional veiled references to the tree's pillars.

The outer pillars reflect extremities, and the middle pillar fuses the energy. This is where an individual finds balance inside inner duality. It is the occult objective of integration of all energies inside the body. It is the alchemist's Great Work. It is also why some people consider the World card to be a metaphorical hermaphrodite. The World card reflects an individual who is the master of balancing and integrating all the essences of who they are. The World dancer represses nothing. She moves and expresses herself just as she is. Because nothing is repressed, everything the individual does corresponds with their true intrinsic nature. Wicked magic ensues. Possibilities unfold. This is why the World card is the highest card of the deck.

Four Parts of Your Soul, Four Suits of Tarot, Four Kabbalistic Worlds

Let's go back to the arcade and our pinball room for a moment. It will make this next part easier to understand. We walk away from our Tree of Life pinball machine and move over to the other side of the dark room. A glowing sign appears, blinking above your head. It says "Tetragrammaton (Name of God)." The sign is glaringly bright. You make out four pinball machines underneath it. Tetragrammaton is indeed the name of God or the Divine. Tetragrammaton is a Greek work meaning "consists of four." The tetragrammaton is made up of four Hebrew letters.

Four pinball machines stand side by side and I plug each one in. They spring to life with bells and lights, ping, ping, ping. Each machine has a different Hebrew letter emblazoned across the top: Yod Heh Vau Heh. Under the glass each pinball machine has a tree and ten glowing Sephiroth, matching the original machine we looked at.

The Kabbalistic world is divided into four parts. The four parts align perfectly with the tarot's four suits. The four Hebrew letters translate into Latin as YHVH. This is where the name Yahweh for God was derived. It is the Old Testament's name for God. Make sense? These four worlds (or pinball machines) express the name of the divine creator. Let's get back and examine what those letters actually mean. Remember when I told you that the Hebrew alphabet is infused with divinity? These four letters together express the Divine. They align to the four parts of the soul and the four suits of tarot. They make up the four parts of the Kabbalistic world.

Let's take a close look at the first letter glowing on the first pinball machine. Yod vibrates in color across the top of the game. The board is filled with symbols of pentacles, as found in the RWS deck. Yod aligns with the suit of pentacles. Inside the game and beneath each Sephira, a tarot image has been placed. The Ace of Pentacles' image is under the crown chakra. Divinity pours out of the crown as it also pours out of the ace of every suit. The aces, like Divinity, spill forth the entire suit. By the time we get to the tenth card, there are results seen in the material world. Everything following the ace is part of the ace. It is the same way you can trace your entire life, day by day, back to the day you were born. You are born with your entirety inside you.

Pentacle court cards decorate the four corners of the pinball machine, the King of Pentacles on the top left and Knight of Pentacles at the bottom left. Queen of Pentacles at the top right and Page of Pentacles at the bottom right. The kings and knights align with the masculine pillar, and the queen and page align with the feminine pillar. The pattern holds true for the following three worlds and tarot suits. These are the four Kabbalistic worlds, four parts of the soul, and how the tarot aligns with the tree.

Physical World: PENTACLES / YOD

Yod is the material world and the world of pentacles. It coincides with Kingdom in the Tree of Life. Here is everything you can touch, taste, hear, and see. Everything connected to the world of pentacles connects to Yod. This includes books, chairs, food, people you love, your long, silky hair, and your beautiful, sweet, aloof cat. This is the material world of form and function.

All of the pentacles' minor arcana cards (ace–king) are found inside Yod, the material world.

Emotional World: CUPS / HEH

Heh is the creative world and the world of cups. This is the place of dreams, blossoming thoughts, and emotions. It is from this lofty place that ideas pass through swords to gain a design and find ultimate substance in the material world. It is an imaginative landscape of fantasy with no boundaries, no laws, and no limitations. It is open and wild, rich and forthcoming.

All of the cups' minor arcana cards (ace–king) are found inside Heh, the creative world.

Thinking World: SWORDS / VAU

Vau is the formative world and the world of swords. This is the mental world of thoughts and ideas. It is the thought process for everything before it actually exists in the material world. It is articulation and calculation. It is the space of the mind. This is the narrative world of story. This is where we formulate the stories we tell about ourselves and others. It is the space of "I think, therefore I am." Observe your thoughts. Craft your narrative mindfully.

All of the swords' minor arcana cards (ace–king) are found inside Vau, the formative world.

Energetic World: WANDS / HEH

Heh is the archetypal world and the world of wands. This is the place where archetypes are born. It is the top of the tower. It is energy, passion, and essence. Associating the top of this pillar with the suit of wands is a reminder that passion comes from a divine source and is the most powerful tool in life. It is the generating space of all life as we know it and carries the power to manifest dreams and nightmares into reality.

All of the wands' minor arcana cards (ace–king) are found inside Heh, the archetypal world.

· · · · · · ·

. . . .

Final Thoughts

Now you've gained insight into the Tree of Life. The tree is but one of many spiritual systems explaining the nature of divinity. The tree and the tarot link perfectly to express the somewhat complex nature of the universe and the material/soul existence inside of it. One might say the Tree of Life is a mathematical, linear, masculine sense of understanding the universe. The same conclusions and experiences might be reached by a gardener who sees the unfolding nature of the universe in her neatly arranged flower and vegetable beds. The Buddhist monk high in the Himalayas may reach similar conclusions inside the context of his language and cultural conditioning.

Tarot is a portal allowing readers to look through the material world and gaze at the interior. They may examine the interior of personal landscape, the interior of others, or the interior nature of the world we all live in. Tarot gifts readers with the ability to look past form, structure, and language and gaze directly at what is. Once forms and archetypes are identified inside tarot, readers discover and recognize these forms everywhere they look. Readers discover the vast interconnectivity of all humanity and realize that spiritual systems in every culture—from Hindus to Muslims to Christians—ask the same questions in different languages and cultural contexts. The stories differ, but the desire is consistent. Why are we here? What is the point of life? Where are we going? What does it all mean? How can we become who we truly are?

Tarot and the tree's structure allow the individual to move up and down invisible worlds at their leisure. Tarot is a tool containing seventy-eight gates through which to explore and examine all parts of the interior life and the external life. Possibilities abound and worlds unfold every time a card is flipped. Infinite questions can be asked of the tarot. A single question shines like Venus rising in the evening summer sky: How high, how deep, how far are you willing to go?

. . . .

Geburah (Strength)
Astrology

Understanding the astrology of the Golden Dawn and how it applies to tarot will enrich your understanding of what symbols were chosen to populate the cards. It will also provide you a rich context for understanding and interpreting the cards. Readers who enjoy predictive tarot reading can use astrology to predict certain dates with each tarot card. Additionally, the astrological qualities assigned to each card can be added to the meaning of the assigned card. Astrology can feel confusing to the non-mathematical mindset. This is a pared-down, basic explanation of astrology using the Golden Dawn astrology system. Consider it a diving board off which you can spring into the mysteries of the celestial sphere.

· ·

Reading the Astrological Chart

To understand and apply tarot's astrological associations, it is vital to grasp the basics of the astrological chart. The chart is a pie-shaped diagram reflecting the movement of the zodiac. The zodiac is the belt of heavens around the earth. It includes the sun, moon, principal planets, and the paths they trace as they spin, revolve, and move. The zodiac contains twelve constellations; therefore, there are twelve divisions, or signs, of the zodiac. It looks like twelve slices of pizza or pie. Everyone's birthday falls under one of the twelve signs. My sister is a Libra, and my daughter is a Sagittarius. Which one are you?

· ·

Cardinal, Fixed, and Mutable Signs

The astrological chart, or pie, is a perfect circle containing 360 degrees. There are four seasons in a single year: spring, summer, autumn, and winter. The four seasons are divided by three zodiac signs each. Each astrological sign contains 30 degrees of the zodiac circle.

· · · · · · · ·

Now that the pie is evenly sliced and named with its associated zodiac sign, we can assign qualities to each pie slice and sign. It is the same process as assigning meaning to a tarot card to provide depth and understanding. The difference is, instead of assigning a quality like "curious" to describe the pages of tarot, astrological signs are given something different. Their qualities come under one of three headings: cardinal, fixed, and mutable. Each court card quality is assigned an astrological heading except for pages. Pages serve as the throne, or seat of power, for the ace.

Cardinal Signs

- Tarot queens rule Aries, Libra, Cancer, Capricorn

Aries marks the beginning of the zodiac circle and is placed at spring equinox. Spring, the season of rebirth and renewal, is the starting point of the zodiac. What better place to begin? Directly across the pie from spring equinox, at 180 degrees, is the autumn equinox. Libra marks the beginning of autumn equinox.

Aries and Libra are referred to as cardinal signs. They are the hinges upon which the solar year rotates. The other two cardinal signs are Cancer (assigned to the summer solstice) and Capricorn (at the winter solstice).

Cardinal energy represents fresh, new, original thinking. Cardinal energy is like a burst of fresh air. To remember what a cardinal sign means, think of birds called cardinals. Birds fill daybreak with their bright and beautiful songs. It is exactly how cardinal signs begin the zodiac and each season. The essence of excitement infuses these signs.

Fixed Signs

- Tarot knights rule Taurus, Scorpio, Leo, Aquarius

A fixed sign follows fresh cardinal energy. A fixed sign is found in the center of a season, sandwiched between the cardinal and mutable signs. The fixed sign in spring is Taurus, while its opposite, the fixed sign of autumn, is Scorpio. Fixed is the energetic center of the season. The fixed sign of summer is Leo, and the fixed sign of winter is Aquarius.

Fixed energy is the least likely to change. Fixed signs stay true to their nature and are intense and unwavering. You can remember this by recalling the word *fixed* can mean a thing or object holding firm.

Mutable Signs

- Tarot kings rule Gemini, Virgo, Sagittarius, Pisces

Mutable signs are like bookends marking the end of a season. Gemini ends spring, Virgo ends summer, Sagittarius ends fall, and Pisces ends winter. Mutable energy is bendy, like its title. It is flexible and about to change. Remember what a mutable sign means by recalling that mutable sounds like the word *mutation,* meaning "changing."

Decans

A cardinal sign is followed by a fixed sign and then a mutable sign, followed by cardinal, fixed, and mutable again. The sequence keeps revolving like the Wheel of Fortune. Each individual sign is then divided into three intervals of 10 degrees each. These are called decans.

Temperament and Signs: MASCULINE AND FEMININE

The zodiac signs are given masculine and feminine character. Their temperament is directly related to the four elements. Masculine signs are associated with fire (wands) and air (swords). These masculine signs tend to be expansive and extroverted. These signs "man spread" across the zodiac. Standing in contrast are the feminine signs of earth (pentacles) and water (cups), which tend to be receptive and introverted. These signs are receptive across the zodiac. Use the classic masculine / feminine symbolism of the suits to recall their meaning. Sword and wand symbols are pointed, phallic, and extroverted, while the feminine suits of cups and pentacles are soft and receptive, like containers.

Triplicities: EARTH (PENTACLES), AIR (SWORDS), FIRE (WANDS), AND WATER (CUPS)

Each element corresponds with three signs; this is called the "triplicity of the element." The triplicity of fire includes Aries, Leo, and Sagittarius. Aries is a fire force, which is either creative or destructive. The fire of Leo the Lion is an energy that is inexhaustible. The fire of Sagittarius is like a burning ember surviving all weather conditions, staying alight, burning eternally.

The triplicity of air includes Gemini, Libra, and Aquarius. Gemini is the air of emotion, like a refreshing breeze that clears away fleeting negativity. The air of Libra is the crisp, refreshing autumn wind that lets us know something marvelous is soon to arrive. The air of Aquarius is the gentle, still, crisp air of white winter.

The triplicity of earth includes Taurus, Virgo, and Capricorn. The earth of Taurus is warm, open, and fertile, like the tilled fields of spring. The earth of Virgo is hot and productive, springing forth the flowers and vegetables of summer. The earth of Capricorn is cold and frozen, yet it preserves precious items, goods, and ideas.

The triplicity of water encompasses Cancer, Scorpio, and Pisces. Cancer is the thoughtful, placid water of a still pond. Scorpio is the churning, cloudy, dark and deep-running ocean waters. The water of Pisces is akin to streams of ideas, fantasies, and fancies, impossible to ever stop or slow.

Court Cards and Decans

Court cards rule over three decans; however, the signs overlap. Each court card rules over a third of a single sign and two thirds of the next. Each court card has two major arcana cards

· · · · · · ·

and three minor arcana cards assigned to it. The Golden Dawn assigns esoteric titles to each of the court cards. The reader can choose a significator card (a card describing the subject of the reading) using a birthday or specific date.

QUEEN OF WANDS

- Queen of the Thrones of Flame; Water of Fire
- Moon, Emperor
- Ten of Cups, Two of Wands, Three of Wands

KNIGHT OF PENTACLES

- Prince of the Chariot of Earth; Air of Earth
- Emperor, Hierophant
- Four of Wands, Five of Pentacles, Six of Pentacles

KING OF SWORDS

- Lord of the Winds and Breezes; Fire of Air
- Hierophant, Lovers
- Seven of Pentacles, Eight of Swords, Nine of Swords

QUEEN OF CUPS

- Queen of the Thrones of the Waters; Water of Water
- Lovers, Chariot
- Ten of Swords, Two of Cups, Three of Cups

KNIGHT OF WANDS

- Prince of the Chariots of Fire; Air of Fire
- Chariot, Strength
- Four of Cups, Five of Wands, Six of Wands

KING OF PENTACLES

- Lord of the Wild and Fertile Land; Fire of Earth
- Strength, Hermit
- Seven of Wands, Eight of Pentacles, Nine of Pentacles

QUEEN OF SWORDS

- Queen of the Thrones of Air; Water of Air
- Hermit, Justice
- Ten of Pentacles, Two of Swords, Three of Swords

KNIGHT OF CUPS

- Prince of the Chariot of Waters; Air of Water
- Justice, Death
- Four of Swords, Five of Cups, Six of Cups

KING OF WANDS

- Lord of the Flame and the Lightning; Fire of Fire
- Death, Temperance
- Seven of Cups, Eight of Wands, Nine of Wands

QUEEN OF PENTACLES

- Queen of the Thrones of Earth; Water of Earth
- Temperance, Devil
- Ten of Wands, Two of Pentacles, Three of Pentacles

KNIGHT OF SWORDS

- Prince of the Chariot of the Winds; Air of Air
- Devil, Star
- Four of Pentacles, Five of Swords, Six of Swords

KING OF CUPS

- Lord of the Waves and the Waters; Fire of Water
- Star, Moon
- Seven of Swords, Eight of Cups, Nine of Cups

PAGE OF WANDS

- Princess of the Shining Flame; Earth of Fire

· · · · · · ·

Page of Cups

- Princess of the Water; Earth of Water

Page of Swords

- Princess of the Rushing Winds; Earth of Air

Page of Pentacles

- Princess of the Echoing Hills; Earth of Earth

. . . .

Golden Dawn Astrological Assignments

Uranus: Fool

Discovered in 1781, Uranus is named for the ancient Greek god of the heavens.

Astrologically, Uranus rules rebellion and revolution. Originality and individuality are its hallmarks; it loves to break with tradition. Uranus is a massive energy that provokes daring inventions and new technological breakthroughs.

- Rules: Aquarius (Star)
- Element: Air

Mercury: Magician

Mercury is the planet of communication. It is the winged messenger of the gods and is sometimes portrayed as a trickster. Mercury's energy infuses everything it touches. It keeps things moving. Mercury represents the mind and how an individual perceives their life story.

In astrology Mercury acts as the messenger, ruling daily interpersonal correspondences. This includes writing, speech, media, emails, and contracts. Communication aspects of Mercury are perceived to go awry during a Mercury Retrograde, when the planet appears to reverse its path across the sky.

- Rules: Gemini (Lovers) and Virgo (Hermit)
- Element: Air

Moon: High Priestess

The moon is the closest celestial body to our earth. It is the nocturnal reflector of the sun's light. The sun and moon are often paired together. The moon reflects the shadow self, dreams, and nighttime visions. Early man relished the moon, who would shed light in the foreboding darkness. The moon controls the tides of the oceans. Mankind has looked to the moon's changing face for omens and portents of future events.

In astrology the moon is used to examine the depths of an individual's psychology. The moon reflects personal habits that correspond to the moon's own cyclical habits of waxing, growing full, waning, and becoming dark. The moon indicates unconscious needs that exert a gravitational pull in an individual's life toward the things that they most desire.

- Rules: Cancer (Chariot)

- Element: Water

- Classical planet

Venus: EMPRESS

Venus is known as the "evening star" due to its brilliance in the night sky. It is the planet of love, romance, and harmony. It relates to shared pleasure, how pleasure is offered, and how it is received. Physical delights and all aspects of beauty connect to Venus.

In astrology Venus rules over love and money. Professional tarot readers say love and finances are the two most popular topics of their readings, the top priorities of the clients who visit them. The Empress card is associated with Venus. Venus symbols are often found decorating the card in various decks. How does the astrological meaning of Venus's pleasure qualities enhance or transform your understanding of the Empress's traditional meanings of creativity, motherhood, and femininity?

- Rules: Taurus (Hierophant) and Libra (Justice)

- Element: Earth

- Classical planet

Aries: EMPEROR

Aries is Latin for "the ram." Rams and horns are often ingrained into the imagery of various Emperor cards. Aries is the sign of bravery, laser-like focus, and confidence. Aries reflects the pioneering spirit. Honest and passionate, Aries displays leadership qualities. American president Thomas Jefferson, financier J. P. Morgan, and author Maya Angelou were all born under this sign. Aries influences the first house of the self. Consider how these personalities integrate with the Emperor card.

- Quality: Cardinal

- Element: Fire

- Ruling Planet: Mars

Taurus: HIEROPHANT

Taurus comes from the Greek *Tauros,* which means "bull" or "steer." The symbol of Taurus can be found on various Hierophant cards. Dependable and stable qualities define the sign of Taurus. Taurus reflects a methodical and dedicated spirit. Consider the intersection of Taurus's qualities along with the Hierophant's meanings of tradition, order, and ritual. Taurus is also considered the most sensual sign of the zodiac and one who takes full command of the five senses. Pope John Paul II, William Shakespeare, and Sigmund Freud were all born under this sign. Taurus rules the house of money and possessions. Consider how these personalities integrate with the Hierophant card.

- Quality: Fixed
- Element: Earth
- Ruling Planet: Venus

Gemini: LOVERS

Gemini is the Latin word for "twins." Gemini twins represent the yin and yang of life and all it encompasses. A couple is almost always placed on the image of the Lovers, representing opposites who come together. Geminis are fiercely intellectual, playful, and curious. Gemini reflects an adaptable and imaginative spirit. Delightful and flirtatious, Marilyn Monroe, Josephine Baker, and Harriet Beecher Stowe were all born under this sign. Gemini rules the house of communication, siblings, and elementary education. Consider how these personalities integrate with the Lovers card.

- Element: Air
- Quality: Fixed
- Ruling Planet: Mercury

Cancer: CHARIOT

Cancer is the Latin word for "crab." The crab is a crustacean who lives under an exoskeleton in and near water. The charioteer is often depicted inside a protective chariot. Cancers are considered moody and emotional, as their watery nature would suggest. They tend to be sensitive and intuitive, which are traits closely linked to the element of water. Malala Yousafzai, Frida Kahlo, and Helen Keller were all born under this sign. The fourth house of the zodiac reflects home life, family, and nurturing influences. Consider how these personalities integrate with the Chariot card.

- Element: Water

- Quality: Fixed

- Ruling Planet: Moon

Leo: STRENGTH

Leo comes from the Latin word for "lion." The archetype of lion has been associated with strength, agility, and royalty since the dawn of man. Creatures of such great power appear supernatural. Additionally, they contain feline associations, including stealth, cunning cleverness, and elegance. Qualities of Leo include great determination and bravery in the face of all obstacles. Leo is the epitome of the energetic spirit. The fierce and charismatic Julia Child, Madonna, and C. G. Jung were all born under the sign of Leo. Leo influences the fifth house of pleasure and creativity. Consider how these personalities integrate with the Strength card.

- Element: Fire

- Quality: Fixed

- Ruling Planet: Sun

Virgo: HERMIT

Virgo comes from the Latin word for "virgin." Historically, the word virgin meant a woman who was not married and therefore not owned by any man. The archetype of the Hermit also implies a person (often depicted as male) who sequesters himself, avoiding all human contact, in order to concentrate on spiritual pursuits. Virgo traits include deep loyalty and aching kindness. They contain a hardworking and practical spirit. The profound Mother Theresa, Greta Garbo and Agatha Christie were all born under the sign of Virgo. The sixth house of health is influenced by Virgo. Consider how these personalities integrate with the Hermit card.

- Element: Earth

- Quality: Mutable

- Ruling Planet: Mercury

Libra: JUSTICE

Libra derives from the Latin word for "balance." Scales represent the tension between two opposing forces. The sign of Libra comes at the season of fall, and the figure can be understood as balancing light and darkness or day and night. Scales are the classic symbol of governmental justice. The qualities of Libra include a social and dynamic personality who is outgoing. The enigmatic John Lennon, Jesse Jackson, and Julie Andrews were all born under the sign of Libra.

Harmony and peace are hallmarks of the Libra spirit. The seventh house rules partnerships and is influenced by Libra. Consider how these personalities integrate with the Justice card.

- Element: Air

- Quality: Cardinal

- Ruling Planet: Venus

Scorpio: DEATH

Scorpio is Latin for "scorpion" and translated as the "creature with burning sting." The scorpion archetype bears ancient roots. The oldest arachnid fossil is a scorpion. It is the quintessential symbol of transformation, negotiating darkness in their burrows and hunting under night's darkness. Scorpio is legendary for its secretiveness and seduction. Resourceful and brave, Pablo Picasso, Martin Scorsese, and Theodore Roosevelt were all born under this sign. This is the place of endings and beginnings, the cycles of human life, and the nature of human sexuality. The eighth house reflects sex and death and is influenced by Scorpio. Consider how these personalities integrate with the Death card.

- Element: Water

- Quality: Fixed

- Ruling Planets: Pluto and Mars

Sagittarius: TEMPERANCE

The word *Sagittarius* comes from Late Old English and from the Latin *archer,* meaning "pertaining to arrows," and *sagitta,* meaning "arrow." The archetype of the archer from early hunting man to the modern concept of a heart struck by love's arrow reminds us of the hunting magic inherent in this symbol. Sagittarians are considered curious and energetic. They embody the adventurous spirit. Innovative Ludwig van Beethoven, Winston Churchill, and Walt Disney were all born under this sign. This is the place to examine an individual's dreams and aspirations. It is also the integration of what is learned and expressed at higher levels. Consider how these personalities integrate with the Temperance card.

- Element: Fire

- Quality: Mutable

- Ruling Planet: Jupiter

Capricorn: DEVIL

Capricorn is Late Old English, from Latin *Capricornus,* meaning "horned like a goat." Goats are known to be feisty, temperamental, and independent creatures. These qualities all apply to the sign of Capricorn, who is known as determined and ambitious. J. R. R. Tolkien, Richard Nixon, and Joan of Arc were all born under this sign. Ancient mythologies assign sexual virility and potency to the goat, such as the Greek god Pan. The Judeo-Christian West turned the goat into a devil-like figure, creating a cloven-footed, bearded, horned man who is associated with sexual lust and black magic. This wicked figure is seen or implied on many a Devil tarot card. The tenth house reflects career and social status and is influenced by Capricorn. This house reflects the role we choose and how we inhabit it. It also indicates how our ego is massaged by others. It is also the house of the father figure. Consider how these qualities integrate with the Devil card.

- Element: Earth

- Quality: Cardinal

- Ruling Planet: Saturn

Aquarius: STAR

Like *aquarium,* meaning "pertaining to water," Aquarius means "water carrier." The Star card is almost always shown pouring water or next to a body of water. The sign of Aquarius is known for the qualities of truth and imagination. Affection and intelligence shine through the Aquarius spirit. Revolutionaries Virginia Woolf, Rosa Parks, and Abe Lincoln were all born under the sign. The eleventh house of social groups, causes, and technology is influenced by Aquarius. This is the house that reflects an individual's tribal sense and the ideas that bind people together. Consider how these personalities integrate with the Star card.

- Element: Air

- Quality: Fixed

- Ruling Planets: Uranus and Saturn

Pisces: MOON

Pisces is the Latin word for "fishes." The Moon card often depicts a water creature emerging from a dark pool to greet the moon's rays. "Imaginative" and "creative" are often used to describe Pisces. Pisces reflects a spiritual and transformative soul. Nurturing and intuitive, Edgar Cayce, Auguste Renoir, and Elizabeth Taylor were all born under this sign. The twelfth house of secrets and desires is influenced by Pisces. It is the shadow self, deep nature, and hidden worlds. Consider how these personalities integrate with the Moon card.

· · · · · · ·

- Element: Water

- Quality: Mutable

- Ruling Planets: Neptune and Jupiter

Sun: SUN

The sun is life. It is the center of the solar system. The sun is the sustaining force of the physical world as we know it. Sun symbolism is found on everything from golden royal crowns to fruit cartons. Solar rays are seen as containing the magical properties of life, birth, and possibility. Ancient rituals celebrate the return of the sun each year as the days grow longer. The sun is the star that makes all life possible.

The sun, in astrology, reflects the ego and the self. The sun is the center of the solar system, just as we are the center of our own lives. People and events revolve around us as mini solar systems. This is why the sun represents the will to live and the creative forces at play in our life. Consider how the astrological meaning of the sun integrates with traditional meanings of the Sun card.

- Element: Fire

- Rules: Leo (Strength)

- Classical Planet

Pluto: JUDGEMENT

Science may have revoked Pluto's planetary status but that doesn't deter astrologers. They still count on this celestial body who rides on the far reaches of our solar system. When it was discovered in 1930, it was named after Greek mythology's Pluto, who ruled the underworld. Pluto takes about 248 years to complete its orbit around the sun.

Pluto rules the subconscious in astrology. Renewal and rebirth are all aspected by this transformative planet. This means that Pluto is the place of deep energetic reserves and surprising resources that make all transformations possible. It is a subtle yet wildly powerful planet. Consider how the irreversible internal change of Pluto associates with the Judgement card.

- Element: Fire

- Rules: Scorpio (Death)

- Modern Planet/Celestial Body

Saturn: WORLD

Saturn is often called the "jewel of the solar system" due to its thousands of gorgeous rings made of crystals, ice, and rock. It is named after the Roman god of agriculture.

· · · · · · ·

In astrology Saturn can be seen in opposition to Jupiter. Where Jupiter reflects expansion, Saturn brings restrictions and boundaries. Metaphorically, the two planets hold each other in check or balance each other like the Temperance card balances energies. Rather than looking at Saturn's restrictions as negative, recall that boundaries are required in life. They keep things from spinning out of control. One can also examine this from an artistic standpoint. An artist experiments, blurts, writes, rehearses, and plays with a variety of creative options. This is very Jupiter-like. Once the artist discovers what works and what doesn't, Saturn energy is brought in through editing, refinement, and finishing touches. This is how the two energies work in tandem. Consider how the astrological association of Saturn enhances your understanding of the World card, whose traditional meanings include completion, success, and travel.

- Element: Earth

- Rules: Capricorn (Devil)

- Classical Planet

Aces

The aces in astrology are the birthplace or explosion of the element, just as they are the root or seed of the suit in tarot.

ACE OF WANDS IS THE ROOT OF FIRE

The Ace of Wands is the seed of fire. It is the explosion of the sustaining and destructive expansion of fire. It is the color of human blood. It is the warmth in our bones on cold winter nights. It is the instinct pointing us toward the things we want before we know we want them. It is the rush of animal attraction, the stirrings of sexuality. It is the nerves in your belly when standing up for something you believe in. Everything an individual feels passion, fire, and love for is found in fire and in the suit of wands.

- Qualities: Passionate, daring, driven

- Signs: Aries, Leo, Sagittarius

ACE OF PENTACLES IS THE ROOT OF EARTH

The Ace of Pentacles is the seed containing everything that is manifested in the material reality of what an individual considers concrete words: bodies, houses, mud, dirt, mountains, furniture, cars, people, friends, family, foes, forests, books, computers, animals, cities, towns, entire continents. Everything an individual can touch, taste, see, and feel is found in earth and the suit of pentacles.

- Qualities: Practical, hardworking, logical

- Signs: Taurus, Virgo, Capricorn

. . . .

ACE OF SWORDS IS THE ROOT OF AIR

The Ace of Swords is the seed that contains everything manifested in the world of thought, calculation, and mental acuity. The root of air contains the words spoken to other people and the narrative constructed inside an individual's head. Events play out in life, we decide what they mean or we react, all due to the element of air. Communication forms here: letters, speeches, emails, books. Everything the individual thinks and expresses is found in air and the suit of swords.

- Qualities: Logical, witty, independent

- Signs: Gemini, Libra, Aquarius

ACE OF CUPS IS THE ROOT OF WATER

The Ace of Cups is the seed containing every feeling and emotion a human is capable of. The root of water is the transformative place of human imagination. It holds the individual's capacity to dream, vision, and empathize. It is where we feel love and connection, anger and sadness, hope and joy, despair and boredom. Every emotional response is felt through the lens of water and the suit of cups.

- Qualities: Emotional, empathetic, artistic

- Signs: Cancer, Scorpio, Pisces

Aries

- Explosion of Fire (Cardinal Fire)

TWO OF WANDS—MARS IN ARIES—LORD OF DOMINION

Aggressive Mars meets assertive Aries and the Lord of Dominion is born. To dominate is to take control, exercise influence, and make oneself and one's intentions clear. This card is often illustrated with an individual who is seen plotting and planning an enterprise.

THREE OF WANDS—SUN IN ARIES—LORD OF ESTABLISHED STRENGTH

The explosive and nuclear energy of the sun meets independent Aries and the Lord of Established Strength is born. Established strength reflects an individual who has already proved themselves worthy and powerful. This theme is often seen in the Three of Wands, where a wealthy merchant sets his ships out into the world or, conversely, is waiting for his ships to return with his riches.

FOUR OF WANDS—VENUS IN ARIES—LORD OF PERFECTED WORK
Beautiful Venus meets successful Aries and the Lord of Perfected Work is born. There is inherent symmetry, beauty, and charm in any form of work done to the best of an individual's ability. The theme of perfected work is often seen in the Four of Wands, in the construction of four wands brought together in a celebratory canopy, or chuppah.

Taurus

- Slow and Steady Wins the Race (Fixed Earth)

FIVE OF PENTACLES—MERCURY IN TAURUS—LORD OF MATERIAL TROUBLE
Perceptive Mercury meets stubborn Taurus and the Lord of Material Trouble is born. Who and what we resist has a tendency to persist. The Five of Pentacles often portrays people who are fraught with peril or challenge.

SIX OF PENTACLES—MOON IN TAURUS—LORD OF MATERIAL SUCCESS
The intuitive moon meets pleasure-seeking Taurus and the Lord of Material Success is born. How does intuition foster advancement? How does pleasure serve us in our professional lives? Images of charity are often found on this card.

SEVEN OF PENTACLES—SATURN IN TAURUS—LORD OF SUCCESS UNFULFILLED
Restrictive Saturn meets down-to-earth Taurus and the Lord of Success Unfulfilled is born. How do boundaries restrict us? Being grounded and focused can sometimes distract us from seeing the big picture. The Seven of Pentacles often shows a successful individual who desires more.

Gemini

- Rapidly Changing (Mutable Air)

EIGHT OF SWORDS—JUPITER IN GEMINI—LORD OF SHORTENED FORCE
Expansive Jupiter meets dynamic Gemini and the Lord of Shortened Force is born. The electrifying energy radiating through this card means that it takes minimum effort for maximum effect. This card is often illustrated with an individual who is blindfolded and bound.

NINE OF SWORDS—MARS IN GEMINI—LORD OF DESPAIR AND CRUELTY
Powerful Mars meets mischievous Gemini and the Lord of Despair and Cruelty is born. Omnipotent forces mingle with transgression, and the results are oftentimes disastrous, however fleeting. This card is often illustrated with late-night mental suffering.

TEN OF SWORDS—SUN IN GEMINI—LORD OF RUIN

The explosive sun meets double-sided Gemini and the Lord of Ruin is born. Duplicity often blows up when light is shined on it. This card is often illustrated with an individual who has been killed or stabbed, yet sometimes the card holds a secret clue or message revealing there is more to come.

Cancer

- Bubbling Emotion (Cardinal Water)

TWO OF CUPS—VENUS IN CANCER—LORD OF LOVE

Romantic Venus meets sensitive Cancer and the Lord of Love is born. Enchantment and fascination ensue when two open souls meet. This card is often depicted with a romantic pair coming together in mutual admiration.

THREE OF CUPS—MERCURY IN CANCER—LORD OF ABUNDANCE

Communicative Mercury and friendly Cancer meet and the Lord of Abundance is born. An expressive nature and openness is a recipe for growth, which spurs more of the same. This card is often illustrated with three people dancing, celebrating, and laughing.

FOUR OF CUPS—MOON IN CANCER—LORD OF BLENDED PLEASURE

The moody moon meets empathetic Cancer and the Lord of Blended Pleasure is born. Cups dip into all sides of the emotional spectrum. This card is often illustrated with a person who is offered a cup or opportunity; however, they do not see it.

Leo

- Stable Passion (Fixed Fire)

FIVE OF WANDS—SATURN IN LEO—LORD OF STRIFE

Laborious Saturn meets domineering Leo and the Lord of Strife is born. Powerful personalities and highly charged energy can provoke conflict or disagreement, yet these are the very challenges that push an idea forward into required evolution. The Five of Wands is often portrayed with five youths sparring.

SIX OF WANDS—JUPITER IN LEO—LORD OF VICTORY

High-level-thinking Jupiter meets charismatic Leo and the Lord of Victory is born. Achievement and success take a combination of many elements. This card is often illustrated with a victory parade.

Seven of Wands—Mars in Leo—Lord of Valor

Dynamic Mars meets action-oriented Leo and the Lord of Valor is born. Courage lies dormant until it is called upon. We only know our strength when challenges test us. This card is often illustrated with an individual taking an offensive or defensive stance.

Virgo

- Quakes and Tremors (Mutable Earth)

Eight of Pentacles—Sun in Virgo—Lord of Prudence

The sustaining sun meets Virgo the leader and the Lord of Prudence is born. Sagacity and common sense infuse the word prudence, which is fueled by solar energy. This card is often illustrated with an individual deeply invested in work.

Nine of Pentacles—Venus in Virgo—Lord of Material Gain

Gorgeous Venus meets creative Virgo and the Lord of Material Gain is born. The gathering of material possessions is a pleasing pursuit when we do not fall under the spell convincing us that this is all there is. This card is often illustrated with an attractive woman lingering in a vineyard.

Ten of Pentacles—Mercury in Virgo—Lord of Wealth

Logical Mercury meets clever Virgo and the Lord of Wealth is born. The nature of wealth exceeds finance and includes the people, animals, and places we inhabit. This card is often illustrated with a multigenerational family.

Libra

- Fresh Ideas (Cardinal Air)

Two of Swords—Moon in Libra—Lord of Peace Restored

The intuitive moon and peaceful Libra meet and the Lord of Peace Restored is born. A sensitive nature treated with care and respect will find its equilibrium, and clarity will ensue. This card is often illustrated with a person wearing a blindfold; however, it is not a prison but rather a gateway to inner peace.

Three of Swords—Saturn in Libra—Lord of Sorrow

Restrictive Saturn meets harmonious Libra and the Lord of Sorrow is born. The edge of harmony cuts like a knife. This card is often illustrated with a heart pierced by multiple swords.

Four of Swords—Jupiter in Libra—Lord of Rest from Strife

Fortunate Jupiter meets gracious Libra and the Lord of Rest from Strife is born. Peace often results from stillness. This card is often illustrated with a resting knight or knight's effigy.

· · · · · · ·

Scorpio

- Deep and Eloquent (Fixed Water)

FIVE OF CUPS—MARS IN SCORPIO—LORD OF LOSS OF PLEASURE

Forceful Mars and hardcore Scorpio meet and the Lord of Loss of Pleasure is born. Can two equally powerful energies cancel each other out? This card is often illustrated with a forlorn figure.

SIX OF CUPS—SUN IN SCORPIO—LORD OF PLEASURE

The glowing sun meets sexual Scorpio and the Lord of Pleasure is born. This combination magnifies the energy of the senses. This card is often illustrated with the giving of gifts.

SEVEN OF CUPS—VENUS IN SCORPIO—LORD OF ILLUSORY SUCCESS

Enchanting Venus meets deeply imaginative Scorpio and the Lord of Illusory Success is born. Things that hypnotize us are not always what they seem. This card is often illustrated with cups floating in the air like a vision.

Sagittarius

- Flickering Flames (Mutable Fire)

EIGHT OF WANDS—MERCURY IN SAGITTARIUS—LORD OF SWIFTNESS

Perceptive Mercury meets extroverted Sagittarius and the Lord of Swiftness is born. Speed of the mind and action of the heart make for great haste and the turning of events. This card is often illustrated with wands flying through the air toward an unknown destination.

NINE OF WANDS—MOON IN SAGITTARIUS—LORD OF GREAT STRENGTH

The subtle moon meets enthusiastic Sagittarius and the Lord of Great Strength is born. Energy bursting from unseen reserves can result in amazing feats. The card is often illustrated with the figure of a person moving through a gate.

TEN OF WANDS—SATURN IN SAGITTARIUS—LORD OF OPPRESSION

Authoritarian Saturn meets optimistic Sagittarius and the Lord of Oppression is born. A domineering personality can feel like death to a person who is open and free. This card is often illustrated with an individual who carries a very heavy load.

Capricorn

- Fresh and Fecund (Cardinal Earth)

TWO OF PENTACLES—JUPITER IN CAPRICORN—LORD OF HARMONIOUS CHANGE

Spiritual Jupiter and helpful Capricorn meet and the Lord of Harmonious Change is born. An effortless and pleasurable alteration is a joy to behold. This card is often illustrated with a juggler who balances two balls.

· · · · · · ·

THREE OF PENTACLES—MARS IN CAPRICORN—LORD OF MATERIAL WORKS

Driving Mars meets determined Capricorn and the Lord of Material Works is born. What type of effort is required to construct something in the material world? This card is usually expressed with three people collaborating.

FOUR OF PENTACLES—SUN IN CAPRICORN—LORD OF EARTHLY POWER

Regenerative sun meets ambitious Capricorn and the Lord of Earthy Power is born. The power of earth lies in its ability to produce, nurture, and regenerate. The Four of Pentacles is often illustrated with a figure who grasps his belongings.

Aquarius

- Stillness (Fixed Air)

FIVE OF SWORDS—VENUS IN AQUARIUS—LORD OF DEFEAT

How does the meeting of stunning Venus and imaginative Aquarius spur the Lord of Defeat? The two are set in their ways. They refuse to budge and are so protective they become dangerous to themselves and others. This card is usually illustrated with a fight showing clear winners and losers.

SIX OF SWORDS—MERCURY IN AQUARIUS—LORD OF EARNED SUCCESS

Intellectual Mercury and innovative Aquarius meet and the Lord of Earned Success is born. How is earned success different from inherited success? Which is more valuable? This card is often illustrated with figures crossing a body of water in a boat.

SEVEN OF SWORDS—MOON IN AQUARIUS—LORD OF UNSTABLE EFFORT

The fickle moon meets eccentric Aquarius and the Lord of Unstable Effort is born. What makes an effort unstable? Is it lack of planning, bad luck, or a plan doomed from the beginning? This card is usually illustrated with a thieving figure.

Pisces

- Rippling Waves (Mutable Water)

EIGHT OF CUPS—SATURN IN PISCES—LORD OF ABANDONED SUCCESS

Authoritative Saturn meets gentle Pisces and the Lord of Abandoned Success is born. What does it mean to abandon personal success? Can leaving achievements behind be a good thing? This card is often illustrated as a person beginning an upward journey.

NINE OF CUPS—JUPITER IN PISCES—LORD OF MATERIAL HAPPINESS

Lucky Jupiter meets generous Pisces and the Lord of Material Happiness is born. Luck and generosity meet delicious results. This card is often illustrated with a magic genie on the verge of granting a wish.

· · · · · · ·

Ten of Cups—Mars in Pisces—Lord of Perfected Success
Instinctual Mars meets compassionate Pisces and the Lord of Perfected Success is born. Fire meets love with spectacular results. Usually the card is illustrated with a "happily ever after" ending.

. . . .
The Golden Dawn Astrological Timing

Seasons

Aces: Wands	Summer
Cups	Autumn
Swords	Spring
Pentacles	Winter

Moon Cycles

Pentacles	New Moon
Swords	Waxing Moon
Wands	Full Moon
Cups	Waning Moon

Times of the Day

Pentacles	Midnight to Sunrise
Swords	Sunrise to Noon
Wands	Noon to Twilight
Cups	Twilight to Midnight

Major Arcana Timing

The Fool	Uranus/Aquarius	January 21–February 20
The Magician	Mercury/Gemini and Virgo	May 21–June 20 and August 21–September 20
The High Priestess	The Moon/Cancer	June 21–July 20
The Empress	Venus/Taurus and Libra	April 21–May 20 and September 21–October 20
The Emperor	Aries	March 21–April 20
The Hierophant	Taurus	April 21–May 20
The Lovers	Gemini	May 21–June 20
The Chariot	Cancer	June 21–July 20
Strength	Leo	July 21–August 20
The Hermit	Virgo	August 21–September 20
The Wheel of Fortune	Sagittarius	November 21–December 20
Justice	Libra	September 21–October 20
The Hanged Man	Neptune/Pisces	February 21–March 20
Death	Scorpio	October 21–November 20
Temperance	Sagittarius	November 21–December 20
The Devil	Capricorn	December 21–January 20
The Tower	Mars/Aries	March 21–April 20
The Star	Aquarius	January 21–February 20
The Moon	Pisces	February 21–March 20
The Sun	The Sun/Leo	July 21–August 20
Judgement	Pluto/Scorpio	October 21–November 20
The World	Saturn/Capricorn	December 21–January 20

Minor Arcana Timing (approx. dates)

Two of Wands	March 21–30
Three of Wands	March 31–April 10
Four of Wands	April 11–20
Five of Pentacles	April 21–30
Six of Pentacles	May 1–10
Seven of Pentacles	May 11–20
Eight of Swords	May 21–31
Nine of Swords	June 1–10
Ten of Swords	June 11–20
Two of Cups	June 21–July 1
Three of Cups	July 2–11
Four of Cups	July 12–21
Five of Wands	July 22–August 1
Six of Wands	August 2–11
Seven of Wands	August 12–22
Eight of Pentacles	August 23–September 1
Nine of Pentacles	September 2–11
Ten of Pentacles	September 12–22
Two of Swords	September 23–October 2
Three of Swords	October 3–12
Four of Swords	October 13–22
Five of Cups	October 23–November 2
Six of Cups	November 3–12
Seven of Cups	November 13–22
Eight of Wands	November 23–December 2
Nine of Wands	December 3–12
Ten of Wands	December 13–21
Two of Pentacles	December 22–30
Three of Pentacles	December 31–January 9
Four of Pentacles	January 10–19
Five of Swords	January 20–29
Six of Swords	January 30–February 8
Seven of Swords	February 9–18
Eight of Cups	February 19–28
Nine of Cups	March 1–10
Ten of Cups	March 11–20

. . . .

Timing Using the Court Cards

Queen of Wands	March 11–April 10
King of Pentacles	April 11–May 10
Knight of Swords	May 11–June 10
Queen of Cups	June 11–July 11
King of Wands	July 12–August 11
Knight of Pentacles	August 12–September 11
Queen of Swords	September 12–October 12
King of Cups	October 13–November 12
Knight of Wands	November 13–December 12
Queen of Pentacles	December 13–January 9
King of Swords	January 10–February 8
Knight of Cups	February 9–March 10

CHAPTER SIX

Tiphareth (Beauty)
The Major Arcana

. . . .

The Fool

STORIES CAN BE sung, some painted, some written
in poetry or prose. But all stories can be told, and
told so that every human being can understand them.

Pamela Colman Smith[32]

Sacred

The Fool is infused with the energy of dawn and the possibility of a new day. He walks in pure optimism. The Fool brings life as he stands at the forefront of unfolding consciousness. The Fool is so pure, so fresh, that he carries the number of ultimate potentiality: zero. He is the human soul manifest and aware of itself in the material world. He is so fresh that he does not think ahead of himself or place preconceived judgments on the world around him. The Fool is the state of the soul as it enters the world.

Waite says of the Fool, "He is the spirit in search of experience." Waite could be describing each of us. Aren't we all searching for experience? Experience defines us. It teaches us who we are. The Fool's journey is the adventure shaping each and every one of us on the planet. Every day brings us possibilities and opportunities ranging the spectrum from pleasant to challenging. The Fool greets every experience head-on. Doing so, the experience tempers who the Fool becomes as he travels through the tarot and down the road of life.

32   "Made Veteran Humorist Laugh."

. . . .

MISS ELLEN TERRY

THE FOOL.

The RWS pulls from earlier Fool symbolism. The Fool's upturned face, sack, and canine jumping on his heels is reflected in the Tarot of Marseille (below right). Pamela's Fool symbolism appears in her post-RWS illustration in The Book of Friendly Giants, 1914 *(above left). Pamela's symbolically adopted mother, Ellen Terry, is photographed with her favorite dog (above right), the likely inspiration for the dog on Pamela's Fool card.*

The Fool is a clearinghouse of the senses. He is perception, feeling, and experience. He is the way in which he organizes the world inside the body. The Fool looks at the world in pure innocence and without predetermined labels. He never tires of looking, seeing, and observing because the world is continually new under his step.

The Fool contains every card of the tarot deck inside of him the same way you are the unique container for your personal life experience. An individual's life appears to occur outside because we view others from an external viewpoint. Life, however, occurs within each individual's interior life. Individual consciousness processes events, happenings, and relationships on the inside, not the outside. Buddha says, "Peace comes from within. Do not seek it without."

The Fool is the first card of the RWS deck. The number zero connects the Fool to the World card, acting as a jewelry clasp between cyclical endings and beginnings. The Fool's placement in tarot has changed over the decades. Ancient decks carried an unnumbered Fool. Eighteenth and nineteenth-century decks placed the Fool between Judgement and the World. The Golden Dawn placed the Fool at the front of the major arcana, which allowed the corresponding astrology to line up with the cards. The most usable tarot deck of the twentieth century was born.

Waite speaks to the Fool's expression when he says, "His countenance is full of intelligence and expectant dream." His statement reminds us the Fool is not a simpleton. The Fool is an energetic creature who desires stimulation and adventure. Waite calls him "a prince of the other world." The other world is the invisible world. The Fool passed through the veil from supernatural to natural, from subconscious to conscious. Waite says, "The sun, which shines behind him, knows whence he came, whither he is going, and how he will return by another path after many days." Waite's statement posits the sun as the source of all life and magic. Waite speaks of the Kabbalistic journey of emergence and return when he states the Fool will return by another path. The Tree of Life's paths are each connected to specific tarot cards. The journey of emergence begins at the top of the tree and moves downward until the soul, idea, or thing is made manifest in the material world. The journey of return occurs as the Fool moves back up the tree to convene with the divine energy pouring though the top of the tree. Like the child who grows up and leaves home only to return home as a fully formed adult, so will the Fool move forth into the unknown to discover who he is.

Symbolic

Esoteric Function: No function

Hebrew Letter: Aleph

Element: Air

Astrological Association: Uranus

· · · · · ·

The Fool's tunic displays ten circles. The circles represent the ten emanations (Sephiroth) on the Hebrew Tree of Life. These emanations or circles connect the major arcana's Kabbalistic paths. A careful examination of the circles reveals an eight-spoked wheel inside each circle. Just as the pentacle's star represents four elements and the human spirit, the eight-spoked wheel represents the Golden Dawn's symbol for spirit.

A red feather sprouts from the Fool's cap. Historically, a feather marks the Fool. The Visconti-Sforza deck's Fool carried a slew of red feathers in his hair. Ancient Italian and Christian art used the feather, particularly peacock feathers, as symbols of immortality. The RWS deck's placement of red feathers on the Fool, Death, and Sun cards strings together the narrative of occult expression. The three cards are intimately connected. The Fool's feather marks the occultist moving through degrees of initiation and experience. The Fool is emergence, Death signifies rebirth, and the Sun card merges the occultist with divinity.

Waite describes the Fool's reaction to the gaping cliff before him, stating, "The edge which opens on the depth has no terror; it is as if angels were waiting to uphold him." Innocence protects the Fool. Many interpretations suggest the cliff continues to regenerate under the Fool's light step. The Fool, impervious to any danger the cliff represents, embodies a person unconcerned with external threats.

The Fool is assigned the Hebrew letter Aleph and the element of air because he is the "Breath of Life." The Fool's dog is drawn in the same shape of the Hebrew letter Aleph, which is considered to be the animating principle of life. Geraldine Beskin, proprietress of the Atlantic Bookshop in London, discovered Pamela's source material for the Fool's dog, who is none other than Ellen Terry's favorite pet. Famed actress Ellen Terry took Pamela under her wing after Pamela's father passed away. In addition to Ellen being the muse for many of Pamela's cards, so was her favorite pooch.

The Fool carries a bag fastened to the end of a stick. The Fool's bag reflects the experience he brings with him into his new life. We may be done with the past, but is the past done with us? His bag reminds us how as new cycles begin, we bring the past with us. Experience and past events may be hidden, even forgotten, yet their imprints remain. The Fool's bag of experience includes past lives, genetic inheritance, and any event an individual has experienced.

The Fool walks from right to left. His movement imitates the Hebrew alphabet, also written and read from right to left. The World dancer moves right to receive the Fool's energy. Only the Death card moves directly into the Fool card, reflecting the end of the physical journey and the beginning of the spiritual journey.

The Fool's left hand holds a white flower, yet he looks in the opposite direction. Does he acknowledge what he holds? Perhaps he does not see his gift. Alchemical white reflects purity, while flowers represent manifestation. The white flower thus becomes a potent symbol of seeking what already lies within. As the Fool, each of us enters our journey and life cycle innocently. Experience forges us into who we become. Each person we meet, challenge we face, and obstacle we overcome teaches us more about who we are. The Fool's white flower is the glistening potential inside each and every one of us. It is the pursuit of this flower and the people and places we touch along the way that truly matters. In the end, no matter how wild the journey, we come back to ourselves. Like Dorothy of Oz, we find there is no place like home. The home and flower we sought were inside us all along.

Profane

Optimism. Innocence. Adventure. New cycle. Clean slates.

> **Waite's Divinatory Meanings:** Folly, mania, extravagance, intoxication, delirium, frenzy, bewrayment.

> **Reversed:** Negligence, absence, distribution, carelessness, apathy, nullity, vanity.

Asana

The Fool card aligns with yoga's mountain pose, or tadasana, or samasthiti. The Fool reflects pure consciousness and contains every tarot card inside of him. The same can be said for mountain pose, the place from which all movement issues forth and eventually returns. Mountain pose usually begins a practice, and it is also the physical posture we often take in regular life as we greet the world beyond the mat. The Fool is symbolically placed on a mountaintop landscape, further aligning it with mountain pose. Mountain pose offers a moment to balance ourselves, come to the present moment, reflect upon spiritual clarity, and consider the heights to which we aspire to ascend. The card and the pose also prepare us for the looming adventure lying ahead of us, both in our practice and in our life, which, of course, are one and the same.

· · · · · · ·

THE MAGICIAN.

The Magician on the Visconti-Sforza deck, the earliest known tarot, depicts the magician at his table with the four instruments (suits) of tarot. The RWS deck adheres to this tradition.

. . . .

The Magician

IN A FEW lines
tell your story.

Pamela Colman Smith[33]

Sacred

The Fool is consciousness awakened. The Magician marks the point at which the individual becomes master of his or her consciousness. The Magician holds a powerful key for both tarot and life. His key is mastery of the self. The Magician's experience is strictly in his control. This is the reason all four suits of tarot sit ready and waiting upon the Magician's table. A Magician chooses both thoughts and tools wisely. The Magician doesn't control his "outside." He doesn't control the weather or the stock market or wield maniacal influence over the actions of others. The Magician is in control of his interior experience. Doing so, he decides what his experience of life will be. It is a mental process used consciously and unconsciously by millions of people, from dancers to athletes, from scientists to yogis, from students to teachers. No individual can control external events. However, we are free to control and determine our response to external events, people, and places. This is how a jailed prisoner may experience complete freedom behind bars. Roman emperor Marcus Aurelius said, "You have power over your mind—not outside events. Realize this, and you will find strength." The Golden Dawn was well aware of the Magician's secret. Now you hold the key to his magic. It is a tool you have always possessed. You have complete control over your experience of life once you have control over the mind and emotion.

The Magician exudes a wild charisma, yet he works not for the crowd. Energy radiates through his pores because he is an electric channel, like a power cord buzzing with intensity, looking for an outlet. He uses his wand to siphon energy from the celestial realm above. The energy floods his body and moves through him as he directs it toward the ground, the place of manifestation. The Magician thus becomes the channel for three levels of existence: the upper spiritual world, the middle "real" world of reality (the one we all live in), and the lower world of dreamtime. He embodies the goal of various spiritual traditions as the divine union of energetic connection. The Magician embodies the Sanskrit word *yoga*, meaning "union."

---

33   Smith, "Should the Art Student Think?" 417.

. . . . . .

The Magician and ordinary individuals differ only in the awareness of their act. Attention is energy. Our body is a device controlling energy at every moment of every day. We conserve and build energy at night as we sleep. Our energy is spent during waking hours on people, places, and things. We turn our attention to something and we light it up. The Magician, who already resonates with innate personal power, collects additional energy from above. His posture mimics a flower opening to receive solar rays. His posture reflects the yogi in a sun salutation posture who infuses herself with solar energy. His wand acts like the tip of a cathedral spire, church steeple, or pyramid channeling divine energy from above. This electricity moves through his physical form and is infused with his awareness. The energy exits his body through his pointed finger. He directs it toward the ground, aligning it with his clear intention.

His stance aligns with the great esoteric truth "as above, so below." The phrase expresses a complex and evocative idea. What is true for the macrocosm (the world) is true for the microcosm (the individual). What exists on the inside (interior world) exists on the outside (exterior world). Observe this axiom at work in a negative individual who harbors an angry worldview. Your irritable and annoyed neighbor holds an inner filter of experience making the world look depressing and dark. The individual's irritable inner feelings are projected on the outside world. You see a beautiful sunset while they see a wasted day. We can identify the inner filter acutely when recalling the experience of falling in love. The world is aglow with magic and excitement when under love's epic spell. The flowers sing, days breed excitement, nights harbor erotic mystery. The opposite holds true during extreme periods of tragic grief where time slows and sorrow washes over once-colorful days that fade to black and white. In every circumstance, the exterior world has barely changed. The interior world decorates the outer world. The Magician who recognizes this truth becomes aware of her projection. She stops fighting against external elements and surrenders to them. By giving up the ghost and surrendering—even to a painful circumstance—she cultivates freedom. Discovering this power, she begins working to master the alignment of her inner life to the outer life and discovers a transformation on every imaginable level. Aware of how the inner and outer world works, the Magician directs her energy anywhere she chooses. The Magician's life becomes an enchantment of her own making.

Waite describes the Magician in *Tarot, A Wheel of Fortune* as a man on whom "the spark from Heaven has fallen." These sparks, seen as electric yellow drops on various other cards, are called the sparks of Yod. They carry enlightenment from the highest source. Yod is the holy active principle. Waite speaks of the Magician's posture: "It is known in very high grades of the Instituted Mysteries; it shows the descent of grace, virtue and light, drawn from things above and derived to things below." The "high grades of Instituted Mysteries" is the Golden Dawn. The "descent of grace, virtue and light" is the drawing down of energy and descriptions of the light. "Derived to things below" reflects where the Magician channels his energy. Waite

• • • • • • •

describes the items on the Magician's table as "the four Tarot suits, signifying the elements of natural life." Here are the four elements, the material world displayed. It is earth (pentacles), air (cups), fire (wands), and water (cups). These are the Magician's tools. They contain everything in the material world including the four directions, north, south, east, and west.

Waite points to the symbolic nature of the flowers: "Beneath are roses and lilies, the *flos campi* and *lilium convallium*, changed into garden flowers, to show the culture of aspiration." *Flos campi* and *lilium convallium* are Latin for "the flower of the field" and "the lily of the valley." This phrase comes from the Song of Songs (Song of Solomon) written on one of the last scrolls of the Hebrew Bible and found in the Old Testament. It is a unique piece of holy scripture celebrating sexual love. In the Hebrew Bible it is an allegory of the love between King Solomon and the Queen of Sheba or Israel and Yahweh (Hebrew God). Early Christianity adopted it and expressed the allegory between church as bride and Jesus as bridegroom. Waite uses the symbolism to express the union of the Magician with "attainment of the spirit." He goes on to say "This card signifies the divine motive in man…its union with that which is above." As above, so below.

Symbolic

Esoteric Functions: Life and Death

Hebrew Letter: Beth

Astrological Association: Mercury

Waite tells us, "Above his head is the mysterious sign of the Holy Spirit, the sign of life, like an endless cord, forming the figure 8 in a horizontal position." Waite refers to it as the lemniscate, a sideways figure eight. It represents the eternal flow of energy. He describes the various associations to the number eight: "The mystic number is termed Jerusalem above, the Land flowing with Milk and Honey, the Holy Spirit and the Land of the Lord. According to Martinism, 8 is the number of Christ." Waite associates the number eight with multiple forms of divinity and worship. Jerusalem is a holy city for Jews, Christians, and Muslims. Multiple biblical events are ascribed to it. Martinism is a branch of Christian mysticism aimed at integrating humanity with its divine source.

The number eight associates with Mercury, Egyptian god Thoth, and Hermes Trismegistus (meaning "three times great"), along with the Hebrew letter Beth, which aligns with Mercury and qualities of quick-witted communication, cleverness, learning, and writing. Waite references the Magician's belt: "About his waist is a serpent-cincture, the serpent appearing to devour its own tail. This is familiar to most as a conventional symbol of eternity, but here it indicates more especially the eternity of attainment in the spirit." The snake eating his own tail

• • • • • • •

echoes the message of infinity as "repetition without end." Waite's phrase "attainment of the spirit" reflects the occultist's intentional journey of return back up the Tree of Life in order to merge with the forces that gave birth to him, thus completing the eternal circle. The soul finds itself reflected in the eyes of divinity.

The Magician card's flowers reflect the results of the Magician's ceremonial magic. Blooming flowers represent effective and workable spells and incantations. Use the body, mind, and spirit to channel energy. Achieve desired results by allowing the energy of the universe to flow through you. Do not resist. The etchings on the table sides reflect ancient knowledge at your fingertips. The Magician's wand is the instrument of intention. Dual wands are held by the figure in the World card. The Fool emerged as consciousness. The Magician awakens to his power. He is aware and in control. The next stage unfolds as darkness brings the High Priestess to the fore.

Profane

Charisma. Magnetism. Electricity. Center of attention. Intention. Purposeful magic. Asserting one's will. Creating change on the material level. If a yes-no question, the answer is: yes, you wouldn't have it any other way.

> **Waite's Divinatory Meanings:** Skill, diplomacy, address, subtlety; sickness, pain, loss, disaster, snares of enemies; self-confidence, will; the Querent, if male.

> **Reversed:** Physician, Magus, mental disease, disgrace, disquiet.

Asana

The Magician card aligns with yoga's sun salutation, or surya namaskar. The sun salutation is a dynamic pose, matching the Magician's energetic stance. The sun salutation channels solar energy from above and invites it into the body, just as the Magician channels divine energy through his body and into the material world via his magic wand. The energetic flow of each differs slightly. The Magician acts as a conduit who moves the energy into the ground beneath him, whereas the yogi channels the sun's solar energy into their own body, keeping it there to build internal heat. The yogi's energy is ultimately released into the world after their practice in their subsequent thoughts and actions.

The High Priestess

SUNSETS FADE FROM rose to grey, and
clouds scud across the sky. The cold
moon bewitches all the scene.

Pamela Colman Smith[34]

Sacred

The High Priestess issues forth thunderous silence and exists in a realm beyond articulation, words, or speech. She is the space of devotion. She is felt, intuited, understood. The High Priestess is the place where you stop thinking and start doing. The High Priestess contains everything making you unique. She is a pure source of personal authenticity. The High Priestess is the litmus test inside of you. She is the space you move to when you ask yourself, "Is this what I really want?" Her throne is the seat of your soul; her waters, your life energy. The moon gracing her head and feet remind you of the ebb and flow of life. Her gentle lunar energy reminds you she is always there, always constant, no matter your outer state. Inside you she is malleable, she shapeshifts, she reminds us to find, awaken, and access her deep wells of wisdom.

The High Priestess is the blueprint of the soul and container of sacred depth. The book of your life rests upon her lap. The book cannot be read. It must be lived. Every single event and experience that you have had or will have is marked in her scroll. Thoughts from your highest self to your murky shadow self are recorded on creamy white parchment. The book writes and rewrites itself as intentions and actions alter past, present, and future.

The High Priestess's eloquent silence fosters the space for a creative response to any situation. She is the gap between self and spirit. Inside the chasm is the container of possibility. Slipping into High Priestess silence allows words, confusion, and distraction to fall away. The ego is relinquished. Perception is mastered. The third eye awakens. Wisdom ushers forth. Intuition graces the senses. Authenticity of the soul is attained as you align with your unique true purpose.

Waite calls her "the Queen of the borrowed light, but this is the light of all." He references lunar qualities, as the moon borrows its light from the sun when it reflects solar rays toward the earth. Waite says, "She is the Moon nourished by the milk of the Supernal Mother," meaning she is the child who gains sustenance from the mother. The Supernal Mother refers to the

---

34   Smith, "Pictures in Music," 635.

THE HIGH PRIESTESS

The RWS deck pays homage to the Visconti-Sforza tradition of the female pope. Pamela replaces the papal triple crown with a triple moon crown. The book of life that rests in her lap is transformed by the RWS deck into a scroll.

Divine and to the highest trinity on the Tree of Life, called the supernal triad. Waite tells us she is the child of the deity. He says, "In a manner, she is also the Supernal Mother herself—that is to say, she is the bright reflection." Waite means she, like us, reflects the divine nature which creates us. Divinity is like a parent whose children reflects them. But Waite puts her above all others, stating she is the "Spiritual Bride of the just man." She is the all-encompassing spiritual nature that is evocative, sensual, and silent. Waite says, "When she reads the Law she gives the Divine meaning." His powerful statement suggests she gives substance to spiritual meaning. She acts like a power generator, infusing all material things with spiritual light. The mysteries and the ecstasy of spiritual transcendence are contained within the High Priestess. Giving the High Priestess his highest accolade and assigning her the utmost importance inside the deck, Waite says, "There are some respects in which this card (the High Priestess) is the highest and holiest of the Greater Arcana."

Symbolic

Esoteric Functions: Peace and War

Hebrew Letter: Gimel

Astrological Association: Moon

Waite infuses meaning into her cloak, which partially hides a scroll. He mentions the scroll: "It is partly covered by her mantle, to show that some things are implied and some spoken." Waite describes the essence of his text, *The Pictorial Key*, in this sentence. Waite is bound by oath to uphold the secrets of the Golden Dawn. He can only imply certain secrets of his rectified tarot. The reader can garner secret information through personal observation.

Waite describes the High Priestess's pillars: "She is seated between the white and black pillars—J. and B." Her placement is of paramount importance. The High Priestess's body becomes the center pillar of the Tree of Life. The dual flanking pillars, one black and one white, align with the Chariot card's black and white sphinxes, with the charioteer as center point. The color contrast between black and white reflects the oppositional nature of masculine and feminine qualities. Masculine and feminine qualities integrate at the center pillar. This idea is exemplified in the highest arcana, the World card. Occult circles consider the final card to be a gender-fluid hermaphrodite containing an ideal integration of masculine and feminine qualities inside a single body.

The letters J and B stand for Jachin and Boaz, the names of the two pillars standing at the front of King Solomon's temple in Jerusalem. All references to King Solomon are additional links from tarot to Freemasonry. Masons use the construction of Solomon's Temple for rituals, stories, and lessons. The pillars are described as 27 feet tall. This would make the High

· · · · · ·

Priestess a megalith, a massive 25-foot-tall figure. Lilies adorn the top of the pillar (recall the Magician's lilies). It was said Solomon's Temple contained a netting embroidered with pomegranates between the pillars, just as the High Priestess sits before similar fabric. Waite tells us that "the veil of the Temple is behind her: it is embroidered with palms and pomegranates. The vestments are flowing and gauzy, and the mantle suggests light—a shimmering radiance." The fruits on the High Priestess's veil form the graphic symbol of the Tree of Life. The veil is a widely used symbol of a threshold that makes the space between two realities and the place where two worlds meet.

The High Priestess's dress reflects celestial fluidity, lunar qualities, and the moon's effect on tidal waters. Her dress is the font of water flowing through the entire tarot deck. Tarot waters follow the direction of the Magician's channeled energy. Waite describes the "lunar crescent at her feet," another lunar symbol. He points out "a horned diadem on her head, with a globe in the middle place." The High Priestess's crown reflects the three phases of the moon: waxing, full, and waning. The graphic structure of her crown connects the moon to the symbol of Pisces, two crescents joined by a single line.

Waite says the High Priestess's scroll is "signifying the Greater Law, the Secret Law and the second sense of the Word." It is the "word" of divinity. Waite says "she is also the Supernal Mother herself—that is to say, she is the bright reflection." The High Priestess as the reflection of the Supernal Mother is the highest, holiest, and top triad of the Tree of Life. A scroll is a symbol of secret information and ancient wisdom.

The Hebrew word *Tora* inscribed upon the scroll means "teachings," "interactions," and "doctrines." Waite's High Priestess holds his beloved secret doctrine, aligning with Waite's intellectual and esoteric knowledge. Waite, who considered himself the occult keeper of secrets, dispelled information only to those he deemed worthy. Her secret book contains the mysteries of our lives. She is the key to who we are as individuals and sentient beings.

A cross is placed across her chest and heart chakra, denoting religion and spirituality. The symbol of a cross is a celestial pole, marking the exact location of the body in relation to the universe. The High Priestess, as acute intuition and the blueprint of the soul, marks the point at which the soul animates the body. The High Priestess is where the unseen self inhabits the physical form and our borrowed body.

Profane

Inner knowledge. Silence. Secrets. Intuition. Subtlety. Knowing who you are. Personal authenticity. In a yes-no question, the answer is yes; it always was and always will be.

> **Waite's Divinatory Meanings:** Secrets, mystery, the future as yet unrevealed; the woman who interests the Querent, if male; the Querent herself, if female; silence, tenacity; mystery, wisdom, science.
>
> **Reversed:** Passion, moral or physical ardour, conceit, surface knowledge.

Asana

The High Priestess aligns with intention setting and the opening chants or mantras in a yoga practice. The yogi quiets the mind, settles into their practice, focuses on their breath, and begins devotion to their practice. These actions align the yogi with the interior self and their true purpose. Yoga's powerful metaphor is that physical alignment breeds spiritual alignment and truth. Intentions brings acute attention to our actions, on and off the yoga mat, to aid us in stripping away the false layers, confusion, fears, and blockages so we can arrive at our true self. The authentic, deep soul self is exemplified by the High Priestess. We embrace her every time we take stock, set an intention, and begin the yoga practice.

THE EMPRESS.

The RWS Empress follows in the essential symbolism of the Marseille Empress (above), yet her shield is transformed into a heart with the sign of Venus, and her crown is crafted with the twelve stars of the zodiac.

. . . .

The Empress

BEAUTY. BEAUTY OF thought first, beauty
of feeling, beauty of form, beauty of color,
beauty of sound, appreciation, joy, and
the power of showing it to others.

Pamela Colman Smith[35]

Sacred

The Empress is Mother Nature, the driving force of all creation and the archetypal Mother who cares for all things. She seeks to nourish all. With a stroke of her finger and a single glance and thought, she infuses life, vibrancy, and fecundity. The Empress contains all sensate qualities of earth and gifts them to us. She tastes of chocolate spice, her touch is velvet silk, she smells of lavender and mint, she sees all colors, she conducts symphonies of evening crickets and sends the wind whistling through the trees. The Empress colors, crafts, and infuses the spirit once the High Priestess evokes the soul's design.

The Empress reflects the creative process and pure femininity. She sets everything free and unlocks hidden potentials of beauty in the world. She is the vine shoot seeking sunlight, the artist meeting the canvas, the poet meeting language. The Empress is pure desire. Her expression is passion. She is love and instinct. Her eyes reflect golden morning sunshine and her voice murmurs purple twilight evening.

The Empress surrounds you at all times. She feeds the soul with her brilliance and beauty of the night sky. Mountain landscapes, rolling hills, and ocean waves rise like the curve of her hips. Her breath is the warm air of summer, her cool palms are the willow tree's shade. She is the peace of mind of a walking meditation. The Empress fills you with the entirety of the world's beauty if you let her in. She shows you, in no uncertain terms, that you are never, ever alone. You are part and parcel of the glistening, pulsating world of energetic and beatific connection. You are her and she is you. She is everything and everything is you.

Waite begins his description of the Empress with "a stately figure, seated, having rich vestments and royal aspect, as of a daughter of heaven and earth." Stately figures are heads of state, political and royal. The the royal right to rule is tied the idea of being ordained or chosen by the Divine. The crown is a direct symbol of divine connection. "Daughter of heaven and

---

35   Smith, "Should the Art Student Think?" 419.

. . . . . .

earth" suggests a male heaven and a female earth. The Empress is the child of the ecstatic sexual union of heaven and earth, the offspring of the spiritual and physical union. The Empress is conceived as heaven and earth collide. She exists in the physical and material world. The Empress is everything you can touch, taste, feel, and hear, while the High Priestess operates in unseen realms.

Waite says, "She is the inferior Garden of Eden," meaning she reflects the state of the garden after the fall. She is "the Earthly Paradise, all that is symbolized by the visible house of man." Waite suggests she is the imperfect world. She contains holistic forms of beauty including faults, sins, dark and light, all sides of the human condition. She is humankind and all its messiness. Waite continues, "She is not *regina cilia*." The Latin translation of *regina cilia* is the "Queen of Heaven," an ancient Latin hymn typically sung during vespers or evening prayers. Waite stresses explicitly that the Empress is not to be understood as the "Holy Mother" or a perfect, unattainable goddess. Instead, she is everything human. She is, in his own words, "the fruitful mother of thousands." He also states, "She is above all things universal fecundity," which is fertility. The Empress is the pregnant doorway into the earthly world. She is "the door or gate by which an entrance is obtained into this life."

The Empress's gate swings both ways, into both the physical and invisible world, but Waite says that "the way which leads out therefrom, into that which is beyond, is the secret known to the High Priestess." It is the High Priestess who guards the secret of all things. The Empress births these secrets into the earthly world. She gives birth to children, brimming with potentialities and talents so they might grow, evolve, and become aware of themselves in the dance of life, only to return someday from whence they came. It is the give and take, yin and yang, birth and death cycle by which the universe expands, unfolds, and becomes aware of itself.

Symbolic

Esoteric Functions: Wisdom and Folly

Hebrew Letter: Daleth

Astrological Association: Venus

Waite moves through the symbols of the cards, noting "the scepter which she bears is surmounted by the globe of this world." This is no ordinary scepter. It is the world in her hands. She actively holds it as if to show, bless, or demonstrate to the reader her power over the material world. "Her diadem is of twelve stars" reflects the twelve signs of the zodiac. "The symbol of Venus is on the shield," connecting her to the implicit beauty and sensuality of Venus. The string of white pearls around her neck, pillows, and robes all contain symbols of Venus, goddess of love and pleasure.

The Empress's wheat sheaves are sacred to ancient corn goddess and Greek grain mother Demeter. The silent reaping of an ear of corn was a central symbol to the ancient cult of Eleusinian mysteries. Cultures dependent on grain as a staple food source typically viewed wheat as a symbol of life. The goddess Ceres, the Greek embodiment of Venus, held sheaves of grain. Pamela Colman Smith's self-published magazine was titled *The Green Sheaf*. Her magazine title is grounded in the allegory of creative fertility.

It is often assumed the Empress displays a pregnant belly beneath her dress because she is the archetypal mother. Her pregnancy can be construed as literal or metaphorical when interpreting the card. All creative acts—from bearing babies to building a life to reading tarot cards—reflect the core and essence of creation. The waterfall to her right denotes energetic fusion from above to the space below. The Empress is wild creativity unleashed in the material world.

Profane

Soft and gentle touch. Femininity. Sensuality. Fertility and birth. Creativity. Reinvention. Expansion. Love and adoration. Physical beauty and grace. Motherhood. If a yes-no question: yes, no one could do it better.

> **Waite's Divinatory Meanings:** Fruitfulness, action, initiative, length of days; the unknown, clandestine; also difficulty, doubt, ignorance.

> **Reversed:** Light, truth, the unravelling of involved matters, public rejoicings; according to another reading, vacillation.

Asana

The Empress aligns with yoga's triangle pose, or trikonasana. The Empress bears the number three, which is the numeral of creativity, and the triangle contains three points. This aligns the highest triangle on the Tree of Life, the supernal triad, while additionally aligning with the sacred trinity pattern found in cross-cultural religions. Triangle pose offers a physical expansion, inviting in the nectar of life to enter the body of the yogi. The body opens like a flower, soaking in creative rays of solar energy from above. The heart expands, stretching its muscles wide open for deeper love, expansive compassion, and unbound creativity. The feet remain grounded to remain perfectly still and solid while the body expands outward into possibility and freedom. It is a pose of trust, devotion, and ecstatic love, asking the yogi to reveal themselves as they are to the world. These are the endearing and essential qualities of the Empress.

THE EMPEROR.

© 1971 U.S. GAMES SYSTEMS, INC.

Pamela reveals an introspective side of the Emperor archetype in her post-RWS illustration in The Book of Friendly Giants, *1914 (above). The Visconti Emperor (below right) sits with an orb in his left hand, and the RWS (below left) follows tradition with the long white beard, reflecting ripened wisdom, age, and maturity.*

The Emperor

But how shall I find it?
Look for it.

Pamela Colman Smith[36]

Sacred

The Emperor gives form and shape to the Empress's world. The Empress is the archetypal Mother who explodes life and color. The Emperor is the archetypal Father who orders everything into its proper and rightful place. The Emperor is the Empress's four-cornered canvas and the structural glue holding the physical world together. He provides form and shape. The Emperor reflects Newton's rules, Einstein's physics, and atomic molecules. He is the weather system forming around you. He is the bubble of atmosphere that hugs the planet, making human life possible. Life would be a continual series of never-ending big bangs without the Emperor. He places limits on human consciousness and creativity so they don't spin out of control. Limits are essential for existence. It is impossible to process every sensation entering our body, impossible to follow every creative impulse. Life as we know it, physics and manifestation, all require limits. This is how the Emperor maintains the physical structure of the universe.

The universe carries a mathematical and physical structure that makes it livable for human beings. The Emperor reflects this need and becomes the place where habits are formed and broken. He is the boundary of duality that keeps things moving forward amidst containment. He reflects the narrative structure inherent to the human mind. The Emperor creates beginning, middle, and end. He is the binding force of tarot, archetype, and habit.

Waite tells us "he is executive and realization, the power of this world." Waite is describing the organizing power of the material world. It is only through structure and organization that the material world is possible. This is where laws of physics, sacred geometry, and numbers organize those things. Therefore, the Emperor is the very act of organization. Waite offers a sensual metaphor, saying, "He is the virile power, to which the Empress responds." The metaphor suggests the Emperor opens the Empress's gate—that she responds to his forceful energy like silk flower petals opening to the sun.

36 Smith, "Should the Art Student Think?" 417.

Waite illuminates the Emperor and Empress's relationship by describing him as "he who seeks to remove the Veil of Isis; yet she remains *virgo intacta.*" The Veil of Isis covers nature's secrets. *Virgo intacta* is the Latin translation for a virgin whose hymen is intact. He paints the Emperor as the constant suitor who exists in a perpetual state of seduction yet who never fully gains what he seeks from the Empress. Were the Empress to succumb, her actions would unhinge the natural order of the physical world. The Emperor and Empress dance, flirt, and court one another. Their courtship brings the world into being. Their mutual desire is never fully satisfied, their love is never satiated. The Empress remains virginal, just out of his reach. The Emperor keeps courting and calling her. The material world evolves through their dance.

Waite says the Emperor and Empress "do not precisely represent the condition of married life, though this state is implied." They could be husband and wife, mother and father. Waite's reading suggests they stand for "mundane royalty." He suggests the Emperor is "the intellectual throne" and "the lordship of thought." In this light, the Emperor acts as our logical brain making sense out of the creative and sensorial world as it flies into our perception.

Symbolic

Esoteric Function: Sight

Hebrew Letter: Heh

Astrological Association: Aries

The Emperor's gleaming armor implies a history of battles waged and won. Waite describes the "*crux ansata* for his scepter and a globe in his left hand." *Crux ansata* is the Latin word for a cross with a handle at the top. This is the symbol of the ankh and the talisman of gods and pharaohs. The globe in his left hand reflects dominion over the natural world. The Emperor holds an ankh in his right hand to represent immortality. This Egyptian symbol for soul can be understood as the sun rising (the circle at the top of the cross) or the union of the male and female energies and the union of opposites, two halves becoming whole. The ankh is a legendary symbol of esoteric knowledge.

The Emperor carries the astrological association of Aries, the powerful ram. Four rams decorate the Emperor's throne. The rams sit on the top left and right corners and also below the Emperor's hands on his armrests. The image of ram horns is embroidered upon the Emperor's left shoulder. The Emperor's crown reveals ram horns sprouting from the top.

The Emperor's robes are vibrant red. The Golden Dawn assigns red to the sign of Aries as well as to Aries's ruling planet, Mars. Red is the alchemical color of transformation. Massive cliffs and mountain peaks reflect the Emperor's domain and the safe harbor he has created. These epic chasms protect him from the dangers of the outside world.

. . . . . .

The Emperor's esoteric function is sight. Sight makes the world visible; each individual holds a specific view of the world. No one else on the planet sees what you see. No one else carries your unique viewpoint. No one experiences this particular moment as you do. The sounds tickling your ears, the light entering your eyes, your perception and inner voice reading my words inside the inner recess of your mind. My fingers fly across the keyboard behind you, in the past. I'm whispering, writing this book into your consciousness, but it is you in the present who hears it, interprets it, and sorts it in your own unique way. Life, although a shared experience, is ultimately an individual experience.

The Hebrew letter Heh is assigned to the Emperor, and it means "window." Our eyes are the window to our world. It is through this window that each of us is our own Emperor. We create and destroy habits, patterns, and thoughts. We create the kingdom of our life just as the Emperor does. We court, flirt, and engage creativity. We decide where it begins and ends. Life occurs through the shifting sands of the boundaries we erect. Our actions construct our world. Our perception is our window, and each of us is the monarch of our life.

Profane

The Emperor acts as our habits and strategies. He reflects all order and stability, from paying monthly bills on time to our cleaning habits. The Emperor often reflects the type A personality, a domineering personality, or a father figure. He is the authority who allows or prevents possibilities. He is ultimate control. Domination. Asserting boundaries. Taking the lead in any situation. Establishing rules and regulations. Knowledge in ability. Self-possession. Self-control. Fatherhood. Intense discipline. If a yes-no question: yes, you wouldn't have it any other way.

> **Waite's Divinatory Meanings:** Stability, power, protection, realization; a great person; aid, reason, conviction; also authority and will.

> **Reversed:** Benevolence, compassion, credit; also confusion to enemies, obstruction, immaturity.

Asana

The Emperor aligns with yoga's chaturanga dandasana pose. *Chaturanga* means four limbs and *danda* means staff. The Emperor is assigned the number four, and he traditionally holds a staff. The dynamic pose requires strength, control, and agility, which are Emperor qualities emblematic in his suit of armor. Chaturanga builds the stability needed for a demanding physical practice, and stability is the hallmark of the Emperor. Chataranga poses often repeat, linking several sequences together in a practice. Like the Emperor, they reflect foundation, habit, dynamism, and ultimate power.

· · · · · ·

THE HIEROPHANT

The RWS deck heavily draws upon Tarot of Marseille symbolism (above). It retains the triple papal crown, the sign of benediction, and the dual pillars and dual monks at the foot of the Pope.

. . . .

The Hierophant

I HAVE HEARD it said that half the world
has nothing to say. Perhaps the other
half has, but it is afraid to speak it.

Pamela Colman Smith[37]

Sacred

The Hierophant teaches the secrets behind the world the Emperor and Empress create. He is the pope, priest, cleric, shaman, yogi, guru, and rabbi. The Hierophant exists as an opening to the mystery of life. He reflects humankind's historical attempt to explain and understand the deep and spiritual subtleties. The Hierophant quantifies, explains, and concedes the mystery of existence. Hierophant figures are found in all religions and spiritual systems. He is the exterior symbol of organized religion, recognizable to all.

Religion, the supernatural, and magic are irrevocably linked. Religion and magic each ascertain, explore, and interact with an unseen world. Religion and magic are each grounded in ritual. "While religion is exoteric (intended for the many), magic is esoteric (directed at the few)."[38] The Hierophant is a symbol of the exoteric and stands as a culture's religious identification. He is all forms of religion and laws in regular life. He is the holy books, the psalms, and the sermons. He is the outer form of church, temple, and ritualistic meeting place. The Hierophant's container holds all acts of human sacred behavior done in the name of the spiritual world of any culture.

Children do not differentiate between real and "unreal," mystery and "non-mystery." They accept all things at face value. Maturity and learning, while essential for a child's growth, usually separate the seen from the unseen. The Hierophant stands before its culture as the gateway or harbinger of mystery and religious experience. Spirituality is ultimately a personal experience, different for everyone. Regardless of an individual's inner state, the Hierophant stands up before the public as an archetype of spiritual guidance. He is the generic and societally "approved" symbol who stands as the doorway to the holy.

The Hierophant bears multiple visual similarities to the High Priestess. He is a graphic representation of the Tree of Life who sits between two pillars. He too wears a triple crown. She

---

37   Smith, "Should the Art Student Think?" 419.

38   Dell, *The Occult, Witchcraft and Magic.*

. . . . . .

wears the triple moon crown; he wears a triple gold crown. Waite says the pillars "are not those of the Temple which is guarded by the High Priestess." Waite marks the distinction between the two, telling us the Hierophant is "the ruling power of external religion, as the High Priestess is the prevailing genius of the esoteric, withdrawn power." This remarkable distinction informs us the High Priestess marks inner, individual worlds. She is what we know, feel, and intuit about ourselves, our spiritual relationships, and everything around us. The Hierophant is the external billboard aspect of religious and spiritual tradition. He is scripture, sutra, dogma, temple, candle, incense, hymn. The Hierophant requires disciples, followers, and a congregation to exist. The High Priestess needs only herself.

Waite says the Hierophant is *"summa totius theologiæ,"* which is a classical book of philosophy and religion. It was written by Thomas Aquinas as an instructional book for Christian theologians. The book describes a cycle of divinity. Divinity sparks and appears, creation follows, man exists, Christ emerges, the sacraments appear, and then it circles back to divinity. Waite moves further, saying the Hierophant acts as a channel for those unable to see or detect the spiritual truths behind reality, for "he is the channel of grace belonging to the world of institution as distinct from that of Nature." Nature is distinct and separated because nature is sacred in and of itself. The sanctity of nature requires no definition or explanation. Nature exists independent of man. The Hierophant is a channel of grace for those without eyes to see the garden for what it really is. As such, the Hierophant is every form of manifested religion and dogma.

Symbolic

Esoteric Function: Hearing

Hebrew Letter: Vau

Astrological Association: Taurus

The Hierophant is assigned the Hebrew letter Vau. It looks like the letter Y. This shape is hidden on the card. It is placed across the chest of the Hierophant and across the backs of his monks' garments. The Golden Dawn translates the letter Vau into the English letters of U, V, and W. The U appears in the two pillars next to the Hierophant, next to his head. V is located within the Roman numeral five at the top of the card and is also reflected in the shape of the dual keys at the bottom of the card. W is placed on the Hierophant's crown. W additionally stands for Waite's initial. The Taurus symbol, a circle with a crescent moon shape above it, is hidden on the Hierophant's throne. A circle with a dot in the center is seen on each side of the Hierophant's head. This is the alchemical symbol of gold.

The supernal triad and holy trinity are created by the placement of the three figures on the card. The Hierophant's monks' heads are shaved in the practice of tonsure, the act of shaving one's head to display religious devotion. It was a popular practice in medieval Christianity. The Three of Pentacles also includes a monk with a tonsure. The card's right monk displays white lilies on his clothing. The left monk displays red roses, which are also found in the Magician card. The symbol of crossed keys unlocks dogmatic secrets. It reminds us tarot is a key for unlocking mysteries and secrets. Remember, Waite's own book is titled *The Pictorial Key*. A symbol is a key to a door. A door marks a threshold. A threshold marks a new reality, and so forth. Traditional Catholicism uses the key symbol to reflect the keys to heaven, derived from St. Peter in the Roman Catholic tradition. The Hierophant makes the sign of benediction, a blessing, with his right hand. This gesture is also made by the Devil and the fallen figure inside the Ten of Swords.

The Hierophant card contains multiple crosses. Three vertical crosses mark the center of his robe and reflect the Christian cross, and the number three reflects the trinity. The trinity of crosses is repeated on the triple staff seen in the Hierophant's left hand. The staff is reserved for popes and spiritual leaders and contains three crosses laid on top of one another. The trinity is further alluded to in his threefold crown. The High Priestess wears a triple lunar crown while the Hierophant's golden tiered crown is crafted with the solar properties of the sun. The holy trinity is cemented with the use of three figures inside the card.

Profane

Religious dogma. External spirituality and all things that signify the holy life. Spiritual figures in your life and procession. Teachers and students. Mentorship. Doorways to sacred secrets. Religious systems used to control rather than empower. Spiritual tools like candles, incense, music, etc. Outer tools enhancing the inner experience.

> **Waite's Divinatory Meanings:** Marriage, alliance, captivity, servitude; by another account, mercy and goodness; inspiration; the man to whom the Querent has recourse.

> **Reversed:** Society, good understanding, concord, over kindness, weakness.

Asana

The Hierophant card aligns with pyramid pose with reverse prayer or utthitta parsvottana-sana. This eloquent, devotional posture echoes gratitude in the presence of divine holiness. Universally, a prayer is a symbolic gesture uniting polarities with the left and right palms coming together. Bowing is an act of ultimate reverence. The reverse prayer reflects duality, opposition, a coming and going, yin and yang, and the balance and harmony of the heart. The triangular shape of the legs and ultimately the entire body echoes the graphic trinity of the Hierophant between his two pillars, the trinity of his crown and staff, and the trinity implied between himself and his monks.

· · · · · · ·

Waite switches the Marseille traditional Lovers card (above) to make it fit with the Golden Dawn's astrological association of Gemini. The single man who makes a choice between two women is swapped out for a naked couple standing beneath an archangel Raphael.

. . . .

The Lovers

THERE IS A garden that I often see, with moonlight
glistening on the vine-leaves, and drooping roses
with pale petals fluttering down, tall, misty trees
and purple sky, and lovers wandering there.

Pamela Colman Smith[39]

Sacred

The Lovers card is the source of manifestation and the point of human existence. As the ultimate form of creativity, love is what we are here to experience. Love is the source of all life. The Emperor sets up physical boundaries. The Hierophant exerts external "authority" of all things spiritual and dogmatic. The Lovers card rescues every last one of us. The Lovers card is a metaphysical reminder that we are not confined to our physical body. Love and lust are natural drugs. The Lovers evokes the most potent force known in the universe. Our physical, biological, and spiritual goals are expressed in the Lovers card. It reflects how we are sunlike, full of fire, fury, and passion, when engaged in the act of love.

Sex is a transcendental, occult, and metaphysical experience. The self is lost. Acts of love between consenting adults achieve the same results as transcendental meditation and magic. Love and passion come on like a freight train when pierced by Cupid's arrows. It heightens our senses and tears at our emotions. Love opens channels of communication where no words exist. Sexual experience and psychedelic drugs are similar. Love and drugs light up the same parts of the brain. Love and psychedelics make you feel as if you've ascended the highest point of a mountain peak. Your view is expanded. The world is altered. You see and feel farther than you ever had before. Just as a yogi seeks to condition the body and expand consciousness, passionate love expands every sliver of our experience of the world.

Erotic, passionate love is transcendent yet fleeting. Few experiences in life equal the first few weeks and months of romantic love. Extreme passion teaches us about states of pure love. Once the individual experiences this overwhelming, soul-shaking state of being, we need not mourn it as it slips away or transforms into something different. It is up to each and every one of us to infuse passionate love, affection, and attention into every aspect of our life and relationships long after the flame has flickered. Cultivating this state is a worthy and pleasurable

---

39   Smith, "Pictures in Music," 635.

. . . . . .

pursuit even when external factors do not push us there. Passion reveals what is possible, not what is sustainable. The Lovers' intensity reminds us of this valuable lesson.

Waite explains in no uncertain terms that the Lovers' picture illustrates the biblical "Adam and Eve when they first occupied the paradise of the earthly body." He tells us the tree behind the man is the Tree of Life and the tree behind the woman is the Tree of the Knowledge of Good and Evil along with its famous snake. Each tree is part of the Adam and Eve story and each is described by the book of Genesis. The apple is the symbol of the fruit of temptation, though the book of Genesis does not explicitly state it. Waite tells us, "The figures suggest youth, virginity, innocence and love before it is contaminated by gross material desire." Waite equates desires of the flesh with the attachment to material things. It includes seeking to control another or imbalance due to jealousy, anger, or boredom. The Lovers reflects an "ideal" state of innocent love.

Waite switches to a different meaning when he says "this is in all simplicity the card of human love." He speaks to a pure love uncomplicated by sex. He states, "In a very high sense, the card is a mystery of the Covenant and Sabbath." A covenant is an agreement between God and humans, while the Sabbath is a time for rest.

Waite describes his female figure not as being a temptress but as "working of a Secret Law of Providence." Providence is the name for God's intervention in the world. He assigns woman aspects of divinity, yet he suggests her "imputed lapse" or her "error" is being the thing which "man shall arise" and "only by her can he complete himself." In this sense, the woman is akin to the state of the natural world, complete in herself yet required by man. Waite says the card is "concerning the great mystery of womanhood." This mystery may be defined in many ways. Waite has already claimed the Empress is the gateway to the Divine, yet the Emperor never takes full possession of her; she remains a virgin. The Lovers card is illustrated prior to sexual union. Waite says it is the divine nature of the female that makes man complete. The great mystery of womanhood is the full intentional integration of masculine and feminine energies, the nature of divinity. The power of life and birth are secure inside the female. It is the core, the "mystery" of woman, that man has grappled with for centuries. The man gazes at the woman inside the Lovers card. Rather than meet his gaze, she looks above to the angel as she completes the cycle of spiritual trinity.

Symbolic

Esoteric Function: Smell

Hebrew Letter: Zain

Astrological Association: Gemini

· · · · · · ·

Waite describes "a great winged figure pouring down influences." Forty-five sun rays spring from archangel Raphael. Raphael is the angel of healing. His presence dispenses the healing properties of love to the couple below. Love carries restorative properties. His hair is aflame, as fiery as the sun behind him and the flaming tree below. Fire elements express momentum and sexual desire.

Waite admits he had thrown out a previous incarnation of the card that typically bore two women and one man (as in the Marseille Tarot). Waite favors a card with two figures who align with the Golden Dawn's astrological assignment of Gemini. The previous version of a man between two women gave the card the divinatory meaning of choice. The RWS card offers a trinity as seen between the three figures echoing the supernal triad. The snake behind the woman is a dual symbol. It is temptation and also reflects the occultist moving up the Tree of Life. Distant mountain peaks foreshadow the occultist's spiritual ascent expressed in later cards. Clouds appear below the angel, expressing divine manifestation, as seen in all four aces.

Lessons of ecstatic spiritual divine love are encoded in the card. The male figure looks toward the female, while the female's eyes are focused on the angel above her. This subtle hint whispers a secret. It tells us our human experience of transcendental love is a mere fraction of the love and passion felt by the force creating us. Ecstatic love is what bore us. Ecstatic love is what we will return to. This radiant love is at hand. It is with us in this life, in our experience and encased inside the present moment for those who seek it.

Profane

Sex. Love. Passion. Ecstasy. Romance blossoms. Attraction. Eros in action. Sensuality. Electricity of love. Spiritual ascension. Making a choice. Choosing a mate. Soul mates. If a yes-no question, the answer is yes.

> **Waite's Divinatory Meanings:** Attraction, love, beauty, trials overcome.

> **Reversed:** Failure, foolish designs. Another account speaks of marriage frustrated and contrarieties of all kinds.

Asana

The Lovers aligns with yoga's camel pose, or ustrasana. The yogi balances on her knees, reaches back for her feet, and offers her heart to the sky in this exquisite heart-opening pose. It is a gesture of extreme vulnerability and tenderness. The Lovers card reflects how we offer ourselves to another when we engage in acts of love and creativity. Camel pose evokes the trust of love and giving as the yogi offers her heart to the world around her.

Pamela's post-RWS illustration for The Book of Friendly Giants *(above)* reveals a landscape identical to the Chariot card's city towers, walls, tree line, and rushing river. The RWS adheres to the structure of the Marseille *(below right)* with its cube-like carriage and drapery, dual animals, golden scepter, the shoulder plates of Urim and Thummin, and white center shield.

. . . .

The Chariot

"HIGH OVER CAP" on a fairy horse—ride on
your Quest—for what we are all seeking.

Pamela Colman Smith[40]

Sacred

The cards preceding the Chariot reflect humanity's unfolding conscious realization. It is the individual's sense of self as a sentient and sensual being. The Chariot gathers these lessons, places them in his vehicle, and forges ahead. Historical chariots are imbued with military impact and suggest power and domination over the material world. The Chariot tarot card fosters the ability to spread personal gifts, intentions, and passions. Self-determination rather than military domination issues forth as you take control over your life. Your hands grasp leather reins and you are the master of your destiny through personal thoughts, choices, and actions. The Chariot appears as you forge ahead, demonstrating motivation, daring, and movement.

A curious paradox is presented in the Chariot card. The Chariot reflects movement and speed, yet the vehicle is carved from a cube of stone. The driver is mysteriously bonded to the cube as if he were a toy figure inside a cement box. The cube is flat against the grass. The golden wheels could never move this vehicle. Why would the Chariot, a symbol of speed and movement, be crafted from a heavy object that could never be pulled? Why not illustrate a traditional chariot figure who races with his horses? The answer lies in the level of existence Waite's context of understanding reflects.

Psychologist Carl Jung and Hindu mythology say chariot symbols reflect the self. Waite's Chariot exists in the material world, yet for Waite the material world reflects the lowest level of understanding. Waite considers spiritual movement to be paramount, the ultimate goal of human existence. In Waite's mind, an individual could travel the world and physically dominate everything in a literal sense but remain spiritually starved, ignorant, and stuck. This is the lesson of the unmovable chariot.

Waite describes the Chariot as "princely" but not "heredity royalty and not a priest." Waite explains the Chariot's true nature unequivocally: "He is above all things triumph in the mind." Triumph in the mind differs than triumph of the mind. Triumph in the mind is the decision to take control, action, or make change. Triumph of the mind reflects the ability to follow through that decision, as demonstrated in Strength, the following card. For example, you decide to start

---

40   Smith, "Should the Art Student Think?" 419.

. . . . . .

a healthy course of eating by adding loads of fruit and vegetables to your diet. This decision is reflected in the Chariot card. The follow-up and maintenance of the decision is reflected in the Strength card. Triumph in the mind suggests the individual has made a decision. There is no going back. You don't just want to do it, you are officially committed. Nothing will prevent you from attaining your goal, yet the actions have yet to unfold.

The charioteer points his vehicle and theoretically moves toward his desired destination. The Magician's pointed finger contains the same pointed intention. Waite continues to make the clear distinctions between the material and spiritual plane, planting his Chariot card firmly in the former camp. Waite says, "the planes of his conquest are manifest or external and not within himself…if he came to the pillars of that Temple between which the High Priestess is seated, he could not open the scroll called *Tora*, nor if she questioned him could he answer." The Chariot bears no relevance in the spiritual world. He could come face to face with the High Priestess and she would remain a mystery, invisible to him. The function of the Chariot is displayed in the individual's will toward practical matters and nothing else.

Waite says we should understand the Chariot although "the tests of initiation through which he has passed are to be understood physically or rationally." Waite explains the Chariot does not undergo initiation in the metaphysical sense. He once again confirms the presence of the Chariot as an agent of the physical world. Occult initiation is a supernatural experience occurring on the internal and interior level of human experience. The Chariot reflects the external self. The interior self is embraced inside the following card, Strength.

Symbolic

Esoteric Function: Speech

Hebrew Letter: Cheth

Astrological Association: Cancer

Waite's Chariot is an agent of the physical world, yet the charioteer is draped in rich esoteric symbolism. His left and right shoulders carry Urim and Thummim, whose profiles look up toward the sky. Historically, Urim and Thummim possess oracular power; ancient priests used them to identify sinners in a crowd. Urim and Thummim appear in the book of Exodus, where they exist on a Hebrew high priest's breastplate. Joseph Smith, founder of the Mormons and the Church of Jesus Christ of Latter-day Saints, claimed to receive divine information from two seer stones called Urim and Thummim in 1827. Smith wrote the Book of Mormon, the church's religious text, based on this information. The Mormons are now over fourteen million strong, according to the church's website. Smith was a Freemason who utilized Masonic structure to create and organize the Mormon Church, just as the secret chiefs used Masonic structure to create and organize the Hermetic Order of the Golden Dawn.

Speech is the esoteric function of the Chariot. Words and language infuse the Chariot. Words have the power to imprint the mind. Language carries knowledge and intention. The Hebrew letter Cheth means fence, wall, barrier, or wild beast in a field. The high wall enclosing the background city reflects a barrier. The Chariot's battle armor and his vehicle additionally reflect a barrier. Language operates as a barrier as well as a blessing. To name something is to give it limits, to nail it down. Language becomes a barrier when expressing an experience or feeling of something beyond description. Art, poetry, and metaphor save us when language fails. Negative language reaps negative impact on the mind and body, whereas positive language results in positive results, thus the barrier of language is both a blessing and a curse.

Cheth is associated with astrological Cancer. Cancer's symbol is the crab, an oceanic crustacean whose soft body is protected by a hard outer shell. The charioteer bears a similar shell in his vehicle and protective armor. Cancer is ruled by the moon. Dual moon profiles appear on the charioteer's shoulders. The belt of the Chariot holds five symbols, two of which contain the moon and Cancer.

Waite explains the mystery of the Chariot's sphinxes. They are concerned with "a Mystery of Nature and not of the world of Grace." He means to say the mystery of the sphinx concerns the material world, not the divine world. The sphinx's black-and-white colors match the High Priestess's black-and-white pillars. The sphinxes immediately become the graphic depiction of the outer pillars on the Tree of Life with the charioteer as the middle pillar, reminding the reader of duality and integration.

Profane

Taking the reins. Being in the driver's seat. Knowing where you are going. Keeping your eye on the prize. Movement. Speed. Travel by car. Moving across great distances. Focusing on a singular objective. Thinking outside the box. Domination. Moving from point A to point B. If a yes-no question, the answer is yes, as long as you know what you are about to do.

> **Waite's Divinatory Meanings:** Succour, providence; also war, triumph, presumption, vengeance, trouble.

> **Reversed:** Riot, quarrel, dispute, litigation, defeat.

Asana

The Chariot card aligns with chair pose, or utkatasna. This dynamic pose echoes the posture of the Chariot's vehicle. The pose engages the dynamic opposition of the cube. The arms reach up. Power and balance are required. This seated chair pose is often held for long periods of time. This challenging pose speaks to the Chariot's fortitude and the effort it takes to set a goal and move directly toward it without distraction.

· · · · · ·

VIII

STRENGTH.

© 1971 U.S. GAMES SYSTEMS, INC.

The RWS adheres to Marseille symbolism (above) as a female in flowing garments demonstrates finesse by using gentle force over the fierce lion's jaw. Her physical placement above the lion additionally reflects humanity's dominion over its own base animal instincts. The RWS takes the symbol of the s from the brim of the Marseille hat and places it literally floating over the RWS maiden's head.

. . . .

Strength

UGLINESS IS BEAUTY, but with a difference,
a nobleness that speaks through all
the hard crust of convention.

Pamela Colman Smith[41]

Sacred

Strength is the quality needed to sustain and meet each and every challenge once the Chariot sets the individual off on their path. As its title implies, Strength is physical, emotional, and intellectual fortitude. Strength filters through the world daily via human action, fostering possibility, stability, and healing. Strength is felt keenly and tested in times of uncertainty. Strength illuminates moral fibers, decisions, and actions. The figure of Strength expresses kindness to her beastly animal friend. Strength is recognized in the way we treat ourselves, other people, animals, and our environment. The strongest of souls often express strength through subtlety rather than overt control.

Traditional Strength cards depict a female taming a wild lion. Pamela's card reflects a lion who has already been tamed. The beast is putty in her hands. "Her beneficent fortitude has already subdued the lion, which is being led by a chain of flowers," Waite says. This small yet significant change reflects the maintenance of Strength, not the struggle. Waite is coy in his decision to switch Strength with the traditional placement of the Justice card for his deck, "For reasons which satisfy myself, this card has been interchanged with that of Justice, which is usually numbered eight." Waite, in fact, switched Strength and Justice to align with MacGregor Mathers's Kabbalistic attributions. Mathers realized by placing the Fool at the beginning of the deck and switching the placement of Justice and Strength that the tarot would perfectly match the astrological attributions located inside the Sefer Yetzirah, an ancient book of Hebrew mysticism explaining the formation of earthly reality via the Tree of Life.

Waite writes that the card represents "the strength which resides in contemplation." Contemplation is the practice of quieting the mind, similar to meditation. Strength of mind is a powerful step, moving us closer to strength in personal actions. It is to embrace the contemplative mindset and allow thoughts to drift away like clouds without becoming attached to them. Notice thoughts and feelings as they come and go. Thoughts and emotions become freed from

41   Smith, "Should the Art Student Think?" 418.

. . . . . .

our automatic reaction to them. Once we obtain mastery of our thoughts, we embody the figure on the Strength card. We are the female figure and our mind is the lion. Thoughts lose their control over us. Instead, we control them. We become the outside observer who experiences freedom of self and the freedom to determine our course of action in all circumstances.

Once contemplation is achieved in private, it may be used in everyday life. It is especially helpful during fraught emotional situations, fights, or moments of fear. This tool is brought to foster space for a creative response to any situation, no matter how upsetting or destructive. The ability to filter the mind's experience and choose our reaction invokes the freedom to dictate our experience of every life event. For example, a person who is fighting a tobacco or food addiction practices contemplation. A craving hits. She notices her first thought is to satisfy herself with a cigarette or sugary sweet cupcake. Rather than acting upon her impulse, she observes her thought. She allows the thought to slip away without acting on it. Each time she prevails over her thoughts, she becomes stronger. This process applies to any situation or challenge.

Strength through contemplation encourages the space of possibility. One who practices contemplation is able to stay inside of an experience. It fosters attention in the moment. This ability allows the individual to discover possibility, thus making their world fresh and new in every situation. This practice becomes paramount to interpersonal relationships, where destructive habits and patterns are born. The practice helps us strengthen relationships between the people we love most. For example, you find yourself in an exciting new relationship with the person of your dreams. However, you suspect they are cheating because you suffer from past trust and intimacy issues. You have zero evidence to support your claim, but you are plagued by the idea they will find someone better than you. Wild thoughts drive you crazy. These thoughts force you to prowl their social media. You sift though photos of ex-girlfriends and violate their privacy by searching their emails. You accuse your dreamboat of not wanting you. Eventually, you break up because of your lack of trust and wicked insecurity. Your thoughts created a self-fulfilling prophecy, and you became a willing slave to them. The contemplative mindset helps one who is self-aware, who notices the feeling of fear of abandonment rising. Once noted and recognized, it is allowed to slip away. No action is taken. Like ignoring a cruel taunting child on the playground, eventually such thoughts lose all power over you. You become free to enjoy a healthy, trusting relationship. This is the essence of Strength.

Symbolic

Esoteric Function: Taste

Hebrew Letter: Teth

Astrological Association: Leo

· · · · · ·

Waite speaks of the higher spiritual meaning of the Strength card when he says, "They are intimated in a concealed manner by the chain of flowers, which signifies, among many other things, the sweet yoke and the light burden of Divine Law." The flowers wrap around the female's head, resting upon her golden curls. A yoke is a crosspiece fastened upon animals so they can pull a plow or cart. Waite's "sweet yoke" is the nature of divinity and the metaphorical link of an individual and their connection to divine nature. "Divine Law" is the spiritual law or agreement made between the practitioner and divinity as they understand it. The yoke applies to any idea or practice the practitioner engages upon, such as gratitude, devotion, or, in Waite's case, the occultist's law.

The lion is the astrological symbol of Leo, assigned the Hebrew letter Teth. Leo's astrological symbol is hidden inside the lion's curling mane. Lions are a Christian symbol for the resurrection of Jesus. Early Christians believed lions slept with their eyes open, like Jesus in his tomb between death and resurrection. The lion symbol appears in the Wheel of Fortune's lower left corner.

A lemniscate appears above Strength's head, just as it did in the Magician card. It is representative of the infinite nature of energy, life, and the divinity of the human soul. A distant rising mountain suggests spiritual heights. It foreshadows the spiraling journey up the Tree of Life that is to take place in the coming cards as the occultist moves higher and higher toward their divine nature.

Profane

Intense personal strength. Doing the right thing. Gentle control over a situation. Effortless action. Past challenges foster present strength. Your actions prevail. If a yes-no question, the answer is yes because you earned it.

> **Waite's Divinatory Meanings:** Power, energy, action, courage, magnanimity; also complete success and honours.
>
> **Reversed:** Despotism, abuse of power, weakness, discord, sometimes even disgrace.

Asana

The Strength card aligns with yoga's warrior II pose, or virabhadrasana II. The yogi imitates the posture of an advancing warrior shooting energy out of both arms. The Strength card reflects internal vitality. Warrior ll energizes and empowers the body. Like the Strength card, it invokes gentleness combined with stunning power.

· · · · · ·

Hermitlike isolation and internal enlightenment combined with the symbolism of the mountainscape bringing humanity closest to the upper worlds of divine presence is exemplified by Pamela's post-RWS illustration for The Book of Friendly Giants (above). The RWS borrows direct symbolism from the Visconti-Sforza deck (below right). It reflects identical posture, including the hunching shoulders of old age. The Hermit's walking stick remains the same, as does the white beard. In the RWS (below left) Pamela transforms the hourglass into a lantern containing the six-pointed star.

. . . .

The Hermit

IN CITIES LARGE—IN county lane,
Around the world tis all the same;
Across the sea from shore to shore,
Alone—alone, for evermore.

Pamela Colman Smith[42]

Sacred

The Hermit cultivates stillness by removing himself from society. Stillness feeds his soul. This stillness fosters a space of discovery and wisdom. Life's circumstances remain in a constant state of flux while inside, from age six to sixty, we remain essentially who we are. We move closer toward our authentic self, immune to the influence of others, when we know who we truly are and reclaim what was long ago forgotten. The Hermit gives us the space to encounter his spiritual sister, the High Priestess. He is our doorway to her threshold. He opens the passage leading us back to our true self.

All life is a viable energetic exchange. The clever Hermit removes himself from society and the company of others because he understands the body is a device for giving and receiving energy. Each of us acts as energy vampire, empath, and caregiver who constantly affect ourselves via personal actions. People, activities, and actions either stoke our energy or diffuse it and break it down. Certain people make us feel wonderful, while others darken our spirit. Engaging in positive activities bolsters us, while negativity and depression bring us down. Physical exercise builds our energy, while inactivity breeds tiredness. Human connection is inspiring or damaging, depending on who an individual surrounds themselves with. Amidst the noise of everyday life and the influx of distraction, it can be hard to separate ourselves from others. How do we cultivate a sense of stillness to reclaim who we truly are while engaging with others? The Hermit gives us the answer.

The Hermit discovers, integrates, and understands human nature. He is the examination of personal nature and individual sensate experience. We are the only person who can feel our life for ourselves. Life is completely subjective; the experience is ours alone. We may paint, write, photograph, or share personal experience with others, but it is ultimately our own because we are the ones inside of ourselves experiencing it. Spiritual and sensual natures are intimately

---

42   Smith, "Alone," 9.

. . . .

connected. The spiritual and sensual inform the experience of the outer world entering our inner body. One person is inspired by jazz music while another is inspired by walking in nature. One person responds to church hymns while another chants on her yoga mat. The Hermit is the place we go to, time and time again, to check in with ourselves.

Waite is clear and direct in the symbolic meaning of the Hermit's lamp. "It is a star which shines in the lantern...His beacon intimates that 'where I am, you also may be.'" The Hermit has found, captured, and displays the shining light of hope, inspiration, and guidance. A star is a universal symbol of hope. Waite's Hermitic statement gives voice to the card: "Where I am, you also may be." Pamela's Hermit expresses the idea that hope, light, and guidance can be yours. You too can move through a spiritual journey to cultivate truth and light. The guru exists inside you.

Waite discards previous occult interpretations of the Hermit, including the idea of "occult isolation." He states, "It did not refer to the intended concealment of the Instituted Mysteries, much less of their substitutes, but—like the card itself—to the truth that the Divine Mysteries secure their own protection from those who are unprepared." Waite's statement explains how he is able to publish the deepest secrets of his secret society without truly revealing what those secrets are. The most powerful occult secret is right in front of you. There is no need to keep it secret. Those who can't see it, won't. Those who are not ready to experience "the truth that the Divine Mysteries secure" won't detect them. They won't see them. They will fail to understand them. Divinity is in front of every person at every moment, yet most remain blind.

Waite's statement reveals Tarot's greatest secret. Tarot's mysteries will unfold before you only when you are ready. Mystery continues to unfold before you every day of your life if you are paying attention. With each card, revelations appear. Waite acts as Hermit, holding his shining light—or, in Waite's case, the shining tarot—up for all the world to see. Here is the true nature of tarot as well as the divine mysteries of nature, reality, and time. Two people gaze at a garden. One person sees veggies and flowers. The other sees the entire universe.

Symbolic

Esoteric Function: Sexuality (Touch)

Hebrew Letter: Yod

Astrological Association: Virgo

The Hermit's lantern contains a six-pointed star, two triangles representing the intersection of heaven and earth. Virgo, the astrological association of the Hermit, is the sixth sign of the zodiac. Waite wrote a book titled *Lamps of Western Mysticism: Essays on the Life of the Soul in God*. The lamp, a powerful symbol for Waite, suggests the guiding light of spiritual truth. The

Hermit's star shines a bright yellow in contrast to the other colors on the card, suggesting the appearance of warmth in coldness. The star glows like a Sephiroth of the Tree of Life.

Like the Hermit, the Fool and the Eight of Cups carry a staff. The Eight of Cups may be the Hermit embarking on his journey up the mountain. The mountain peak on which the Hermit stands reflects spiritual ascension and great heights. Snow-covered mountain peaks further convey the high altitude, heightened awareness, and clarity. The clear whiteness of the snow reflects a blank page and fresh start. The Hermit's shaggy gray beard denotes wisdom. The same beard is found on the grandfatherly gentleman in the Ten of Pentacles. The Hermit's cloak-covered head is a sign of devotion and respect of spiritual power residing above.

The first ten cards of the RWS deck describe the process by which we become at home in ourselves. Each card marks the evolution of humanity and unfolding psyche and self. Standing on his high mountain peak, the Hermit uses his shining lamp of wisdom to guide us home.

Profane

Withdrawal from the outer world. Avoiding the fray. Quality time spent alone. Reflection leading to wisdom. The spiritual practice of silence. Cultivating personal energy. Spending time alone in nature. Reordering personal boundaries. Shining the light of hope to the world around you. Introspection. Self-knowledge. Meditation. Spiritual heights. If a yes-no question, the answer is yes, but quietly.

> **Waite's Divinatory Meanings:** Prudence, circumspection; also and especially treason, dissimulation, roguery, corruption.

> **Reversed:** Concealment, disguise, policy, fear, unreasoned caution.

Asana

The Hermit aligns with yoga's plow pose, or halasana. The yogi lies on her back and swings her legs over her head, keeping her legs straight while the top of her feet rest on the floor behind her. Plow pose brings the practitioner directly to the heart chakra. There is no avoiding it. What happens when you are confronted by the nature of your own heart's attitude toward itself? Can you love yourself as you love another? Can you offer and speak kindness to yourself as you would to a child?

The Hermit sequesters himself to confront himself. It is only when one accepts, loves, and integrates every aspect of the self that he can then begin the cultivation of ancient wisdom. The doorway to infinity lies within the body, your dwelling place and portal of experience. To love and accept the world, you must first love and accept yourself. You are the world and the world is you. Plow pose's internal gaze is often held for long periods of time. It is ultimate introspection unlatching the gate to the infinite possibilities of the soul's integration with the universe.

· · · · · · ·

WHEEL ᴏꜰ FORTUNE.

The Wheel of Fortune is an ancient allegory of the nature of fate, fortune, and destiny. The RWS Wheel (left) adheres to earlier translations of the symbol that reflects humanity's fate rising and falling upon the wheel as seen in the Visconti-Sforza (right).

. . . .

Wheel of Fortune

ONCE IN A long-before time…

Pamela Colman Smith[43]

Sacred

The Wheel of Fortune is the symbol of cosmic momentum. The Wheel of Fortune echoes the cycles in our life—our sunrises, lunch breaks, evening twilights, and slumbering dreams. We sleep, wake, eat, socialize, and move through our day to the tick-tock of our rhythmic time-keeping clocks. Our bodies are made of circular cells; we live on a circular planet traveling a circular path around the sun. Cyclical time is made of decades, years, months, days, hours, and seconds. Time keeps coming at us, one new moment after the next. The question is, how do we surf waves of time? Each second, like a snowflake, is different from the last. Every moment carries the opportunity of newness embedded inside. How do we access this opportunity once we recognize it?

The wheel, like ancient Chronos, is the personification of quantifiable time. Time is linear and countable, yet time exists on multiple levels and is pliable. The individual bends time every day. All of us experience inner and outer time. Outer time is calendar and clock time. Inner time is reflected by the creative imagination. A businessman sits in a meeting at noon. He nods along with the boss, his eyes on the speaker, yet inside he's reliving last night's date. He's thinking how foxy Stacy looked sitting across from him at dinner and how her breasts shifted when she crossed her legs. He thrills at how soft and inviting her lips felt when he kissed her goodnight. He is halfway inside the meeting he sits in. Last night and his present moment exist together. Inner and outer time coexist.

The experience of deep time, exemplified by the World card, is the state where all time disappears and the individual engages in complete immersion. Einstein proved time is relative. It slows down and speeds up. This is why humans can't travel at the speed of light. The closer you are to a center of gravity, the faster time will pass. If you have a twin who lives high in the mountains while you live at sea level, at the end of your lives, she will be a few milliseconds older than you.

Buddhist mandalas, chakra wheels, and meditative labyrinths are examples of sacred circles. The sacred circle offers wisdom about the nature of life and acts as a powerful learning and

43   Smith, *Annancy Stories*, 51.

. . . . . .

healing tool. Contemplation of the circle provides deep insight regarding the nature of time, life, and reality. The Wheel of Fortune is an excellent contemplation tool. The reader can look deeply into the card and imagine the self in the center point of the circle. The wheel spins, the scaly snake slithers down, the jackal heads up. Clouds blow through the sky. The entire solar system revolves in a single card.

Waite admits he doesn't use Golden Dawn inspiration for the wheel. He looks to an older occultist. "I have again followed the reconstruction of Éliphas Lévi." Lévi was the first occultist to place the tarot at the center of all occult science. Lévi's Wheel of Fortune expresses the tetragrammaton, the four-letter name of God in Hebrew. The four letters are woven into Waite's image. The letters represent the divinity's name, four elements, four alchemical symbols, four angels, and the word ROTA, which is arranged around the wheel.

ROTA	TETRAGRAMMATON	ELEMENT	ALCHEMY	CORNER ANGEL
R	Yod	Water	Azoth	Man
O	Heh	Earth	Salt	Ox
T	Vau	Air	Mercury	Eagle
A	Heh	Fire	Sulfur	Lion

Waite explains his use of Egyptian symbols inside this card and others: "Use Egyptian symbolism when this serves our purpose, provided that no theory of origin is implied therein." Europe's obsession with Egyptology reached a fever pitch at the turn of the nineteenth century, after Napoleon's invasion of Egypt. Expeditions raiding Egyptian tombs brought new treasures back to Europe. Occultists and the general public were entranced by Egypt's dazzling mysteries. King Tut's tomb was unearthed thirteen years after the RWS was published. Antoine Court de Gébelin, a earlier occultist who popularized tarot by seizing upon public ignorance, falsely claimed tarot was Egyptian in origin. He asserted the deck contained Egyptian secrets to life. Waite reassures his reader that his Egyptian figures are purely metaphorical.

Waite is clear about the meaning of this card: "The symbolic picture stands for the perpetual motion of a fluid universe and for the flux of human life." He claims, "The Sphinx is the equilibrium therein." All symbols of the card, including the above chart, express "Divine Providence," the mark of divinity in the material world. The Wheel records traces of the deity at every level of life, from sips of coffee to the cries of a newborn child. Waite suggests occult explanations including "principle, fecundity, virile honour, ruling authority, etc." are silly and ridiculous due to the holy nature of the card. He advises these meanings are better left to the "findings of common fortune-telling." Once again, Waite makes a case for the dual meanings, sliding fortunetelling interpretations next to his occult interpretations. A wise reader will adopt a wide and ever-expanding system of meanings to their tarot repertoire.

· · · · · · ·

Symbolic

Esoteric Functions: Riches and Poverty

Hebrew Letter: Kaph

Astrological Association: Jupiter

Symbolic representations of the Wheel of Fortune icon are found worldwide, especially in Europe, and predate tarot. The wheel as an allegory of life's ups and downs struck a deep chord for the medieval general public. They lived in a highly stratified social class with little mobility. Those born into a peasant life with no chance of escaping it make fate, fortune, and destiny a viable trinity.

The wheel's circle reflects the nature of the physical and spiritual universe. A material circle, or sphere, is detected in the quality and shape of the sun, planets, moons, molecules, eyeballs, wheels, dinner plates, clocks, and a million other objects. The spiritual wheel is detected in humanity's evolution, the span of human life from infant to geriatric, the energetic body, emanations of love, and the aura of the human body.

Clouds billow in the corners of the card, echoing divinity and manifestation. Like tarot's aces, something appears out of nothing. The mystery appears and traces of divinity are made manifest, as exemplified by the creatures in the corners representing the tetramorph. The tetramorph is based on the four biblical tetramorphs found in the first chapter of Ezekiel who have the heads of a man (Mathew the Apostle), lion (Mark the Evangelist), ox (Luke the Evangelist), and eagle (John the Evangelist). The creatures each hold an open book, a symbolic representation of history, religion, and destiny.

The Wheel of Fortune's astrological association is Jupiter, god of the sky. Kabbalistically, Jupiter connects to the number four, which is echoed in the fourfold nature of the card as seen in the previous chart. The wheel has eight spokes, twice the number four. Upon the spokes are three alchemical symbols and one astrological symbol. Starting at the top and moving clockwise, find mercury, sulfur, Aquarius, and salt. The word *rota* is Latin for "wheel."

Profane

Fate, fortune, and destiny. Past, present, and future. Hindsight, insight, and foresight. Go with the flow. Make every effort to stay centered. The nature of life is change. Release attachment to past behaviors and habits. Embrace each moment as it arrives. A change in your luck for the better. If a yes-no question, the answer is yes, and quickly.

Waite's Divinatory Meanings: Destiny, fortune, success, elevation, luck, felicity.

Reversed: Increase, abundance, superfluity.

· · · · · · ·

Asana

The Wheel of Fortune aligns with yoga's upward bow (wheel) pose, or urdhva dhanurasana. Wheel pose is a standing backbend challenging the yogi to emulate the shape of an archer's bow or a wheel. It connects to the symbolic shape of the Wheel of Fortune while aligning with the wild energy of universal forces. Backbends work the nervous system, the network connecting the brain, spinal cord, and nerves, and can feel like a roller coaster. Upward bow can seem intense, scary, even terrifying. This is precisely why it aligns with Wheel of Fortune energy. Anything shaking our presumed stability can rattle us to our core while offering valuable lessons.

Yoga's physical challenges gift practitioners with the ability to stay focused no matter what life throws their way. The Wheel of Fortune card asks the reader to do the same. The yogic gaze, or drishti, is the specific place a yogi is taught to focus her attention. No matter the emotional or physical experience inside the body, a soft yogic gaze will give the yogi a focus point so her greater concentration remains inside her body and her experience. The drishti aligns with the center point on the Wheel of Fortune. Staying centered inside the present moment without escaping to the past or future, simply staying put in the experience of whatever is happening to the body or in your life, is the ultimate lesson of upward bow and the Wheel of Fortune card.

· ·

Justice

FIRST MAKE SURE in your own mind
you know what end you wish to
work for. Do you know?

Pamela Colman Smith[44]

Sacred

Justice reflects the material world's inherent logic and all the trappings attached to it. Justice represents courts, laws, and public systems of justice used to keep order and control chaos. Determinations of "good" or "bad" mark the quality of efforts made. Justice reflects the societal rules of all cultures. Interior justice is where we measure personal actions. We each carry a Justice card within us, acting as our moral code. It is the place we cultivate personal right or wrong, our moral system and inner compass. We explore personal limits of justice in early childhood to discover what we can get away with. We discover how it feels to lie, cheat, or steal by comparing the experience to kinder, gentler actions. Exploration continues during teen years as we test different behaviors. Eventually justice matures and reflects the place where we hold ourselves accountable. This is where we answer to ourselves.

Justice is where we make value judgments about other people. Justice's scales can be used as a weapon when we compare ourselves to another person or group of people. We cultivate a false sense of satisfaction when putting down other people to inflate our own ego. Speaking ill of others, judging their actions, decisions, and lives, is a slippery slope of negativity turning to bitterness and even hatred. Conversely, we use Judgement's scales against ourselves to support a negative self-image. We might compare ourselves to others to make us feel insecure and unworthy. We can say to ourselves, "I'll never look like her" or "He'll never love someone like me" or "I'll never be as brilliant and successful as them." Justice can be used as an unattainable ideal to perpetually hold the self back and therefore never suffer the failure that is attached to risk. No matter how Justice is wielded, if you use the scales as a weapon, put them down and begin practicing the art of compassion, both toward yourself and others. Empower the scales of Justice by placing yourself on one side of the scale and your High Priestess on the other side. Weigh yourself against yourself. Check in and discover if you are being honest and true to who you really are.

Waite tells us "the figure is seated between pillars, like the High Priestess." Waite becomes poetic. He speeds past the traditional interpretations of Justice as it pertains to fairness and

---

44   Smith, "Should the Art Student Think?" 417.

· · · · · ·

XI

JUSTICE .

The RWS (left) instills Marseille symbolism (right) in Justice with the pillar-like throne and draping throne, a sword in the right hand, and scales in Justice's left hand.

rules of law. He tells us, "It seems desirable to indicate that the moral principle which deals unto every man according to his works—while, of course, it is in strict analogy with higher things." It appears that Justice is intertwined with the High Priestess and the card contains a moral imperative of right and wrong. However, it "differs in its essence from the spiritual justice," which would be the High Priestess. He states, "The operation of this is like the breathing of the Spirit where it wills." The "breathing of the Spirit" is direct divine intention, and "where it wills" is the Divine's choice of where it arrives. This suggests the natural talents and sensitivities we are born with. Everyone carries special and unique talents. These traits are found in the authenticity of the High Priestess, who holds your inner blueprint.

Waite explains divine mystery: "We have no canon of criticism or ground of explanation concerning it." According to Waite, it is impossible to explain divine mystery and its appearance or absence in anyone. Waite says the best analogy is "the possession of the fairy gifts," meaning supernatural powers or the "high gifts" and "gracious gifts of the poet." These are the natural gifts a person is born with. The High Priestess is the place where the gift reveals itself in the individual. Waite claims of personal gifts "we have them or have not," meaning to him there is no rhyme or reason to the supernatural talents operating within us. He says "their presence is as much a mystery as their absence," meaning there is no explanation for how or where they appear or are absent in people.

Waite states "the pillars of Justice open" like a door into the material world. The High Priestess's pillars open to the invisible world. Justice is the moral principle the individual enacts in his or her life. It dictates personal action or inaction in the material world. The High Priestess is the spiritual. This knowledge offers opportunity. The Justice card reminds us, regardless of our natural talents, if we practice and devote ourselves to any pursuit with diligence, we will find results in the material world.

At this point Waite has identified three doorways or gates between worlds. The High Priestess is the essence of the soul in relation to the divine and spiritual world. The Empress is the physical door through which the physical body is manifest in the material world. Justice is the doorway to the logic, high or low action, and activity of talent we make use of in the material world.

Symbolic

Esoteric Function: Work

Hebrew Letter: Lamed

Astrological Association: Libra

Waite says, "This card follows the traditional symbolism and carries above all its obvious meanings." Traditional decks portray Justice unblindfolded, holding a scale in the right hand, a sword in the left. The sword points upward in the direction of truth and can assume all the

• • • • • •

qualities of the suit of swords: articulation, calculation, and mental activity. The figure is synonymous with traditional statues of Justice except the eyes are revealed rather than blindfolded.

Libra's scales of Justice in the left hand connect to the Hebrew letter Lamed. Waite switches the card with the traditional placement of Strength to line up the association of Libra. A jewel in the middle of Justice's crown marks the third eye, indicating the ability to seek truth with a higher consciousness. The posture gently echoes the Magician and Justice's left forefinger pointing toward the ground as energy moves toward manifestation.

Profane

Our inner thoughts and judgment calls. Moral ethics. Work. Reaping the results of effort you have put forth. Universal karma. Legal systems and lawsuits. Contracts and lawyers. Doing the right thing regardless of immediate consequence. Making the world a better place. If a yes-no question, the answer is yes; however, you bear all responsibility for your actions.

> **Waite's Divinatory Meanings:** Equity, rightness, probity, executive; triumph of the deserving side in law.

> **Reversed:** Law in all its departments, legal complications, bigotry, bias, excessive severity.

Asana

The Justice card aligns with yoga's hand to big toe pose, or utthitta hasta pagangusthasana. The yogi stands straight, takes their toe, and extends their leg to the front, side, and back to the front. The yogi creates a perfect intersection of horizontal and vertical lines, a 90-degree right angle with the body. This multiple breath posture creates a statue-like physicality imitating iconic blindfolded Justice, whose figure graces many state and federal buildings.

The Scales of Justice usually represent dual sides in a court case. Embrace the scale's symbolic value and enter inside the heart of true balance evoked in hand to toe pose. This echoes the complexity of weighing opposing sides and opinions but also marks the coordinates of the body in the physical world. Mastery of the pose reflects working with opposing forces, masculine/feminine, light/shadow, material/invisible. We are always suspended between the polarities of who we are. Our intersection changes by the moment. Sometimes we stand strong, while other times we can't find our footing. Our center point, like a butterfly, is in constant motion. But to become aware of the balance and dichotomy of your life is to begin the work of becoming the active observer. Acute observation of the self calms emotional urges to react to others or situations. Active observers give the self room to make the better decisions and allow others the freedom to be who they are. It provides you with the space to gain control over your experience of life. Your interior experience is the one and only thing you have control over. The Justice card and hand to toe pose remind you to make the most of it.

. . . .

. . . .

The Hanged Man

USE YOUR WITS,

use your eyes.

Pamela Colman Smith[45]

Sacred

The Hanged Man's stasis is a visual trick. He is anything but still. He reflects a moment's pause, a brief interlude, an examination of the world, your situation and everything seen from a new point of view. Looking through the kaleidoscopic eyes of the Hanged Man is like taking a psychedelic drug. The Hanged Man's internal life pulsates and moves. Trees whisper, walls bleed crimson, crickets scratch your skin with song. A forest breathes in unison with you. Senses come alive as predetermined definitions fade back into human memory. Cookie-cutter definitions fade to black. The world is encountered with newborn eyes, like a vampire spying immortal nightfall for the very first time.

The Hanged Man is a signpost in the road of your life. He tells you things are about to get interesting. He is the harbinger of mysticism and transcendence. The ego falls away. Truth is revealed. His stasis draws you in. He asks you to look closer. The Hanged Man's body is immobile, yet his consciousness radiates. Internal life, imagination, and illumination pulsate and glow yellow around his head. His posture indicates a brief interlude. He examines the situation from an entirely new point of view. He is saturated in silence and completely present in the moment.

It is said traitors were once hung at crossroads as a warning to would-be thieves and vagabonds. The Hanged Man issues forth a warning, yet he is not a harbinger of light or darkness. Each end of the spectrum contains unique gifts. The Hanged Man's wooded cross evokes choices at the crossroads of our lives. Hecate, goddess of magic and witchcraft, is found at the crossroads, illuminating midnight with her blazing torch. A choice is to be made. Energies convene. New roads emerge. Possibilities develop. Which way will you go?

The Hanged Man often indicates sacrifice. What are you willing to give up that no longer serves you? How can you literally, like the Hanged Man, rise above the situation? Often, our best option is not to act at all. Human nature and habit find us constantly inserting personal needs and desires into events and situations. It is only natural to assert your point of view, yet

---

45   Smith, "Should the Art Student Think?" 419.

. . . .

THE HANGED MAN.

The Visconti-Sforza (right) shows us a man hanging by one foot, with his second foot bent behind, a calm face and hands gently at his back. The RWS image (left) stays consistent with the Visconti image yet brings his gaze toward the reader and illuminates the Hanged Man's head.

often if we step back and watch and wait, things will resolve in a unique and unexpected way that exceeds our expectations.

Waite describes the figure as "the seeming martyr." Waite's description reminds us not to take the image at face value. This is no martyr, no traitor hung at a crossroads; he is something else altogether. Waite gives his reader three points to consider. "(1) that the tree of sacrifice is living wood, with leaves thereon." The falling leaves are a manifestation of the Tree of Life. Just as leaves grow and fall, indicating manifestation in the suit of wands, the Hanged Man's tree is alive with energy. Waite is also referencing Noah's ark. "(2) that the face expresses deep entrancement, not suffering." The figure gazes at an inverted world, like a yogi on his head, entranced by what he sees. But what does he see? What do *you* see? "(3) that the figure, as a whole, suggests life in suspension, but life and not death." Waite describes a figure who is betwixt and between, a figure between worlds. Cross-cultural spiritual dogma suggests a three-fold world. The lower world is the place of death and regeneration, the middle world is the place of life and the material world, while the upper world contains celestial beings and freedom. If the Hanged Man is not part of the worlds of life and death, he must be located in the upper world, the place of the spiritual awakening.

Waite reflects on the rampant misunderstandings of the true secret of this card. He coyly states, "I will say very simply on my own part that it expresses the relation, in one of its aspects, between the Divine and the Universe." He tempts further with "he who can understand that the story of his higher nature is imbedded in this symbolism will receive intimations concerning a great awakening." Waite says the person who has experienced spiritual awakening will know that in "the sacred Mystery of Death there is a glorious Mystery of Resurrection." Nothing ends. Energy never dies; it merely transforms. He also speaks of the death and resurrection implicit in occult initiation, where the initiate's former self "dies" and "resurrects" with occult and experiential knowledge.

Waite dangles a giant occult secret like a carrot in front of his readers. His secret is immanence. The Hanged Man peers into the essence of immanence. Immanence is the appearance of the sacred and divine in each and every manifest molecule, part, piece, and shadow of the world. Life becomes rich, infused with meaning, when peering into immanence with Hanged Man eyes. Every stone, animal, and person is infused with possibility. A breezy rainy day, a boring afternoon, or a tedious morning commute is infused with sacred energy. The sacred essence of life filters out of every molecule, sound, and smell. Life is transformed.

Symbolic

Esoteric Function: No function

Hebrew Letter: Mem

Element: Water

• • • • • • •

Waite describes the wood on the card as the "Tau cross." A Tau cross is a Christian symbol of the Old Testament. The cross bears a vertical and horizontal line looking like the letter T. He describes a "nimbus about the head." Christian iconography uses the nimbus, a glowing sphere around the head, to reflect supernatural creatures, saints, and holy figures. Forty spokes spring from the nimbus around the Hanged Man's head. Numerical Kabbalah assigns the number forty to the Hebrew letter Mem, which is given to the Hanged Man. The Hanged Man is the twelfth card of the major arcana. Twelve is the inversion of number twenty-one, the World card. The Hanged Man's physical posture is a direct inversion of the World card's posture. Each figure bears a crossed leg. The Hanged Man and the World are intimately connected, as the Hanged Man foreshadows the eventual fruition and cultivation of the World's wisdom, insight, and transformation. The Hanged Man offers a brief flash of truth that will bear fruit in the coming cards.

The line from his crossed foot to his knee, from knee to elbow, and from right elbow to left is a graphic depiction of energetic movement shooting between the left and right pillars of the Tree of Life. The Hanged Man's image is true to earlier renderings in historical decks. The Visconti-Sforza's Hanged Man has his hands crossed at back, crossed legs, open eyes, and a relaxed face. The Hanged Man's tunic is blue, matching the Hebrew letter Mem's association with the element of water, further offering ideas of suspension and depth of knowledge and insight.

Profane

Pause and stillness. Coming to rest. Reevaluation. Sacrifice toward a greater goal. Creativity. Understanding. The solitary path of the individual. Unique point of view. The halfway point. The visionary. Things are about to get interesting. If a yes-no question, the answer is to ask again later.

> **Waite's Divinatory Meanings:** Wisdom, circumspection, discernment, trials, sacrifice, intuition, divination, prophecy.
>
> **Reversed:** Selfishness, the crowd, body politic.

Asana

The Hanged Man aligns itself with all yogic inversions, especially supported head stand, or sirsasana. Inverting the body allows us to find balance and strength while flipping our world on its head. Examine the nature of the universe, your location on the planet. There is no right-side up or upside down. All points of view are relative, yet we become so ingrained in our habits and points of view that it can take a supported headstand or the Hanged Man to literally turn our world upside down so we can view the world through a fresh pair of eyes.

· · · · · · ·

. . . .

Death

BANISH FEAR, BRACE your courage, place your
ideals high up with the sun, away from the dirt and
squalor and ugliness around you, and let that power
that makes dirt and squalor and ugliness around you
enter your work—energy—courage—life—love.

Pamela Colman Smith[46]

Sacred

The Hanged Man is witness to the divine spark inherent in all things. Death, marching on his horse, is the divine nature in the material world as the essential and unequivocal force of change. Death is traditionally the most feared card in tarot. The public takes the Death card at face value, thinking it portends actual death. Like all great stories—from myth to fairy tales, from biblical texts to sacred poetry—the tarot draws ultimate power from metaphorical value. One who believes the Death card signals literal death fails to see what the occultist sees. Death makes life possible. Death is the nature of energetic change, generation, and evolution. For anything to live, something else must die. Every flower occupies space in the dirt. Every blade of grass needs nutrients from the soil. Death is the evening sun setting, the fiery transformation of autumn's golden leaves, the thundering silence of a long winter night. Death is what gives structure to the human mind and narrative storytelling with the finality of an ending. Death is the exhaling breath of the universe rising up to meet the inhaling breath of birth.

Death's metaphor comes in many forms. We experience the loss of a loved one. We say goodbye to the old year as a shiny new one beckons. An idea, person, or behavior fades from consciousness. To be fully alive, one must discard the past so as not to be muddled by it. Death is releasing old, unneeded habits. Letting go offers the ability to anchor inside the present moment. Doing so allows you to act in accordance with your true nature and the nature of the universe.

Entropy, loss, and renewal echo inside Death's image. Waite says, "The veil or mask of life is perpetuated in change, transformation and passage from higher to lower." A veil or mask is the skin concealing the nature of divinity. Divinity reveals itself as the transformation of all things in the material world. We receive glimpses of the skin of reality being pulled back when

---

46   Smith, "Should the Art Student Think?" 419.

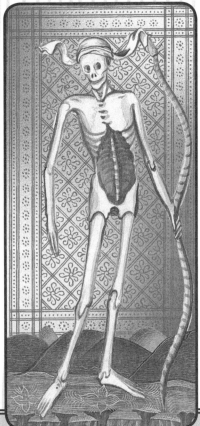

The graphic depiction and the figure of the young girl in Pamela's post-RWS illustration for The Book of Friendly Giants (above) bears striking similarity to her Death card. The skeleton is the universal symbol of death and mortality. The Visconti Death skeleton (below right) is naked, reflecting the reader's eventual and inescapable fate, while the RWS (left) clothes Death in a suit of arms and shows an active death march.

we experience the loss of a loved one or unexpected tragedy. Tragic moments remind us life's journey is short; actions and words count. Love matters. Our experience of life is a gift. We should take nothing for granted. Extreme beauty, natural landscapes, and deep feelings of love will reveal what lies before our eyes at all times. The trick is to walk through daily life secure in this knowledge when it's not staring you in the face.

Waite boasts his rectified tarot contains a better demonstration of Death's activation using an "apocalyptic vision" rather than the traditional "reaping skeleton" tarot image. "Behind it (the skeleton) lies the whole world of ascent in the spirit." The Hanged Man's eyes spy the divine nature of the world and sacred nature of immanence. Death's horsebound figure, like a horse pulling a cart, brings this vision into the world behind him. The skeleton is an ancient symbol of death. Pull back or poke your very own skin to remember the bones underneath. The material world tricks some into thinking that we are different, but at our core we are all the same. Our skeletons match, regardless of the color of the skin covering us. Even gender dissolves as the body decomposes, leaving nothing but bones.

A pair of white towers stand in the distance. The towers echo the two outer pillars of the Tree of Life. The rising sun reflects the middle pillar. The glowing orb reflects the ascension of the spirit. It is a visual representation on working up the Tree of Life, aka the Journey of Return. It is the awakening of the occult soul. The soul's awakening is the point of resurrection. Only through awakening can the soul move upward to greet the essence of what made them.

A small black cave is drawn into the cliffs above the sailboat. Jesus was said to have been placed inside a cave after his crucifixion. His body lay inside the cavern for three days. On the third day—note the symbolic use of the number three—his resurrection occurred and he rose from the dead. It is the same path for the occultist. Enter into darkness and rise as the light. Confusion to clarity, regeneration to fruition, just as winter gives forth to spring.

Waite points out that actual death "may be one form of his progress." The end of life is only a singular form of death. For both Waite and the occultist, death comes in many forms. Initiation is symbolic death. The initiate dies so he can be reborn through his ordeal or experience. Waite explains "mystical death" as a "change in the form of consciousness." Mystical death requires no coffin. It is the evolution or "passage into a state" that leads to a spiritual state of being. Mystical death is "an exotic and almost unknown entrance" into a new state of being while you are alive. The layman doesn't understand because he is used to taking metaphors literally.

Symbolic

Esoteric Function: Movement

Hebrew Letter: Nun

Astrological Association: Scorpio

Waite points to the horseman's black banner to tell us it is "emblazoned with the Mystic Rose, which signifies life." It is a Rosicrucian symbol. The four figures before Death reflect the court cards, the family, the tetragrammaton, and the elements:

Pope	Father	Yod	Fire
Woman	Mother	Heh	Water
King	Son	Vau	Air
Child	Daughter	Heh	Earth

The child is the only figure on the card who does not back down or look away from the specter of death. The king's crown is tossed aside in a symbol reflecting a new order. Fallen kings are a standard symbol of Death's march and are found in ancient renderings of the Death card. A woman bearing a striking resemblance to the female Strength card turns her face away from Death. A pope-type figure wearing a cross upon his garments makes a mysterious gesture. Is he praying for mercy and redemption or does he welcome Death's menacing figure?

Skulls and crossbones decorate the horse's harness. Astrological Scorpio is assigned to the Death card, and the entire illustration is symbolic of regenerative Scorpio. A red feather connects Death to the Fool and the Sun child. Each card is a distinct stage of evolution marking the beginning, middle, and end of the occultist's journey. Death and the Sun child each ride upon the back of a white horse. The distant ship is a symbol of energy proceeding on as usual, unaware of what it does not see, like the layman. The background towers and sun reflect the ascent up the Tree of Life. The associated Hebrew letter Nun means snake or eel. The image of a snake winding up the Tree of Life is synonymous with the soul's movement toward the supernal triad.

Profane

The end. Finale. Finished. Done. Terminus. Moving to a higher level. Transformation and evolution. Putting a situation to rest. Making way for the new. If a yes-no question, the answer is no, the situation must come to an end.

Waite's Divinatory Meanings: End, mortality, destruction, corruption; also, for a man, the loss of a benefactor; for a woman, many contrarieties; for a maid, failure of marriage projects.

Reversed: Inertia, sleep, lethargy, petrifaction, somnambulism; hope destroyed.

Asana

The Death card aligns with yoga's corpse pose, or savasana. The yogi literally assumes the posture of Death's deep sleep. The yogi lies like a corpse on the yoga mat at the end of her practice. Rest and stillness is as important as effort and output. Corpse pose invites you to move deeper into the interior of the Death tarot card because it aligns precisely with Death's valuable lessons.

Transformation lies at the heart of the Death card. Yoga's purpose is to transform the body, mind, and soul. True bodily death allows the soul to slip free of physical constraints, to move into invisible realms, to mingle with angels, entities, and archetypes. Many yogis describe a similar out-of-body experience during corpse pose.

Unilaterally, the yogi is transformed by the end of the practice, never departing the mat in the same mind-state as was entered. The yogi embraces the journey of the occult initiate with every yogic experience. Asana practices are akin to initiations where the practitioner partakes in a journey ending in symbolic death. Corpse pose ends once the practitioner opens her eyes. She finds herself altered, changed, and marked through her interior experience. She is reborn, ready to rise and remake the world as she sees fit. Take death into your own hands. Respect, encourage, and engage in death's transformational process to support your wild, unique, unfolding soul.

TEMPERANCE.

The RWS Temperance (left) draws off the Marseille image (right) of an angel pouring celestial fluid from one pitcher into another.

. . . .
Temperance

HEAR ALL THE music you can, good
music, for sound and form are more
closely connected than we know.

Pamela Colman Smith[47]

Sacred

The Death card marks the ascent of the Hanged Man's vision up the Tree of Life. Death lays this vision at the foot of Temperance as if bestowing a gift. Temperance picks it up and merges the energy like a cat's cradle. Temperance is the winged creature of balance and integration. It reflects the activation of energies, merging and flowing. Above all, it is fusion. It moves from the right cup to the left cup, from the foot on water to a foot on land. Its path carries us from sea level to high mountain peaks.

The base level of Temperance reminds us of the ability to cope with any situation. The angel is interchangeable with an individual's autonomy and balance. The juggler on the Two of Pentacles is elevated to divine status inside the Temperance card. Balance is cultivated and maintained on the material level. Temperance grasps this energy and transforms it in the fusion of every level of consciousness.

Temperance is the gift of complexity in personal evolution via differentiation. Differentiation accounts for gray areas of the world that lie beyond comprehension. Things are not right or wrong, simply different. Differentiation is understanding and respecting other people and foreign points of view. Others intuit the world differently than we do. Complexity is the art of holding two oppositional ideas together and feeling comfortable while maintaining opposition and duality. Complexity is the act of holding both anger and compassion toward one who has wounded you. Complexity is holding fast to personal beliefs while respecting the differing opinions of others. Complexity is recognizing multiple sides of an argument. Complexity fosters new forms of communication and understanding. Integration is the gift of owning who you are as an individual with the differentiation of others. It bears the mark of human interpersonal, political, and cultural significance. Complexity is essential because once we are capable of holding two opposing thoughts, we are free in how we respond to them. Rather than caving to an emotion or reaction, we foster a creative response to any situation.

47   Smith, "Should the Art Student Think?" 418.

. . . . . .

Just as we navigate familial and personal relationships, we must also navigate the landscape of who we are as spiritual beings. We experience complexity as the spiritual self inhabits the container of our body, which navigates the physical landscape of the material world and the earth. We blend and balance our emotional and physical needs along with our romantic, financial, and practical needs. Each of us is a mystery inside our very own body. Temperance fuses the complexity of physicality, relationships, and spirituality. This leads each of us up Temperance's path to the golden crown. The crown contains the intriguing and curious, rich, and satisfying experience of an examined life.

Waite describes archangel Gabriel, who is "pouring the essences of life from chalice to chalice." His placement is of "one foot upon the earth and one upon waters, thus illustrating the nature of the essences." The essences of life are the energies of life and death, the movement of yin and yang, the space between silence and fluidity. It is the interchange of the spiritual self and earthly self. To flow in step with these energies without pressing one's agenda and needs, but rather of aligning oneself in tandem with such energies, is a delicate dance rooted in the power of mindfulness.

Waite describes the distant path moving up the mountain and how "above there is a great light, through which a crown is seen vaguely. Hereof is some part of the Secret of Eternal Life, as it is possible to man in his incarnation." This heavy sentence is laden with Christian overtones. Eternal life is a Christian idea that promises a reward after death for adhering to its religious dogma. Waite's idea of Eternal Life contains the ideal of being "spiritually" reborn. In Waite's case it is the "individual awareness" of man's temporality. It is the ideal of "initiation," Waite's personal relationship to the Divine, which guarantees Eternal Life. This idea reverberates through Temperance and the entire RWS deck. Tarot offers a way to invoke our divine nature.

Waite offers additional interpretations of Temperance while moving away from spiritual aspects. He says Temperance is "changes in the seasons, perpetual movement of life and even the combination of ideas." The sacred is infused even in a mundane description. Nothing expresses the idea of evolution and adaptation as well as changing seasons. The human capacity for understanding and accepting life's perpetual movement provides meaning, wisdom, and richness. It echoes the yogi on her mat. Just as she moves from one pose to another using breath to connect her asanas, so does the earth revolve in a state of permanent change. Life is different one day to the next. If we are not brave enough to flow with the ever-changing nature of life's cycles, we are at risk for becoming stuck. We can align ourselves to this intelligence and hold various thoughts and realities while accepting change as the only thing we can count on. It is complexity in action.

Ultimately, Waite states, "It is called Temperance fantastically, because, when the rule of it obtains in our consciousness, it tempers, combines and harmonizes the psychic and material natures. Under that rule we know in our rational part something of whence we came and whither we are going." Waite speaks of Temperance as a verb, fusing understanding between the psychic and material. We realize we ourselves are like angels on earth, here for a short time. The dance of our imagination and intuition is unseen, yet it is keenly felt. It fuses logic with the illogical. Waite implies if we maintain both, if we observe deeply, we will understand our relation to our spiritual self. His use of the word *temper* suggests a learned skill of repetition, again and again, like a blacksmith who tempers his sword in fire. With each pass, the blade is forged sharper, our understanding deeper. Doing so, we recognize ourselves as eternal divine sparks residing on earth to become the fullest incarnation of ourselves. This idea is expressed by a pond, which is a rich biosphere of manifestation, depth, and life. The path leads from manifestation up to the mountains to the sacred place where the godhead resides.

Symbolic

Esoteric Function: Anger

Hebrew Letter: Samekh

Astrological Association: Sagittarius

Archangel Gabriel is the messenger angel and the intermediary between the sacred and profane. Waite describes him as "a winged angel, with the sign of the sun upon his forehead." The circle upon the angel's head reflects the sun's solar power. The sun is the source of all life and energy in our solar system. The circle with center dot is the alchemist's symbol for gold. The angel's head glows with a halo, a symbol of divinity that can be traced to ancient sun gods. "On his breast the square and triangle of the septenary." Septenary relates to the number seven. Temperance is number fourteen, twice seven. Waite tells us "the figure is neither male or female." This is a reminder of the occult aim to merge and balance the masculine and feminine energies of the self. Pamela's artistic androgyny allows the viewer to easily project gender fluidity onto Temperance.

Temperance is one of the four cardinal virtues identified by Plato and Aristotle. Temperance is a cross-cultural concept. Temperance is part of Buddhism's eightfold path. The Hindu word for temperance is *dama*. Dama evolved in Sanskrit literature and yogic texts as part of an ever-evolving list of essential virtues. Temperance, cross-culturally, is the ability to exercise self-control and self-restraint.

The traditional figure of Temperance as a female pouring sacred fluid predates the RWS deck. It is a common theme of Renaissance art. Symbolically, a woman controls the changing nature of emotion, thus echoing fluidity. It directly relates to the suit of cups and the emotive element of water. The temperance movement, an effort to criminalize alcohol consumption and eradicate drunkenness, found a perfect symbol in Temperance.

· · · · · · ·

Both the Temperance and Moon card's landscapes mirror one another, each containing a pool and a path. The former card reflects expansive solar energy while the latter card reflects introspective lunar energy. The pool of water is a symbol of new life and the subconscious. The yellow irises growing amidst the pond reeds are significant. Greek goddess Iris was the intermediary between gods and humans (playing the same role as archangels) and is often portrayed in ancient art as a winged goddess with a jug. As a link between heaven and earth, gods and humans, Iris's symbol was the rainbow. The fully bloomed iris flower reflects manifestation in the material world as a result of Temperance's activity. The glowing yellow crown above the path is a reference to the divine spark at the top of the Tree of Life, the first Sephira. It reflects humanity's connection to its original source. Waite calls it "part of the Secret to Eternal Life." Waite's metaphor of death and resurrection are adapted by the occultist. The secret is that eternal life exists here and now on earth. There is no need to wait for physical death. Waite's tarot does not presume to tell afterlife stories. His ideas, based on ancient medieval texts, lead the occultist to an inspired, enlightened, and powerful life of their own making.

Profane

Balancing fun and responsibility. Going with the flow. Rolling with the punches. A natural state of harmony. Practice makes perfect. Honing personal talents. Finding unique and winning combinations. If a yes-no question, the answer is yes, based on your ability to maintain control of the situation.

> **Waite's Divinatory Meanings:** Economy, moderation, frugality, management, accommodation.

> **Reversed:** Things connected with churches, religions, sects, the priesthood, sometimes even the priest who will marry the Querent; also disunion, unfortunate combinations, competing interests.

Asana

The Temperance card aligns with yoga's seated spinal twist, or ardha matsyendrasana. The Temperance card's fluids are fused in front of the angel's sacral chakra, located three inches below the navel. Like the Temperance card, the sacral chakra is associated with water, emotions, and creativity. Seated spinal twists work the sacral chakra to encourage the body to become flexible and fluid. Flexibility encourages complexity, which heals and expands the world, benefiting all creatures. It is the ability to hold two opposing thoughts at the same time and to make room for other's points of view without demonization and scapegoating. The inner flexibility of the sacral chakra moves outward as space is fostered and created for yourself and others. The yogi's body becomes the physical metaphor of the Temperance card.

· · · · · · ·

. . . .

The Devil

SURELY IT IS through evil
that we realize good.

Pamela Colman Smith[48]

Sacred

Satan is an enduring archetype of literature, religion, and cultural life. The Devil is the world's most famous scapegoat, having been blamed for wrongdoings, mistakes, and faults for centuries. Why look within yourself when you can blame someone else? Is it any coincidence the Devil is called "the Horned Goat" by Waite? He is a convenient symbol who holds the projections of humanity when they can't bear to take responsibility for their own actions. The Devil reflects a base level of a disorder of the mind or psychic entropy. The Devil may represent anger, rage, jealousy, and a powerful wellspring of pain, negativity, and seething anger. His presence sucks attention away from meaningful experiences. He burns precious time and life energy as fuel for his appetite raging out of control like a wildfire.

The Devil stands as the absolute projection of human evil. History is rife with entire societies and individuals who are demonized, used as scapegoats and punished, reaping disastrous consequences. The Jews were blamed for economic depression and approximately six million were killed during the Holocaust. Tens of thousands (if not more) women were executed under the charge of medieval witchcraft. Anything and anyone classified as "other"—immigrants, women, the poverty stricken, people of color—have been demonized and punished for it by those who seek power and control. Who and what are you demonizing in the present moment? Do you take personal responsibility for your life or do you blame circumstances and other people? Can you see as history repeats itself over and over again ad infinitum?

The Magician and Devil share the exact same posture. The Magician channels a pure state of energy while the Devil seeks to control it. He is intoxicated by a false sense of power. The Magician's precise wand becomes the Devil's flaming torch that sets the human on fire. Energy must flow. It cannot be controlled. Energy can be nudged and encouraged. It can be nurtured and cared for. Like the flowing rivers moving through multiple tarot cards, both water and energy will always find their own ways regardless of human interference. Don't try to contain them. The dam will eventually crack; the river will flood. This is why emotions, feelings, and

48   Smith, "Should the Art Student Think?" 418.

. . . . . .

155

Visual inspiration for the RWS Devil card is taken from Éliphas Lévi's rendering of the Devil in his famous work Transcendental Magic: Its Doctrine and Ritual, *for which Arthur Waite wrote the preface. Note the figure's posture, inverted pentagram on the forehead, wings, horns, and his placement on a cube.*

urges should be acknowledged, confronted, and sifted through. Repression yields disastrous consequence. There is no need to act out every urge or desire but repression makes it stronger. Acknowledging truth fosters healing because secrets develop a unique consciousness of their own when stashed in the dark.

The Devil knocks when extreme control is exercised over any situation. This includes all forms of control: seeking intellectual or physical power over another, obsessive behavior, compulsive cleaning, manipulating people and situations. Which end of the spectrum are you on? Do you attempt to control others or do you let others control you? Perhaps a little of both? Ultimately, the only thing we can control is ourselves. We command our response to the external world by controlling our interior life. Once you step back and observe your thoughts, desires, and emotions without acting or reacting to them, you begin to assert control and responsibility over yourself.

Waite explains the Devil "is the Dweller on the Threshold." The Dweller on the Threshold carries a significant role in magical rituals of enlightenment. Just as Death reflects the metaphorical ascent of the spirit, the journey of return up the Tree of Life, the Dweller on the Threshold appears when the initiate breaks into the subconscious. The dweller, or Devil, is the changeable part of human consciousness, protecting the ego. Acts of domination and control over others feed the ego. The shadow figure is created by all things dwelling in the subconscious. He appears like a monstrous video game boss who must be defeated in order to win the game. The dweller looks different to each of us depending on what we store inside our subconscious.

Both the Devil and the dweller are overcome by looking it straight in the eye. Shine your light on the Devil. He will no longer exist in shadow. His power lies in the ability to hide through secrets, repression, and our darkest emotions. Once brought into the light, the Devil is like the vampire who is vaporized by sunlight. The conscious self can communicate directly with the higher self once the Devil is met, confronted, and integrated. Nothing need be filtered through the subconscious. Consciousness is free to interact with the higher self without interference. This is why a sense of relief prevails in telling the truth. It is usually with ourselves, not other people, that we need to become honest with.

Waite points out the graphic similarity between the Devil and the Lovers, saying the Devil card reflects how "the Mystical Garden" has been left behind. The Mystical Garden is the material world left behind as the initiate moves higher to meet the Dweller on the Threshold or the Devil. Waite confirms Éliphas Lévi's theory that "the Baphomeeic figure is occult science and magic." The Devil holds the key to occult science and magic because he is the Dweller on the Threshold. Once greeted and slayed, the gates of possibility are thrown open to infinite potential unfolding before you.

. . . .

Symbolic

Esoteric Function: Laughter

Hebrew Letter: Ayin

Astrological Association: Capricorn

The karmic power of three operates within the trio of figures of this card. The figures reflect sadness. The powerful Devil does not revel in his demonic activity; rather, he holds an expression of cowering fear. He looks like a dog caught and ashamed of stealing the family's steak off the dinner table. The witch's rule of three states that which you do unto others will revisit you with three times as much power. Karma's energetic effects mark the inside of a human as much as it does the outside.

The Devil infects the figures below with his power. The male and female sprout small goat horns as the Devil's venomous power surges through them. The subtle horn symbols are a stark reminder of familial cycles of abuse. Children often revisit parent and caregiver abuse on others or themselves. Cycles of violence, oppression, and sexual dysfunction often repeat as child victims become adult perpetrators. The cycle can only be broken when light illuminates the situation. Just as the Dweller on the Threshold evaporates when he is exposed to the light of acknowledgment, so are generations of addiction and abuse broken when actions are acknowledged and responsibility is assumed. The victim is often the one to break the cycle. The victim is taxed with the dual responsibility of healing their internal wounds of abuse but also speaking out and calling light to the situation. They often suffer the consequences of extreme anger of those who want to keep secrets, often the people they love most. The victim engages in a vicious two-front battle. They are taxed with healing the most sensitive and deeply wounded parts of themselves while acknowledging the light of truth surrounding the acts that caused it. Ultimately, the victim should be named warrior. These brave souls step forward to end cycles of destruction, violence, and sexual deviancy. They are warriors of the soul who transcend the flesh and blood shed on battlefields. Their brave actions and willingness to speak the truth clear a path of possibility for future generations. Like Katniss Everdeen or Luke Skywalker, challenges are the process through which we discover who we are and what strength resides within. This is why every obstacle, from a pedophile in the family to the bully of the playground, becomes the wound that lets in the light. These demons show us what we are truly made of.

The Devil's white beard evokes Hermit wisdom but in a beastly, animalistic, inverted fashion. His intellectual superiority is used as a weapon against others. The female's tail sprouts eleven grapes, suggesting intoxication and the loss of control. Waite tells us the couple is "Adam and Eve after the Fall." This is the time period after Eve has tasted the forbidden fruit. The chains

• • • • • • •

reflect the "fatality of the material life," yet the rusted neck chains are large enough to remove. The man and woman could free themselves at any moment. The power of escape is theirs. Have they locked themselves in his dungeon willingly? Are they handing their power to the Devil? Do you give your power away to others?

Graphically, the Devil card takes all visual cues from Éliphas Lévi's illustration of the Devil in his book *Transcendental Magic: Its Doctrine and Ritual*. The Devil is archangel Uriel. His wings are bat wings, agents of darkness. Waite tells us he is "standing on an altar," implying holiness. The Devil's lesson must be learned. His uplifted palm matches the Magician's hand and additionally evokes the Hierophant's sign of benediction, also seen on the Ten of Swords. The symbol of Saturn, the planet of boundaries, embeds the Devil's palm. An inverted pentacle upon the forehead suggests distortion of the natural world. The esoteric function of the Devil is laughter. The Devil, in certain circumstances, reflects a riotous good time. After all, the Devil wants to indulge your every desire, whim, and fantasy. He appears in film and literature under the guise of temptation, offering you money, fame, sex, and pleasure. But when is enough enough?

Profane

Issues of power and control. Addiction and negative behavior. Being a slave to your desire. Abuse and neglect. A fear shutting down all possibility. Giving your power over to another. Treating others with anger and disrespect. Focusing on the negative. You must find an exit strategy. Ignoring personal responsibility. Leave the current situation. Confronting frightening aspects of yourself in order to foster new growth. Shadow work. Facing what frightens you. In a yes-no question, the answer is yes, only if you are willing to assume complete responsibility for your actions.

> **Waite's Divinatory Meanings:** Ravage, violence, vehemence, extraordinary efforts, force, fatality; that which is predestined but is not for this reason evil.

> **Reversed:** Evil fatality, weakness, pettiness, blindness.

Asana

The Devil card aligns with yoga's crow pose, or bakasana. Crows are shapeshifters, transformative creatures who, like bats, reflect darkness and shadow realms. The Devil sprouts bat wings while balancing on top of his cube. Crow pose is a similar arm balance, and yogis often employ mind over matter to achieve this difficult pose.

The Devil card and crow pose remind us to examine our constant struggles and interior wars. Is your darkest demon nothing more than a habit? An illusion? Ideas, assumptions, and self-limitations are only real if you believe them. What can you discard? What false truth do you abide by? Set your bats and crows skyward. Free yourself from the cycles of the past. Embrace the shimmering present and the glorious possibility and freedom it contains.

• • • • • • •

The RWS (left) pulls symbolism from the Marseille Tower (right) with energy streaming from the upper right of the card to strike a crown off a tower. A trio of windows is set in the tower, and two figures (scaled larger than what would actually fit inside the tower) fall to their demise.

. . . .

The Tower

LIFT UP YOUR ideals, you weaklings, and
force a way out of that thunderous clamor.

Pamela Colman Smith[49]

Sacred

Lightning strikes a great tower. Smoke and brimstone billow as two figures fall to a merciless, jagged death. Brilliant illumination reflects the rocky landscape. Transformation occurs in the flash of an eye, demonstrating genius of the mind and the power of thought. Immediate understanding radiates through body and soul. The Tower card is the ultimate *aha* moment. Truth breaks through the carefully constructed story you've been using to protect the ego. Earth-shaking knowledge rushes forth with tsunami-like speed. Life will never be the same.

You've danced with the Devil and lived to tell, but universal forces aren't finished yet. The lightning marks a moment of no return and unexpected upheaval. It is the ultimate masculine orgasm, an energetic opening of epic proportion. Goosebumps erupt across the skin as the tectonic plates of life shift. It is the bolt of illumination, the moment that everything changes. Something you've heard a million times makes sense in a new way. Understanding and certainty lock into place. The Tower reflects ultimate freedom, which is terrifying to behold and evolutionary to embody.

The Tower reflects the shattering of false pretenses. These falsities are destroyed by acceptance of the shadow self and destruction of the Dweller on the Threshold. Waite reminds the reader not to take this card literally: "I do not conceive that the Tower is more or less material than the pillars which we have met with in three previous cases." He is referring to the pillars of the High Priestess, Hierophant, and Justice. These pillars are not real but metaphorical. Therefore, the Tower is not an actual card of physical catastrophe in the reader's life. The card does not forebode being struck by lightning, hit by a bus, or falling out a window. Waite says it is "a ruin of the House of We," meaning the ego is destroyed. All that remains is the active observer.

Waite says the card favors "the materialization of the spiritual world." The occultist's lifestyle and worldview are altered forever as the spirit world is made manifest. Nothing can ever be the same once the occultist peeks beneath the veil. Waite asks the reader to examine the two figures falling from the Tower as analogies: "one is concerned with the fall into the material and animal state, while the other signifies destruction on the intellectual side."

---

49   Smith, "Should the Art Student Think?" 419.

The red-caped former figure "is the literal word made void." Nothing is as it seems or can be taken at face value. The crowned, blue-gowned figure is "false interpretation." The Tower thus reflects the moment when the individual realizes the world is not real, it is but an illusion. They have misjudged the nature of reality and the self. He claims it "may signify also the end of a dispensation," suggesting the old order has fallen and a new world begun.

Literary giant W. B. Yeats penned *Is the Order RR&AC to Remain a Magical Order?* in 1901 amidst Golden Dawn disarray. The order was splitting into numerous factions. Yeats eloquently made a case for Golden Dawn unification or irrevocable and dire consequences. Inside the pamphlet, Yeats starkly describes the order's work. His text specifically describes the Golden Dawn's symbol of the lightning bolt in conjunction with the Tree of Life. He states the "ascent to the Supreme Life," the movement up the Tree of Life, creates a "double link." The double link enables occultists to move up the tree. The link is a gate that swings both ways. He describes great supernatural beings, "teachers and wise ones," and energetic bodies moving down the tree and through the gate. The downward motion of wise ones "is symbolized by the Lightning Flash." He says, "We receive power from those who are above us by permitting the Lightning of the Supreme to descend through our souls and our bodies." The lightning bolt is the illumination of wise ones permeating the occultist's body as if electrified by the energy of a Jesus or Buddha figure. He says, "The power is forever seeking the world," meaning spiritual power, wise ones, and supernatural entities always seek to manifest in the material world. These energies want to break through and be known and shown. Yeats's fear is that splintering factions risk alienating other members and vying for their own power, thus perverting the creatures who wish to become manifest. "It consumes its mortality because the soul has arisen to the path of the Lightning." He finishes his statement referring to the power grab inside the Golden Dawn saying, "The soul that separates itself from others, that says 'I will seek power and knowledge for my own sake, and not for the world's sake,' separates itself from that path and becomes dark and empty."

The lightning flash for Yeats is not simply a symbol of knowledge destroying the occultist's old world as he moves up the tree but is the acute energy of divine beings permeating the occultist's body and soul, therefore the world at large. Sadly, Yeats's eloquent words were not heeded. The Golden Dawn ultimately disbanded. The Tower remained a potent symbol for Yeats. He purchased and lived in a tower from 1921–1929. It is now called the Yeats Tower. He continued writing and working long after the Golden Dawn fell into disarray and leaves a vast legacy of art and literature behind him.

• • • • • • •

Symbolic

Esoteric Functions: Indignation and Grace

Hebrew Letter: Peh

Astrological Association: Mars

The symbol of a circle (crown) knocked off a square (tower) by the lightning bolt is an eloquent reminder of the destruction of what never fit to begin with. Catastrophe brings ultimate catharsis, resolution of the unbalanced balancing itself. The lightning is an arrow. Specific and direct intelligence aimed from an unseen archer above. Mars, god of war, carries the astrological association for the Tower. The Mars symbol is a circle with protruding arrow as seen by the lightning bolt. The body of the lightning bolt is an energetic symbol of Tree of Life emergence and return. It zigzags just as energy and the occultist move up and down the Tree of Life from left to right pillar and back again. The Hebrew letter Peh is assigned to this card, meaning mouth. The mouth is the place where sustenance is taken in and words, feelings, thoughts, and emotions flow out. It operates like Yeats's metaphorical gate. The three flaming windows reflect trinity and the supernal triad. Twenty-two Yod flames reflect divine fire, operating as seeds and sparks of creative life falling to the earth.

Profane

A flash of insight. A breakthrough of epic proportions. Light-bulb idea. The shattering of illusions. Truth revealed. A shakeup. Unexpected results. Everything you know changes in a second. Upheaval stemming from things that never fit to begin with. A breakdown. A turning point. There is no going back from this moment. In a yes-no question, the answer is yes, and mayhem ensues.

Waite's Divinatory Meanings: Misery, distress, indigence, adversity, calamity, disgrace, deception, ruin. It is a card in particular of unforeseen catastrophe.

Reversed: According to one account, the same in a lesser degree; also oppression, imprisonment, tyranny.

Asana

The Tower card aligns with yoga's tree pose, or vrksasana. Tree pose requires the yogi to balance on one leg while lifting the arms to the sky, invoking the shape of a tree and the Tower. Doing so, the yogi becomes stable in the three worlds (lower, middle, and upper). They are rooted in the ground, stretch though the material world, and reach toward spiritual ascension. To master tree pose and the Tower card, the middle and lower self must remain stable, no matter the storms, havoc, and chaos at the top.

• • • • • • •

The RWS deck (left) literally interprets the symbolism of the Marseille Star (right) with a naked maiden who pours fluid on earth and water. Her posture is replicated, as are her blond locks. The overhead stars retain their original Marseille formation, and a bird sits happily on a tree.

. . . .

The Star

KEEP AN OPEN mind to all things.

Pamela Colman Smith[50]

Sacred

The Star is divine light we can engage with directly. We look to the stars; the stars twinkle back. Inspiration from above infuses the body, the brush, the life with purpose. The Devil and the Tower rattled us to our core. The Star soothes with calm clarity like calm settling over a wildflower field after a thunderstorm has passed. The Star foreshadows the innocence of the child seen in the Sun card and the brilliance of the world to come as exemplified in the naked World dancer.

The loss of self-consciousness permeates every level of the Star card. Children are naturally unselfconscious. A "child's mindset" breeds freedom. Children are free to employ innate trust in the space around them. Before the ego is developed, they see themselves as an extension of the world, not as a separate creature. This encourages wholeness of sight, sound, and experience. Self-consciousness consumes innate psychic energy. Releasing self-conscious notions frees the spirit. Engaging in vulnerability and revoking the ego, you are free to focus on the world around you. You concern yourself with the project or issue at hand rather than dealing with the ego, who prefers the forefront and demands attention by screaming *look at me, feed me, see me and only me*. The Devil and the Tower eradicated the ego so that when we meet the Star, we can engage in cosmic unity.

Glimmers of celestial radiance manifest in starlight, mini suns light-years away from where our feet touch the earth. Each is a pinpoint reminder of magic, life, and connection. The sun is the pure source of energy, life, and magic. To gaze into the face of our own sun would render us blind. To merge with starlight is to space travel across light-years. Stars are suns. Planets are reflections of those suns. Even mysterious Jupiter reflects back the light of our own sun like the moon.

Waite is direct in his expression of the card: "The figure expresses eternal youth and beauty." The Star's beauty is more than skin deep. To Waite, what she "communicates to the living scene is the substance of the heavens and the elements." She is truly made of star-stuff. She is matter illuminating the far reaches of an infinite universe and four earthly elements: earth, air, fire, and water.

50   Smith, "Should the Art Student Think?" 418.

. . . . . .

Waite tells is she is the "Waters of Life freely." Waite's phrase evokes religious baptism, as the Water of Life is a reference to the Christian holy spirit. Water is used to represent the life force. The Star is pouring forth the waters of life; doing so, she is "irrigating sea and land." It is a reference to flow and the illuminating powers of life she reflects; of course there is no need to irrigate the ocean. Waite tells us the Star has "Gifts of the Spirit," which are supernatural gifts bestowed unto ancient Christians to fulfill the church's needs. The New Testament, Romans, contains seven Gifts of the Spirit, one for each white star in the Star card's sky. The first gift is Prophecy, fitting with themes and ideas surrounding the tarot. The remaining six gifts are Serving, Teaching, Exhortation, Giving, Leadership, and Mercy.

Waite explains the figure is "the type of Truth unveiled. Glorious in undying beauty, pouring waters on the soul." He finishes by saying she is "the Great Mother in the Kabbalistic Sophia Binah, which is Supernal Understanding, who communicates to the Sephiroth that are below." She is the female nature of eternal compassion. The Star is like a champagne fountain whose inspiration flows freely. In doing so she reflects the nature of stellar energy. She pours divine, compassionate light on all the Sephiroth below her and the material world, imbuing it with grace and inspiration. The two streams of water are her energy pouring through the left and right pillars of the Tree of Life. The Star's naked body is the center pillar of integration.

Symbolic

Esoteric Function: Imagination

Hebrew Letter: Tzaddi

Astrological Association: Aquarius

The Star's nudity reflects vulnerability and trust. She is the symbolic center pillar. She hovers above the pool magically. Waite tells us "her right foot is upon the water," and this is the Water of Life. These waters stem from the "Great Mother in the Kabbalistic Sophia Binah, which is supernal Understanding." Waters are the heart and soul of compassion. Water reflects the life-sustaining amniotic fluid birth waters. The entire suit of cups is filled with this liquid. The great and lesser stars in the sky are never identified by Waite; however, the seven white stars do align with the number of "Gifts of the Spirit." The golden-centered eight-spoked star, distant hills, flowers, and trees are all traditional Star card symbols stretching back through to Marseille decks to the Visconti-Sforza cards.

A bird takes residence in the tree behind the female figure. Its long beak evokes an ibis, the sacred bird of Egypt. The ibis is seen in Egyptian mythology as the head of Thoth (Hermes), the god of logic, reason, thought, and intelligence, adding additional sacred qualities to the Star card. Birds also signify the connection between the celestial realm and life on earth due to their wings and ability to fly.

The Golden Dawn system assigns the astrological sign of Aquarius to the Star. Aquarius is the water bearer. The water to her left breaks into five small rivulets, but the significance is never explained by Waite. The Hebrew letter Tzaddi means "fishhook" and thus aligns with the aquatic nature of the card. The esoteric function aptly describes the Star as inspiration and imagination.

Profane

Inspiration and renewal. Rejuvenation of the mind, body and spirit. Endorphins releasing. The artist and the muse. Connection and intense creativity. Inner peace. You find contentment. Flowing cosmic connection. Celestial influence. Quiet after the storm. Emotional flow. Clarified hope. You are free. In a yes-no question, the answer is yes, but gently.

> **Waite's Divinatory Meanings:** Loss, theft, privation, abandonment; another reading says hope and bright prospects.

> **Reversed:** Arrogance, haughtiness, impotence.

Asana

The Star card aligns with lotus pose, or padmasana. The lotus flower's symbolic value of a flower rising from the mud transcends culture and religion. Lotus is the ancient and traditional cross-legged meditative pose of India. Lotus pose is often performed at the beginning and end of a yoga practice, and the legs may move into lotus inside other postures. Seated in lotus pose, the yogi clears the mind, focuses in the breath, and allows the benefits and energy of the practice to move freely through the body.

Lotus echoes the Star card in every way, especially when performed at the end of the practice, after challenges have been met and endorphins flowed. This is the moment of reaping all benefits. Energetically, the yogi becomes aligned with what is above and below, with herself as the center pillar. Just as the Star card filters the sacred waters of the universe, so does the yogi bask in the sacred nature of her being, her sweat, her effort. The essence of the Star card can feel like a peaceful silence after the storm has passed, reflecting the clarity of the soul, a clean slate, and newly born space.

We often gaze at the night sky in amazement, but what we don't often realize is that the night sky is gazing back. The stars want to be seen. Darkness wants to be felt. Vastness wants to enter your soul. Starlight wants to infuse your essence. Rise like a lotus flower. Invite the universe inside of you.

Pamela's white moon towers are on full display in this 1910 illustration taken from MacDonald's "Fairy Faith and Pictured Music of Pamela Colman Smith" (above). Pamela listened to Beethoven's Symphony No. 5 while crafting this. The Moon retains Marseille symbols (right) in the RWS deck (left), including the rising crawfish, dual beasts, double towers, identical face in the moon, and lunar rays.

. . . .

The Moon

TOWERS, WHITE AND tall, standing against the
darkening sky. Those tall white towers that one
sees afar. Topping the mountain crests like crowns
of snow. Their silence hangs so heavy in the air.

Pamela Colman Smith[51]

Sacred

Vampires linger, werewolves howl, on her broomstick a witch's silhouette zips through the
moonlight. The Moon is the card of myth and monster, of altered states and deep internal
landscapes. Dreamlike visions pass through the imagination of sleepers, artists, and seekers.
Dark prophesies are uttered. Spells are cast. Devils leap like flames at the crossroads. Intense
psychic energy and the binding nature of intuition, placid and peaceful in the High Priestess, is
now electric, undeniable, permeating the lunar landscape.

The Moon's body circles the earth, its cycles echoing the transitory nature of human life,
menstrual cycles, and the nature of all things. Life is a constant state of flux and flow. The
Moon is an eloquent reminder that no matter what we face, given time, it will change. No
circumstance lasts forever. Good, bad, or indifferent, life's nature, the psyche's energy, ebbs and
flows, hustles and grooves, like the ocean's tides. "Yes," the Moon says. "Things get weird, scary.
The unknown is terrifying. Unimaginable things occur. But not forever. Nothing is forever."

Encounter the Moon's wild creatures. Learn to speak their tongue. Boldly move between the
glowing luminescent towers. In doing so, dare those hiding above and inside to peer down at
you. Explore paths appearing before you. Strange turns and uncanny moonlit moments transform the familiar into the grotesque. Use weirdness and unfamiliarity as opportunities to reexamine current beliefs and understandings in a new context. Just because you don't recognize
something does not mean it is dangerous or bad. The sun will rise eventually and cast rays of
new understanding. Once awake, you'll have seen more than you ever imagined.

Waite expresses dual meanings when he states the Moon is "increasing on the side of mercy."
The moon waxes or grows larger from the right as it grows toward its state of fullness. The
card reflects the natural state of waxing lunar power. The moon's energy becomes brighter
and more luminous each night toward the right. The Moon gazes at the right pillar of the card.

---

51   Smith, "Pictures in Music," 635.

. . . . . .

This is the feminine pillar of mercy on the Tree of Life, aligning with the black pillar, Boaz, on the High Priestess. The opposite pillar is masculine and the pillar of severity—Jachin on the High Priestess. The crawfish's path between the towers is the center, the equalizing pillar of mildness integrating the forces and energies.

Waite says of the Moon that "it has sixteen chief and sixteen secondary rays." He points out the specific number because added together they equal thirty-two, the number of paths in the Tree of Life in Yetzirah. Yetzirah is the world of formation and imagination, thus connecting to lunar qualities. Waite explicitly states, "The card represents life of the imagination apart from life of the spirit." Imagination plays a paramount role for occultists. Artists and writers mine the imaginative landscape for work; the mystic and occultist follows suit to explore invisible spiritual realms. Sacred imagination grounded in symbol laid the landscape for all the Golden Dawn's work, including astral travel, tattwas, tarot, etc.

"The path between the towers is the issue into the unknown," says Waite. This is a symbolic journey of the unexplored path. He tells us "the dog and wolf are the fears of the natural mind in that place of exit…" The animals reflect the mental terror of movement from known into unknown. It is the threshold of madness. However, he finishes his statement saying it is a fear existing in a place "when there is only reflected light to guide it." Reflected light is moonlight as opposed to direct sunlight.

To exit the known in the direct light of the sun is to avoid the descent to madness. Therein lies our safety net. We stay in control of our mental faculties and avoid the raving lunacy of a mad person. Waite says, "The face of the mind"—meaning the face in the moon—"directs a calm gaze upon the unrest below; the dew of thought falls." The dew of thought is the fifteen Yod symbols looking like yellow tears. "The message is: Peace, be still; and it may be that there shall come a calm upon the animal nature, while the abyss beneath"—the pool of water—"shall cease from giving up a form." In other words, the direct light of the sun, as seen in the next card, will bring about the peace that will quiet the fears of the mind.

Waite is an occultist, yet he maintains a Victorian mindset. Consider what unrest and animal nature meant to a culture who wore top hats and modest dresses and adhered to specific societal rules even as fields of psychology were being charted and explored. The Moon connects to your shadow self. It reminds us to confront secrets, shadows, and dark fantasies to heal them. Illuminate without judgment or action. The light of the sun shines upon dark qualities and such things are acknowledged powerless. Darkness and animal nature pass back through the richness of the psyche if they are examined and considered rather than feared and oppressed.

Waite tells us "intellectual light is a reflection" and in doing so aligns our mental, decisive, and calculating thoughts as symbolized in the suit of swords with the moonlight. Beyond our intellect lies "an unknown mystery." The mystery is beyond our powers of comprehension, i.e.,

· · · · · · ·

the mystery of the Divine. It is impossible to intellectually understand the true nature of the Divine without losing one's mind. Imagine the human mind equipped with the ability to look through every state of consciousness at once, from your dog's perception to a bumblebee's. Waite suggests this would lead to madness. He suggests we do not have the capacity to understand it. Our confusion is beheld in the reflection, which, according to Waite, "will allow us to behold our animal nature, that which comes up out of the deeps, the nameless and hideous tendency which is lower than the savage beast." Ultimately, it "sinks back whence it came" into the depths of the water and into primordial ooze.

Symbolic

Esoteric Function: Sleep

Hebrew Letter: Qoph

Astrological Association: Pisces

To summarize the Moon card's rich symbolism, the path between the towers is the imagination's journey into the unknown. The dog (left) and wolf (right) are fears present in the natural mind. The dog, wolf, and crawfish also symbolize animal nature. It is the place where the imagination takes flight. The two glowing towers are the left and right side of the Tree of Life; the path, its integrated center. The pool reflects the depths of the subconscious. The Sepher Yetzirah assigns the Hebrew letter Qoph to the function of sleep, invoking dreams and all lunar qualities, including the card's esoteric function of sleep.

The Moon and the Sun's images are graphically combined to demonstrate the moon's reflection of the sun. The path's journey is guided only by the reflected light of the sun and, above all, the intuition. In this way, the Moon is the path into the unknown illuminated by the High Priestess's lunar glow. Trust should reign in this space. Recall the High Priestess and the eternal self already know the outcome; it is the physical and temporal selves who fear the journey toward our inevitable destiny.

Profane

Mysterious times and personal unease. Shamanic and meditational journeys. Twilight and walking between worlds. Betwixt and between. Witchcraft and sorcery. Paying careful attention to evocative dreams in order to unravel the secrets of your subconscious. Mythical undertakings. A journey begins. Trials test you. The fluctuations of the moon and lunar cycles. Oceanic tides pull you in strange directions. Uncanny feelings and intense psychic flashes. An opportunity to examine familiar things in a new light and from a new perspective. In a yes-no question, the answer is not yet.

· · · · · · ·

Waite's Divinatory Meanings: Hidden enemies, danger, calumny, darkness, terror, deception, occult forces, error.

Reversed: Instability, inconstancy, silence, lesser degrees of deception and error.

Asana

The Moon card aligns with yoga's half moon pose, or ardha chandrasana. This pose combines the fiery essence of the sun with the cooling essence of the moon and thus echoes the sun and moon depicted inside the Moon card. The half moon speaks of a specific lunar phase. It is either the first or the last quarter, depending on whether the moon is waxing (growing larger) or waning (growing smaller). The first quarter waxing moon reflects a time of decision-making and action. The last quarter of the waning moon is a time of gratitude and sharing. No matter if you pull the Moon card or embody a moon pose in yoga, you can use it as a reminder to consider your current life cycle in the context of the lunar phase.

Note the graphic balance of the moon's dual towers and two beasts. Golden energy falls in perfectly aligned drops, and even the grass near the pond contains symmetry. Half moon pose offers the yogi the same balancing benefits. A yoga practice echoes the ebb and flow of lunar cycles. The yogi's experience on the mat morphs and changes, flying effortlessly one day, feeling weighted down and heavy the next. Yoga, like the moon, reflects the nature of time, the gifts of grounding inside the present moment. Yoga and the Moon card meet us in malleable and ever-changing forms.

. . . .

The Sun

THINK GOOD THOUGHTS of beautiful things,
colors, sounds, places, not mean thoughts.

Pamela Colman Smith[52]

Sacred

The Sun represents fertility and pregnancy due to the child on the card. The manifest nature of sunlight brings forth all life. The card often marks literal pregnancy. Expansion in all areas is implicit; the heat of pleasure, long summer days, and wanton sunflowers. The peaceful face of the sun evokes kind advice, as if to say no matter what happens, you'll be okay. It evokes an endless summer's day, gentle flower-filled breezes, and the earth's caressing nature.

The sun is the engine making all life possible. Solar power is so bright and beguiling, daylight is thought of as the normal state of the universe while nights are slept away without a thought. Yet summer noon sky is not the normal state of the universe. The myriad of midnight stars on a crystal-clear night comes closer to the true nature of the universe. About 95 percent of the known universe is filled with darkness: dark energy and dark matter. Awareness is thought of as light, and light as awareness. Humanity's high states of being are considered "light." The phrase "love and light" is a commonplace expression of blessing derived from sunlight itself.

Waite's "The Tarot: A Wheel of Fortune" explains that the horse-bound child on the Sun card complements the horse-bound skeleton on the Death card, saying "the Sun is the symbol of light and revelation. It is the glory of all worlds. The naked child mounted on the great horse is the complement by antithesis of the thirteenth card—which is Death, also mounted." This "complement" is a metaphor for Christ's resurrection. It is the process of death to rebirth using the child as a Christ figure. Spiritual ascension is illustrated on the Death card via the sun between two towers in the background of the card. The sun moving up between the pillars echoes the occultist's ascent up the Tree of Life. The occultist experiences resurrection through trials of initiation.

Waite tells us "the sun is the consciousness of the spirit." The human soul consciousness is the place where the soul becomes aware of itself. The soul is aware of its true nature because the ego and the shadow have been vanquished. The soul now becomes aware of itself in the integration of divine light, understanding itself as interconnected divinity.

---

52   Smith, "Should the Art Student Think?" 418.

. . . .

THE SUN .

© 1971 U.S. GAMES SYSTEMS, INC.

The RWS deck (left) keeps the placement of the Marseille sun (right) and retaining wall, reflecting boundaries. The twins are swapped for a child on horseback as the Golden Dawn relocates the sign of Gemini on the Lovers card. The Sun is given the astrological attribute of the sun.

He compares and contrasts by saying the Sun is as bright and alive as the Moon is murky, base, and animal, "direct as the antithesis of the reflected light." He explains, "The card signifies, therefore, the transit from the manifest light of this world, represented by the glorious sun of earth, to the light of the world to come." The sun's actual movement and energy empowers the occultist. The "world to come" is not a heavenly biblical afterlife. The world to come is right around the corner in the World card. It will be experienced as the supernal triad's explosion as experienced via the World, not through physical death and resurrection, but through interior enlightenment and the intense experience of divine love on every possible level.

Symbolic

Esoteric Functions: Fertility and Barrenness

Hebrew Letter: Resh

Astrological Association: Sun

A red feather connects the Fool, Death, and Sun child. The feather reflects a state of innocence in the Fool. It is transformed by Death. It is reborn in innocence in the child of the Sun. The child's innocence vastly differs from the Fool's innocence. The Sun's child, in Waite's own words, is only "a child in the sense of simplicity and innocence in the sense of wisdom." The soul had to lose its innocence in order to regain it through the process of maturation. Choice and knowledge imply wisdom against the finite background of experience. This Sun child knows exactly what it is doing, where it is going, and what its intentions are. Waite explains that "he signifies the restored world." This is the restored self.

Waite specifically changes traditional Marseille symbols for the Sun in the RWS. Traditional Sun cards were assigned to the astrological sign of Gemini and illustrated with two children or twins. The Golden Dawn system makes the sun the astrological attribute of the Sun. They relocate Gemini to the Lovers card. A single child is placed on the RWS card, and there is no need for a second. The brick wall is a traditional symbol from older Sun cards and represents boundary lines. The Hebrew letter assigned to the Sun, Resh, means "face." The peaceful face on the radiant yellow sun is a reference to the Hebrew letter; however, an anthropomorphic sun is a traditional symbol appearing on many versions of this card, beginning with the Visconti-Sforza. The Sun is a symbol for a Sephiroth on the Tree of Life. Sunflowers are reference to solar power, and the child's flaming red banner reflects flickering solar flames.

Profane

Growth and expansion. Pregnancy, either real or metaphorical. A happy love affair. Your horizons broaden and opportunities surround you. It is safe to let your true self shine forth in vulnerability and beauty. Glowing health abounds. Magnetism and passion are exhumed through

• • • • • • •

every pore. Bodily enjoyment and long summer days. Accumulation of material things, making your life pleasurable. An energetic power boost adds an extra spring to your step and the stamina you need to complete a task. In a yes-no question, the answer is an unequivocal yes.

Waite's Divinatory Meanings: Material happiness, fortunate marriage, contentment.

Reversed: The same in a lesser sense.

Asana

The Sun card aligns with child's pose, or balasana. The body assumes a fetal position, thus aligning the posture with the child illustrated on the Sun card. The restorative pose is available to the yogi at any point during the practice as a resting point. It soothes the solar plexus and calms the body. Yoga can be strenuous. It is important to work hard for the things you care about. However, the counter point to effort is ease. Balance infuses every inch of the yoga practice and exists inside the tarot deck. Balance exists inside the polarities of your body and in the intricacies of your life.

Yoga channels solar energy from the first sun salutation. How you work with the energy is entirely up to you. You might channel it inward for personal growth. You may use it to build physical strength and emotional stamina. You might use solar energy to fuel the burning at the core of your soul so you may burn with the fire of a thousand stars. Regardless of how you choose to work with the sun's energy, it falls upon you effortlessly. It creeps into your bedroom in the morning to wake you up, it generates the food you eat, it makes all life possible. It is always there. It doesn't have to be worked at all the time. Allow your child's pose, like the Sun card, to become a place of absorption and effortless pleasure. Take child's pose and feel the energy of the sun coursing through your exquisite body. Allow it to foster a sense of interconnectivity between you and all living things.

. . . .

Judgement

FOR IT IS a land of power,
a land of unkempt uproar—
full of life, force, energy.

Pamela Colman Smith[53]

Sacred

Judgement is a monumental point in life. Boundaries, walls, and encasements are destroyed. Doors open, possibility comes knocking, intuition flows freely. The tectonic plates of change move like giants beneath your feet and alter the landscape forever. Gaping holes of darkness give way as dirt, rock, and stone cave into the abyss of a yawning earth. You have reached the point of no return. There is no going back. The train leaves the station. The airplane's aloft. Change permeates beneath the surface of everything in life.

The difference is felt in small and large ways—clothes don't feel right, the house feels ill at ease. Things that used to bring joy leave you blank. New qualities fill your life with pleasure. The trumpet's song is a true calling, a wake-up sign, the right song coming on the radio at the right time, just when you needed to hear it. Our personal evolution impacts the people around us. A single shining truth echoes from this card. It is unaltered in the infinite definitions and understandings of Judgement. It whispers, screams, and sings the message, "There is no going back."

Waite says yes, the card reflects the literal image of biblical judgment: "Last Judgment and resurrection of the physical body." The archangel blows his horn and the dead rise. He says if you want to use the biblical interpretation of judgment, feel free. But he also asks "those who have inward eyes" to look deeper. Those with "eyes" will discover this card can be compared to Temperance's divine fusion of energies.

He asks point-blank, "What is that within us which does sound a trumpet and all that is lower in our nature rises in response—almost in a moment, almost in a twinkling of the eye?" He asks, in his thick sentence, where is the calling inside yourself? Does it come from art, nature, poetry? From where does it stem? What is loud enough for the "lower nature" or the material and earthbound selves to hear the call of the Divine? He suggests it happens in a flash, in a moment, before cognition occurs. Danger is often felt before it is seen. The body

---

53   Smith, "Should the Art Student Think?" 419.

. . . . . .

JUDGEMENT.

The RWS (left) takes literal symbolic inspiration from the Marseille Judgement card (right) with a trumpeting angel appearing above souls rising from coffins against a backdrop of mountains.

knows you've fallen in love before the mind realizes it. Knowledge and truth arrive to us from unknowable places.

Ultimately, it is "the card which registers the accomplishment of the great work of transformation in answer to the summons of the Supernal." In other words, it is more than the physical body rising and responding to the call of the Supernal (god). It is the entire earth rising to the call of the Supernal. Remember, "as above, so below." You are the world and the world is you. You bring the earthly world with you as you rise to embrace the nature of divinity. You transform not only yourself but the entire world along with you.

Symbolic

Esoteric Function: No function

Hebrew Letter: Shin

Element: Fire

Archangel Michael, the angel of protection, faith, and will, sounds his trumpet above the figures below. Pamela's card is symbolic of the Last Judgment in the biblical sense. It can be read using all of its metaphors and allegories. The Last Judgment has been painted the world over by artists, from Michelangelo to William Blake. Dozens of films and works of literature mark the end of the world. Judgement's iconic use, whether comical, serious, or biblical, always marks the ending on the known world.

The figures' nudity expresses vulnerability. The children reflect innocence. Families represent unity. The mother, father, and child represent the trinity. Upward-facing and open arms suggest an invitation and opening. Fire and the Hebrew letter Shin are associated with this card. Shin is the first letter in the Hebrew word meaning "heaven" or "sky." Fire is reflected in the red wings of Michael and the red cross on his banner. The cross exemplifies the axis mundi, the center point of the universe where heaven and earth meet. The red and yellow flames of Michael's hair also suggest the element of fire. The angel appears out of clouds, like all of the ace cards. Coffins represent death. The distant mountain peaks reflect spiritual heights, as always, yet these mountains are covered in white snow, suggesting great altitude, pristine understanding, and clarity.

Profane

Judgement is an official wake-up call. Your life must change. Old ways of doing things slip by the wayside. Your family is affected by personal actions. You stand as an example for others, demonstrating what is possible. An opportunity is staring you straight in the face. Will you heed the call? Judgement reflects the truth rising to the surface. You are asked to interview for

· · · · · · ·

an important, life-changing job. You are expected to deliver a result. You are required to rise to the challenge. In a yes-no question, the answer is yes, if you take the highest road possible.

> **Waite's Divinatory Meanings:** Change of position, renewal, outcome. Another account specifies total loss through a lawsuit.

> **Reversed:** Weakness, pusillanimity, simplicity; also deliberation, decision, sentence.

Asana

Judgement aligns with yoga's warrior I pose, or virabhadrasana. The yogi reaches toward the sky in an physical imitation of the mythological Hindu warrior Virabhadra, who rose from the earth with two swords, one in each hand. The Judgement card is illustrated with bodies emerging from floating coffins. They rise from the grave in the ultimate act of reanimation and rebirth, just like Virabhadra.

Transformation, evolution, and growth results in a more fully realized version of yourself. It creates more of YOU for the world to enjoy and absorb. Just as teenage hormones did the work of transforming our bodies, we become stewards of internal transformation by fostering an open, curious, and attentive attitude to the world around us. We place our attention, our most powerful asset, on things mattering to us. We don't avoid fear but choose to move through it. Transformation occurs in fits and starts, all at once or slowly. Sometimes we feel the internal rotation and gears of change; other times we are oblivious. Certain yogic poses, like some tarot cards, channel acute attention and energy toward transformation. They can be used to power up, jumpstart, and infuse growth. Warrior I pose and the Judgement card both require you to stand up, pay attention, and heed the call. The fire, fury, and effort of the card and the pose is akin to a birthing mother's final push. It is you who is reborn. Are you ready to greet a new world entirely of your own making? What are you waiting for? Will you leap into paradise?

. . . .

The World

Learn from everything, see everything,
and above all feel everything!

Pamela Colman Smith[54]

Sacred

The World card reflects you as the World dancer moving in a state of sheer perfection. The nature of the universe is now embodied inside your skin and bones, in your actions and gestures, your thoughts and feelings. Opposing qualities are integrated. Self-consciousness is cast aside. Complete trust is formed. You are the dazzling essence of who you are meant to be. Your talents, qualities, and sensitivities infuse every action. A glorious moment of completion. Beauty and brilliance are as profound as the possibility that was birthed in the Fool. Your pattern is forever altered. Salutation occurs. You are the universe. You are the most creative and magical act you will ever partake in.

The loss of self-consciousness as foreshadowed by the Star is no loss but a gesture toward complete immersion. All psychic energy is infused and given in the form of love, attention, and focus in the World card. The individual becomes what they focus on. Sublime transcendence occurs as complete intention moves past experience of a thing and into the embodiment. The ego dissolves. Deep time is experienced. Clock time vanishes. The major arcana's grand finale is foreshadowed in the Wheel of Fortune card. The wheel spins like the World's wreath, four creatures mark the corners of the card, clouds fill the blue sky.

Divinity craves your attention at all times. Divinity is the lover who never tires of your gaze. How do you create a devotional space? How do you let divinity know you see it? Do you focus on what moves your soul? How do you embody love and compassion in the simplicity of day-to-day life? Implicit trust in the blueprint inside you brings you to the World card repeatedly. Move past the ego; ground yourself in the present. Trust the soul's desire and deep intuition. The true magic of the universe will be unleashed inside and outside of you.

According to Waite, the World is "the state of the restored world when the law of manifestation shall have been carried to the highest degree of natural perfection." The Magician succeeds in his spell. His will is aligned in the true manifestation of the divinity. Yet, Waite tosses this idea aside and challenges us to move higher: "It represents the perfection and end of the Cosmos" as well as "referring to that day when all was declared good, when the morning

---

54   Smith, "Should the Art Student Think?" 417.

. . . . . .

THE WORLD.

The RWS borrows heavily from the Marseille
World card (right). An androgynous female is
placed inside a wreath, while four creatures,
the tertramorphs, decorate the four corners,
reflecting the four suits and directions.

stars sang together." Waite links the end of the cosmos or the universe to the primordial myth. Doing so, he evokes the endless circle of life.

Waite says the World card is "the rapture of the universe when it understands itself in God." The Judgement card depicts biblical judgment and the resurrection of the dead. The occultist and thereby the earth (as above, so below—human is the earth, the earth is human) has raptured itself to the heavens. To Waite's point, it is now the universe's turn. The universe mirrors and responds to your awareness. The universe raptures itself back to you. The connective and energizing force is love / god / deity. It is the supernal triad and the essence of trinity.

Lovers mirror each other; parents and children reflect each other; friends, muses, and colleagues inspire one another. Out of all these interactions, new possibilities occur. The center activating agent is love (divinity). Spiritual trinity: earth, universe, divine; the supernal triad; father, son, holy ghost; maiden, mother, crone; past, present, future; the threefold world of upper, middle, and lower expand in unison. Everything sees each other. The Sun (you) rises to embrace the Judgement card (the universe). The universe (divinity) sees you seeing it. Divinity responds when it is recognized. Divinity wants to be noticed. It wants to be "seen." Divinity craves your attention as much as the client wants her tarot reader to "see" her. It is the reason the infinite universe will never stop expanding. It is why you enjoy unlimited potential in every second of your life. Divine response occurs as you recognize it and rise up to greet it. Divinity, once embraced and acknowledged, is embodied in the World card. The World card is the universe's response to being seen. Perfect. Complete. New. Fresh. Unlimited. It is the big bang. It radiates orgasmic consciousness.

Symbolic

Esoteric Functions: Power and Servitude

Hebrew Letter: Tav

Astrological Association: Saturn

The World dancer's naked body reflects complete trust and vulnerability. Her posture, foreshadowed by the Hanged Man's inverted body, echoes Saturn's planetary symbol, the cross in the circle. Occult interpretations suggest the scarf warping around her body conceals male genitalia. The World dancer as a hermaphrodite exemplifies a perfected union of masculine and feminine energy. The four corner figures are tetramorphs, a biblical reference to the first chapter of Ezekiel, reflecting a man, lion, ox, and eagle. The four creatures represent the four corners / directions (north, south, east, west) and the four suits of tarot (wands, cups, swords, pentacles). Her green wreath is oval and in the shape of a zero, the number of the Fool, who rises to meet her. The oval also suggests the female birth canal through which new life moves. The wreath's oval shape is used by the Golden Dawn's tattva tradition, which uses symbols and invocations while rising through initiatory grades. This shape is the akasha tattva, also assigned to Saturn and the Hebrew letter Tav, meaning "mark." The bluish-violet color of the scarf is associated with the letter Tav.

The World dancer holds dual magic wands in opposition to the Magician, who holds a single wand. The Magician opens and directs the flow of spiritual energy. This essence flows through the entire deck like a humming stream and is reflected in tarot's rivers. The World holds two wands and in doing so allows the energy to move through her uninterrupted. She acts as a human energetic clearing house, capturing the energy, as symbolized by the green wreath around her. She infuses this energy and knowledge into every action, movement, and thought. She discards what is not needed without hesitation, free to meet each moment fresh. The World card is the ideal state of grace and complex alignment between the soul and the universe. The World is the ultimate integration as the left and right pillar fall away and become a circle. She perfectly integrates all aspects of the personality, both male and female, becoming the idealized center pillar. Additionally, she walks in each world, sacred and profane, spiritual and material. She is the ultimate integration of all things, all qualities, and all truths.

Profane

The World card reflects living in the moment. It is success, euphoria, and completion. The end of a cycle. Travel, movement, and excitement beckon. Your goals are achieved. You enjoy the freedom of movement and expansion of life. Laughter, pleasure, and contentment are yours. You are free to bask in the glory of all your hard work. You make plans for a trip. You reap success in love and at work. You enjoy sound mind and a supple, healthy body. In a yes-no question, the answer is yes, as long as you stay true to yourself.

> **Waite's Divinatory Meanings:** Assured success, recompense, voyage, route, emigration, flight, change of place.
>
> **Reversed:** Inertia, fixity, stagnation, permanence.

Asana

The World card aligns with yoga's down dog pose, or adho mukha svanasana. Down dog is often the first pose taught to the beginning yogi. It may seem counterintuitive to align a seemingly basic yoga pose to the World card, the most highly esteemed card of tarot, yet World card delights, like down dog, are repeatedly available to us. World card properties are not reserved for a chosen few or the most enlightened but infuse every moment of our life. The World card, like down dog pose, offers the integration of the highest and lowest, expansive and introspective, and every infinite space in between. It's right before your eyes. Can you feel it? Do you see it? Do you want it? Claim it.

• • • • • •

Netzach (Victory)
The Minor Arcana

- - - - - - - - - - - - - - - - -

RWS Suits

Tarot's four suits offer an extraordinary way for the individual to understand themselves and the world around them. Waite and Pamela illustrated their suits to align with the Golden Dawn's Kabbalistic interpretations.

The RWS is the first tarot since the Sola Busca deck to illustrate the minor arcana. The minor arcana of older decks employed only symbol and number. The Six of Swords in an older deck would likely contain six swords, the Five of Swords would reflect five swords, and so forth. Pamela was the first modern illustrator to fill the minors with scenes. The cards became like moving pictures. Anyone could look at the cards and create a story from them. They became easy to interpret. The cards could now be shuffled, read, and retold with infinite outcomes and possibilities. The Six of Swords became an evocative image. A mysterious boatman ferries two souls across a river. The Five of Swords became a battlefield with clear winners and losers. Pamela's images are beguiling and ambiguous. They are moving pieces of a story that can be told and retold each time the reader shuffles.

Suits reflect earth's four elements and directions:

Pentacles	Earth	West	The place of manifestation and growth
Swords	Air	North	The place of clear thinking
Wands	Fire	South	The place of heat
Cups	Water	East	The place of new beginnings

The elements reflect *you.*

- - - - - - -

Pentacles/Earth

Everything you can see, smell, feel, taste and touch (material world)—this is your physical body, dog, car, mom, boyfriend, dinner, money, closet full of clothes, garden, airplanes, family. Pentacles are your flesh, bones, blood, and DNA. It is everything in the material world.

Pentacles and earth are represented by the quality of loamy, fecund earth, dirt, soil, matter and compost, tectonic plates, mountains—earth.

- Remember pentacles' attribution by recalling a pentacle looks like a molecule and molecules make up all earthy matter.

Swords/Air

Your thoughts, ideas, and stories. The way you think about things. The decision you made last week. It is words, language, and articulation. How you speak to people and how other's words affect you. It is your mind. How you speak to yourself. It is the yogic breath, your inhales and exhales. Control your breath and you can control emotion. You constantly engage in the energetic exchange of air and the suit of swords when you breathe. It is life and death. This is why the suit of swords appears frightening.

Represented by the quality of wind, oxygen filling the lungs, humidity, icy cold and thermal hot temperatures—air.

- Remember swords' attribution by recalling a sword moves through the air quickly. Like weapons, words can wound, heal, or protect.

Wands/Fire

Your passion, everything that gets you out of bed in the morning, your desire to travel, your romantic attractions, your deepest desires, intentions, and beliefs. Wands are the heat, the internal fire, the passion informing your life and directing your actions. Wands are where the individual emulates the sun itself. Through the element of fire, we germinate and grow all things.

Represented by the quality of fire, crackling, consuming, cooking, burning embers, hot coals, a match in the darkness, candles, incense, forest fires, volcanic lava—fire.

- Remember wands' attribution by recalling a magic wand with electrical fire passing through it or the heat of the sun.

Cups/Water

Your feelings, imagination, and dreams. The appreciation of art, love, beauty. Every single emotion from raging anger to all-encompassing love. The highs and lows, darkness and light are all expressed by the element of water. It is the place of compassion.

Represented by the ever-changing nature of water, from quiet ponds to raging seas, rivers, clouds, mist, ice, snow, rain…it is all the quality of fluid water/fluid emotion—water.

- Remember cups' attribution by recalling a cup is a container for holding slippery, elusive water.

. . . .

Important RWS Kabbalistic Note on Suits

The RWS minor arcana is designed in accordance to the Kabbalistic Four Parts to the Soul associated with the tetragrammaton. These make up the four Kabbalistic Worlds. Each world springs from the ace. The ace is the root of that world. All the minor arcana cards spring from the ace like flowers from a seed.

Pentacles	Earth	Assiah, the Material World
Swords	Air	Yetizrah, the Formative World
Wands	Fire	Atziluth, the Archetypal World
Cups	Water	Briah, the Creative World

Note: The accompanying poetry comes from Waite's *Shadows of Light and Thought* (1906)—four years before the tarot deck, when he was enmeshed in the Golden Dawn.

. . . . . .

ACE of WANDS.

. . . .

Ace of Wands

Kether of Atziluth—Root of the Power of Fire

IF THOU HAST the gift of soul to bear,
A glimpse of the secrets of earth and air.
As an outward sign of the heart's desire,
Thy little parcel of sacred fire.

Arthur Waite, *Collected Poems*

The Ace of Wands reflects the initial spark of desire—the rush of fire ignited by romantic attraction. It is the energy of passionate obsession, the instant of beguilement and amazement, and your heart moving from zero to sixty miles an hour in the space of a second. The Ace of Wands gets you out of bed in the morning. It fills you with excitement as your eyes flutter open. It is the famous movie closeup where the character realizes what they want. The story is set in motion. Luke Skywalker gazes longingly across the desert in *Star Wars*. Jack spies Rose in *Titanic*. Baby sees Johnny grinding on the dance floor in *Dirty Dancing*. The Ace of Wands is a blossoming desire with the power to change the course of your life.

In a deeper sense, the Ace of Wands is the seed, the sprout, and the beginning of the element of fire. It reflects toe-curling longing. Fire marks our blood, passions, hungers. It is the suit of careers, desires, and spirituality. It is pure energy. The energy of fire's flames will nurture and warm us when used safely. Fire contains the power to singe or burn when used carelessly or allowed to rage out of control. It carries the potential to engulf, devour, and incinerate everything if not contained. The Ace of Wands is the internal fire yogis stoke during their physical practice. It is the spirit felt by pulpit preachers spouting fire and brimstone to their spiritually starved congregations. Fire is the combustible, unavoidable element making life worth living. It often gets us all into trouble. It ultimately defines who we are.

Waite states the obvious when he tells us, "A hand issuing from a cloud grasps a stout wand or club." Pamela takes her direction from the *Book T*: "A WHITE Radiating Angelic Hand…" The stark whiteness of the hand is apparent. The whiteness, as pale as a blank sheet of paper, marks a stark contrast to the skin color of every other character Pamela draws in the deck. A spiky electrical field with thirty-six spikes glows around the fist and wrist, depicting additional radiance. All of the deck's ace hands match up in color and display radiant qualities with differing numbers of spikes.

. . . . . .

The palm's grip is tight. It forcefully holds the masculine element of fire (wands) and air (swords). This is oppositional to the feminine element of earth (pentacles) and water (cups), where the pentacle rests gently in the palm. Pamela crafts an especially phallic wand for her deck. The phallus is an ideal symbol for the masculine suit of fire. It reflects the outward nature of masculine energy as opposed to the feminine receptivity.

The *Book T* says the Ace of Wands is "issuing from clouds, and grasping a heavy club, which has three branches." Pamela has followed these instructions precisely. The *Book T* describes three leaves sprouting from the left and right branch, although the text calls them "flames." It also describes four leaves on the top branch. These leaves or "flames" counted together equal ten and represent the ten Sephiroth on the Tree of Life. The symbol of the wand is the token of the suit of wands. The wand is also placed on the Magician's table alongside the three other suits.

The posture of the Ace of Wands matches the Ace of Cups. Each hand extends from clouds on the right side of the card. Additionally, the Ace of Wands and Cups both depict water in the environment surrounding and supporting the card. In opposition, the Ace of Pentacles and Swords extend from the left side of the card and no water is seen within their landscape. The Ace of Wands is the only ace to reflect a home. The house or castle reflects humankind, domesticity, family life, and security. Waite tells us the Ace of Wands is the virility behind family, origin, and birth. The river's moving waters reflect a journey away from home. It is forward flow, the journey we embark on when heeding the work and call of our passions.

> **Waite's Divinatory Meanings:** A natural force, strength, vigor, energy, beginning, source, family, origin, creation, invention, enterprise, power of virility.
>
> **Reversed:** Decadence, ruin, perdition, clouded joy.

. . . .

Two of Wands

Lord of Dominion—Mars in Aries

WITHIN THE CHARMED walls is a place of delight,
And a world from its windows
shines strange to the sight.

Arthur Waite, *Collected Poems*

Energy is realized and recognized in the Two of Wands. The energy of the Ace has doubled. "It is our light, not our darkness that most frightens us," says Marianne Williamson. "Our deepest fear is not that we are inadequate. Our deepest fear is that we are powerful beyond measure."[55] Personal intention permeates the suit of wands. The Two of Wands reflects electricity stirring the soul to action and contemplation. The Two of Wands reflects the duality of basking in permeating light. The internal fire is stoked and plans are laid.

Interpret the image of the Two of Wands literally. The world is in your hands. Now is the time to plot and plan. The energy of passion doubles and swings in your favor. Make alliances, list goals, create a vision board and write out your plan for action. Outline the novel you've always wanted to write. Make the business plan for your company. This is the card of weighing options carefully. Dual opportunities come your way. Choose between romantic entanglements. Find a partner whose passion equals yours. This is the card of cleverness and daring, not of folly. A well-executed plan combines passion, knowledge, and timing. Hold these elements firmly in your grip as you move forth.

Pamela is faithful to the card's esoteric title, "The Lord of Dominion." The figure emulates the Emperor card who surveys his kingdom. The Two of Wands surveys the landscape while holding a globe in one hand (the Emperor holds a globe). The character holds a wand in the other (just as the Emperor holds his ankh). Both the Emperor and the Two of Wands are adorned in fiery red and orange clothing. The figure is placed between two wands, like the High Priestess and Justice cards. Graphically, the figure becomes the middle pillar standing inside the two outer pillars of the Tree of Life, represented by dual wands.

Waite makes a special note: "The Rose and Cross and Lily should be noticed on the left side." The rose and lily are alchemical symbols for the sun and the moon. The three colors of

---

55   Williamson, *A Return to Love.*

. . . . . .

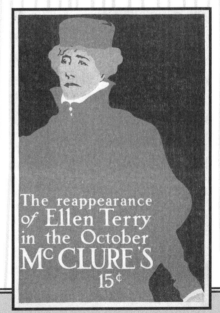

The Lyceum's 1907 production of The Merchant of Venice likely inspired Pamela's rendering of her Two of Wands card. Here we see two examples of Ellen Terry as lead character Portia.

black, white, and red are classic alchemical colors. Black reflects the base material level, red is the energy of transformation, and white is the color of purification. Roses and lilies are the same flower blooming around the edges of the Magician card, whose energy flows and ignites each card. Illustrated in this manner, the flowers on the Two of Wands become a "Rosy Cross." Waite created his own organization, the Fellowship of the Rosy Cross, in 1915. White lilies are found beneath the Ace of Pentacles. White lilies are also embroidered upon the luminous cloaks of the Hierophant's monks.

The figure strikes a powerful posture by holding a globe in hand. It reflects having the world at your fingertips, the power of intention-setting and careful planning. The globe is a subtle reminder of the World card and ultimate attainment. The landscape of the card evokes the mountainous island of Jamaica, where Pamela spent her childhood years. The distant beach marks the threshold of known meeting unknown and a boundary line. The mountainscape reflects the duality of spiritual heights, while the ocean reflects emotional depths. It reminds the reader to keep a foot in each world. A plowed field, rich with ripe, freshly tilled soil, reflects fecundity and generative growth toward the issue at hand. The figure stands upon a battlement offering a wide-ranging view. Examine all aspects of the situation at hand and from as many vantage points as possible.

Pamela adorns her character in costuming similar to the Lyceum Theater's production of *The Merchant of Venice*. Her figure emulates Ellen Terry in the role of Portia and Henry Irving as Shylock. The play is set in Venice. Cool blue Aegean waters may be pictured on the card. Shakespeare's *Merchant of Venice* contains an actual reference to wands. Shylock tells Antonio, "The skillful shepard peeled me certain wands. And in the doing of the deed of kind, he stuck them up before the fulsome ewes." Shylock's story is a reference to the story "Thistorie of Jacob" found in the book of Genesis. It was a popular visual tale seen on multiple Renaissance engravings, woodcuts, and tapestries. Jacob uses his "wands" to divide and bring order to his flocks of sheep. A wand, in this sense, is used as an object of power and discernment, much like a sword. It is also a story of thrifty business bearing weight on the forthcoming Three of Wands card, where we discover a new merchant sending his ships out into the world in an act of trade and commerce.

> **Waite's Divinatory Meanings:** Between the alternative readings there is no marriage possible; on the one hand, riches, fortune, magnificence; on the other, physical suffering, disease, chagrin, sadness, mortification. The design gives one suggestion; here is a lord overlooking his dominion and alternately contemplating a globe; it looks like the malady, the mortification, the sadness of Alexander amidst the grandeur of this world's wealth.

> **Reversed:** Surprise, wonder, enchantment, emotion, trouble, fear.

• • • • • •

Three of Wands

Lord of Established Strength—Sun in Aries

So THEREFORE DAYS and nights dissolve
By this low-breathing sea,
While here I pause and still revolve
Voyage and venture free!

Arthur Waite, *Collected Poems*

The Three of Wands reflects the triplicity of fire. Leaping, glowing flames of desire are coaxed into the hypnotic dance of fire. The sorceress casts her spell. Offerings are made. A prayer is whispered. Incantations abound. The send button is hit. Messages and communications fly toward their target, invoking the power of three. Energy is sent flying into the world. Like-minded people gather to aid you in your goal. If the Two of Wands suggested careful planning, the Three of Wands reflects the first stages of the plan's execution. Plans are in motion. Ripples of cause and effect are visible.

The Tree of Life's three pillars are graphically reflected by the wands and character standing between them. The figure grips a wand with his right hand, the active hand. This reflects an understanding and active usage of deep esoteric knowledge. It deepens your experience of the world. Your deeds and actions grow richer and more effective. Expansion and creation dance before your eyes. You are now the active participant, no longer willing to sit passively and watch. You stand at the fore, taking responsibility for what has been generated. It reflects a maturity of the self.

T. S. Eliot references the Three of Wands in his epic 1922 poem *The Waste Land*. The Three of Wands are found inside the poem's first section, "The Burial of the Dead," where Eliot says, "Here is the man with three staves."[56] He soon makes a prophecy of the poem by telling the reader to "fear death by water." Out of water we crawled. Into water we shall one day return. Eliot suggests we face our own mortality when we face the water. He raises the timeless existential question: How does knowledge of death inform our life? The Three of Wands is a card of action. The number three suggests creativity, and the merchant faces the water while sending out his ships. Eliot's usage of the card provides a deep context in which we can examine our

56   Eliot, *Collected Poems 1909–1935*, 59–79.

own accountability in life. Are we doing what we were put here for? What do today's actions, seemingly insignificant, add up to in the end?

Eliot tells us in his notes to *The Waste Land*, "The Man with Three Staves (an authentic member of the Tarot pack) I associate, quite arbitrarily, with the Fisher King himself."[57] The Fisher King is a character from Arthurian legend. The Fisher King is a wounded king who is healed not by medicine but by insight. This association reminds us of the healing power of insight and contemplation. It reminds us of the true power of the tarot. It is a reminder of the healing power of questioning well and the introspective life.

Waite gives us the keys to unlock the mystery of the three ships. He allows us a peek right inside them when he says that "those are his ships, bearing his merchandise, which are sailing over the sea." The ships are a clear metaphor for desires, intentions, and material goods being set forth. Waite suggests the figure is "looking from his side toward yours with a view to help you." In this way, the card suggests you will receive help in achieving your goal. Help often arrives in surprising and unanticipated ways; an old friend reappears, a patron appears to fund your creative project, a family member steps in to offer you a loan, or synchronicity appears from out of the blue to help you along. The title "Lord of Established Strength" suggests protection and power are assured. It is a strong, stable card. As surely as the figure's wand offers support, you can stick to your guns. Your actions reflect strength. The posture of the Three of Wands reflects stamina and fortitude at your disposal.

> **Waite's Divinatory Meanings:** He symbolizes established strength, enterprise, effort, trade, commerce, discovery; those are his ships, bearing his merchandise, which are sailing over the sea. The card also signifies able co-operation in business, as if the successful merchant prince were looking from his side toward yours with a view to help you.

> **Reversed:** The end of troubles, suspension or cessation of adversity, toil and disappointment.

---

57   Eliot, *Collected Poems 1909–1935*, 59–79.

· ·

Four of Wands

The Lord of Perfected Work—Venus in Aries—Stage Card

AND THE WORLD to the walls
the high carnival came,
Bright eyes full of rapture,
bright faces aflame.

Arthur Waite, *Collected Poems*

The Four of Wands reflects a happy home, marriage, and celebration. Shower sparks of midsummer fertility magic, fire festivals, and passion's fourfold stability radiate through the card. The card's appearance marks a return to the natural world, being in touch with the earth when at the height of its radiant power. The passionate stability of fire does not consume but kindles. Fire cultivates pleasure for all who seek its warmth. It signifies a revelrous time, summer festivals, parties and weddings. At the very long last, you have something to celebrate. The hard work is done; you've worked well. Now it is time to rejoice.

Humanity has participated in fire rituals since fire was cultivated. The Vestal Virgins cared for Rome's sacred flames, runners pass the Olympic flame, and the simple lighting of a candle with an intention evokes a fire ritual. Fire's cinnamon and jasmine incense smoke carry messages to the gods. Ceremonial fires are stoked with herbs and plants to conjure and release their magical properties. Fires purify and release what is burned, be it sacred wood, yule logs, or sacrificial elements. Crackling fireplaces and wood stoves were a common source of heat in 1909, when the RWS deck was created. The average citizen stoked fires for cooking and warmth. Flickering torchlight filled dark city streets; candles and oil lamps lit homes. The general public had a direct and immediate connection to the element of fire.

Pamela's wands run like scenes from a novel. An idea sparks in the ace; a plan is conceived in the two and implemented in the three. The four breeds celebration and reflects the human need to share feelings and enthusiasm. Shared joy is richer than happiness experienced alone. The Four of Wands reflects the desire to share happiness and good fortune. The card suggests you inspire others by gifting them with the same treasures and qualities empowering you with joy.

Ancient spring rites suggesting celebration are painted on the scrim of the stage. Venus is symbolized by the roses in the garland and in the bouquets of summer revelers. Blooming flowers reflect manifestation of desire. Waite is clear in his description: "Two female figures

· · · · · ·

uplift nosegays; at their side is a bridge over a moat, leading to an old manorial house." The bridge is a symbol of passage between dual realities. Waite's description of a moat and manor house carries ancestral overtones. The stories of those who have gone before us, our parents and grandparents, help us to find how we fit into our life matrix. Discovering familial roots— be it through story, pictures, and genealogy—helps us to figure out who we really are. While family lineage never defines us completely, examining our roots helps us to excavate pieces of ourselves. We can look and see what we have inherited from those who have gone before karmically, energetically, and genetically. Once we see familial patterns, just like tarot patterns or habits, we are free to fix them however we choose by healing ourselves. In healing ourselves, even if we do not have the means to examine our family history, we retroactively heal those who have come before and those who will come after. This is a magic and a power each of us possesses. The Four of Wands reminds us of this gift.

Once internal spaces are healed, we venture forth into the greater space and interconnectivity of the entire world. Our joy amplifies to all those who draw close to us. Joy and pleasure pour through our actions and intentions. The human race is our family, and the earth is our home. As above, so below. Never forget the power of the present to heal the past and create a new future.

The esoteric title, "The Lord of Perfected Work," is aptly given to this card. The job is accomplished. The Emperor's rock-like structure is buried deep within the card. Underneath the licking flames of passion, we see our passionate pursuits take shape in the world. The goal has been met, the intention has manifested, and the dream has come true, yet it is early in the cards. We are only at number four. There is plenty more to come. Unexpected, unanticipated consequences both good and bad are yet to unfold. We will reach higher, find new objectives, and face a new set of challenges as a new day begins.

> **Waite's Divinatory Meanings:** They are for once almost on the surface—country life, haven of refuge, a species of domestic harvest-home, repose, concord, harmony, prosperity, peace, and the perfected work of these.
>
> **Reversed:** The meaning remains unaltered; it is prosperity, increase, felicity, beauty, embellishment.

· ·

Five of Wands

The Lord of Strife—Saturn in Leo

FROM OUT OF the depth and vastness of the dark,
Brought voices wild which stirred within the soul.

Arthur Waite, *Collected Poems*

The unity of Four of Wands is divided, scattered, and combusted. Everyone fights for themselves. Five young people raise wands against one other. Each takes a solid stance, feet flat on the ground. The Five of Wands appears when it feels like everyone is out for blood at work or at home. It is the incendiary nature of the sparks of a fire building toward combustion. This is seen when crowds are on the verge of violence, when a peaceful protest becomes dangerous, or when skirmishes unexpectedly break out. It is the point in a long-term relationship when the flames of desire are replaced with the intensity of agitation and conflict.

Primordial myths tell us fire is the essence of power. Precious fire is stolen from the gods by Greek Titan Prometheus as a gift to mankind. He suffers eternal punishment at the hands of angry Zeus for his deed. Cherokee myth portrays Grandmother Spider, who hides fire in her clay pot, while for Creek Native Americans Rabbit steals fire from the Weasels. Fire's many valuable qualities include agitation and friction, often leading to explosive results.

The lighter side of the Five of Wands reveals an enjoyable challenge, scrimmage, or lively debate. Personal passion changes minds and influences events and others. A secret of this card is revealed by looking into the future. The five figures come together and form the shape of a magical pentagram with their wands. It is proof positive of the uniting power of passion and accepting and respecting differing opinions and views. Waite describes their action "as if in sport or strife." He claims their skirmish connects to the "battle of life." His statement begs the question of what you fight against. What is the source of struggle between yourself and others? What do you feel is worth fighting for? Do you embrace a challenge or fight the challenge itself? The *Book T* calls this card "violent strife and boldness."

The esoteric title, "Lord of Strife," is defined as a bitter disagreement over fundamental issues, thus the incendiary nature of this card. A single spark carries the potential to consume or nurture. The transformative ability of passionate beliefs is exercised and explored. The question remains. What direction will the energy move in? Will it create or consume?

· · · · · · ·

For those who do not wish to engage in fighting and those who shy away from conflict, a moment of truth may be upon you. Will you stand up for what is right? Can you express your opinions and thoughts without hurting those who oppose you? Can you avoid becoming part of the problem? How is it possible to surrender to a situation yet remain strong? The answer lies in anchoring yourself in the present moment. Eckhart Tolle tells us,

> Accept your here and now totally by dropping all inner resistance. The false, unhappy self that loves feeling miserable, resentful, or sorry for itself can then no longer survive. This is called surrender. Surrender is not weakness. There is great strength in it.[58]

To follow this advice and free yourself from the energetic skirmish of the Five of Wands, surrender to the moment. Stop inserting the ego and allow yourself to observe. Doing so offers new options and creative solutions. Because you are not being angry, reactive, and retaliatory, the freedom of creative response is at your fingertips. You are impervious to the slings and arrows, insults and enemies of others. Your freedom lies in responding in any way you choose, any way you see fit. You rise above and beyond the situation.

> **Waite's Divinatory Meanings:** Imitation, as, for example, sham fight, but also the strenuous competition and struggle of the search after riches and fortune. In this sense it connects with the battle of life. Hence some attributions say that it is a card of gold, gain, opulence.

> **Reversed:** Litigation, disputes, trickery, contradiction.

58 Tolle, *The Power of Now*.

- -

Six of Wands

The Lord of Victory—Jupiter in Leo

IN THE POMP of deep night and high glory of day,
Where the long golden prospects
stretch shining away.
With pennons and banners the pageants pass by,
And the crash of their music goes up to the sky.

Arthur Waite, *Collected Poems*

When the Six of Wands appears, it lets you know you have something to celebrate. A figure carries a staff and rides his horse in a celebratory parade. The crowd waves five wands into the air. Victory parades evoke national, team, and individual success and jubilation. Sporting events culminate in victory marches for winning teams in their respective cities. Fire is the vital essence used in celebration the world over. The Six of Wands reflects the image of a victory march. Success is yours. Mission accomplished. Onward movement commences.

Waite tells us "footmen with staves are at his side." The figures marching forward in victory are part of a processional, yet a crowd is nowhere to be seen. Is the victory real or imagined? The card stands as a reminder of the people who surround you and support you. No success is obtained alone. You are supported every step of the way, whether or not you realize it.

It is the card of achievement, but as in all minor arcana six cards, the story is far from complete; there is more to come. Waite's article "The Tarot: A Wheel of Fortune" describes this card as "crowned with hope and confidence." Having, maintaining, and exhuming hope and confidence can be seen as a victory in itself. The card issues forth the magnanimous feeling that helps us obtain any goal. It fills us with energy. It is a card of inspiration regardless if you are reflected by the figure on the horse or if you stand in the crowd. Deep down, you discover anything is possible.

Waite admits the card has many meanings. He offers a surface reading describing happy news and hope. He neglects to mention the deeper esoteric meaning of the number six, which corresponds to the heart center of the Tree of Life. As such, this is the space of compassion, kindness, and infinite love.

Pamela clearly illustrates the esoteric title, "Lord of Victory." The horse in her card eerily matches the posture of the horse in the Knight of Cups of the Sola Busca deck, where the horse

- - - - - -

The Sola Busca Knight of Swords' horse (right) turns his head with a mysterious and knowing look. Pamela re-creates the horse's curious glance in her Six of Wands (left).

conveys a message of its own with his turned head. It is as if the horse senses or sees something the rest of us do not. Indeed, as cards numbered five bear challenge, six cards usher respite and success. Sixes bear reward for experience and through the challenging times reflected in previous cards. It also reminds you it is only through experience that we discover what we are made of. No victory exists for things arriving easily or automatically. Waite's card follows the *Book T's* seamless description of "victory after strife."

Sixes in the minor arcana each imply separation and hierarchies between people. One figure towers over the rest. It suggests issues of separation, authority, and positions of power. Sixes reflect caste or social systems whereby people are organized due to external attributes. On the subtle level, the nature of the minor arcana plays out in the progression on the number, growing bigger, larger, and closer to its final goal of complete manifestation in the ten. The number six connects to the Chariot card, who rides above and over all of us in his advance. The appearance of any six asks the reader to consider whether they are giving or receiving.

> **Waite's Divinatory Meanings:** The card has been so designed that it can cover several significations; on the surface, it is a victor triumphing, but it is also great news, such as might be carried in state by the King's courier; it is expectation crowned with its own desire, the crown of hope, and so forth.

> **Reversed:** Apprehension, fear, as of a victorious enemy at the gate; treachery, disloyalty, as of gates being opened to the enemy; also indefinite delay.

. . . .

Seven of Wands

Lord of Valor—Mars in Leo

AND THE SUBTLE hint of invisible wings
Tense expectation thrills and swings.

Arthur Waite, *Collected Poems*

The Seven of Wands is the card of confrontation. The animating nature of fire helps us to stand up for what we believe in, even if we feel alone in our battles. Instincts come to our aid when defending passionate and political causes. Fire's friction heats up. We expand like a balloon or puffer fish gaining strength the moment it is needed. We must be wary of fire's bloodlust consuming us when fighting a battle, even one begun with the best of intentions. If we give in to base instincts, we may win the battle but we have lost the war.

Does the figure on the Seven of Wands ambush the Six of Wands' victory parade as it passes below him like a thief hiding in the woods? Does he fight off invaders? Is he defending his higher ground from an angry mob, like Mary Shelley's Frankenstein? Has he imagined the entire scene? Is he like Don Quixote attacking windmills of his mind? The minor arcana sevens are highly weighted cards. A situation has developed. The objects and ideals at stake are worth fighting for. We stand like the figure on the Seven of Wands when we feel threatened and we defend our personal actions or creative work.

Waite tells us plainly, "It is the card of valor, six are attacking one." Waite lifts the definition from the *Book T* and it matches the esoteric title, "Lord of Valor." Waite adds that the card indicates intellectual discourse and the rapid exchange of quick minds. It suggests a court case, fighting for your rights, or defending a political position. Human nature inserts personal ego into situations. Are we giving others too much credit or, even worse, undeserved power?

Pamela places a visual clue on her figure. He wears mismatched shoes, one boot and one slipper. It suggests a rapid exit, potential deceit, or absconded clothing. An element of distrust or desperation cloaks her figure. The shoes reflect the pull of differing choices and potential imbalance.

. . . .

Waite's Divinatory Meanings: It is a card of valour, for, on the surface, six are attacking one, who has, however, the vantage position. On the intellectual plane, it signifies discussion, wordy strife; in business—negotiations, war of trade, barter, competition. It is further a card of success, for the combatant is on the top and his enemies may be unable to reach him.

Reversed: Perplexity, embarrassments, anxiety. It is also a caution against indecision.

. . . .

Eight of Wands

Lord of Swiftness—Mercury in Sagittarius

FLOWING FROM VALES beyond,
and yet beyond from the hills,
A sense magnetic of expectation fills.

Arthur Waite, *Collected Poems*

Eight wands fly across the sky. A fertile land lies beneath. A river meanders and a house sits atop a hill. The power of intention is made manifest, visible and alive, in the Eight of Wands. This card echoes the "call and response" of the universe. An intention is made known through an invocation, prayer, or spell. Others call it synchronicity or coincidence, but the reader knows it is the universe acting in perfect accordance to its laws. It lets us know we chose well. It is the card of karmic action. Intentions sent into the world return to the sender three-fold.

We envision our desire in the mind's eye just as mythological Artemis strings and aims her bow and arrow. The Sagittarius archer, the card's astrological association, links to intuition and wisdom. Eight of Wands echo the space between wish and culmination. The wands are mid-flight, their final destination unknown. The following card in a spread will almost always contain information regarding the Eight of Wand's final destination and ultimate resting place.

Cupid's bow and arrow seeks the vulnerable heart. The Eight of Wands often signifies messages of love. Are you vulnerable to love's arrows? Are you the sender or receiver? The phallic nature of a penetrating wand seeking its target is multiplied by eight, the number of synchronicity. It suggests great speed and events unfolding lightning-fast. Plans, ideas, and directives are midway, like a lightning bolt midstream, yet the landing place is unseen. Hamlet's "slings and arrows of outrageous fortune" place us firmly on the receiving end of the eight flaming wands.

The esoteric title, "Lord of Swiftness," is aptly applied to the image. Waite tells us, "That which they signify is at hand; it may be even of the threshold." A threshold is a barrier space where two realities meet. In this case, wands act as a gate, carrying with them the power to transport the reader to an entirely new reality. It may be a change in location or career. He calls it "the immovable," reminding us there is no going back once the intentions have been set forth. Once out there, it's out there. You can't take it back. The wands move in the same direction as the Magician's channeled energy, from the top left of the card to the bottom right. This

. . . .

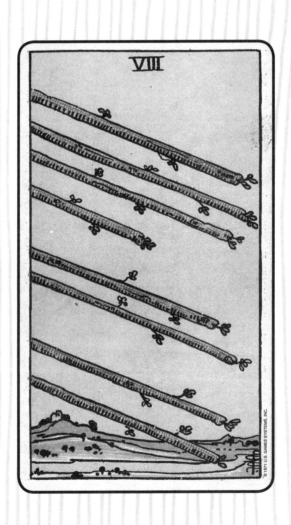

suggests a natural energetic ease, a comfort and familiarity. Ultimately, the card reflects change, movement, and travel. It is the energy that moves up to a new place both metaphorically and literally.

> **Waite's Divinatory Meanings:** Activity in undertakings, the path of such activity, swiftness, as that of an express messenger; great haste, great hope, speed toward an end which promises assured felicity; generally, that which is on the move; also the arrows of love.

> **Reversed:** Arrows of jealousy, internal dispute, stingings of conscience, quarrels; and domestic disputes for persons who are married.

. . . .

Nine of Wands

The Lord of Great Strength—Moon in Sagittarius—Stage Card

HAS WALK'D IN a waking dream apart from
the gates and the walls which fence
The common life of a world enswathed
in the dreamless swoon of sense.

Arthur Waite, *Collected Poems*

The Nine of Wands is a threshold card. Thresholds mark the passage between here and there in time, space, and place; a boundary line between the inner and outer, betwixt and between. It is the veil separating worlds, realities, and possibilities. The number nine is the number of wish fulfillment and concrete results. Eight wands are painted on the scrim like a fence while a figure steps through holding the ninth wand. He glances to his side. What is he looking for?

It is the card of pushing barriers, shattering a glass ceiling, and taking energetic reserves and moving into a space of transformation. It reflects moving from a childhood home, going off to college, beginning a new job, becoming a first-time mother. The Nine of Wands is where you push yourself past all comfort zones. The risk pays off. The action contains real and true consequences in your life. It is the bravery to stick up for yourself in the place where you used to cower. It is an exciting creative experience. You see or do something completely new. It is the moment you have received what you have fought long and hard for. You wonder, what now? What have I gotten myself into?

The bandage on his head is a reminder that every wound carries a lesson. What does not kill you builds character and makes you stronger. Risk marks us in visible and invisible ways. If we are wise, we realize wounds let in the light. We bear a scar from the abusive relationship teaching us inner ferocity and strength. Recovery from an addiction reflects our depth, brilliance, and vulnerability. Fighting for independence teaches us its innate value. The card echoes the need for inner expansion. A goal is attained, and we move on to the next. We never stop. Goals themselves are thresholds leading to new objectives and new potentials.

The figure holds the wand firmly in his grip. It suggests he maintains his ideals and passion. He glances to his right, the place of the past when the cards are laid upon the table. A lush green mountain range reflecting unlimited potential stands in the distance.

. . . . . .

Waite offers little guidance on the card, mentioning only, "The figure leans upon his staff and has an expectant look, as if awaiting an enemy." Pamela adapted the image from the *Book T's* description of "recovery from sickness," as seen with the bandage on the fellow's head. She even takes a cue for his facial expression: "Victory, preceded by apprehension and fear." Depending on the surrounding cards, the Nine of Wands may display an unwillingness to trust others.

Esoterically, the ninth position on the Tree of Life is the place where all things are pulverized before entering the material world. Viewed in this way, the threshold is specifically that place between the spiritual and the physical, an actual doorway. C. S. Lewis gave us a wardrobe in the Chronicles of Narnia, and Pamela Colman Smith gives us the Nine of Wands in the RWS deck.

> **Waite's Divinatory Meanings:** The card signifies strength in opposition. If attacked, the person will meet an onslaught boldly; and his build shews, that he may prove a formidable antagonist. With this main significance there are all its possible adjuncts—delay, suspension, adjournment.
>
> **Reversed:** Obstacles, adversity, calamity.

. . . .

Ten of Wands

Lord of Oppression—Saturn in Sagittarius—Stage Card

HIS FLAGGING WINGS athwart the story and stress
Of hostile current wildly forward press.

Arthur Waite, *Collected Poems*

Wands stoke the spirit, boil the blood, and thrust us into action. Wands, as the essence of erotic love and passion, are a dazzlingly electric suit. The incendiary nature of wands can't burn forever. The energetic process breeds deep soul exhaustion when flames reduce to embers. The individual ravaged and drained by the intensity of wands is displayed in the Ten of Wands.

The Ten of Wands reflects the final stage of energetic reserves. A cycle is completed. The fellow walks away. This reflects taking what remains and departing. He grasps ten wands in his hands and arms, bearing responsibility for his actions. It is cleaning up what one has amassed. His back is bent and his head falls into the wands, signaling a need for rest. A blue sky hangs over a small estate and a neat patch of trees; safe haven awaits. A plowed field, ready for planting and rich with possibility, signals fresh beginnings as the suit renews itself in the ace. The cycle and situation has culminated for now. New prospects soon beckon.

Pamela uses the Sola Busca's Ten of Swords to inspire her design for this card. She mimics the hunched back and body language as the figure bears the weight of ten swords. Her rendering reflects hard work's toll on the body and physical tiredness. Examine issues of exhaustion and treat the body kindly.

The esoteric title of this card is "The Lord of Oppression." Waite describes "a man oppressed by the weight of the ten staves he is carrying." Waite offers more to the meaning of this card by explaining it as "a card of many significances" with multiple meanings. He claims, "I set aside that which connects it with honor and good faith." Waite brushes aside the positive connotations of the card in order to examine the card's darker side.

Moving into the idea of unexpected consequence, he says, "The chief meaning is oppression simply, but also fortune, gain, any kind of success, and then it is the oppression of these things." Waite speaks about the unintended consequence of gaining what is desired or an ideal you thought you desired. He reminds us to be careful of what we wish for. Wish fulfillment, at the end of its cycle, carries its own unique set of challenges. A desire for fame results in a loss

. . . . . .

The Ten of Swords from the Sola Busca deck (right) inspired Pamela's Ten of Wands (left).

of freedom, the desire for riches brings crushing responsibility, an obsessive love wears off as daily reality sets in.

Waite becomes cryptic when he states, "The place which the figure is approaching may suffer from the rods that he carries." His sentiment suggests the figure may visit harm to those whom he approaches. In this case, the card literally becomes the explosive nature of wands in its ultimate fire and fury before flickering into inky darkness.

> **Waite's Divinatory Meanings:** A card of many significances, and some of the readings cannot be harmonized. I set aside that which connects it with honour and good faith. The chief meaning is oppression simply, but it is also fortune, gain, any kind of success, and then it is the oppression of these things. It is also a card of false-seeming, disguise, perfidy. The place which the figure is approaching may suffer from the rods that he carries. Success is stultified if the Nine of Swords follows, and if it is a question of a lawsuit, there will be certain loss.
>
> **Reversed:** Contrarieties, difficulties, intrigues, and their analogies.

ACE of CUPS.

© 1971 U.S. GAMES SYSTEMS, INC.

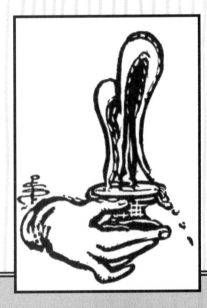

The Ace of Cup's W is seen in reverse as an M (above) and Pamela's Ace of Cups leaps to mind looking at her illustration of a tiny fountain (below) in Pamela's post-RWS illustration from The Book of Friendly Giants.

. . . .

Ace of Cups

Kether of Briah—Root of the Powers of Water

THE ALMOND BLOSSOMS in thy breath; the red
Lies richer on the rose;
Earth yields up fragrant incense; where we tread
Baptismal water flows.

Arthur Waite, *Collected Poems*

The Ace of Cups bursts with emotion, love, and intimacy. It is the perfect state of emotional flow. The overflowing baptismal water literally reflects the emotions of life pouring forth and the state of emotional openness and vulnerability. It is the ability to give and receive. The cup receives the dove's gift as its waters pour forth. It is the card of rejuvenation, the water washing us physically and metaphorically. The energy erupting reflects the fresh energy of a shower, a waterfall, or even a good cry. The card evokes the auditory sound of bubbling, cascading water. The Ace of Cups is the yogic heart opener of the deck and is connected to the heart chakra, the place we each experience and express love, vulnerability, and peace.

The element of water, reflected by the suit of cups, is the suit of emotions, feelings, and art. Pamela's cups cards portray happy and heartwarming images. The reader should recognize, however, the nature of emotions runs a full spectrum from light to dark. Anger and fear linger where there is joy and expansion. Not every emotion feels wonderful; some emotions are uncomfortable and strange. It is wise, especially in the suits of swords and cups, to keep this in mind. Tarot's images, whether on the RWS deck or any other deck, are only a single facet of what the card actually represents. A tarot card is like a single snapshot or photograph of you. It only grazes the top of what inhabits the space beneath.

Pamela follows both the *Book T* and Waite's instructions, though there is a disconnect between Waite's description and her illustration. The *Book T* states, "A WHITE Radiant Angelic Hand, issuing from clouds, and supporting on the palm thereof a cup." Pamela makes a faithful representation of this idea. The stark whiteness of the hand is apparent. The whiteness, as pale as a blank sheet of paper, marks stark contrast to the skin color of every other character in the deck. A spiky electrical field glows around the fist and wrist, depicting additional radiance. All other ace hands match in color and all display radiant angelic and celestial qualities.

. . . . . .

Lotus flowers and water lilies dot the water beneath the Ace of Cups, aligning with the *Book T's* directive. The Golden Dawn embraces the lotus symbol. The lotus carries cross-cultural associations of death and resurrection. Ancient Egyptians used blue lotus flowers in art and hieroglyphs. They considered it a symbol of rebirth because the flower disappears at night, only to bloom again when the sun beams across the morning sky. The Egyptian Book of the Dead contains a resurrection spell. It turns the corpse into a lotus, thus giving the soul an opportunity to rise in immortality.

The Ace of Cups is laden with Christian symbolism. Waite calls the Ace of Cups the "Holy Table" in *The Pictorial Key*. The Holy Table is part of the Christian Eucharist (note the dove with wafer appearing on the card). The Holy Table is an altar in other spiritual traditions. In Christian rites it occurs during Catholic mass. The New Testament describes the Eucharist occurring during Jesus's Last Supper. He gives his disciples wine and bread. He tells them to continue doing so in memory of him. Jesus explains to them the bread is his body and the wine, his blood. Remembering Jesus's sacrifice, churchgoers line up to receive a sacramental wafer (his body) and sip of wine (his blood) from the priest.

The Ace of Wand's dove, communion wafer, and cup reflect the Eucharist. The dove, a Christian symbol for peace and the Holy Spirit, descends toward the cup bearing the communion wafer or sacramental bread. Birds represent communication between mankind and the Divine due to their soaring ability. A Christian symbol of a cross moline or a cross potent decorates the wafer.

The cup streams five rivers of water; however, Waite's description of the card differs: "the cup, from which four streams are pouring." Artist and creator were not on the same page regarding this image. Some have suggested Pamela was given free rein to design the minors, while Waite was more concerned with the majors. The "W" reflects either Waite's name, the element of water, or an inversion of the Hebrew letter Mem, which is assigned to the element of water. The palm is receptive and open like the feminine element of water (cups) and earth (pentacles). The cup rests gently in the palm. This can be viewed oppositionally to the masculine elemental suits where the palms tightly grip the wand (fire) and sword (air).

Waite's Divinatory Meanings: House of the true heart, joy, content, abode, nourishment, abundance, fertility; Holy Table, felicity hereof.

Reversed: House of the false heart, mutation, instability, revolution.

• • • • • • •

. . . .

Two of Cups

Lord of Love—Venus in Cancer—Stage Card

I WILL NOT speak of love to thee,
For having looks in eyes like thine,
Past love's inscrutable mystery,
Something more sacred, more divine
And undeclared than love I see;
And what those secret depths infold,
That, in my heart, for thee I hold.

Arthur Waite, *Collected Poems*

The Two of Cups is the soul mate card. The charming Two of Cups echoes the heart's emotional recognition in another. It is a meeting of the like-minded and finding your other half. Duality of the soul and discovering the heart's mirrored desire. You meeting someone for the first time, yet it feels like you've known each other forever. Conversely, old friends come together, no matter how many months or years have passed, and it feels like you saw each other yesterday. The two of you pick up right where you left off.

The card is structurally similar to the Lovers. Two figures face one another while a being floats above. The landscape rises behind the Two of Cups as does the mountain in the Lover's card. Each figure is dressed as if attending a Shakespearean wedding. If the cups may be filled with liquid or drink, we do not see what it is. The two could be Romeo and Juliet uttering secret marriage vows.

The couple's costumes are colored with alchemical symbolism. The male is dressed in red and yellow, symbolizing fire (a masculine element also associated with wands), while the female dons blue, white, and green, the colors of water (a feminine element associated with cups). The female wears a laurel wreath, which is an interlocking set of bay leaves representing victory.

The red lion suggests the element of air. Waite tells us, "Above their cups rises the Caduceus of Hermes." The symbol of a caduceus is a winged rod with two snakes winding around it. It is a symbol of the Greek god Hermes (Roman Mercury). The caduceus has long been associated with Hermes, known as the messenger of the gods. Acting as intermediary between humans and gods, Hermes is able to traverse the boundaries between the natural and supernatural. Greeks viewed him as the dream god. They made their last daily offerings to Hermes at

. . . .

bedtime, linking Hermes with the dreamlike and ephemeral quality of the suit of cups. Is the card a vision? Has the couple dreamt each other into existence?

The two snakes are the dualistic symbol of business, negotiation, and the balance between them. It speaks heavily to the legal structure of marriage existing beneath warm emotions. It could even be construed as an arranged or predestined marriage. The wings atop the staff are a nod to Hermes and the speed at which he delivers his messages. A wider view sees dual snakes as a combined effort of moving up the Tree of Life as embarked upon by the Golden Dawn.

Waite describes "between the great wings of which there appears a lion's head. It is a variant of a sign which is found in a few old examples of this card. Some curious emblematic meanings are attached to it, but they do not concern us in this place." The lion on the Two of Cups, according to author David Allen Hulse, is a symbol for the alchemical homunculus, a small yet completely formed human being. It first appeared in alchemical writings in 1537, but the idea reaches back further into folklore and history. The idea posits that an alchemist can mix certain properties, namely human semen and blood, to create miniature creatures. This Frankensteinish idea was reported inside the Masonic *Die Spinx*, a book written by Italian mystic Count Johann Ferdinand von Kufstein and a Rosicrucian cleric named Abbé Geloni. An entire chapter is devoted to a "true account" of ten homunculi grown inside of sealed jars in 1775. It was said each homunculi had its own distinctive personality. The homunculi foretold future events to those who visited them. This tale gives us an idea of the contents of the manuscripts, alchemical grimoires, and mixture of occult and Masonic activity that individuals like Arthur Waite spent hours examining and rewriting inside the British Museum.

Pamela took into account the *Book T's* description of this card as "harmony of masculine and feminine united." The astrological associations of Venus in Cancer is woven into this card. Venus is expressed via the love implied between the couple. Cancer governs the home that is painted onto the scrim between them.

The Two of Cups, devilishly simplistic, holds layers of meaning. It speaks to the occult and alchemical idea of merging the masculine and feminine side of oneself. This integration, akin to the center pillar of the Tree of Life, is the spiritual creature known as the hermaphrodite, as seen in the final card, the World.

> **Waite's Divinatory Meanings:** Love, passion, friendship, affinity, union, concord, sympathy, the interrelation of the sexes, and—as a suggestion apart from all offices of divination—that desire which is not in Nature, but by which Nature is sanctified.
>
> **Reversed:** No reversals are listed.

• • • • • • •

Pamela's romantic, loose, and flowing garments for many of her female tarot characters are similar to costuming at the Lyceum Theater, where she was a costume and set designer. This photo shows Ellen Terry in The Amber Heart, *a Lyceum repertory play.*

o . . . .

Three of Cups

Lord of Abundance—Mercury in Cancer

I KNOW SUCH spirits though the starry spaces
Subsist for ever with increasing graces!

Arthur Waite, *Collected Poems*

The Three of Cups carries a simple and straightforward interpretation. The celebration is yours and shared with friends. The deep bonds of friendship, moving in harmony with others, and the creative nature of emotion in its highest element. Happiness is greatest when shared with others. The threefold law of return states what you put out returns three times in strength. Share with others what you hope to receive. Give to others what you wish you had. The more you give, the more you receive.

The abundant Three of Cups reflects the triplicity of pleasure and flow. Creativity abounds as consorts of the goddess spin, twirl, and dance. The three maidens cheer each other. The lush field bursts with harvest bounty as manifestation multiplies. Macbeth's three witches embrace summer's intoxication in a circular dance. The three Graces ritualize summer with their graceful choreography. It is merriment, joy, and happiness.

The Three of Cups is a reminder to surround yourself with people who lift you up. All life is an energetic exchange. Stop to consider how you spend and conserve personal energetic reserves. Are you surrounded by people who support you or beings who deplete you? Make adjustments accordingly.

Visually, the three cups are arranged as the upper triad in the formation of the first three Sephiroth of the supernal triad on the Tree of Life. The maidens take on the elemental association of each Sephiroth, the left maiden as air (Kether), the center maiden as fire (Chokmah), and the right maiden representing water (Binah). The top three spots of the Tree of Life, the beginning of spiritual life, dance in celebration. Romans cultivated grapes, which are sacred to Bacchus, the Roman god of agriculture, wine, and fertility. The grapes held in the hand of the right maiden are a reference to intoxication and can also be found on the female's tail in the Devil card. The grapes evoke the Nine of Pentacles and the woman who stands inside her vineyard, as well as the King of Pentacles.

Waite offers up no clue and tells his readers what we can see for ourselves: "Maidens in a garden-ground with cups uplifted, as if pledging one another." The *Book T* offers a narrative

. . . .

which Pamela adapted in her design. It explains, "Binah of HB:H (Plenty, hospitality, eating and drinking, pleasure, dancing, new clothes, merriment)." The Golden Dawn's title, "The Lord of Abundance," is apparent in the design as well. Pamela places an Elizabethan tone to the card as if this were a vision in the field of a midsummer night's dream, where fairies prance circles in the moonlight, leaving circles of mushrooms and toadstools in their wake.

> **Waite's Divinatory Meanings:** The conclusion of any matter in plenty, perfection and merriment; happy issue, victory, fulfilment, solace, healing.

> **Reversed:** Expedition, dispatch, achievement, end. It signifies also the side of excess in physical enjoyment, and the pleasures of the senses.

· ·

Four of Cups

Lord of Blended Pleasure—Moon in Cancer

HERE IN GLADE and dingle sweet
Ye may find a close retreat:
Can ye find a softer bed
Thank the moss that here is spread?

Arthur Waite, *Collected Poems*

The Four of Cups reflects the contemplative mind because the stability of the emotions is expressed via number and suit. Four offers emotional structure. Calm thoughts prevail. A still mind creates space for discovery and possibility. The figure sits beneath a tree. A magical hand holding a cup materializes out of thin air. Buddha, the founder of Buddhism whose Sanskrit name means "awakened one," is said to have sat beneath the bodhi (bo) tree to gain enlightenment. He achieved enlightenment through the quieting of his mind. To quiet the mind and meditate, the practitioner allows emotions and thoughts to come and go without acting upon them. They become the active observer of their own consciousness.

Buddhism's Four Noble Truths can be applied to each of the four cups. The first is the truth of suffering (life is painful). The second is the truth of the cause of suffering (others and ourselves). The third is the truth of the end of suffering (control of our mind and senses). The fourth and final truth is the truth of the path that leads out of suffering (transcendence). Ultimately, these truths lead us back to the simple yet complex notion that each of us is in control of our inner life. We can embrace this truth only when we release the ego, which seeks identification through outer means, patterns, and habits. Cups' emotional qualities, especially deeper, darker emotions like irritation, resentment, and anger, are often the source of great pain. Learning to control thoughts surrounding pain, or, conversely, letting emotions pass without reacting to them, brings us closer to the Buddhist ideal.

The thoughtful Four of Cups is often interpreted as a card of complacency. A simple message moves through the card, reminding the viewer to look up. Notice what is right in front of you. An opportunity is at hand, but it may be missed. It is impossible to observe everything happening around you at once. We can only focus on a few things at a time to avoid sensory overload. However, we can choose what we focus on. We can decide what is worth our

· · · · · ·

227

attention and energy. The Four of Cups offers an opportunity to re-examine potentials surrounding you. It reminds us to remain open to the unexpected.

Waite tells us the figure is unsatisfied when he states, "His expression notwithstanding is one of discontent with his environment." The *Book T* offers a clue to Waite's reasoning: "Success or pleasure approaching their end…some drawbacks to pleasure implied." Waite goes on to explain, "This is also a card of blended pleasure," and in doing so shares the esoteric title of the card. Blended pleasure can be an experience of delight complete with the knowledge that it will soon end. It is the infusion of pleasure with other qualities.

The Golden Dawn grew alongside the Theosophical movement, which drew heavily upon Buddhist practice. Pamela would have been aware of yogic and Hindu tradition. Pamela inserts a mini ace into her illustration with a mysterious hand appearing from a cloud. Three cups sit at the bottom of the card. All cups are empty. As with all emptiness, you are free to fill the cup with whatever quality you like or leave it open to creative possibility.

> **Waite's Divinatory Meanings:** Weariness, disgust, aversion, imaginary vexations, as if the wine of this world had caused satiety only; another wine, as if a fairy gift, is now offered the wastrel, but he sees no consolation therein. This is also a card of blended pleasure.

> **Reversed:** Novelty, presage, new instruction, new relations.

• • • • • •

. . . .

Five of Cups

Lord of Loss in Pleasure—Mars in Scorpio—Stage Card

BUT IF THE perfect joy of daily life
Some transient sorrow sears,
Thy holy function falling on the strife
Melts pain to happy tears.

Arthur Waite, *Collected Poems*

The Five of Cups is filled with a dark and deviant presence. Emotional challenges reverberate through the card. The Five of Cups is often considered the card of addiction due to the emotional and chemical basis of dependence. Three cups, turned to the side, represent loss. They ooze a mysterious liquid. Two standing cups remain to the figure's right side. It is unclear what they hold. The figure considers the abyss while draped in melancholic black. His back is turned to the upright cups. Will the figure embrace the cups or will he move toward the bridge stretching across the river? Does salvation exist on the other side? How many of us have worn the cloak of sadness and tears? Will he embrace transformation and choose light instead of dark or will he return to learn this lesson again? If we are wise and learn from our deepest sorrows, they will provide context for happiness. Do we go back for more or do we say enough is enough?

Rivers mark distinct boundary lines; they are often the thresholds between lands and countries. Rivers and bridges are metaphorical devices offering the opportunity to "cross over" or to traverse a "bridge over troubled water." They provide movement between lands, from the living to the dead, between the conscious and unconscious or from bad to good and vice versa. Bridges help us cross to a new form of being when moving from the known to the unknown. A bridge, like a door or a gate, offers the possibility of leaving something or someone behind.

Waite writes of the Five of Cups in his article "The Tarot: A Wheel of Fortune." He states it is "the card of heritage diverted," suggesting an inheritance or legacy, symbolized by the manor house across the river, was denied. Yet nothing stops the figure from moving across the bridge to claim what is rightfully his. This card can represent a person who is feeling sorry for themselves or a person who feels as if life owes them something. Waite describes a "life emptied of joy," matching the dark quality of the cloak.

. . . . . .

Waite notes in *The Pictorial Key* that for "some interpreters it is a card of marriage, but not without bitterness or frustration. " His explanation links the Five of Cups with the Five of Pentacles, also often seen as a marriage card linked with the idea of traveling with another person through "thick and thin." Both cards reflect the challenging downsides of long-term relationships.

Struggle is apparent in all of the minor arcana five cards because the five marks the halfway point. Struggle ensues. Challenge erupts. The esoteric title of the card is "Loss of Pleasure." The *Book T* states this card is "Death, or end of pleasure." Joy has vanished. The essence of flow embodied by the Ace of Cups has run its course. Celebration turns to desolation. The question remains: how will you fill the void? How long will you don the cloak?

> **Waite's Divinatory Meanings:** It is a card of loss, but something remains over; three have been taken, but two are left; it is a card of inheritance, patrimony, transmission, but not corresponding to expectations; with some interpreters it is a card of marriage, but not without bitterness or frustration.

> **Reversed:** News, alliances, affinity, consanguinity, ancestry, return, false projects.

Six of Cups

Lord of Pleasure—Sun in Scorpio

OLD VOICES GROW faint, from the summit they fall;
Your measures enchant me, I come at your call.

Arthur Waite, *Collected Poems*

After the darkness and despair of the Five of Cups, hope is reborn inside the Six of Cups. Two childlike figures express gifts of the heart and the warmth of the soul blossoms like flowers. Cups, once empty, now overflow with beauty. The tangible nature of flowers and foliage suggest the manifestation of desire and results you can count on. The Six of Cups contains the antidote to the bleakness and despair implied in the Five of Cups. Give to others what you wish to receive. Make the first gesture, make your move.

Implied separation and hierarchy exists between the two figures, just as in all minor arcana six cards. The boyish figure towers over a diminutive girl. Their positioning indicates separation, authority, and the assumption of power. The minor arcana demonstrates a progression of numbers, each growing higher, larger, and closer to its final goal of complete manifestation in the tenth card. The maturity, lessons, and history are now evolving among the higher cards. With this gift comes great power and wisdom. It reflects the nature of the linked Sephiroth on the Tree of Life, each flowing into the next.

A figure, a soldier or adult suggesting authority and law, walks away from the scene. It marks the exiting factor of the situation. The past loosens its grip. A habit has been banished. Limits are removed and freedom ensues. Qualities of safety and protection are evoked from the protective courtyard. It is one of only four cards of the seventy-eight-card deck Pamela drew inside the environs of a town—the Ten of Pentacles is at the threshold, and the King of Pentacles and Two of Wands reside inside a tower or wall.

Waite describes the card as if looking at a different picture when he writes "children in an old garden." The children are obviously in a courtyard or town square, not a garden. This comment and others have led tarotists to believe that Waite was only interested in the design of the majors. They posit the minor's designs were entirely in Pamela's capable hands.

Waite offers dual interpretations for the Six of Cups. His first is nostalgic: "A card of the past and memories, looking back…but coming from the past; things that have vanished." Framing his nostalgia as coming from the past offers an explanation that lacks the maturity of hindsight,

Giant feet walk through a town strikingly similar to the courtyard of the Six of Cups in Pamela's post- RWS illustration for The Book of Friendly Giants.

so the card simply speaks of what has disappeared. The second offering, "new relations, new knowledge, new environment and then the children are disporting in an unfamiliar precinct," suggests the children are delighting in the quality of newness. It is as if the cup is reborn as a new toy or object of fascination now that a challenge has been overcome.

> **Waite's Divinatory Meanings:** A card of the past and of memories, looking back, as—for example—on childhood; happiness, enjoyment, but coming rather from the past; things that have vanished. Another reading reverses this, giving new relations, new knowledge, new environment, and then the children are disporting in an unfamiliar precinct.

> **Reversed:** The future, renewal, that which will come to pass presently.

• • • • • • •

. . . .

Seven of Cups

Lord of Illusory Success—Venus in Scorpio

FOLD ALL THY jewell'd shores in mist
From Cape to austral pole:
With brilliant, topaz, amethyst,
Tempt eyes—but not the soul!

Arthur Waite, *Collected Poems*

The beautiful, beguiling Seven of Cups shows a figure gazing at seven cups floating in the sky. Eden Grey's definition of this card, "building castles in the air," is a simple catch-phrase. It is easy to associate with the image. It suggests unreal flights of fancy and wishful thinking. It matches the esoteric title of the card, the "Lord of Illusory Success." Every great invention and achievement was imagined before it became real. You can't desire a thing or create something new if you can't first imagine yourself having it. Our imagination is our most valuable asset.

The Seven of Cups offers a wide variety of choices, options, and opportunities for the reader. The image might call to mind a movie theater where a man stands silhouetted against a projected screen. Filmmaking was still in its infancy when the RWS deck was created. London's first movie house opened in 1896, thirteen years before the publication of the RWS deck. It showed grainy, silent, black-and-white short films. Given the esoteric title of the card, "Lord of Illusory Success," and Waite's own description as "images of reflection, sentiment and imagination," it is helpful to look at this card as a moving picture. Is it a theatrical projection or is the reader projecting the cups from their imagination? Have they drawn these cups before them like cards in a reading? Does the image spring from the figure or a higher power? Are we focusing on what we want for ourselves or listening to others who think they know better?

Waite calls this the card of "fairy favors." Waite would later edit the book *Poems and Songs of Fairyland*, a European collection of fairy poetry and songs. Each cup specifically connects to a major arcana card. Examine the Seven of Cups image before reading any further. See if you can figure out which major arcana card each cup connects to. Pamela offers visual clues and astrological hints.

Waite did not order planetary associations. Mathers ordered them in alignment with the Hebrew alphabet.

. . . . . .

Beginning from the top left and moving right:

Cup #1—The female head corresponds to the Empress and the planet Venus (recall the sign of Venus on the Empress's garments).

Cup #2—The veiled and glowing figure is the High Priestess and the Moon (recall the High Priestess's Moon crown).

Cup #3—The snake who escapes the cup is the Magician and connects to Mercury (recall the Magician's snake belt that devours itself around the Magician's waist).

Beginning lower left and moving right:

Cup #4—The castle on high rocks reflects the Tower card and connects to Mars (recall how the Tower is placed atop a mountain peak).

Cup #5—Glittering jewels reflect the Wheel of Fortune and connect to Jupiter (recall that the wheel represents fate, fortune, and destiny).

Cup #6—The wreath reflects the World card and connects to Saturn (recall the World dancer's wreath). The skull is the illusion of success holding deceptive qualities.

Cup #7—The crouching dragon reflects the Sun card and connects to the sun itself (recall that dragon's breath holds the incendiary power of the sun).

Waite's Divinatory Meanings: Fairy favours, images of reflection, sentiment, imagination, things seen in the glass of contemplation; some attainment in these degrees, but nothing permanent or substantial is suggested.

Reversed: Desire, will, determination, project.

. . . .

Eight of Cups

Lord of Abandoned Success—Saturn in Pisces—Stage Card

NOW THE MILD moon wax and dwindle,
Voice of winds keep calling,
While the long paths wind before me,
Falling, rising, falling.

Arthur Waite, *Collected Poems*

The Eight of Cups carries powerful magic and evocative quiet. Waite tells us the card "speaks for itself on the surface." A figure moves upward. Silent water ripples beneath a sun and moon. A strange twilight of mystical colors is on the card, a rare solar eclipse as the moon passes before the sun, blotting out light and casting strange double shadows on the landscape. Did the figure materialized out of a cup? Two stacks of cups lie at the forefront. The figure walks away from them. A close inspection reveals the line of the scrim. The Eight of Cups is a stage card. We are looking at a painted backdrop, not a real figure at all. Is the situation an illusion or does it depict reality?

The "Lord of Abandoned Success" is the esoteric title of the Eight of Cups. This reading suggests the figure leaves behind what is no longer needed even if it was something he fought for. Are you satisfied with what you have created? Would you be willing to abandon all? Will you search for something more or stick with the status quo? The element of risk inherent in abandoning all is an essence of bravery. The number eight connects this card to the Strength card. Rumi tells us, "Don't grieve, anything you lose comes round in another form." It is brave to walk away from a situation, person, or thing that you value and be secure in the knowledge that something similar or better will come into your life. When we are brave and test this principle, we find it to be true. We find love again. Happiness comes back around. We leave what is comfortable, secure in the knowledge we can do better, strive harder, and create something extraordinary. Our faith and hard work are rewarded. The Eight of Cups implores us to release bonds of fear and desperation to forge new ground.

The card's figure connects to the Hermit card, reflecting the Hermit at the beginning of his journey up the mountain. Walking stick in hand, the Hermit moves toward a lofty summit, away from what has been gained. It is the essence of pilgrimage, the sacred journey of religious devotion. He moves toward spiritual heights, away from worldly goods. It is the "high road"

. . . . . .

© 1971 U.S. GAMES SYSTEMS, INC.

and "the road less traveled" and all that those phrases imply. What roads have you traveled? What is your current path? Where are you going? Have you plotted your course? What is it you must do this very moment? What can you leave behind?

Waite reminds us the man "is deserting the Cups of his felicity, enterprise, undertaking or previous concern." What was once important has lost its luster. We focus on something new. Waite says that "a matter which has been thought to be important is really of slight consequence." The transitory nature of life reveals this lesson repeatedly. When what was important, even immediate, fades away, we are confronted with new challenges and opportunities. The lessons we carry bear import and move us higher than we ever imagined.

> **Waite's Divinatory Meanings:** The card speaks for itself on the surface, but other readings are entirely antithetical—giving joy, mildness, timidity, honour, modesty. In practice, it is usually found that the card shews the decline of a matter, or that a matter which has been thought to be important is really of slight consequence—either for good or evil.

> **Reversed:** Great joy, happiness, feasting.

· · · · · ·

. . . .

Nine of Cups

Lord of Material Happiness—Jupiter in Pisces

EASY COMES AND easy goes
Tinkles, twitters, sparkles, flows;
Nothing matters, no one knows.

Arthur Waite, *Collected Poems*

The gleeful Nine of Cups says, "Your wish will come true!" Your dream is granted. A genie sits, arms crossed, and with a wink and a nod to make your fantasy a reality. Nine cups, the number of wish fulfillment, fan behind the genie in an arc shape. The cups foreshadow the cup rainbow shape appearing in the Ten of Cups card as the cycle nears completion. The nine cups sit on a blue curtain that hangs over a table. Could there be additional hidden meaning to a seemingly simplistic card?

Waite teases readers with an esoteric hint, saying, "The picture offers the material side only, but there are other aspects." The number nine on the Tree of Life is the Hebrew word Yesod, meaning "foundation." It is the place where intangible becomes manifest in the material world. Foundation is the gateway, the doorway through which anything becomes "real." Because cups reflect invisible qualities (as do swords and wands) like emotions, feelings, and creativity, cups will manifest themselves in the form of something wished. The wish comes true in a tangible way. A romantic partner appears. You find the house of your dreams. The trip is booked. Something longed, wished, and worked for stands in front of you in its final form.

Waite describes "physical *bien-être*," the French term for "well-being." Pamela is clever in her illustration. She chooses not to display a character who languishes in delight, like the Nine of Pentacles or the Ten of Cups. Instead, she involves the viewer directly, using an excellent intuitive trick. The genie seems to speak and directly engage the viewer. The reader becomes an active participant in the deck. The card immediately asks you, *begs* you to answer the questions, "What do you want? What is your desire? If you could wish for anything, what would it be?"

The card also reminds the reader to be careful what they wish for. Why should a person exercise care? Wish fulfillment often arrives with unforeseen consequences. The old saying is true, the grass is often greener on the other side. We think something else will be better while the real thing stands before us all along.

. . . . . .

A final contemplation of this card comes in the form of the ninth position of the Celtic Cross spread, which reflects hopes and fears. How can a hope and a fear be two sides of the same coin? If we hope for something, why do we not already have it? The card becomes the marker for the ultimate spiritual and human evolution and a job very well done when we work through fear and deep desires are met.

> **Waite's Divinatory Meanings:** Concord, contentment, physical *bien-être*; also victory, success, advantage; satisfaction for the Querent or person for whom the consultation is made.

> **Reversed:** Truth, loyalty, liberty; but the readings vary and include mistakes, imperfections, etc.

. . . .

Ten of Cups

Lord of Perfected Success—Mars in Pisces—Stage Card

IN THE HOUSE where I was born
Vivid light of rose and gold,
Permeating vast and fair
Vaulted heights of heavy air,
Held netted sunbeams there.

Arthur Waite, *Collected Poems*

The dazzling Ten of Cups is the "happily ever after" card. The cycle of cups reaches its finale. A frolicking family appears beneath an old-fashioned and dazzling rainbow of color. The rainbow evokes feelings of heart and harmony. The dream comes true and a treasure of fairy gold appears. A quaint homestead stands beside a wandering river. The couple gestures to the sky as if they have summoned or are presenting the rainbow. It is the cherry on the cake of their story, the perfect last act.

The Ten of Cups reflects the typical nuclear family. It is the only card in the RWS deck to hold all four positions and stations of the court card family: king/father, queen/mother, knight/teen, page/child. The four figures represent the tetragrammaton (the fourfold name of the Hebrew deity). The female figures, adorned in blue, symbolize the element of water. The male figures, adorned in red, symbolize fire.

The reader should examine the relationship between Two of Cups next to the Ten of Cups. A narrative culmination runs in every minor arcana suit of the deck. The couple has grown and matured into adults with a family of their own. The same house with red thatched roof stands, and trees have grown right alongside their children. Pamela illustrated many books of fairy tales in her career, including her own set of Jamaican folk tales. The Ten of Cups is similar to her illustrations in *The Book of Friendly Giants*. She calls upon familiar mythic landscapes. Always true to her theatrical background, the Ten of Cups denotes the feeling of finality held in the breathtaking moments before the curtain falls and the crack of final applause ripples through the audience.

The rainbow is a celestial bridge linking the spirit to the sky. The three colors of the rainbow recall the three aspects of divinity. Waite describes the scene and states that the rainbow is "contemplated in wonder and ecstasy by a man and woman below, evidently husband and

. . . . . .

wife." The odd formation of his statement supports the idea that Pamela presented an original illustration, free from his direction. It is as if Waite is describing something he has just seen for the first time, rather than describing a card he envisioned for his artist. He points out the children, noting, "The two children dancing near them have not observed the prodigy but are happy after their own manner." His uses the word prodigy in the sense of "archetype" or something amazing. Perhaps the children do not notice the particular magic of the rainbow because children see everything through the eyes of enchantment and wonder.

>**Waite's Divinatory Meanings:** Contentment, repose of the entire heart; the perfection of that state; also perfection of human love and friendship; if with several picture-cards, a person who is taking charge of the Querent's interests; also the town, village or country inhabited by the Querent.

>**Reversed:** Repose of the false heart, indignation, violence.

ACE of SWORDS.

. . . .

Ace of Swords

Kether in Yetzirah—Root of the Powers of Air

WE HAVE PASS'D through the region of omen,
and enter'd a land of sight.

❋ ❋ ❋ ❋ ❋ ❋ ❋

Arthur Waite, *Collected Poems*

The Ace of Swords is the essence of the mind. The Ace of Swords, with swift, clever execution, represents an excellent idea, intellectual instincts, and mental acuity. The Ace of Swords advises the individual to follow their first instinct. It suggests a moment of complete clarity. A problem is worked out. It is known to be true. It happens before others weigh in to convince us otherwise or allow circumstances to influence us. Setting clear intentions each and every day helps to place the Ace of Swords firmly in hand. It directs the will and focuses the consciousness. Intentions, inherited or purposeful, inform everything in life.

Examine this card as if it is a Caesar thumb. Upright, the gladiator lives; down, he dies. The Ace of Swords will appear to tell you if an idea is good or bad or if the surrounding energy is flowing or blocked. Alternatively, upright is a thumbs-down and down, you've totally nailed it. It will advise you to proceed or give the matter more thought. The suit of swords is tricky, and it is no accident that swords are the scariest cards in the deck. Swords and the element of air reflect the mind. Our entire experience of the world takes place in our mind. Anais Nin famously said, "We don't see the world how it is, we see it as we are." Events play out in our lives and we construct narratives around it. This is how two people experience the exact same event in entirely different ways. Two brothers grow up in a family with little money. One views himself as a victim of poverty and resigns himself to it. The other brother is inspired by his financial challenge and uses it as a call to action. He becomes highly successful and reinvents his life as an adult.

Swords are tools at our disposal. Those lucky to possess a sound mind, without chemical imbalance or mental illness, have the ability to choose their thoughts. Choosing thoughts allows destructive emotions or distracting ideas to float away without reacting to them. Attention is like a laser beam: what we focus on receives power. The Ace of Swords reminds us we already have ownership over life's most transformational tool.

Waite explains only, "A hand issues from a cloud, grasping a sword, the point of which is encircled by a crown." The *Book T's* instructions are followed carefully. It states, "A WHITE

. . . . . .

Radiating Angelic Hand, issuing from clouds, and grasping the hilt of a sword…" Pamela crafts a faithful representation. The stark whiteness of the hand is apparent. The whiteness, as pale as a blank sheet of paper, marks a stark contrast to the skin color of every other character in the deck. A spiky electrical field glows around the fist and wrist, depicting additional radiance. All other ace hands match in color and display radiant qualities. The hilt of a sword is the handle of a sword or dagger that remains visible when the weapon is plunged into enemy flesh.

The *Book T* goes on to describe how the sword "supports a White Radiant Celestial Crown; from which depend, on the right, the olive branch of peace; and on the left, the palm branch of suffering." The second half of this sentence holds rich figurative symbols. "Crown" is the Hebrew name for the first Sephiroth on the Tree of Life. The first Sephiroth appears like an ace, where something appears out of nothing or "no thing." An olive branch, hanging to the right of the crown, is a symbol of conciliation and goodwill. The palm branch, hanging to the left of the crown, is a cross-cultural symbol of victory and triumph. The *Book T* likely describes it as the "palm branch of suffering" because in Christianity it reflects the victory of the soul over the flesh. Ancient Christian tombs decorated with palm symbols meant a martyr was buried beneath. A martyr is an individual murdered in the name of their religion via crucifixion, stoning, stake burning, or some other horrific way.

The *Book T* describes how "six Vaus fall from its point." Vau is the sixth letter of the Hebrew alphabet, and it means hook or peg, which is associated with the suit of swords. A sword can be used to pierce anything. There are six images of the sixth letter. Hooks were once used by ancient nomadic peoples to secure their tents as they traveled. Through mental acuity we protect ourselves in the physical world, and the idea of a hook may be used to connect our thoughts to higher realms. Swords are the mental process providing an understanding of the sacred patterns laid before us and our ability to make sense of them.

The *Book T* goes on to say, "It symbolizes 'Invoked,' as contrasted with Natural Force: for it is the Invocation of the Sword." This statement of invoked force is in direct opposition to the Ace of Wands, which is described as a "natural" force. What is the difference between a natural and an invoked force? What is the difference between air and fire? Between swords and wands? The difference is consciousness and mental acuity. Primal fire is a natural instinct. Procreation is instinctual to all living things. It happens without thought. To "invoke" means that one is aware of one's actions. It is the awakening of consciousness. Man posits himself above all other creatures due to his ability to discriminate and intellectualize. Right or wrong, mental ability is what makes up the entire essence of the suit of swords. It is what makes us who we are.

The *Book T* gives us a clue to the Justice card within its description of the Ace of Swords by claiming, "It is the affirmation of Justice upholding Divine Authority…" The Justice card holds an upright sword in the right hand. It reminds us of the divine authority of the sword.

· · · · · · ·

It goes on to offer grave warnings about the nature of the Ace of Swords, echoing the truth of the human condition. "Raised upward, it invokes the Divine crown of Spiritual Brightness, but reversed it is the Invocation of Demonic Force; and becomes a fearfully evil symbol. It represents, therefore, very great power for good or evil." We can remove the moral implications of Spiritual Brightness and Demonic Force and simply look at the destructive or expansive nature of human thought as expressed by the suit of swords.

To harness the "very great power" of the Ace of Swords, we need only to grasp control of the mind. Controlling the mind means we choose which thoughts we focus on and which thoughts we allow to slip away. This is the work of Zen masters. The opportunity exists every moment, every day, even right now. Gaining control over the mind, we run the computer rather than allowing the computer to run us.

The palm's grip on the sword is tight. Aces forcefully hold the masculine elements of fire (wands) and air (swords). This is viewed in opposition for the feminine elements of earth (pentacles) and water (cups), where the pentacle rests gently in a receptive palm.

> **Waite's Divinatory Meanings:** Triumph, the excessive degree in everything, conquest, triumph of force. It is a card of great force, in love as well as in hatred. The crown may carry a much higher significance than comes usually within the sphere of fortune-telling.

> **Reversed:** The same, but the results are disastrous; another account says— conception, childbirth, augmentation, multiplicity.

· · · · · · ·

. . . .

Two of Swords

Lord of Peace Restored—Moon in Libra—Stage Card

AND SWEET INCENSE, each exhaling
From a thurible, ascends,
Drifts, a dim enchanted veiling,
Eastward as the dew descends:
Hence concealed in all that seems,
Truly human nature teems.

Arthur Waite, *Collected Poems*

The Two of Swords reflects stillness and calm. A female figure wears a white gown and sits on a cement cube. Her feet rest flat on the floor. Her arms criss-cross across her chest and heart chakra. Her hands hold dual silver swords pointing to each corner of the card. She wears a white blindfold. A crescent moon, yellowed with reflected light, hangs at the top right. An inlet of water is painted on the scrim behind her.

The Two of Swords suggests blocking out the outer world and holding all intrusive things at bay. It is the card of blotting out distractions, chores, annoying parents, houses full of children, responsibilities, and needy coworkers, bosses, or clients. It reflects a helpful spiritual practice of extreme focus during a problem-solving moment. Alternatively, the Two of Swords can be understood as the card of denial, a refusal to look at obvious facts that are staring you right in the face. Like the Hanged Man, the Two of Swords is a suspended moment in time where events, feelings, and observations are digested.

The duality of the card reflects the ability to hold two opposing thoughts at the same time. It suggests a broad range of thinking and the intellectual advantage of understanding essential truths of human nature. It reflects the empathy of putting yourself in another's place. It suggests the understanding of the existence of a gray area, that no issue is black-and-white but rather shades between. Rising above the situation gives you a bird's-eye view.

Intuitive reactions to this card vary. Some viewers are unnerved by the image. Others find it peaceful. The former feel the fear of danger or bondage as they observe her blindfold and swords. The latter feel she takes a protective stance. They see an individual who has voluntarily blindfolded herself to blot out the outer world like a sleeping mask. She focuses on her internal

. . . .

life and meditation like the yogi who quietly centers herself at the beginning of her practice and sets her intention.

The secret of the Two of Swords is its revelation of initiation into a secret magical society or enlightened way of thinking. The esoteric meaning of a blindfold applies to the Eight of Swords card as well. Blindfolding initiates is a cross-cultural device used in many organizations, from fraternities to Freemasons. Masons call it "hoodwinking." Blindfolds are a highly transformative symbol. The individual is temporarily blinded. The initiate symbolically moves from darkness (incomprehension) to light (enlightenment). The Two and Eight of Swords each reflect moments of intense internal transformation and unique moments in time. It is a purposeful and willing transformation. They are cards of choice and silliness. It is not a reflection of a random circumstance like losing a job or a loved one unexpectedly. The implied transformation is acutely desired by the subject and embraced. The Two and Eight of Swords cards imply acts of personal power, choice, and a willingness to change.

The esoteric title for the card is "The Lord of Peace Restored," and Pamela perfectly illustrates this sentiment with her graphically elegant card. It is highly symbolic, not literal, as no human could hold swords of such length and weight with such perfect symmetry. The two swords point upward. It is the energetic opposite of the Three of Swords' downward-facing crossed swords. The Two of Swords additionally resembles a stripped-down High Priestess card whose esoteric function of "silence" perfectly aligns with "peace restored." The background of each card is almost identical. The veil, pillars, and all decorative elements have been removed from the High Priestess. It looks as if the priestess has become the initiate and vice versa. We see the High Priestess in her youth, moving through the early stage of initiation.

Astrologically, the moon is in the first decan of Libra. Libra rules the Justice card. The Two of Swords resembles the traditional blindfolded Justice. Justice's blindfold reflects impartiality and fairness, although the Justice card in the RWS deck wears none. The two swords imply balance, like Justice's scales. The two cards mirror one another. The *Book T* uses the word *justice* in its description of this card. A moon appears as a fingernail crescent on the Two of Swords. In the northern hemisphere, the moon waxes and grows toward full, from right to left. Pamela's crescent moon reflects the first decan, the first approximate ten days of any astrological sign, further aligning it with the moon in Libra. The water on the scrim reflects a mild agitation from the wind (recall that swords represent elemental air), enough to ripple the water. This suggests an active, changeable, and moving energy toward the situation.

Waite writes a single lonely sentence to describe the Two of Swords: "A hoodwinked female figure balances two swords upon her shoulders." His comment is a digression from the image Pamela created. Her figure is not balancing the implements on her shoulders but holding one in each hand. Once again, the illustration and Waite's description do not entirely match up.

. . . .

Waite's Divinatory Meanings: Conformity and the equipoise which it suggests, courage, friendship, concord in a state of arms; another reading gives tenderness, affection, intimacy. The suggestion of harmony and other favorable readings must be considered in a qualified manner, as Swords generally are not symbolical of beneficent forces in human affairs.

Reversed: Imposture, falsehood, duplicity, disloyalty.

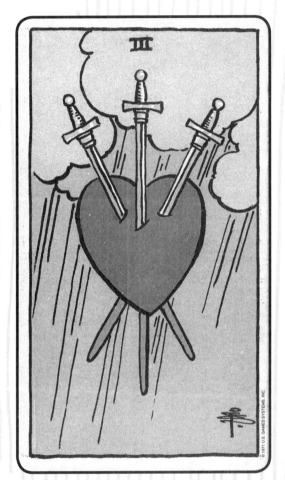

Pamela's graphic design (left) is a direct derivative of the Three of Swords in the Sola Busca deck (right).

. . . .

Three of Swords

Lord of Sorrow—Saturn in Libra

WASTE, WASTE, WASTE,—BUT the
voice in the waste of the sea!
The dread, sheer height of an empty night!
And the heart—Ah, the heart in me!
I know here the deep is wider, I know
of a gloom more dread—
O the waste and the night of the heart,
when the star from the heart has fled.

Arthur Waite, *Collected Poems*

Thunder cracks and lightning strikes as the card of betrayal appears. The Three of Swords is a simple, powerful card expressing heartbreak. It is visually stunning, graphically gorgeous, and a popular tattoo icon. A blood-red heart floats in the air. Three swords pierce the heart with exactitude and precision. Cumulus storm clouds surround the heart. Rain falls in thick sheets. The Three of Swords is one of the scariest cards of the deck. The Three of Swords can tear the heart to shreds, and it usually does.

In relation to our personal life, it suggests discovery or participation in a duplicitous love triangle. The betrayal of friendship tears at the heart. Family members attack our jugular vein. Gleaming swords plunge into a scarlet heart with perfect symmetry. The surgical perfection of the damage suggests the heartbreak is intentional, therefore making it all the more painful. It is the betrayal card, especially in terms of a love triangle. The beauty of this card resides in the wound letting in the light. It is the ability to feel pain and discomfort, which is marked by holistic deep love and compassion on the other side.

Christian iconography portrays the Immaculate Heart of Mary, the heart of the Virgin Mary, as a heart pierced by swords. It is a common devotional image. A devotional image is religious depiction used for prayer or contemplation. It is akin to the use of tarot as a contemplative practice. The sword piercing Mary's heart suggests deep compassion for humanity and is called the "Mother of Sorrows." The Three of Swords extends past our personal grievances and transgressions and becomes the place where we feel compassion, heartache, and despair

. . . .

for the state of the world, the horror and compassion for a human tragedy in a specific place, such as famine, crimes against humanity, and natural disasters.

The number three is a reminder of the threefold nature of energetic return. What we put out returns to us three times in strength. Keeping this thought in mind, the card's message becomes obvious. Reacting from heartbreak's essence could result in hateful, horrid actions. Scary deeds and words are often expressed in the midst of excruciating pain. Crimes of passion occur when the individual reacts to the pain in their heart. The law of three reminds us to wait until the heartbreak subsides and the emotion subdues before we react.

Waite copies his definition practically word-for-word from Mathers's pamphlet *The Tarot*: "Separation, Removal, Rupture" and the *Book T's* "disruption, interruption, separation, quarreling; sowing of discord and strife, mischief-making, sorrow and tears." Waite states, "All that the design signifies naturally, being too simple and obvious to call for specific enumeration." Waite posits you will learn everything you need to know about the card by gazing and reflecting upon it. The same is true for each card in Pamela's deck.

> **Waite's Divinatory Meanings:** Removal, absence, delay, division, rupture, dispersion, and all that the design signifies naturally, being too simple and obvious to call for specific enumeration.

> **Reversed:** Mental alienation, error, loss, distraction, disorder, confusion.

. . . .

Four of Swords

Lord of Rest from Strife—Jupiter in Libra

GOOD-NIGHT; THE HOUR is late, the house is cold,
The fires have smoldered down, the lamps are spent,
And all the visitors that came and went,
Sleep—which I also need—doth now enfold.

Arthur Waite, *Collected Poems*

The Four of Swords reflects rest, repose, and the calm inner sanctum of the mind, no matter the issue at hand. The space of this card offers restoration and sanctuary for the weary soul. The card's advice says relax. Don't worry. It will remind a fervent heart to take a break. Sleep. Things will look and feel better tomorrow. The balance and stability acts in direct opposition to the Nine of Swords. It is a carefully arranged and orderly thought process.

Silence prevails in a peaceful tomb residing in a stone-gray chapel. A single sword is carved into the coffin. Three swords hang above the figure who rests in effigy. A colorful stained glass window lets in the light. Pamela's peaceful Four of Swords is an effigy or funerary sculpture of a fallen knight. He rests inside a tomb or in the corner of a sacred cathedral. This placement suggests a sleep as deep as death, rich and full; as Shakespeare's Hamlet says, "To die: to sleep;/ No more; and by a sleep to say we end/The heart-ache and the thousand natural shocks/That flesh is heir to, 'tis a consummation/Devoutly to be wish'd." The heartache referred to can be seen in direct correlation of the pain of the preceding Three of Swords. The storm clouds have passed, the feelings felt, and time is now for sweet restoration. The card evokes the yogic savasana, or corpse pose, a restorative position. Corpse pose is as important as the extremely physically challenging poses because balance and regeneration are as important as flexibility and strength.

The Four of Swords is a rest well earned and evokes its esoteric title, "The Lord of Rest from Strife." The three swords upon the wall point to three specific chakra points on the figure below: the third eye (intuition), the throat (communication) and the solar plexus (love). The chakra points carry additional hidden Masonic meaning. The story of Hiram Abiff is told to Masons and used as an example of integrity. King Solomon's Master Mason refused to share his Masonic secrets with a murderous group of thieves. He was struck in the head, throat, and chest, slain in cold blood for his silence. His story is also referenced in the Three of Pentacles.

. . . . . .

The Four of Swords draws parallels to Arthurian and Knights Templar legends. Sacred burial sites harbor the secrets of the dead. Many temples and churches are constructed on sacred, ancient Pagan holy grounds.

The stained glass window holds additional hidden meaning. Jesus lays hands on a kneeling follower. A halo looms around the Christ figure's head. The word PAX is written on it. Pax is the "kiss of peace" bestowed upon disciples and objects in the Christian Eucharist. It is named for the Roman goddess of peace, reflecting the historic layers of religious institutions. The halo is a symbol of divinity adapted from ancient sun gods. This tomb, like many sacred sites, is likely placed right on top of an older, ancient religion.

Waite is straightforward in his explanation: "The effigy of a knight in the attitude of prayer, at full length upon his tomb." His understanding derives from the *Book T*, which states, "Rest from sorrow; yet after and through it. Peace from and after war." No matter the situation at hand, you will have respite. Additionally, the number four will always express the stability of the suit; in this case, the stability of the mind.

> **Waite's Divinatory Meanings:** Vigilance, retreat, solitude, hermit's repose, exile, tomb and coffin. It is these last that have suggested the design.

> **Reversed:** Wise administration, circumspection, economy, avarice, precaution, testament.

· · · · · · · · · · · · · · · · · · · ·

Five of Swords

The Lord of Defeat—Venus in Aquarius—Stage Card

AWAKE, REVOLVING MANY troublous themes,
Because of thee I suffer, and in dreams
Am darkly haunted.

Arthur Waite, *Collected Poems*

Razor-sharp gray clouds race across the sky. Three figures appear as if upon a stage. The figure in the foreground holds three swords and turns his face in profile. Two swords lay at his feet. A middle figure stands between the two. The third and final individual rests his face in his hands. A water body is painted on a scrim, and a distant mountain range is seen.

The Five of Swords is the ultimate drama. A terrible fight has broken out. A clear winner, loser, and mediator is seen. The consequences are real, events are set in motion, sentiments have been made. They can't be taken back. Perhaps you were too truthful or just plain cruel. Maybe you were the victim of aggression. A nasty text was sent to the wrong person, and now you are busted. The group nature of this card infers bullying in groups or people ganging up on one another. The man collecting the swords holds a devilish advantage. He takes pleasure in what has been taken by force and caused pain to another. He delights in another's pain.

The Five of Swords reminds you of the power of your words and the impact you can have on others. It is as if the three heart-piercing swords have become human in the Five of Swords card. The suggested metaphor becomes literal. The smallest figure in the background foreshadows the despair of the Nine of Swords. The water's surface and clouds reflect an agitated energy. The karmic implications of the card remind the reader that participating in aggressive acts will inevitably result in you standing in each of the character's shoes. Why cycle through any of these stages? Take the high road, release the ego, and dissolve any energy leading to such disagreements.

Fives in the tarot always present a challenge. Waite wastes no words, saying, "A disdainful man looks after two retreating and dejected figures. Their swords lie upon the ground. He carries two others on his left shoulder, and a third sword, in his right hand, points to earth. He is the master in possession of the field." This aligns with the *Book T's* definition of the card as "failure, defeat, anxiety."

· · · · · ·

Pamela, forever true to her theatrical roots, creates a scene of Shakespearean drama and strife. The card, being in the suit of swords, asks if the reality of the situation is as terrible as it appears in your mind. Are you assigning more manipulation and ill intent than actually exist? Perhaps the situation has nothing to do with you at all.

Waite's Divinatory Meanings: Degradation, destruction, revocation, infamy, dishonour, loss, with the variants and analogues of these.

Reversed: The same; burial and obsequies.

• • • • • • •

. . . .

Six of Swords

Lord of Earned Success—Mercury in Aquarius

Or far in some land remote—
Perchance unfriendly, at least unknown—
Picture the bliss and vision alone;
Here let anchor a stranded boat.

Arthur Waite, *Collected Poems*

The Six of Swords is the card of literal or figurative journey. Passage, crossing, and movement radiate as two figures are ferried across the water. Their faces are hidden. Six swords are stuck at the front of the boat. A distant shore is seen. The water is calm. The weather is still. The appearance of this card often implies "better times lie ahead." The rippled water on the right of the boat and the smooth water on the left reflect the transition from trouble to smooth. The imagined depth of the water and river can be viewed as the emotional depth of the relationship. The card reflects a literal move, such as the purchase of a new home or relocation to a new city, state, or country. It can reflect moving forward and making progress with a child. The appearance of the card also suggests traveling and vacations.

The RWS deck contains many cards reflecting a journey, but the Six of Swords is the only card suggesting movement with other people. It is assumed that the figures in the boat are mother and child. This suggests a journey with loved ones. Is the boatman a father or partner or has he been hired? Each interpretation tells a different story of escape.

A mythic sense envelops the card. It echoes moving into a new plane of existence or to the underworld, netherworld, or otherworld. Charon, the Greek ferryman spirit who transports dead souls over the River Styx to the realm of Hades, haunts the image of this card. According to the myth, dead souls paid Charon a single coin for their passage. Funeral rites included placing a coin in the mouth of the corpse during burial. Corpses without money or plagued by improper burial rites were doomed to wander the riverbed. The implied message reminds the reader to prepare for movement into the unknown. Do not dwell in a single place for too long. The Six of Swords is a deep, eloquent card, no matter if the implied trip is metaphorical, joyful, or painful.

Of all the minor arcana, six cards carry implied separation and hierarchies between people. Each card shows a single figure towering over the rest. The separation suggests authority and

. . . .

positions of power, even a caste or social system whereby people are organized via external attributes. The nature of the minor arcana plays out in the progression on the number, growing bigger, larger, and closer to its final goal of complete manifestation in the ten. In a Kabbalistic sense, this progression is the movement from one Sephiroth on the Tree of Life to the next until it becomes manifest in the material world.

The esoteric title of the card bodes well as "The Lord of Earned Success." Earned success is always more rewarding than a simple or easy success. Both the *Book T* and Waite's *Pictorial Key* suggest this card is "journey by water." At the time and date the RWS deck was published, overseas travel could only be made via ship. Commercial air flights did not exist. Passage via boat or steamship held poignant meaning for travelers depending on the reasons, class, and level of comfort on their ship. The *Titanic* disaster struck three years after the publication of the RWS deck. A journey by water could mean days or maybe weeks or months at sea.

Waite notes that "the work is not beyond his strength." We never confront an obstacle, issue, or challenge that we do not have the power to overcome. In this sense, the card speaks of greeting challenges. This will bring us assured success. It is a reminder that we have what we need at our disposal. If we allow our challenges to transform us, we learn and grow from them. Like the figures in the boat, we will move toward new lands, arriving in a vastly different place. Our personal and spiritual evolution will continue to push past boundaries we can scarcely imagine.

> **Waite's Divinatory Meanings:** Journey by water, route, way, envoy, commissionary, expedient.

> **Reversed:** Declaration, confession, publicity; one account says that it is a proposal of love.

· · · · · · ·

Pamela crafts a figure suspiciously creeping like the Seven of Swords in her illustration for the post-RWS The Book of Friendly Giants *(above)*. The Seven of Swords from the Sola Busca Tarot *(below)*.

. . . .

Seven of Swords

Lord of Unstable Effort—Moon in Aquarius—Stage Card

O SEVENFOLD COSMOS, to the sevenfold man
Responding, set thy veils aside:
Thine inner self confide,
Thy deep-draw plan!

Arthur Waite, *Collected Poems*

The Seven of Swords reflects trickery or betrayal. Are you trying to get away with something? Are you cutting corners at work or school? Have you recently stolen something? Are you snooping behind someone's back? Do you harbor obsessions over things other people have? Do you crave things that are yours alone? If we read the appearance of this card as a betrayal, it invokes the Trickster archetype, exemplified by the Magician card, as someone who defies convention and disobeys traditional rules. When has this type of behavior worked in your favor? Lemon yellow saturates the card. A man wearing a crimson fez hat carries five swords in his hand. Festive tents with open flaps fly cheerful flags behind him. A gathering of individuals or soldiers crowd a campfire in distant silhouette. The man looks behind him as he tiptoes away.

Waite mentions the swords left behind: "the two others of the card remain stuck in the ground." This is what is no longer needed. The Seven of Swords can be understood as the editing card, the action of removing what is no longer needed. This may equate to cleaning out the closet and proofing manuscripts or papers. It can apply to life-changing events and ridding yourself of old habits and things that no longer serve you. Looking through this lens, the two swords behind the figure represent things once serving you but what you no longer need—behaviors, objects, people, relationships, and ideas that are better left behind.

The figure moves of his own volition. It suggests independent gestures, moving without the validation or opinion of others. You are finished checking in or seeking approval. At the same time, you may feel timid and have the instinct to hide your actions or wait to surface until your deed is done. In all matters, this card suggests you move quietly, without fuss, broadcast, or fanfare. Not everything you do needs to be broadcast on social media. Your own approval is most important.

. . . . . .

The figure steals away. The background soldiers suggest rules of law are ignorant of the figure's subterfuge. He moves with five swords, as sharp as his deception, in his hands. The silver blades might slice an apple or pear in half, yet he gently holds them in his warm, soft hands without a single cut. The figure's posture moves in three directions, reflecting future (where he heads), present (where his chest and solar plexus face the reader), and past (the direction he looks back at). The posture echoes a yogic seated spinal twist known for cleansing properties and aligns with the card's interpretation of editing, cleaning, and taking away only what is needed.

The card is an obvious derivative of the Sola Busca Seven of Swords, where a Roman figure steals away with swords. These swords are also benevolent, as his posture embraces them but they do not pierce or slice his skin. The esoteric title is "The Lord of Unstable Effort." This suggests the plan may not work and accounts for the subversive quality of the card. Waite does little more than describe Pamela's playful illustration. He offers no esoteric clues.

> **Waite's Divinatory Meanings:** Design, attempt, wish, hope, confidence; also quarrelling, a plan that may fail, annoyance.

> **Reversed:** Good advice, counsel, instruction, slander, babbling.

. . . .

Eight of Swords

The Lord of Shortened Force—Jupiter in Gemini

THE KNOTS WHICH bind our souls are such
As earthly ties would strain and start;
Each would not hold in each so much,
If ill-content on earth to part.

Arthur Waite, *Collected Poems*

The Eight of Swords is a frightening card to many who behold it. Imprisonment. A woman is blindfolded, marking intense interior life and the shamanic experience. She is bound at the seashore, marking the convergence of elemental threshold space. Her pointed feet hover above sand and water—she is disconnected from the earth and all worldly concerns. An oval prison of swords surrounds her. A turreted castle looms from distant cliffs as if the past slips away in the ocean mist. The woman appears to be held hostage. You could be imprisoned by a domineering relationship, family member, or even be a slave to your own tumultuous inner life. It suggests an oppressive religion or moral code where you feel as if you are unable to express your individuality. Perhaps a situation feels restrictive, the bills are piling up, you are faced with overwhelming confusion, or you feel like you have no good choices. Like the Three of Swords, the illustration leaves little to the imagination. A female figure is held captive in bondage and blindfold. The figure is held in dire straights. Or is she?

An esoteric reading of this card, like Two of Swords, suggests the blindfold signifies transformation and initiation. This is a voluntary act. She is like the caterpillar in the cocoon transforming into the butterfly. The swords are not a prison but mark the boundaries of sacred ritual space. The woman sees with a new set of eyes when her blindfold is removed. A sexual interpretation of this card (aligning with the Devil card) marks a proclivity for S & M, bondage, power, and control. What do you gain when you relinquish all control?

The eight swords in this card are magical in nature, like the Seven of Swords whose blades will not actually slice or the Two of Swords who are light as a feather. These eight swords stick up from the sand with little support. Magical realism inside any tarot deck can be used as a reminder of enchantment, glamour, and unseen forces at play in your life. No thing is actually as it seems. All of life is an interpretation, a story, like the tarot. One card carries

. . . . . .

To
All
Believers

The castle and cliffs in the background of the
Eight of Swords make a return appearance
in Pamela's post-RWS illustration for The
Book of Friendly Giants, *also featuring
the Hermit archetype.*

infinite meanings; one day in your life, a thousand possibilities. A single experience has multiple interpretations.

The esoteric title, "The Lord of Shortened Force," suggests a quick jolt of energy like the ripping of a bandage. Waite comments upon this card in his article "The Tarot: A Wheel of Fortune," where he states the card represents "disquietude, conflict, crisis, sometime fatality," yet he refers to the Masonic ritual of initiation, using the word "hoodwinked" in *The Pictorial Key*. He also supports the initiator aspects by saying that "it is rather a card of temporary durance than of irretrievable bondage." This suggests whatever the issue at hand, its effects will soon be over. It reminds you to be patient, and soon enough the situation will turn to your advantage.

> **Waite's Divinatory Meanings:** Bad news, violent chagrin, crisis, censure, power in trammels, conflict, calumny; also sickness.

> **Reversed:** Disquiet, difficulty, opposition, accident, treachery; what is unforeseen; fatality.

© 1971 U.S. GAMES SYSTEMS, INC.

. . . .

Nine of Swords

Lord of Despair and Cruelty—Mars in Gemini

IT SHOWS YOU that life's scheme
Has more of omen, sign and dream
Than enter into the hearts of those
Who cannot the inner eyes unclose.

Arthur Waite, *Collected Poems*

The Nine of Swords is a card of intense despair, a dark night of the soul. It reflects perpetual slavery to the thoughts running rampant circles in the head. You feel powerless to stop. Falling deeper into darkness, wide awake at 3:30 a.m. with an alarm set for 6:30 a.m., you beat yourself up, chide yourself, second-guess yourself, hyper focus on passive-aggressive situations, and lose sleep. This card signifies insomnia, nightmares, and depression. It also reflects an individual who is holding themselves to impossible standards. When the Nine of Swords appears in a reading, it reminds us to treat ourselves with kindness and compassion instead of judgment and criticism.

A nightmare of epic proportion envelops the imperiled woman who sits up in bed. Her head rests in her two hands. Nine stacked swords rise above her in darkness. Her hair is as white as a sheet. A colorful quilt covers her legs. A scene is carved onto her simple wooden bed. Swords are the scariest suit of the deck because they reflect the mind. They reflect internal dialogue. We often speak to ourselves in ways we would never speak to another.

Pamela includes many hidden treasures inside the card. The woman's white hair is a symbol of stress, although the idea of hair turning white from fright is a myth. It is impossible to lose pigment from hair once it leaves the scalp. Interestingly, there is a condition due to extreme stress where pigmented hair (brown, red, blond) falls out, leaving only gray hair behind. This gives the appearance of a head gone white with fright.

Nine swords on the wall offer an exit, a ladder of sorts. Will it offer a magical escape or slice her feet and hands to shreds? The bed, a symbol of rest and regeneration, has become the holding place of despair. The relief carved onto her bed shows two figures between two trees, each representing a pillar on the Tree of Life. The figure on the right holds a sword above his head and is about to strike the other figure down. The other figure falls back, vulnerable and unable to defend themselves. The carving reflects the woman's state of mind.

. . . .

The blanket is embroidered with forty-two squares. Twenty-one of the squares bear the red rose of Rosicrucianism. The other half bear a random scattering of zodiac and planetary symbols. Moving across as one would read a book, from left to right, the symbols are Mars, Taurus, Cancer, Pisces, Gemini, Leo, Virgo, Scorpio, Moon, Saturn, Aries, Saturn, Sagittarius, Leo, Mars, Aquarius (partial), Mercury, Sun, Gemini, Libra, Jupiter, Pisces, and Taurus (partially concealed).

In *The Pictorial Key* Waite claims she is "seated on her couch in lamentation," which is a strange statement. The woman obviously sits in a bed. It reflects Waite's disconnect with Pamela's image and supports the theory Pamela was given free rein to design her groundbreaking minor arcana images. Waite's description of "utter desolation" falls in line with the card as outlined by the *Book T,* which states it is the card of "pitilessness, malice, suffering." In his article "The Tarot: A Wheel of Fortune," Waite suggests it "should be compared to the former [Eight of Swords]; it is the card of disappointment, well illustrated by the picture."

The reader should note the use of temporary blindness suggested by the figure, who blocks out her own eyes. This figure, like the Eight of Swords and the Two of Swords behind her, is completely in the realm of her very own mind. This action provokes great pain and distress. It is likely that if she were to hop out of bed and gaze up at the night sky, she would quickly realize her place in the scale of the universe. Life is dramatic. The ego loves to be placed in the center of all things. It results in stories and impressions that are often untrue. We torture ourselves with projected possibilities that never unfold. The card reminds us that in a moment of pain or duress, we should take a deep breath and open our eyes. Become grounded in the moment and release everything we have no control over. In the end, you can only control yourself and your reaction to life's ups and downs.

Waite's Divinatory Meanings: Death, failure, miscarriage, delay, deception, disappointment, despair.

Reversed: Imprisonment, suspicion, doubt, reasonable fear, shame.

· ·

Ten of Swords

Lord of Ruin—Sun in Gemini

HOW WILL IT come to us, that great
day? What will the dawn disclose?
Past veils expended, all omens ended,
what truth at the heart of those?

※ ※ ※ ※ ※ ※ ※

Arthur Waite, *Collected Poems*

A golden dawn pushes up against an inky night sky and gray clouds. A man lies on the ground near the threshold of the beach. A mountain range is in the far distance. Ten silver swords pierce his spine, neck, and face. Blood streams from his head. His right hand makes a strange, secret gesture with his fingers and thumb. The bloody nature of the Ten of Swords often inspires fear in the viewer. The card, however, is not as dark as one might imagine. Tens suggest the ending of cycles and stories. The last act. A hushed theater a moment before the curtain falls. The situation at hand is over, whether it reflects pleasure or pain.

Swords represent the mind. The Ten of Swords appears when the mind is made up, finished calculating the situation, and becomes unchangeable. In many ways, this card also reflects things we cannot change about other people. It stands for the actions, opinions, and morals of others, yet the suit of swords is a reminder of the power of the individual mind; we are free every second to choose our thoughts. We can change how we approach the task at hand or way we react to unalterable events even if events or other people can't be altered. The ten swords additionally suggest acupuncture, concentrated chakra work, spinal issues, and themes of physical support.

The yellow dawn breaking above the mountains is an obvious reference to the Hermetic Order of the Golden Dawn. It references the continuation of a cycle that is implied in the Death card. In this sense it is the fresh possibility appearing once a conclusion is drawn. It is a very fresh start and the dawning of a new reality. The alarm rings. Daybreak rips away the evening's magic when you've been out all night long.

The esoteric title is "Lord of Ruin," and Pamela is explicit in her illustration. The card appears as the ending of a Shakespearian revenge play, a sub genre where violent murder, cannibalism, and spectacle is on display. The scarlet fabric in place of blood is a popular stage device. Red ribbons and fabrics are onstage blood symbols used in place of stage blood in violent theatrical

· · · · · ·

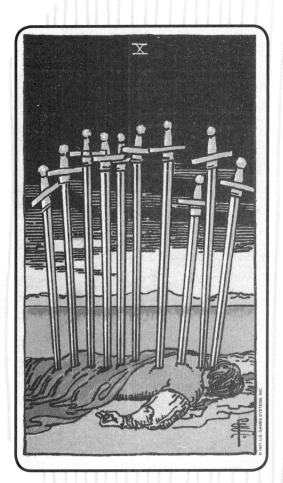

The Ten of Swords from the Sola Busca deck (right) inspired Pamela's Ten of Swords (left).

finales. The ritualistic use of blood makes it a symbol of the life force. The card looks to be inspired by that Sola Busca Ten of Swords, which is directly referenced by the Ten of Wands.

The figure makes a hand gesture matching the Hierophant's sign of benediction or blessing. The hand blessing appears on Christ depictions in early Byzantine art. The benediction is formed with the right hand and with the last two fingers curled down. Gemini also rules the hands. A subversive reading of this image suggests that the speared figure is the Hierophant. This reading implies that the old religions are dead and irrelevant. The old ways are dying. The slain Hierophant makes way for the new order of the Golden Dawn rising above him. It also implies that in life and death we are blessed. However, the hand gesture can only be made with active muscular control. Ultimately, it suggests the figure is not dead. It serves as a reminder that everything in tarot is symbolic and metaphorical.

Waite defines the card in a single sentence: "A prostrate (means lying flat) figure, pierced by all the Swords belonging to the card." In his divinatory meanings, Waite says the reader is free to take meaning from the image, "whatsoever is intimated by the design," but also that "it is not especially a card of violent death." An additional clue lies in his reversed meaning, which states that "none of these are permanent." At last we see that the Ten of Swords reflects the ephemeral nature of life—that nothing lasts. Nothing is forever except the soul or spirit.

> **Waite's Divinatory Meanings:** Whatsoever is intimated by the design; also pain, affliction, tears, sadness, desolation. It is not especially a card of violent death.

> **Reversed:** Advantage, profit, success, favour, but none of these are permanent; also power and authority.

. . . .

Ace of Pentacles

Kether in Assiah—Root of the Powers of Earth

THEN SUDDENLY OUT of the land withdrew,
The savor, the music, the scent, the hue.

Arthur Waite, *Collected Poems*

The Ace of Pentacles sits in an open palm as a gift, specifically the gift of money or inheritance. The Ace of Pentacles reflects the miracle of physical manifestation in the material realm. The garden is the perfected world of cosmic harmony and design. It carries the power of the sun and all its life-giving essence. In this way the card is a reminder of all the natural power already in your possession; a reminder of generative power, of how things blossom and grow. It also reiterates natural states and rhythms of the world. The Ace of Pentacles is the daisy growing through concrete. The Ace of Pentacles asks you what might blossom and bloom if you do not block the sunlight.

A rich and lush garden heralds the element of earth. A yellow pentacle, saturated with the golden nature of solar light, inspires all living things to grow. A pentagram or five-pointed star is drawn inside the double circle. The pentagram is an ancient symbol dating back to 3100 BCE, where it was found on a jar in Thebes, Egypt. Pentagrams were also found on tablets and vases in Mesopotamia during the same time period. Interestingly, in Egyptian hieroglyphs a pentagram enclosed by a circle represented the world of the dead. The RWS pentagram represents the opposite. The pentacle is the very building block of life.

Pentacles symbolically reflect the material world. The pentacle is the circle, the same shape of everything the material world consists of. It is a suitable symbol to reflect those things we can see, feel, and touch. The pentacle is the shape of the sun, the center of our solar system. It reflects the shape of each planet and moon revolving inside the solar system. The pentacle is the shape of the earth. It is the shape of human eyes. It is the shape of coins, human currency, and the original suit in older tarot decks. It is the shape of human molecules. This reminds us when we study something small, we are also examining something quite large. Pentacles are the building blocks of life and all things in the material world.

A gate leads out from the garden and into the world at large. The gate is covered with ivy and flowers. It is the threshold and passage of one plane of reality into another. The safety of the garden is left behind in lieu of adventure and the thrill of the open road. It is the true gate

. . . .

of manifestation—a path upon which all things are possible. What begins as a thought in the mind becomes real in the material world. An idea comes to fruition, a path is revealed, a possibility is encouraged.

Pamela departs from the *Book T's* description of the Ace of Pentacles entirely, while the other three aces closely follow Mathers's script. The same white, angelic hand glows with radiance and is exemplified by white spikes. The palm is receptive. It is open like the feminine elements of earth (pentacles) and water (cups). The pentacle rests gently in the palm. This can be viewed in opposition to the masculine elemental suits, where the palms tightly grip the wand (fire) and sword (air).

> **Waite's Divinatory Meanings:** Perfect contentment, felicity, ecstasy; also speedy intelligence; gold.

> **Reversed:** The evil side of wealth, bad intelligence; also great riches. In any case it shews prosperity, comfortable material conditions, but whether these are of advantage to the possessor will depend on whether the card is reversed or not.

. . . .

Two of Pentacles

Lord of Harmonious Change—Jupiter in Capricorn—Stage Card

WHEN IN THE higher moments of the soul,
Ascending from divided things,
Almost it seems to snatch the whole,
Of that which nature sings.

Arthur Waite, *Collected Poems*

The light-footed Two of Pentacles is the card of making a choice and weighing dual options. The figure literally and figuratively juggles responsibilities and life decisions. Rolling waves behind the figure echo the up-and-down nature of options, choices, and outcomes. The gentle nature of the card and the character's dance indicates the nature of the choice is pleasant. The Two of Pentacles, which can be understood as a lesser Temperance card, has the uncanny ability to appear in spreads and situations where important choices are being made. This includes serious matters of the heart, home, and finance.

The minor arcana cards numbered two, all connecting to the High Priestess, stand as a reminder of the duality in any situation you encounter. It reminds us there is always another side to the story. Nothing is as cut-and-dried as it seems. The Two of Pentacles additionally speaks to how you can manipulate things in the physical world, not in a negative way but by setting yourself up for success. It extends to everything seen, felt, and touched. How do I cultivate peace between people? What physical actions can I take? What monetary or financial choices am I facing? How are things dividing and multiplying in my life? What patterns have I set in motion? What would happen if I stepped aside? How can I rearrange elements in my life so authentic growth occurs naturally and easily?

Waite tells us, "A young man, in the act of dancing, has a pentacle in either hand, and they are joined by that endless cord which is like the number 8 reversed." Waite withholds valuable esoteric information when he neglects to inform his readers the sideways eight is a lemniscate, the symbol reflecting the nature of infinity. This symbol also appears above the Magician's head, thus placing a connective thread between the two cards. The Magician is traditionally called the Juggler in historic decks, adding an additional connection between the two cards. The posture and directional line of energy between the Magician and Two of Pentacles juggler

. . . . . .

© 1971 U.S. GAMES SYSTEMS, INC.

match up. They both siphon energy from the sky and draw it downward and to the right. It is the ease of natural flow.

Pamela places two tall ships traversing undulating ocean waves behind the juggler. In doing so, Pamela offers us a clever double duality. The ships are the physical manifestation of pentacles. The water, like the lemniscate, reflects the energetic and changeable quality of life. Like a wave, what goes up must come down. As with tidal cycles, what retreats will always return. The ship's portents and symbolic nature contain further meaning. In 1909 the only mode of traveling overseas was via steamship. Commercial air travel was nonexistent. The Rider-Waite-Smith deck was published six years after the Wright Brothers made flight history at Kitty Hawk. Travelers crossed the Atlantic on steamships. Pamela's own name appears on multiple steamship passenger lists between the United States and Europe. She made dozens of crossings. Steamship travel took anywhere from four days to a week. Traveling by sea, the friendships, socializing, and experience gave passengers a strong sense of the symbolism and lessons learned only by direct contact with wild weather and ocean waters.

The juggler in the Two of Pentacles wears a "sugar loaf" hat, commonly found in England under the reign of Henry VI (1422–1461). Pamela's theatrical background continues to influence her deck of cards. Shakespeare often used the symbol of the ship in his plays. They serve as powerful symbols and plot tools. Prospero summons a storm in *The Tempest* to wreck a ship and bring characters to his magical island. *Twelfth Night's* Viola suffers a shipwreck where she is separated from her twin brother, thus thrusting the play into action. Ships are objects subject to unknown forces carrying the fate of man. We can gaze at the juggler standing on Pamela's stage and wonder, is it he who juggles or are the forces of fate and the universe juggling him?

> **Waite's Divinatory Meanings:** On the one hand it is represented as a card of gaiety, recreation and its connexions, which is the subject of the design; but it is read also as news and messages in writing, as obstacles, agitation, trouble, embroilment.

> **Reversed:** Enforced gaiety, simulated enjoyment, literal sense, handwriting, composition, letters of exchange.

· · · · · · ·

. . . .

Three of Pentacles

Mars in Capricorn—Lord of Material Works

GRAND-WORD AND PASS-WORD and Number thine,
Grades and Degrees to the height advancing,
And the golden dawn and the glory glancing
Far and away the secret shrine!

Arthur Waite, *Collected Poems*

The enterprising Three of Pentacles is the card of collaboration. It reflects building, manifesting, and invoking creativity in the material world with outside help or expertise. One may embark on garden, home, or professional projects of renovation. Help is assembled for a creative project. A photographer assembles an assisting team. A couple seeks financial advice and guidance. Business collaborations are formed. The card implies growth in all areas, fostered and nurtured by one's own hand.

The Three of Pentacles leaps out viscerally. One can hear the echoes of the chamber, sense the cool stone of the chapel, and detect the faint smell of incense. The figures are theatrically adorned in the colorful costumes, especially on the hooded figure. Pamela crafts a deceptively simple image laced with rich historic symbolism and secret clues.

The card brims in esoteric symbolism, yet Waite is coy when he describes the scene to his reader: "A sculptor at his work in a monastery." What Waite conceals from his readers is that the sculptor is a Freemason. He suggests the reader "compare the design which illustrates the Eight of Pentacles. The apprentice or amateur therein has received his reward and is now at work in earnest." The comparison reveals the Masonic nature of progression and building. The apprentice becomes the master, like the novice reader who becomes the expert, versed in the secrets of the cards.

Monasteries act as containers for sacred space. Historically, chapels and cathedrals were built by operative Freemasons. An operative Freemason is a professional builder, the actively working Mason and stoneworker. Speculative Freemasons are non-builders who join Masonic organizations, like Arthur Waite, George Washington, and Benjamin Franklin. These men participate in Masonic practice and ritual without actually engaging in career Masonry. The Freemason on the card is identified by three Masonic symbols: apron, bench, and tool. The apron suggests work. The bench is an elevated space upon which to perform sacred work. The tool

. . . . . .

is his agent of change. Stop for a moment and think. When and how have you crafted sacred space for yourself? What does it mean to construct and create sacred space? Does sacred space require stone walls or something different? How does one construct an inner temple? What is the higher significance of your work?

A Masonic legend lies beneath this card like Pagan relics buried beneath a Christian church. The story of Hiram is the basis for the Masonic Third Degree. The tale begins as King Solomon appoints Hiram to design and construct his temple. Hiram is culminating his project when three creepy Fellow Craft Masons (Masons who have received their second degree) barge in, demanding Hiram's secrets. Hiram, forever loyal, refuses their requests and is killed. King Solomon declares that the Master Mason's secrets are now gone forever. The moral of the story is fidelity to Masonic secrets. It also speaks to the acknowledgment of the unavoidable death that we all will face.

We don't see fellow Craft Masons on the card. Instead, we see a monk displaying the practice of tonsure, the practice of shaving one's head to display religion devotion. The practice was popular under the reign of Henry VI (1422–1461). Monks with tonsure are seen at the feet of the Hierophant. A figure with a long caped hood (also popular men's fashion during the reign in Henry VI) holds master plans next to the monk. A close examination of the master plan document reveals the outline of the space where they stand.

The card's three pentacles form the shape of the supernal triad (top pyramid or triangle) of the Tree of Life. Inside the three pentacles is a circle with a cross, reflecting two paths on the Tree of Life. Below these symbols is a rose cross, which suggests future development of the tree and the paths that will connect the next two Sephiroth when they appear. This triad is also found in the Three of Cups via the three maidens and their cups. The tree's formation continues to evolve in the stained glass window of the Five of Pentacles. It concludes in complete formation within the Ten of Pentacles.

Pamela deviates from her normal roman numeral design by placing the number three into the card as if it were inside the monastery and part of the design of the delicate arches. This is a special mark as Pamela places the roman numerals on top of the images. The three pentacles' star tips equal fifteen, which is the number for Capricorn in the major arcana, as represented by the Devil.

> **Waite's Divinatory Meanings:** *Métier*, trade, skilled labour; usually, however, regarded as a card of nobility, aristocracy, renown, glory.
>
> **Reversed:** Mediocrity, in work and otherwise, puerility, pettiness, weakness.

. . . .

. . . .

Four of Pentacles

Lord of Earthly Power—Sun in Capricorn—Stage Card

THE GOD-LIGHT FALLS lost, if it shine,
on the eye unresponsive and blind;
While the eye that would see hath no light,
as we tread the dark maze of the mind.

Arthur Waite, *Collected Poems*

A figure sits on a cube. He holds a pentacle at his chest. One pentacle sits atop his crown and two are beneath his feet. A sprawling city is drawn on the scrim behind him. He stares straight ahead. The Four of Pentacles can be interpreted as stability in the material world by plugging in the structural meaning of the number four into the suit of earth. The card reflects having what you need. The card is often interpreted literally as the "miser" card because it looks as if the figure is desperately grasping his financial resources. The city behind him is the symbol for what he has built. It reflects the idea of hard work and clever financial planning as well as the idea of being attached to what is ultimately ephemeral. Buddhists practice the art of non-attachment because nothing in the material world lasts forever. The material world is the ultimate illusion.

Pamela's pentacles are placed on chakra locations for the crown, solar plexus, and two feet of the character. The pentacle placement matches up with the four Hebrew letters Yod Heh Vau Heh of the tetragrammaton. The Zohar, a collection of mystical Jewish writing, indicates the four letters form the shape of man. Waite offers little clue to the card, saying only, "A crowned figure, having a pentacle over his crown, clasps another with hands and arms; two pentacles are under his feet. He holds to that which he has."

Pamela's illustration adheres to her traditional theatrical and Shakespearean context. The figure strongly suggests Richard III from the play of the same name. Richard's character contains a wicked history. Richard III is described as a hunchback with physical deformities who is as crooked as the day is long. He is willing to lie, cheat, and steal his way to the crown. Thomas More describes him in *The History of King Richard the Third, 1513* as "ill featured of limbs, crookbacked, his left shoulder much higher than his right, hard favored of visage." This accounts for the card figure's bizarre and strange arm positions. Certainly Richard and many other royals sought to claim the esoteric title "Lord of Earthly Power" in their lifetimes. The crown is also

. . . .

similar to the ones often seen in stage productions of Richard III, and the figure's hair color matches Richard's black hair. The black cloak is a symbol of melancholy, as in the Five of Cups. His character lies, cheats, and steals his way to the crown, only to be killed by the end of the play. He is one of Shakespeare's great villains who clings to the prizes offered in the material world, only to lose everything in the end, yet another reminder that all life is ephemeral. No matter how hard we grasp material possessions, we, like them, will someday be reduced to dust.

Waite's Divinatory Meanings: The surety of possessions, cleaving to that which one has, gift, legacy, inheritance.

Reversed: Suspense, delay, opposition.

• • • • • • •

. . . .

Five of Pentacles

Lord of Material Troubles—Mercury in Taurus

IF, WHEN WEAKER sentiments invade,
The ragouts of our wintry course,
Abstention and divorce,
Make hearts afraid.

Arthur Waite, *Collected Poems*

The Five of Pentacles reflects a moment when insurmountable challenge lies ahead. All appears lost. It is a moment of angst and anguish not faced by the solo traveler but by a pair. A challenge is faced together. This card often reflects the ups and downs of long-lasting relationships, marriages, friendships, and the tumultuous nature of parenting. Puccini's operatic *La Bohème's* moonlit snowscape is evoked as white snowflakes fall to the ground in somber beauty.

A couple moves through a frigid winterscape. Night falls as quick as snowflakes in an icy blizzard. A woman draws her scarf closed at her neck. A leper on crutches is identified by a bell around his neck. Bells were used in medieval Europe as leprosy affected the larynx and caused a loss of voice. The figure is wrapped in bandages and pleads with the reader as if in great pain. A glowing yellow stained glass window is above them.

The Five of Pentacles contains a centerpiece of shining hope. It hints at salvation in a way that none of the other challenging minor arcana fives of tarot do. The glowing stained glass window of the cathedral contains the upper portion of the Tree of Life. The pentacles represent the tree's Sephiroth. The glowing light of spiritual knowledge fills the window and enlightens the beholder. Salvation is next to the couple. Can they see it? Warmth, rest, food, and shelter is there. Do they smell it? They can find refuge within the safety of the church's walls. Will they? Like the figure in the Four of Cups who is oblivious to the cup, will this couple seize upon an opportunity? This interpretation of the card does not advocate for specific religious dogma but stands as a powerful metaphor. It is a stark reminder. No matter how desolate, horrible, or terrible a situation appears, there is always hope. One must only look for it. Help, hope, and resolution is often closer than we think.

Waite is simplistic in his description: "Two mendicants in a snow-storm pass a lighted casement." A mendicant is a professional beggar, one who begs on the street as a way to survive.

. . . . . .

Waite's wordage may contain a hidden clue. Mendicant orders were Franciscan and Dominican religious orders of traveling monks. During the medieval period, they moved from city to city, assuming a lifestyle of poverty in order to live like Jesus. They would proselytize to the poor. This links the Five of Pentacles to the Six of Pentacles, which also contains a pair of beggars who kneel in mysterious cloaks as if they are concealing their true identity. Regardless of Pamela and Waite's intention, note the center challenge of the number five in the run of pentacles. The suit reflecting money and material wealth contains characters who have lost all material possessions. Examine the entire suit to discover the story of abundance, loss, and renewal. It echoes life cycles, the ebb and flow of energy, and ultimately the fact everything is constantly in motion. Nothing remains in its true form except for love.

> **Waite's Divinatory Meanings:** The card foretells material trouble above all, whether in the form illustrated—that is, destitution—or otherwise. For some cartomancists, it is a card of love and lovers—wife, husband, friend, mistress; also concordance, affinities. These alternatives cannot be harmonized.
>
> **Reversed:** Disorder, chaos, ruin, discord, profligacy.

. . . .

Six of Pentacles

Lord of Material Success—Moon in Taurus—Stage Card

WE SEEM TO wait
Forever at the opening gate
Of resonant, intelligible speech,
And ever still the Word is out of reach.

Arthur Waite, *Collected Poems*

The Six of Pentacles is a deceptively complex card reflecting many layers of meaning and interpretation. In the simplest terms, its appearance suggests an act of charity, gifts to others, and helping less fortunate souls. A well-dressed man stands in stark contrast to two beggars who kneel before him. He drops coins into a beggar's hands and holds a scale over the head of another.

When a tarot card contains multiple characters, it is a useful technique for the reader to discover which figure they identify with in their current situation. Do you identify with the wealthy merchant or the beggars? Are you in a place of lack or abundance? Answering these questions will access the current situation, and additionally, it cracks open the card's many levels. The merchant holds a scale over a beggar's head. This connects the Six of Pentacles to the Judgement card's scales and the act of weighing the pros and cons of a situation. Is the act of charity reflected also an act of reciprocity? Is give and take expected? Does the figure doling out coins contain an ulterior motive? Does his act of charity make him feel superior? Does he give from the decency of his heart or is he expecting a karmic return on his investment?

The Six of Pentacles contains a pictorial image of hierarchy, as do all the minor arcana sixes. One figure towers over others, implying separation. The Six of Pentacle's merchant connects to the Six of Sword's ferryman, the Six of Cups' youthful boy, and the Six of Wands' triumphant rider. The number six connects these cards to the Chariot, who bears the same number and rises above all to reach his final destination. The implied hierarchy additionally marks a visual connection to the number six on the Tree of Life in the place of Tiphareth. Tiphareth is the heart of the Tree of Life, the very center, and as such it implies giving, sharing, compassion, and integration. Therefore, it is the energy of the tree manifesting downward into the material world, sharing all of its gifts. The three figures additionally become a visual representation of the three pillars of the Tree of Life.

. . . . . .

The Six of Pentacles is visually connected to the Hierophant card. The merchant's hand makes the Hierophant's sign of benediction as he drops his coins. The merchant stands in the center of two lower men as the Hierophant towers above his two disciples. The merchant holds scales in his left hand; the Hierophant holds the triple staff. The merchant and Hierophant are both draped in red garments (note the red slip peeking out of the left beggar's pocket). The Hierophant and Six of Pentacles are each ruled by Taurus. The connections speak volumes on the nature of spiritual and material gifts.

Waite tells us, "A person in the guise of a merchant weighs money in a pair of scales and distributes it to the needy and distressed." His use of the word *guise*, which is an appearance that hides a true nature, hints the merchant may be concealing something from us or the beggars. Waite continues, saying, "It is a testimony to his own success in life, as well as to his goodness of heart." Waite speaks in a gentle tone. The *Book T* describes this card as "power, influence, rank, nobility, rule over people." This is an idea blatantly expressed by Pamela's image. This card denotes its esoteric title as the "Lord of Material Success" in all ways. It is always simple to demonstrate material success against those who are less fortunate. Doing so solidifies one's standing in the material world. Judging the inner wealth of an individual, however, is a much harder task.

The bandage on the head of the beggar suggests spiritual duress and redemption as the crown chakra heals. Four coins fall from the hand of the merchant, suggesting stability and evoking the Four of Pentacles. The merchant once clung tightly to his pentacles; now he distributes them freely. Are the beggars a spiritual test of the merchant on the material level? And what mysterious ticket pokes from the right beggar's cloak?

> **Waite's Divinatory Meanings:** Presents, gifts, gratification another account says attention, vigilance now is the accepted time, present prosperity, etc.
>
> **Reversed:** Desire, cupidity, envy, jealousy, illusion.

Pamela's figure in the Seven of Pentacles
is drawn in the same posture as Misero
in Tarocchi of Mantegna (E-series).

. . . .

Seven of Pentacles

Lord of Success Unfulfilled—Saturn in Taurus

AND IT ISN'T intended that men should get
A fuller glimpse of the secret yet.

Arthur Waite, *Collected Poems*

Seven pentacles have grown to fruition in a garden. The gardener pauses to lean on his tool, lost in thought as he looks at his crop. A tendril reaches forth. He reflects on his work. It is time to take stock and evaluate the path you've chosen and the seeds you've planted. Reexamine motives and perceived outcomes. The Seven of Pentacles reflects moments where results are seen. This card successfully poses the question, "Where do I go from here?" A promotion is received, but what comes next? Romantic advances are accepted. Is the person what you expected? Can you do something better, quicker, or in a more efficient way? More will evolve. Will you coax it to receive the ideal outcome? What slight adjustments can be made now that you've observed results?

The idea of placing a farmer or field worker on the card comes directly from the *Book T* stating in its definition of this card "a cultivator of land." Waite describes "a young man, leaning on his staff, looks intently at seven pentacles attached to a clump of greenery on his right; one would say that these were his treasures and that his heart was there." The title "Lord of Success Unfilled" is indeed expressed by the image, where the figure's "treasures" bring him no apparent joy. Waite points out the contradictory nature of the card as meaning "altercation" in one reading and "innocence" in another. He makes no attempt to clarify the meanings.

Pamela is inspired in her design by a version of the Fool card in an ancient deck of cards called the Tarocchi of Mantegna (E-Series). The Tarocchi of Mantegna, circa 1465, contains fifty cards with five suits. It is not a proper tarot deck because it does not contain seventy-eight cards with a major and minor arcana. The first card is called Misero, or beggar, and is the equivalent of tarot's Fool (note the dog at his side). Pamela crafts her Seven of Pentacles field worker in exactly the same posture. He leans on a staff, exuding the same feeling as her field worker. The Tarocchi of Mantegna also influences the following Eight and Nine of Pentacles.

. . . . . .

Waite's Divinatory Meanings: These are exceedingly contradictory; in the main, it is a card of money, business, barter; but one reading gives altercation, quarrels—and another innocence, ingenuity, purgation.

Reversed: Cause for anxiety regarding money which it may be proposed to lend.

. . . .

Eight of Pentacles

Lord of Prudence—Sun in Virgo—Stage Card

TRANSFORM THE WORLD!
Thou inner sense of sight,
Transform my soul!

Arthur Waite, *Collected Poems*

The Eight of Pentacles is the card of master craftsmanship and productivity. A young fellow with curly hair works on a bench. He holds a mallet in his right hand, a carving implement in his right, and wears an apron. Examples of his handiwork line the wooden wall next to him. A city lies in the distance while the artist forges his own unique creative space.

The Eight of Pentacles reflects creative satisfaction. Pride in work permeates the card as the craftsman hangs examples of his handiwork, the pentacles, in a line up the right side of the card as if they were a ladder on which he could ascend to new heights. It is the card of throwing out distractions, battening down the hatches, and getting serious about work. It is hitting the books or the canvas and using whatever tools, real or metaphorical, you use for your job, career, or hobby.

Freemason symbolism permeates this card, as it did in the Three of Pentacles. The Masonic apron (protection), bench (elevated space), and tool (agent of change) are drawn. The addition of Masonic symbolism brings a deeper metaphysical realm to the card. It asks the observer, how are you the architect of your life? What have you built with your talents, thoughts, and actions? The Masonic element speaks to the nature of internship and apprenticeship. Who is your mentor or do you mentor others? Is there an underlying system to the way in which you live your life?

The esoteric title is the "Lord of Prudence." Prudence is one of the four cardinal virtues recognized in classical antiquity, along with Temperance, Justice, and Fortitude (Strength). Prudence is the only cardinal virtue not to appear in the major arcana. To possess prudence means having a practical and discreet nature. The ability to employ the discipline of reason is exemplified by this card. The astrological traits of Virgo include an analytic mind, hard work, and a practical nature.

Waite tells us the artist's work "is displayed in the form of trophies." This informs the reader the work is exemplary and award winning. Pamela's design is inspired by the Tarocchi of

. . . .

The Eight of Pentacles reveals a figure
similar to the Artisan card in the
Tarocchi of Mantegna (E-series).

Mantegna (E series). Her card closely resembles the card of Artixan, or artisan, who is found two cards after the Beggar card that inspired the design for the Seven of Pentacles. The Mantegna card shows an artist hard at work who is shadowed by his younger apprentice.

Apprenticeships in old Europe held a vastly different meaning than the modern idea of internship. Modern interns often gain valuable work experiences, trading pay for work for short periods of time. Older European models of apprenticeships under a Master Craftsman often began in the apprentice's teen years and lasted a lifetime. Once a trade was selected, it was adhered to for life. Decades of dedication to a craft is how any given craft—watchmaking, winemaking, baking, etc.—kept its value and integrity. This is the true meaning of artisan products and artistry. The Seven of Pentacles holds the deepest elements of lineage and dedication.

> **Waite's Divinatory Meanings:** Work, employment, commission, craftsmanship, skill in craft and business, perhaps in the preparatory stage.

> **Reversed:** Voided ambition, vanity, cupidity, exaction, usury. It may also signify the possession of skill, in the sense of the ingenious mind turned to cunning and intrigue.

Pamela's placement of the falcon on the Nine of Pentacles may have been inspired by Zintilomo V in the Tarocchi of Mantegna (E-series).

. . . .

Nine of Pentacles

Lord of Material Gain—Venus in Virgo

BUT FOR YOU a place of wonder
Your own garden ground must be;
'Twist the trees that you stand under,
Seeing what is yours to see.

Arthur Waite, *Collected Poems*

The sumptuous Nine of Pentacles is the card of luxury, wealth, and riches. It is the desire to surround oneself with beauty, not as a status symbol but for the pleasure of refinement and appreciation of craftsmanship. The European vineyard implies inheritance. Traditionally, European vineyards, like castles and large estates, are passed down through generations. The idea of craftsmanship echoing throughout the suit of pentacles with its multiple Masonic overtones adds to the physical nature of the suit. In a certain sense, the pentacles are inherited DNA providing an opportunity for us to examine traits, behaviors, and our personal House of Spirits, with all its gifts and curses. Mihaly Csikszentmihalyi describes the import of ancestors: "To remember a long list of elders, going back a dozen generations, is particularly enjoyable in that it satisfies the need to find a place in the ongoing stream of life. To recall one's ancestors places the recaller as a link in a chain that starts in the mythical past and extends into the unfathomable future." Where do you fit into the chain? What behavior is authentic to you? What belongs to your mother, your sister, or your grandmother? What talents have you been gifted? What traits and behaviors do you wish to cast off?

The female's gown is embroidered with flowers, with the symbol of Venus under her left arm. This connects her to the Empress card's fertility and creativity. The falcon and art of falconry imply loyalty and lineage, and birds in general reflect the human and cosmic spirit intertwined. The snail denotes a slowness requiring plenty of time to develop. The snail shell reflects the infinity of the golden spiral. Rosy purple grapes bursting from the vine imply ripeness and harvest. The woman's hand gently resting across the pentacles marks her gentle touch over them. It is as if the pentacles themselves are bending to her will, falling at her feet and obeying her orders like a well-trained pet. The Nine of Pentacles is a figure with complete manipulation and mastery over the physical world. She acts in accordance to the Strength card. She respects the forces of nature by working in tandem with them, not attempting to bend them to her will.

. . . . . .

Her nature serves as a strong reminder to work in tandem with all the forces and assets of your life. It is also a reminder to appreciate what you already have rather than envying the possessions of others. The figure reflects a woman who is completely at home in herself. She is complete and alone amidst her own pleasures. She defines herself and the moment. Like the World dancer, she integrates without thought to the past or the future. She luxuriates in the present.

Waite describes the card and its "manorial house." Pamela's image is inspired by her many illustrations of actress Ellen Terry, a woman she loved like her mother. The Nine of Pentacles looks specifically like the illustrations Pamela made of Ms. Terry in her role in *The Merry Wives of Windsor*. Pamela drew and colored individual prints of her fellow actors in the Lyceum Theater. She sold them to fans the way movie fans purchase movie stills and posters. Pamela's illustrations of Ellen Terry proved quite popular, and it was likely she used her own illustrations of actors as models for the RWS deck.

> **Waite's Divinatory Meanings:** Prudence, safety, success, accomplishment, certitude, discernment.

> **Reversed:** Roguery, deception, voided project, bad faith.

. . . .

Ten of Pentacles

The Lord of Wealth—Mercury in Virgo

AH, ONE THING more, last gift and best, we wait!
Beyond all type and sign,
Teach us to issue out of Nature's gate
On Thine unveil'd Divine.

Arthur Waite, *Collected Poems*

The Ten of Pentacles reflects the culmination of all things in the material world. The Nine of Pentacles reflects the autonomy of an individual with her wealth. The Ten of Pentacles reflects the entire family. Like all minor arcana tens, the Ten of Pentacles depicts finality and the end of a saga, story, or cycle in one's life. Three generations—a grandfather, parents, and child—are seen. Two elegant family dogs (in contrast to the Fool's mangy dog) are petted by grandfather and grandson. The card implies wealth in all physical things, from finance to family to friends. It is set at the threshold of a city, marking the entrance to a warm interior protected by battlements. It is a safe and protected space. The city is also the place of commerce and a place reflecting the monetary value of the pentacle. The Ten of Cups reflects a pastoral family of the countryside, while the Ten of Pentacles reflects a wealthy urban family in the space of material possessions.

The Tree of Life is encoded onto and across the design of the card. The tree has developed across the entire suit. It appeared as a single pentacle in the ace. It is seen as a triad in the Three of Pentacles' cathedral. Five upper points of the tree appear in the stained glass window of the Five of Pentacles. The entire tree now hangs in splendor.

How does the material world bridge us to the spiritual? We merge with the sublime in various ways. The ace is the simplest, while the ten is most complex. The Ten of Pentacles can reflect a masterpiece, like Vivaldi's *Four Seasons* or Dante's *Inferno*. Great works of art exist on the material level, yet they transport the participant to higher spaces of spiritual joy and acute happiness.

Waite points out the "two dogs accosting an ancient personage seated in the foreground." Could this figure mark the Hermit's return from self-imposed seclusion? If so, the Hermit's gray cloak has been transformed into an amazing Technicolor dreamcoat. His white beard marks maturity and experience. He looks like the many bearded ceremonial magicians of the

. . . . . .

Golden Dawn. Could this figure be based on co-founders William Wynn Westcott or William Woodman? Waite's monogram is cleverly hidden upon the grandfather's cloak. Perhaps the figure is Waite himself. The grapes on his cloak connect to the grapes in the Three of Cups and Nine and King of Pentacles and their bacchanalian properties.

The outside of the city is pale, drawn in black and white, while the figures and the inside are as vivid as the Technicolor in *The Wizard of Oz*. The Tower card is hinted at by the black-and-white tapestry hanging to the left of the threshold. Justice's scales hang in the black-and-white tapestry above the Magician's head. This card secretly connects to the Hermit, Justice, and the Tower. This coloring reflects the final stage of manifestation into the concrete world of reality. The card is truly the "Lord of Wealth."

> **Waite's Divinatory Meanings:** Gain, riches; family matters, archives, extraction, the abode of a family.

> **Reversed:** Chance, fatality, loss, robbery, games of hazard; sometimes gift, dowry, pension.

PAGE of WANDS.

Hod (Splendor)

The Court Cards

. . . .

Page of Wands

Book T Title: Princess of the Shining Flame, the Rose of the Palace of Fire

Elemental Counterchange: Earth (Page) of Fire (Wands), Princess and Empress of the Salamanders, Throne of the Ace of Wands

Astrological: Season of Summer

> TRAVEL, TRAVEL AND search,
> eyes that are eager glisten
> I stand on the marge and listen.
>
> Arthur Waite, *Collected Poems*

General

The Page of Wands, the Youth of Fire, has a red flame protruding from the top of her hat. The red flame denotes all you need to know about the Page of Wands. As the youth of fire, she reflects purity of passion glowing in its primal stages. Put yourself in your prepuberty mindset and imagine yourself around age nine or ten. What activities did you love more than anything? What fascinated and beguiled you? Did the library's endless bookshelves with tasty titles and colorful covers each call out to you like a new adventure? Did dirt and grass baseball diamonds appear like a magical landscape where you could reach immortality with a single solid swing and crack of your bat? What toys and games did you devour? Did Monopoly or Clue, a colored

. . . .

square cardboard, provide hours of fun? What movie or TV show did you watch repetitively? Were you lost in vibrant waxy crayons, dripping paints, and creamy smooth paper? Did the freedom of bike riding—wind in your hair, gravel crunching under your tires—thrill you? The Page of Wands puts what she loves most at the center of her attention. The Page of Wands' life forms and reforms around her passionate bright flame. This flame burns at the center of her existence.

In You

The Page of Wands places her attention entirely on what thrills her, and when you do the same, you embody her. Recall the complete and total attention of your child-self immersed in play. Holding complete awareness on what fascinates you allows you to live in the moment. It releases the ego. The past and future slip away. Each of us is born with unique talents and dreams. We each hold particular sensitivities. We explore our passions, be it dance, cooking, traveling, etc., and we become the Page of Wands. We are born with unique sensitivities and passions that feed our dreams. Exploring our passions allows us to blossom, grow, and evolve. We feed the passion and the passion feeds us. It is a symbiotic relationship of growth and evolution. The Page of Wands can be understood as the pleasurable energetic process leading you deeper into the evolution of your true self.

In Others

The Page of Wands is the good-time girl who exhibits the excitable qualities of fire. She is full of energy, seemingly tireless, and bubbly. She's the type of friend who gets you both into trouble because fire qualities move first and ask questions later. She cheers you up with her charismatic energy, and she's usually wildly popular, with a wide circle of friends. Her essence is infectious. Being near her is like standing close to a crackly, popping fire.

You'll easily observe Page of Wands energy in others when you see someone immersed in what they love. A fiery excitement fills a person when their inner page is activated. Have you felt hot jealousy while watching someone doing something you wish you could do? Envy, a distinct fire quality, is a clear signal that you need to activate your inner page. The feeling of jealousy can be harnessed once it is experienced because it points us toward hidden desires we have repressed or ignored. Allow the jealousy to slip away, but allow the experience to inform your desire and future actions. Get moving on what you want. The Page of Wands' most endearing and enviable quality is her laser-like dedication to passion. Nothing can stop her once she puts her mind to something. She is often found in dance classes and politics, changing the world for the better.

Symbols

Fire salamanders are identified by their black and yellow coloring. Pamela took these colors to heart for the Page, Knight, King, and Queen of Wand's costuming. Each of their garments matches the fire lizard's colors, black and yellow with circular salamanders. Waite tells us about the page by saying, "His tidings are strange." Waite refers to the pages as males, yet most readers assign pages the female pronoun of "she" to reflect energetic balance in the deck. Her gaze focuses on the ultimate act of manifestation at the tip of the wand. A triad of pyramids stand in the background, echoing the page's creative nature. The number three is the essence of creativity, and a triangle has three sides. Three triangles create the invisible portion of the Tree of Life, which produces manifestation in the material world. The page gently holds a wand and gazes at what is blossoming and growing. She is watching the ultimate act of manifestation, and, by doing so, it teaches her how to be in the world.

> **Waite's Divinatory Meanings:** Dark young man, faithful, a lover, an envoy, a postman. Beside a man, he will bear favorable testimony concerning him. A dangerous rival, if followed by the Page of Cups. Has the chief qualities of his suit. He may signify family intelligence.

> **Reversed:** Anecdotes, announcements, evil news. Also indecision and the instability which accompanies it.

KNIGHT of WANDS.

. . . .

Knight of Wands

Book T **Title:** The Lord of the Flame and Lightning, the King of the Spirits of Fire

Elemental Counterchange: Fire (Knight) of Fire (Wands), King of the Salamanders

Astrological: Sagittarius (Mutable Fire)

LIGHT OF THE endless East and West,
Shine on me here as there;
The signs at least of the great quest
Are round me everywhere!

Arthur Waite, *Collected Poems*

General

The Knight of Wands is infused with the explosive, expansive element of fire. He reflects unbridled and uncontrolled passion. He is teenage energy and indignation. The Knight of Wands doesn't stop to think. He acts out first and asks questions later, if at all. His unbridled energy is a powerful force of change but causes trouble if it goes unchecked. Knights often reflect romance, and the Knight of Wands is hot to the touch. He reflects the dangerous love your mother warned you about, burning fast and hot. He is the rush of romantic love that feels like a drug. He is the exhilaration of the first six months of romance. He's the ultimate endorphin rush. Harness Knight of Wands' energy, point it toward any goal, romantic or otherwise, and there's nothing you can't do.

In You

The Knight of Wands is activated when you get really excited. He's the telephone call bringing you unexpected good news. He's the thrill rolling through your body when you lock eyes with an attractive stranger. He's a runner's high and endorphin rush. The Knight of Wands is activated when booking a spur-of-the-moment trip to an exotic destination or a last-minute impulse plan. You'll harness this powerful energy when gathering strength and pushing through the end of a truly challenging task. You also harness his power when you help others. He's that last burst of energy sending you over the finish line of a project or effort.

In Others

The Knight of Wands is the ultimate hotshot. He is captivating to behold when he crosses our path. His incendiary nature grants him extraordinary charisma. He's extremely fiery and

. . . .

impetuous, and as such, he glows from the inside out. It's flat-out sexy. His intense energy can be observed in athletes, actors, and take-charge types. He'll often work in physically demanding jobs like construction or the military as an outlet for his energy. He's a romantic player on and off the field. He'll seduce many and stick around for none. The Knight of Wands lets every emotion play across his face. He contains no filter. Because he operates on a high level, it means no one knows what he might do next, least of all himself.

Symbolic

A red plume explodes from the knight's helmet like a burst of flame. Scarlet gloves cover his fingers. Flames leap from his arms, reflecting a "fired up" individual who is literally hot to the touch. He wears bright yellow costuming covered with black salamanders. His sheath of protective armor, a symbol of security and the history of battle, covers his vulnerable skin. Pyramids in the background denote ancient spiritual knowledge and divinity. The scorched desert sands he gallops across reflect the element of fire. Waite reminds the reader, "The motion of the core is a key to the character of its rider, and suggests the precipitate mood, or things connected with." A horse always indicates the energy of the situation at hand. The Knight of Wands' horse displays a charging, expansive energy that threatens to rage out of control. The energy is fast and immediate. Consider yourself warned.

> **Waite's Divinatory Meanings:** Departure, absence, flight, emigration. A dark young man, friendly. Change of residence.

> **Reversed:** Rupture, division, interruption, discord.

. . . .

Queen of Wands

Book T **Title:** Queen of the Thrones of Fire

Elemental Counterchange: Water (Queen) of Fire (Wands),
  Queen of the Salamanders

Astrological: Aries (Cardinal Fire)

> WHAT IRIS CLIFFS overhang her path, what towers,
> White argent, crumble down,
> And scatter shards and glitter sparks in showers:
> One gems her like a crown.
>
> Arthur Waite, *Collected Poems*

General

The Queen of Wands is the goddess of fire. She embodies mature female passion. It is a passion understanding itself, rather than the rush of excitement felt in younger years. It is the maturity and knowledge to embrace, engage, and cultivate the evolution of passion into its highest and deepest levels. The art of cultivating passion is akin to any other discrimination and discernment. Once passion is harnessed, it can be fully explored and experienced in limitless ways. The Queen of Wands feels and exudes passion in all its manifestations, from ecstatic sexual love to spiritual ecstasy to the nurturing love of family and friends. The Queen of Wands generates fire through her actions, devotions, and work.

In You

The Queen of Wands is activated inside of you during incendiary moments where you push past personal barriers and take charge. While the Knight of Wands raises passion, the queen executes it and expands it in proactive and marked ways. She reflects taking what you love and putting it to work in the world. She is you working with certainty toward things you desire, respect, and admire, enjoying every delicious step of the way. You brainstorm for your business and reach out to others. You make phone calls and create action plans. You put out the feelers for like-minded allies. You shop for supplies, gather what's needed, and lead by example. You know what you love has the ability to transform the world just as it has transformed yourself.

. . . . . .

Pamela had plenty of royal costuming inspiration for her court cards from her time spent as costume and set designer at the Lyceum Theater. Here is Ellen Terry as Queen Katherine of Aragon in a 1902 Lyceum Theater's production of Henry VIII.

In Others

The Queen of Wands is a firecracker. She's the emotive actress (think Julia Roberts in an emotional scene) and passionate performance artist. She's the "fun mom," often wearing flashy clothes and colorful makeup. She usually looks younger than her age. She is a true queen who enjoys coronation ceremonies, putting on a show, and being the center of attention. She is a compelling and life-changing teacher or professor. She brings forth qualities from you that you didn't know were there. She shows you the best parts of yourself.

Symbolic

Waite tells us, "The Queen's personality corresponds to that of the King, but is more magnetic." The queen's magnetism is marked by her sunflower, a symbol denoting the manifested beauty of the sun. Her black cat reflects loyalty, magic, and charisma. Feline qualities also include the power of transformation and sensual beauty. The cat carries the message of aloofness and a "look but don't touch" quality. You will be inspired by this queen, yet she sometimes seems distant. You can't hold her or capture or contain her any more than you can hold a live flame in the palm of your hand. Better to admire from afar. Bask in the heat, beauty, and sustenance from a safe distance.

> **Waite's Divinatory Meanings:** A dark woman, countrywoman, friendly, chaste, loving, honourable. If the card beside her signifies a man, she is well disposed toward him; if a woman, she is interested in the Querent. Also, love of money, or a certain success in business.
>
> **Reversed:** Good, economical, obliging, serviceable. Signifies also—but in certain positions and in the neighbourhood of other cards tending in such directions— opposition, jealousy, even deceit and infidelity.

· · · · · ·

KING of WANDS

The King of Wands from the Sola Busca Tarot.

. . . .

King of Wands

Book T Title: Prince of the Chariot of Fire

Elemental Counterchange: Air (King) of Fire (Wands),
   Prince and Emperor of Salamanders

Astrological: Leo (Fixed Fire)

Stars be his pathway and suns his track,
For the King comes forth and the King goes back!

Arthur Waite, *Collected Poems*

General

The King of Wands is the commander of fire and enjoys extraordinarily charismatic powers. Imagine for a moment what it means to command and control the element of fire. The King of Wands holds the power to heal or destroy, nurture or incinerate. As a steward of the flame, he leads with sweltering emotion. His personality is volatile. He is quick to anger and equally apt to dissolve into fits of laughter. Once his sights are set, there is no stopping him. He works in conjunction with his queen by utilizing all of her expansive energy and reining it in at just the right moment. He is a visionary, a rock star, and an individual who alters the landscape of the world.

In You

The King of Wands is activated in you when taking a leadership position in a passion project. He is you in the act of seduction. The queen languishes and intermingles inside the mystery and quality of intense energy, while the king has his eye set firmly on the goal. No games. Nothing held back. No fear. He states what he wants, why he wants it, and how he wants it. You embody the King of Wands when you are relentless in a scorching pursuit of desire.

In Others

King of Wand's energy is as spiritual as it is sexual. He's the preacher man and the rock star. He spouts fire and brimstone as easily as he sings and grinds to an arena full of screaming fans. The King of Wands carries a guru quality due to his charisma and belief in his convictions, deeds, and words. The King of Wands is the center of attention and loves it. He is a political hero leading people to freedom. Anyone who uses the passion, fire, and spirit of their guiding flame to move the world embodies the King of Wands.

. . . .

Symbolic

Waite points out the King of Wands "connects with the symbol of the lion, emblazoned on the back of his throne." The lion is a symbol of strength and solar energy. Waite also describes this king in "The Tarot: A Wheel of Fortune" by saying he is "ardent, equitable, noble, and represents goodness blended with severity." This old-fashioned, patriarchal idea of kindness blended with harshness when it is for a person's own good is an antiquated Victorian ideal of masculinity. A loyal salamander is placed next to his throne. Salamanders often blend in to avoid detection from predators, while some salamanders project their toxic and dangerous nature by showing orange, red, and black colors. The king is adorned with salamander colors, reflecting his desire to assert his personality and nature. He warns would-be enemies not to cross his path or they will suffer dire consequences. The green collar at his neck and emerald slippers represent the manifestation inherent in wands. He is the fire that breeds results.

> **Waite's Divinatory Meanings:** Dark man, friendly, countryman, generally married, honest and conscientious. The card always signifies honesty, and may mean news concerning an unexpected heritage to fall in before very long.
>
> **Reversed:** Good, but severe; austere, yet tolerant.

• • • • • •

. . . .
Page of Cups

Book T Title: Princess of the Waters, the Lotus of the Palace of the Floods

Elemental Counterchange: Earth (Page) of Water (Cups), Empress of the Nymphs or Undines, Throne of the Ace of Cups

Astrological: Season of Autumn

Stage Card

> AT EVERY GATEWAY of our dream
> Her echo or her rumor seems;
> A tale upon the point of telling
> A prophecy for ever spelling.
>
> Arthur Waite, *Collected Poems*

General

The Page of Cups, the youth of water, evokes a unique and sensitive character. She carries the playful, fluid, and curious nature assigned to the element of water. Water gifts her with heightened intuition and psychic flashes. She does not differentiate between the "real" world and the psychic world because of her innocence. A ghostly presence in her room is as real to her as her best friend. The Page of Cups is the ultimate empath who absorbs the emotions of others, sometimes confusing them for her own. The Page of Cups is a dreamer, spending hours alone in her bedroom, playing or looking out the window, watching the billowing white clouds float past. She is joyful in her actions. Her emotional filter is like a sieve, and she holds no emotion back—they flow like water through her. She is given to emotional outbursts that pass away as quickly as they came.

In You

The Page of Cups activates inside you when playful and open. Insights rush into your awareness. It is the quality of playing with a child. It is the openness occurring when couples horse around in love, the silly open space of play and safety and goofiness. It is the place of artistic play and experimentation where the actors rehearse, the painter collects images and inspiration. This safe space is an open ground for creative manifestation. Nothing is off-limits for the Page of Cups, and her qualities fill you when safely enjoying a space of vulnerability and joy.

. . . . . .

PAGE of CUPS.

In Others

The Page of Cups is the artsy and interesting girl who loves the theater, cultural events, and literature. She is often found engaging in activities allowing self-expression and her rich and varied emotions. She falls in love at the drop of a hat. The Page of Cups makes a dear friend whose advice is kind and effective. She notices qualities and traits in you that others miss. It often seems like she's the only person who really "gets" you. She's the most likely to contact you out of the blue the moment you need a friend to lean on. She communicates with the animal world and has a menagerie of pets. She's often found writing, photographing her adventures, and at the theater.

Symbolic

The cheeky fish popping out of the cup is a symbol of psychic vision. Like the Seven of Cups, where each cup holds a magnificent mirage, so do we see the comical vision of a talking fish. Waite tells us, "It is pictures of the mind taking form." The Page of Cups is assigned the elemental counterchange of Empress of the Nymphs, who are feminine spirits of the natural world. These mini goddesses and minor deities sprang into mythology from lakes, springs, seas, rivers, and waterfalls and morphed into the European tradition of the spirits who inhabit elemental water.

The Page of Cups wears a fourteenth-century tunic and roundlet hat, as does the Page of Pentacles. This was a popular and extravagant style of clothing for men worn under the reign of Henry VIII. It was meant to convey wealth and well-being. The lotus flowers on her tunic are the Golden Dawn symbol for the suit of water. The water painted on the scrim and the fish are additional water symbols.

> **Waite's Divinatory Meanings:** Fair young man, one impelled to render service and with whom the Querent will be connected; a studious youth; news, message; application, reflection, meditation; also these things directed to business.
>
> **Reversed:** Taste, inclination, attachment, seduction, deception, artifice.

KNIGHT of CUPS.

- -
Knight of Cups

Book T **Title:** The Lord of the Waves and the Waters, the King of the Hosts of the Sea

Elemental Counterchange: Fire (Knight) of Water (Cups), King of the Undines and Nymphs

Astrological: Pisces (Mutable Water)

> WHEN I HAVE seen the sunset smoke,
> My heart has longed for thee!
>
> Arthur Waite, *Collected Poems*

General

The Knight of Cups evokes the dreamy quality of water. All knights invoke offerings and indicate romance; however, the Knight of Cups is the archetypal romantic suitor ready to sweep you off your feet. Their appearance suggests action and motion. The horse's gait on any knight card can be used to determine the quality and pace of action surrounding any situation. The Knight of Cup's gentle horse lifts a single hoof. This is a slow and thoughtful energy. He's not moving fast, if at all. The Knight of Cups sometimes reflects the heart and soul of an artist who is forced into a "practical" profession.

In You

The Knight of Cups appears in you when you feel you have a message in need of delivery. It is the card of gift and praise giving. When you approach others in kind and loving ways, you emulate the Knight of Cups. The Knight of Cups is activated when you are charming toward another, using words and gestures to make the other feel like putty in your hands. His presence suggests deep emotion that will be acted upon in the near future.

In Others

He is the dreamer and a high-level poet, artist, and sensitive soul. He's the mate who sings your praises, cries at the drop of a hat, and anticipates your every need. He is a deep and emotional lover. As the Prince of Water, he is supportive and brings a soft touch to any situation. He is, at times, duplicitous, offering little more than charming words and the vapor in his cup. If he appears in a reading as a potential romance, caution should be exercised until his true motives are revealed.

- - - - - - -

Symbolic

Ornate armor covers the Knight of Cups, suggesting experience in battle. The wings of Hermes sprout from his helmet and heels. Hermes is the messenger god. Hermes' wings are a specific reference to speed, incoming intelligence, mail, deliveries, phone calls, and news. Fish are embroidered into his tunic and are emblematic of the suit of cups, the element of water, and the zodiacal sign of Pisces, which he represents. The landscape is desert-like with the sand and rock with orange and yellow hues. A blue river meanders through the landscape like the Death card's river. The knight brings water to the thirsty landscape. He is like a cool, refreshing drink and helps all things become fruitful and lush.

Waite focuses heavily on the dreamlike quality of this card. If the Page of Cups' imagination took shape as the fish in her cup, perhaps the Knight of Cups has imagined his entire landscape. Waite says, while referring to the knight, "He too is a dreamer, but the images of the side of sense haunt him in his vision." Waite also describes the knight as "graceful, but not warlike; riding quietly." Waite's definition falls in line with the *Book T*, which describes him as "sensual" but also as "idle and untruthful." Waite lifts his divinatory definitions almost word for word from Mathers's *The Tarot* pamphlet, which states the Knight of Cups' upright meaning as "Arrival, Approach, Advance" and the reversal as "Abuse of confidence, fraud, Cunning." The reader may decide for herself if the knight gazes into or past the cup.

> **Waite's Divinatory Meanings:** Arrival, approach—sometimes that of a messenger; advances, proposition, demeanour, invitation, incitement.
>
> **Reversed:** Trickery, artifice, subtlety, swindling, duplicity, fraud.

. . . .

Queen of Cups

Book T **Title:** Queen of the Thrones of the Waters

Elemental Counterchange: Water (Queen) of Water (Cups),
   Queen of Nymphs or Undines

Astrological: Cancer (Cardinal Water)

AND THE SEA, with melodious roar,
For ever and ever responds on
the long, pulsating shore.

Arthur Waite, *Collected Poems*

General

The Queen of Cups is the goddess of water, queen of the mermaids, and empress of the sea. She represents mature female energy and is the most empathetic card in the deck. The ocean's depths reflect her understanding of the animal, vegetable, and human experience. She sits with a sacred chalice, the most ornate and only closed cup of the entire deck. She holds the full extent of cup qualities. She is soft and malleable, like water, and is entranced with dreamlike visions. She is the ideal tarot reader in her ability to see through to the bottom of a situation.

In You

Spaces of gratitude activate Queen of Cups qualities. When you care for others, you activate the Queen of Cups. Feeling compassion for other beings, animals, nature, and humanity is a Queen of Cups trait. When you are deep, open, and emotional, you activate the Queen of Cups. She occupies the space of the active dreamer; when you see something you have imagined come to fruition, you are standing at her height.

In Others

The Queen of Cups is a woman you can always depend on for sympathy and compassion, like a nurse or a therapist. She is there to nurture you, hold you, and let you know everything will be all right. She understands the sands of change and reminds you things will be okay. The Queen of Cups is an inspirational figure, a person who makes their dreams come true by making the world a better place.

. . . . . .

England's White Cliffs of Dover (above) drawn by Pamela for her post-RWS illustration for The Book of Friendly Giants. *The Queen of Cups (below) from the Sola Busca Tarot.*

Symbolic

The Queen of Cups' beaches mark the convergence of elementals and threshold space. The white cliffs of Dover behind the Queen of Cups is a specific English landmark, marking Pamela and Waite's adopted country. The cliffs are one of England's most recognizable features. The cliffs face the narrowest part of the English Channel, and it is said one can see the French coast from them when weather permits. The cliffs are white because they are made of millions of years of compacted skeletal remains of plankton. These chalky cliffs are soft and malleable, like the emotional state of the Queen of Cups. The cliffs have faced invasions from intruders such as Julius Caesar. They contain hidden tunnels created by the prisoners of Dover Castle and were later converted for the military during World War II. The Queen of Cups placed before this iconic landscape suggests the Strength-like quality of peace and imagination in the face of aggression.

Cherub mermaids decorate her throne and the engraved clamshell behind her head. A clamshell is the clasp on her cape. The mermaid at the base holds a fish in her hand. Each clamshell is the symbol of her zodiacal assignment, Cancer. Mermaids are water creatures containing the power and potency of the sea. The shell is a feminine symbol of beauty and eroticism. Oysters are aphrodisiacs, hiding treasures of the palate deep within their folds. The queen's dress merges into the water, colored blue and green, like the waters that surround her. It is as if she is an apparition dreamed of the ocean itself, a ghostly vision who welcomes all who approach the English empire.

Waite is explicit in his description of the water queen. He states in "The Tarot: A Wheel of Fortune" that "The Queen of Cups signifies love and devotion, the image of which she sees like visions in her vessel." Again Waite is expressing the dreamlike quality of the suit of cups, first with the page, then the knight, and now the queen. All three gaze intently to their cup as if it were a crystal ball. Waite says she is "a perfect spouse" and a "good mother." The cross on her cup reflects the divine act of love intersecting with the material world.

Waite mentions an important quality of this queen: "she sees, but she also acts, and her activity feeds her dream." This indicates a woman who is not content to fantasize or languish in the visions of her mind. She takes action upon her visions. The queen's activity feeds her dreams, propelling them forward into spaces of shimmering possibility. Were she complacent, the dream would repeat in endless cycles. It is the queen's action moving her dream forward. In this sense she becomes the master of the lucid dream, her days spent in activity and her nights spent in creative play space.

· · · · · · ·

Waite's Divinatory Meanings: Good, fair woman; honest, devoted woman, who will do service to the Querent; loving intelligence, and hence the gift of vision; success, happiness, pleasure; also wisdom, virtue; a perfect spouse and a good mother.

Reversed: The accounts vary; good woman; otherwise, distinguished woman but one not to be trusted; perverse woman; vice, dishonour, depravity.

· ·
King of Cups

Book T Title: The Prince of the Chariot of the Waters

Elemental Counterchange: Air (King) of Water (Cups), Prince and Emperor of
    Nymphs or Undines

Astrological: Scorpio (Fixed Water)

> FAR ACROSS THE melancholy seas,
> The silent keepers of the mysteries;
> Met in their crowds upon that haunted ground—
> And we, the King's Sons, waiting to be crown'd.
>
> Arthur Waite, *Collected Poems*

General

The King of Cups is the commander of water, the lord of the ocean, master of the waves. He is the mature masculine energy of emotion. Look to the water and waves undulating around the King of Cups to understand him. The king navigates the ocean's depths and dangers by remaining fluid. He does not seek to control the ocean but maintains a strong center regardless of the placidity or movement of the ocean's tides. The King of Cups understands when to put a limit on emotions. He is free to act regardless of the deep feelings within him. This makes him incredibly effective in all situations. Versed in the mythology of the sea, hidden realms, and aquatic depths, he can be lighthearted and mysterious. As master of tidal waters, his charisma is hypnotizing.

In You

The King of Cups ignites in you when you bring your creative project to fruition, no matter the obstacle, barrier, or cost. He is activated inside of you when you allow compassion and caring to manifest action. The vision of the King of Cups lies in his ability to look dangers in the face and navigate past them. He marks inner strength and perseverance to pass through frightening emotional territory that previously held you hostage. He navigates your true course.

In Others

Consider the role of the great sea gods Roman Neptune and Greek Poseidon. If you lived in ancient times and were dependent on the ocean for your livelihood, travel, or food, you would make many appeals to the ocean gods. In this context, the King of Cups appears in your life as a

· · · · · · ·

KING of CUPS.

figure who will grant you sustenance and may appear as a boss, parental figure, or investor. The person with the capacity to green light a project or trip. The King of Cups is guided by instincts and emotion yet is not controlled nor manipulated by them. It is best to approach such figures honestly and openly. He is often found working in the spotlight for the public good.

Symbolic

The fish pendant around the king's neck, as well as the ocean and sea creatures, connect to the element of water. He wears scaly fish footwear. The tall ship is a symbol of adventure, stories, and risk. The fish monster on the left side is an ancient symbol of myth, danger, and unconscious fear.

Waite reflects in his memoir *Shadows of Life and Thought* a personal sentiment aptly describing the King of Cups:

> Do I remember on my own part looking, when less than two years old, upon an open, tossing sea, through a porthole of a passenger ship? And I so slight and small that well I might have slipped through it and finished for ever—or perchance for the time being—my tale of earthy life. The sea has authentic secrets, some that it gives away, some that it keeps for a few: did I make unbeknown a beginning of learning the code of its ciphers—as it were—then and there?

The King of Cups is he who would decipher the secrets of the sea. He reflects the emotions of the sea for all to understand and interpret.

> **Waite's Divinatory Meanings:** Fair man, man of business, law, or divinity; responsible, disposed to oblige the Querent; also equity, art and science, including those who profess science, law and art; creative intelligence.

> **Reversed:** Dishonest, double-dealing man; roguery, exaction, injustice, vice, scandal, pillage, considerable loss.

PAGE of SWORDS.

. . . .

Page of Swords

Book T **Title:** The Princess of the Rushing Winds, Lotus of the Palace of Air

Elemental Counterchange: Earth (Page) of Air (Swords), Empress of the Sylphs, Throne of the Ace of Swords

Astrological: Season of Spring

> THE SPLENDID CLOUDS about her burn and glow,
> Through liquid gold she glides,
> On purple crests floats bouyant, or below
> Sinks deep in lilac tides.
>
> Arthur Waite, *Collected Poems*

General

The Page of Swords, the youth of air, is a curious spirit. Air is the element of the mind, and she is gifted with a wild intelligence. She carries a supreme willingness to experiment and play. She is dedicated to finding the truth lying at the heart of any situation. No tool is off-limits as she pursues her goal. The Page of Swords displays logic above all other qualities and relies only on her own cunning and instincts. She never takes others at their word until she can uncover the truth for herself. The Page of Swords is a gifted writer who records experiences and keeps concise records. She is meticulous in all areas. The ultimate sleuth, she allows new ideas to take hold, and she will follow them through to the rightful conclusion. Her intense curiosity regarding life and human nature keeps her passionately engaged in solving puzzles and figuring out one mystery after another.

In You

The Page of Swords is the Nancy Drew archetype of the deck. She shows up when you find yourself reading between the lines. She is the deep, searching part of your psyche who longs to figure things out and put details together in order to see the big picture. Have you ever internet sleuthed? That was the Page of Swords at work. She is the youthful part of your psyche containing an innocence and true sense of curiosity. This is the place where you are open to all ideas. She strikes as you become truly perplexed and intrigued by a situation or event. She also reflects your thrill of the hunt as felt during a game of after-dark hide and seek and watching or reading a delicious mystery.

. . . . . .

In Others

The Page of Swords is the smart girl. She's the typical straight-A student who holds herself to high standards. She takes responsibilities seriously and reads books as if each one will unravel the mystery of life. She sees patterns and codes that others miss. The Page of Swords sees the subtext others overlook. She finds the right words and articulates truth clearly and succinctly. The Page of Swords knows you and can tell if you are lying. She is the friend who will call you out when you are being dishonest to yourself or others. She is often found in libraries, on a computer database, or solving a local neighborhood mystery.

Symbolic

Pamela crafts a ragged high mountain landscape to reflect the quality of air. A flock of birds, symbolic of the connection between humanity and the Divine, fly past. The ground almost looks like water beneath her feet, and blooming clouds tower behind her. Her hair blows in the wind and birds pass at high altitude, marking her connection to the higher self. Waite describes her as "swift walking." Just as we can interpret energy by looking at the gait of a knight's horse, the reader can determine the speed by her fast-footed action. The Page's movement suggests if swift action is taken, results will appear. The mystery will be solved.

> **Waite's Divinatory Meanings:** Authority, overseeing, secret service, vigilance, spying, examination, and the qualities thereto belonging.

> **Reversed:** More evil side of these qualities; what is unforeseen, unprepared state; sickness is also intimated.

• • • • • •

. . . .

Knight of Swords

Book T Title: Lord of the Winds and the Breezes, the King of the Spirits of Air

Elemental Counterchange: Fire (Knight) of Air (Swords), King of the Sylphs and Sylphides

Astrological: Gemini (Mutable Air)

MY SOUL IS set upon an endless quest
To span the bounds of being.

* * * * *

Arthur Waite, *Collected Poems*

General

The Knight of Swords carries the fiery, expansive quality of air. He's fast, he's smart, he's dangerous. The Knight of Swords is so carried away with his own thoughts and ideas, he is often an unstoppable force. Cunning and decisive, this intense character is often overtaking you before you realize what is happening. His temper flares quickly, and he'll cut straight through to the heart of the matter at hand. He appears and people scatter. He is the energy and presence others make room for and whom everyone sits up and takes notice of.

In You

The moment you rush to a person, place, or thing's defense, you feel the Knight of Swords operating inside of you. Moments of aggression are marked by his appearance, as well as temporary insensitivity toward other's feelings. He contains your need to control or navigate a situation. He marks tremendous courage and an ability to risk regardless of consequence. He appears in moments of irony meant to assert control over another or to express domination over a situation that you actually have zero control over.

In Others

The Knight of Swords is a flash in the pan. He leaves as quickly as he appears, often leaving people in confusion. His qualities can be shocking when found in others, in the form of quick talking and aggressive behavior. Romantically, he is the ultimate bad boy, James Dean–style. He's smooth talking, fast riding, a fun-loving guy who knows exactly the right thing to say in order to get what he wants. He could be the great protector, appearing just when you need him. He could be a flash-in-your-hot-pan romance or the aggressor who hurls insults.

. . . .

The Sola Busca Knight of Swords (right) looks like Pamela's knight (left) in the very moment before charging full steam ahead.

Symbolic

Waite says in "The Tarot: Wheel of Fortune" that "The Knight of Swords is even as Galahad on the Quest, dispersing the enemies thereof," meaning he represents a legendary knight of King Arthur's Round Table. Knights always reflect offerings and important messages, and their appearance reflects the fluid energy of any situation. The Knight of Sword's horse moves at a breakneck pace, reflecting hasty results. Waite describes his as "riding full course, as if scattering his enemies."

Waite says "he is really a prototypical hero of romantic chivalry," suggesting this knight is the ultimate archetype of the romancing suitor who would fight for his lady's virtue. His armor, a symbol of protection, is covered with butterfly, seagull, and hooded falcons, linking the Knight of Swords to the element of air.

> **Waite's Divinatory Meanings:** Skill, bravery, capacity, defence, address, enmity, wrath, war, destruction, opposition, resistance, ruin. There is therefore a sense in which the card signifies death, but it carries this meaning only in its proximity to other cards of fatality.

> **Reversed:** Imprudence, incapacity, extravagance.

The Queen of Swords from the Sola Busca Tarot.

. . . .

Queen of Swords

Book T **Title:** Queen of the Thrones of Air

Elemental Counterchange: Water (Queen) of Air (Swords), Queen of the Sylphs and Sylphides

Astrological: Libra (Cardinal Air)

WRAP ME, YE Winds,
away to some wild place.

Arthur Waite, *Collected Poems*

General

The Queen of Swords is the goddess of air, queen of the clouds, and mistress of the winds. She expresses a mature intelligence. Her analysis is rarely off the mark. She speaks the truth as she sees it. She reaches her hand out to those who approach. She is the honest and articulate queen whose words, deeds, and actions speak to the heart of any situation. Embodying the feminine nature of intelligence, she is wise and to the point. She tosses all unimportant information and distractions aside. She keeps a full schedule and checks off her to-do list with satisfaction.

In You

The Queen of Swords appears inside you when you address any situation with clarity and poise. She reflects personal power and speaking the mind. The Queen of Swords is activated when a clear strategy is required, when action is needed and plans are to be laid. She reflects you being your own best advocate. The Queen of Swords is inside you when you take personal responsibility for your life, your actions, and attitudes. This queen understands we hold power when we control our inner thoughts. As the keen observer of inner thoughts, she writes the story of her life like a brilliant novelist, and so should you.

In Others

The Queen of Swords shows up as a force to be reckoned with in your life. You may feel equally intimidated and inspired by her presence. She takes herself and her work so seriously it may come as a surprise that she also carries a soft, sensitive side. Her dedication to quality and truth help her stand out from a crowd of mediocrity. She's often the topic of discussion. Her professions include writer, editor, teacher, doctor, psychologist, and the unbeatable lawyer.

. . . .

Symbolic

Waite's definition of widowhood has long haunted this card. It is a reminder of the gender stereotypes plaguing the time when this deck was created. It is almost as if the queen's profile, as sharp as her sword, is somewhat responsible for her aloneness. Waite suggests the Queen of Swords carries "familiarity with sorrow." Who doesn't? He calls her "scarcely a symbol of power" and includes the description of "sterility," which he does not offer to her male counterpart.

The Queen of Sword's crown and throne are decorated with butterflies, a symbol of air. A single bird, the symbol of human and cosmic spirit, soars above her crown, matching her lofty thought. Her cloak is dotted with clouds, matching her background. A cherub's head appears on her throne above the waxing and waning moon, suggesting change is afoot. Her posture emulates the Justice card. Her head is literally above the clouds, demonstrating clear and concise thoughts and actions.

> **Waite's Divinatory Meanings:** Widowhood, female sadness and embarrassment, absence, sterility, mourning, privation, separation.

> **Reversed:** Malice, bigotry, artifice, prudery, bale, deceit.

. . . .

King of Swords

Book T **Title:** Prince of the Chariot of the Winds

Elemental Counterchange: Air (King) of Air (Swords), Prince and Emperor of the Sylphs and Sylphides

Astrological: Aquarius (Fixed Air)

> THE ONE TRUE place for a King's repose,
> And, long though he travel the outward track,
> That the King came forth and the King goes back.

Arthur Waite, *Collected Poems*

General

The King of Swords is master of the air, lord of the sky, and king of the western winds. He is the mature and masculine articulation of mental processes. The inner workings of the King of Swords' mind is responsible for mankind's scientific and mathematic advancement. He is the nature and rule of law and the power of logic in the mind. Like the Queen of Swords, he carries a sensitive side rarely seen by those outside of his inner circle. He states what he wants and has little patience until results are delivered. Above all things, he values truth and will stop at nothing until he receives the results he wants.

In You

The King of Swords operates within you as you work to meet a deadline. It is bold thinking, belief in the task at hand, and the quality of the mind. He represents having the utmost respect and ownership for your inner life, clearly listening to the tremblings inside of you and then making them known. He is a major authority figure, so when you lay down rules and regulations and when you reprimand others, you are activating this king. He's at work when you find just the right words to express yourself and in that beautiful moment when you have the perfect verbal response to a situation.

In Others

Answers come quickly to the King of Swords, who shows up as a boss or father figure. He can be an intellectual and mature lover—the "older man." His professions match the Queen of Swords; doctors, lawyers, and psychologists carry this mindset. The King of Swords also represents the archetypal military man or scientist.

. . . .

KING of SWORDS.

© 1971 U.S. GAMES SYSTEMS, INC.

Symbolic

Waite mentions how, like the Queen of Swords, the king emulates "the conventional Symbol Justice." He adds the King of Swords contains the "power of life and death." It all adds up to quite an imposing figure. His throne carries butterflies, and he has billowing clouds matching the sky along with the rest of his royal sword family.

He sits in judgment, holding the unsheathed sign of his suit. He recalls, of course, the conventional symbol of Justice in the major arcana, and he may represent this virtue, but he is rather the power of life and death, in virtue of his office.

> **Waite's Divinatory Meanings:** Whatsoever arises out of the idea of judgment and all its connexions—power, command, authority, militant intelligence, law, offices of the crown, and so forth.

> **Reversed:** Cruelty, perversity, barbarity, perfidy, evil intention.

· · · · · · ·

PAGE of PENTACLES.

. . . .
Page of Pentacles

Book T **Title:** Princess of the Echoing Hills; Rose of the Palace of Earth

Elemental Counterchange: Earth (Page) of Earth (Pentacles), Princess and Empress of the Gnomes, Throne of the Ace of Pentacles

Astrological: Season of Winter

> IN THOSE MOMENTS, rarely known,
> When the soul feels her wings,
> Emblazoned upon star and stone
> There flash immortal things;
> Through Nature's gates, wide open thrown,
> A wild voice sings and sings.
>
> Arthur Waite, *Collected Poems*

General

The Page of Pentacles, the youth of earth, is beguiled and entranced by everything she sees, feels, touches, and smells in the material world. She studies butterflies and crickets, makes playhouses beneath willow trees, and crafts fairy castles from cool slate stones and damp green moss. She is found in flower fields and deep woods, in mountains and glens. Nothing escapes her watchful eye and curious imagination. Nothing distracts her from earthly delights. The Page of Pentacles is the archetypal student. Once she is absorbed in a subject or book, play or project, nothing distracts her keen and careful attention.

In You

The Page of Pentacles is activated inside you while engaging in sensorial activities. The imagination is activated through tactile sensations such as crafting, painting, cooking, gardening, and activities involving exploration. All sense of "normal time" slips away. Responsibilities and concerns retreat to the background as you immerse yourself in your pleasure. The Page of Pentacles is activated when you are thrown into a new course of study or an engaging exercise regimen. You laser-focus on what lies before you, the ego slips away, and you enter a state of timelessness. Page of Pentacles activities lead to physical and quantifiable results because pentacles reflect the material world. Page of Pentacles results often include a finished creative product or diploma.

. . . . . .

In Others

The Page of Pentacles is a princess type of girl with pockets full of pentacles. She usually has lots of money to purchase her heart's desire. She loves fashion, accessories, and makeup. Don't think she's shallow just because she's quick to grab red lipstick and a designer bag. She is the most grounded of all pages because she connects to the element of earth. She is fascinated by physical transformations in herself and others and is often engaged in sports, movement, and exercise. As a friend, she offers practical advice and down-to-earth conversation. Her energy can be slow and sensate, yet when she sets her sights on a goal, she always fosters success. She can be found daily walking in nature, hiking, and exercising as easily as she is found shopping and cooking. To top it all off, she's an excellent student who pairs perfectly as your study partner. She will always show you something you've never seen before.

Symbolic

The Page of Pentacles stands on an earthen landscape near a plowed field. She holds a pentacle. The pentacle appears like a seed she might plant in the rich farmland behind her and reflects the page's potential for growth and generation. The pointed tip of the right foot demonstrates grace and a gentle touch. The grove of trees in the distant background provides protection, should she need it. The distant mountain peak shows spiritual attainment as evoked by the powers of earth: "as above, so below." The green landscape and yellow sky reflect a warm and nurturing environment. Seeds will germinate. All potentialities are possible.

Waite explains how the Page "moves slowly, insensible of that which is about him." A slow-moving quality is applicable to all pentacle court cards. The quality of earth is slow and steady, not quick like air (swords) or flammable fire (wands). The element will often reflect the energy of the situation at hand. In "The Tarot: A Wheel of Fortune," Waite also describes the page as "looking at a talisman." A talisman is an object or charm whose presence contains a powerful influence on human feelings and actions. The appearance of the Page of Pentacles card suggests it is time for you to discover your own personal talisman. It is time to find a symbol, piece of jewelry, art piece, or new tattoo. The tarot deck operates as a powerful talisman. Waite claims this card "really typifies a scholar" and further expresses the ideal student archetype of this card.

Pamela pulls from her deep knowledge of stage costuming as she fashions the page's clothing. She is wearing a Shakespearean-style tunic and roundlet. A roundlet is "a stuffed roll of cloth joined into a circle, with a long strip of cloth laid across it, a long end hanging down, and a short one standing up in a cockade or drooping. This hat was common in Italy, where also the

Fez-shaped cap (generally red) was worn in the fourteenth century."[59] See the Seven of Swords for the Fez appearance.

> **Waite's Divinatory Meanings:** Application, study, scholarship, reflection another reading says news, messages and the bringer thereof; also rule, management.

> **Reversed:** Prodigality, dissipation, liberality, luxury; unfavourable news.

---

59   http://www.shakespeare-online.com/plays/romeoandjuliet/romeocostumes.html.

· · · · · · ·

KNIGHT of PENTACLES.

. . . .
Knight of Pentacles

Book T **Title:** Lord of the Wild and Fertile Land, King of the Spirits of Earth

Elemental Counterchange: Fire (Knight) of Earth (Pentacles), King of Gnomes

Astrological: Virgo (Mutable Earth)

AND THE EARTH no more is barren: from the seed
A harvest springs, and the whole
land is filled with plenty.

Arthur Waite, *Collected Poems*

General

The Knight of Pentacles is the expansive quality and heavy energy of earth. The Knight of Pentacles is a slow landslide of momentum gathering toward inevitable manifestation. He is the stability of the ground beneath your feet. He brings about needed and lasting change. He is slow, steady, and thoughtful. The Knight of Pentacles listens for things in unexpected places. He senses what people and places need. Physicality is important to this sensual knight who is comfortable in his skin and bones.

In You

The Knight of Pentacles is activated when you act with care. You examine all options before proceeding. He is activated when you attend to worthy work. Worthy work makes your heart sing and your soul happy. It leaves its mark in the world. It could be a garden, a house, a foundation, or a school. He is a natural introvert who gains inspiration from the natural world. You'll activate him during moments when you draw a hot cup of tea close and stare out your window while figuring out a problem or curl up in a hammock under your favorite backyard tree.

In Others

The Knight of Pentacles reflects a slow and deliberate romantic suitor. The pentacle in his hand reflects a gift similar to the Ace of Pentacles, given to you by someone you admire and respect. He is the slow and careful financial planner. He is the farmer that feels the land to determine what he will plant. He is the medical intuitive or talented masseuse who intuitively knows where to move his hands and where to find the pain. He heals.

. . . .

Symbolic

The expansive plowed field behind the Knight of Pentacles reflects the secret of the card. It is the largest planting field in the entire deck and what the knight chooses to plant shall grow to fruition. His brilliant green plume which is a symbol of growth and manifestation reminds us of his generative properties. His nurturing energy brings all things to fruition. Look to the horse's gate on any Knight card to determine the quality and pace of action. His horse matches his master's motion as a slow and steady animal of tremendous strength. The horse, a Clydesdale—who is traditionally used for farming, logging, and carriage pulling—reflects power and steadiness. The horse reflects the energy of the situation at hand is slow moving. The knight's armor is heavy and protective expressing the knight's experience in battle. Waite points out "He exhibits the symbol, but does not look therein." Readers often examine the card and believe he is gazing into the Pentacle. It is the difference between looking at an object or focusing on the object's potential result. According to Waite, the Knight is most concerned with results he can see, feel and touch.

> **Waite's Divinatory Meanings:** Utility, serviceableness, interest, responsibility, rectitude—all on the normal and external plane.

> **Reversed:** inertia, idleness, repose of that kind, stagnation; also placidity, discouragement, carelessness.

. . . .
Queen of Pentacles

Book T **Title:** Queen of the Thrones of Earth

Elemental Counterchange: Water (Queen) of Earth (Pentacles),
   Queen of Gnomes

Astrological: Capricorn (Fixed Earth)

THE DUSK QUEEN waits.
Sustain, sweet mother, Earth.

Arthur Waite, *Collected Poems*

General

The Queen of Pentacles is the queen of earth, goddess of the garden, and mistress of the mountains. As such, she wields power over all that is seen, felt, and touched. Her grace is evident though our sights, sounds, and tastes. Every physical thing is reflected in her eyes, and she represents the beauty of the physical world. Beauty opens the spirit and the soul, like laughter. Beauty resides inside the eye of the beholder. New, challenging, and unique forms of beauty take shape every day. These are the doorways opening new worlds and new possibilities for us. Every flower in a summer garden, every pebble glistening in the surf, and every orange sunset bears her touch.

In You

The Queen of Pentacles is operational within you when you are decorating your apartment, shopping at the market, and cooking dinner. The queen is there as you tidy and clean your house, thus rearranging your personal energy. Theoretically, you rearrange your space and rearrange your world. The Queen of Pentacles is the ultimate homemaker; she's there as you chop, slice, and dice dinner. She's you as you shop at Trader Joe's. She's even there when you order junk food delivered to your front door. She operates over the entire spectrum of health, the body, and self-care.

In Others

The Queen of Pentacles appears when you encounter an individual who dedicates themselves to the physical comfort of others. This nurturing quality shines through while renovating the home and helping out little ones with homework. She may run food pantries and organize

. . . . . .

The Queen of Pentacles from the Sola Busca Tarot.

gift drives and fundraisers, as she is excellent at managing and raising money. She instructs cooking and gardening classes, and she often works as an interior designer or architect.

Symbolic

Waite describes his mother in his memoir *Shadows of Life and Thought*. He does not specifically connect the Queen of Pentacles but he writes of pentacle-like qualities "how above all my Mother—without experience—acquired the art of living in a minute income and yet having food enough, garments for three to wear and rooms that were not slums will not be told on earth." His mother found a way to make everything work despite having little money. This is the hallmark of the Queen of Pentacles.

The Queen of Pentacles is illustrated inside a lush garden. The animalistic symbol of fertility, a bunny rabbit, sits next to her. She could be the Empress, yet she focuses only on the material world while the Empress is the doorway of two worlds. A goat, the symbol for Capricorn, is on the armrest of her throne, and to the right is the figure Pan, half man, half goat, playing his pipes. Pan, a nature god, symbolizes fertility and is the god of wild places, forests, glens, and mountains.

Waite notes the Queen of Pentacles treats her pentacle in opposition to the knight as she "contemplates her symbol and may see worlds therein." These eight simple words hold tremendous magic for those with eyes who want to look deeper. To examine or observe any object, the closer you gaze, the more you will see. Nothing ends at its surface. Placing our attention and focusing on something will allow new worlds to appear and discoveries to be made. It is how a painter looks at a subject or landscape, seeing the colors beneath the colors, the muscles, tendons, and structures beneath the skin. It is how the mystic discovers an entire universe in a single blade of grass. This is how the Queen of Pentacles looks at the world. It is her greatest secret. Now it is yours.

Waite's Divinatory Meanings: Opulence, generosity, magnificence, security, liberty.

Reversed: Evil, suspicion, suspense, fear, mistrust.

KING of PENTACLES.

. . . .
King of Pentacles

Book T **Title:** Prince of the Chariot of Earth

Elemental Counterchange: Air (King) of Earth (Pentacles), Prince and Emperor of the Gnomes

Astrological: Taurus (Fixed Earth)

> AND OVER A thousand changeful turrets and towers,
> The morning glory of heaven blooms over and calls
> To morning glories of earth in a thousand bowers.

Arthur Waite, *Collected Poems*

General

The King of Pentacles is the king of earth, master of money, and ruler of the material world. The King of Earth wields seismic power. He consciously commands each and every molecule of manifestation on the earth. His energy reverberates through caves and caverns; he casts tectonic plates like runes. As the king of manifestation, he is in every growing and every tactile object. He reminds us of the physical power we have over our bodies and the objects in our lives through the choices we make. He is the master of finance and builds kingdoms of security.

In You

The King of Pentacles is activated in you when you take small steps toward accomplishing large goals or massive changes in behavior. The smallest changes often usher the largest consequences. The King of Pentacles, who is slow, methodical, and purposeful, understands this perfectly. He hangs back while others rush foolishly ahead. You also activate this king when financial planning.

In Others

This king looms large, like a Viking: full of power, potency, and fecundity. While he may not be a man of many words, his quick mind is always working underneath the surface. His physical stature makes him ideal for the physical demands of fire fighting, farming, and carpentry. He is the archetypal farmer or winemaker using years of experience and an authentic and intuitive knowledge of the land on which he works.

. . . . . .

Symbolic

Waite mentions the King of Pentacles being "lethargic in tendency," which is a nod to slow-moving, earth-like qualities. He says the "bull's head should be noted as a recurrent symbol on the throne." The bull, four of which are placed on the king's throne and one beneath his foot, is the symbol for Taurus. Bulls were often the sacrificial animal for early agricultural societies as they were highly valued and considered a meaningful offering to the gods. His frock is covered with grapes, and the wall behind him denotes security while the buildings and city suggest commerce and wealth. He appears to grow from nature itself.

Waite is coy when he tells the reader earlier versions of this card deal with money specifically but that "the consensus of divinatory meanings is on the side of some change, because the cards do not happen to deal especially with money." He is not letting on to the fact pentacles reflect the element of earth and the nature of the entire material world.

> **Waite's Divinatory Meanings:** Valour, realizing intelligence, business and normal intellectual aptitude, sometimes mathematical gifts and attainments of this kind; success in these paths.

> **Reversed:** Vice, weakness, ugliness, perversity, corruption, peril.

Yesod (Foundation)
How to Read the Cards

Reading tarot is a lifelong pleasure and practice evolving and growing right alongside you. We each bring all of our beautiful life experiences and unique sensitivities to tarot. We are natural-born storytellers. Read the cards with a quiet, focused mind and a vulnerable heart. Maintain a curiosity allowing your imagination to run wild with the cards.

There really is no difference between a beginner and advanced reader, although the latter will have more experience, knowledge, and familiarity of the cards. Experience and knowledge of tarot can be as much a hindrance as it is helpful. Think of all that we sacrifice as we grow from innocent children into experienced adults. Doesn't the adult often seek their inner child? Don't we struggle to maintain our childlike focus, pleasure, and the ability to live in the present like we did when we were six? Bring your tarot deck to a child. Have them pick a card, and ask them to tell you a story about what they see on the card. I guarantee you will be stunned, if not thrilled, by the tale and insight they will weave for you. (This is also an excellent technique to use if you are reading tarot for party guests and a child approaches your table.)

It may feel overwhelming when you first begin reading tarot. Allow yourself to feel whatever emotion rises to the surface. Let it pass. Then get to the business of reading the cards. Tarot is the story of you. Tarot is the greatest novel you will ever read. Tarot is the infinite story reflecting every facet of your being. Tarot changes moment by moment, just as you do. The cards want you to project yourself all over them. When you are done projecting yourself onto the cards, turn to the scholarly tarot books whispering the history and usage of the cards. Use everything you can to gain knowledge and comfort with the deck.

There's no right or wrong way to use and learn the cards. Sign up for classes, read source material, and practice the cards on your friends like crazy. Trust me, everyone *loves* to have their cards read, even when you are first starting out. Why? Because everyone's favorite subject is themselves. Your friends and family will be lining up for practice readings from you. Volunteer to read cards at events and local fundraisers for practice. Take your cards into nature and pull for messages from trees and flowers. Play games by finding cards matching up best with the people in your life. Select a deck and write the meanings of the cards yourself as if you were authoring a book on tarot. Whatever and however you choose to work with the deck, the most important part is to have fun and keep exploring. This will keep you coming back to the cards again and again.

Arthur Waite gives excellent advice on the art of card reading in *The Pictorial Key*:

Notes on the Practice of Divination
1. Before beginning the operation, formulate your question definitely, and repeat it aloud.
2. Make your mind as blank as possible while shuffling the cards.
3. Put out of the mind personal bias and preconceived ideas as far as possible, or your judgment will be tinctured thereby.
4. On this account it is more easy to divine correctly for a stranger than for yourself or a friend.

. . . .
Card-a-Day Practice

A card-a-day practice is a simple, single five-minute activity. It will teach you almost everything you want to know about the cards. Many consider it to be one of the most pleasurable tarot activities. Cartomancers often continue a card-a-day practice over the course of a lifetime. Anyone can pull a daily card; no knowledge of tarot is required. It can be performed at any time of day but morning is preferable. Some pull it with morning coffee or tea, others pull the card before or after a yoga practice, some pull a card before a morning walk or commute. Pull in any way your heart desires.

To perform a card-a-day reading, clear your mind and shuffle your cards. You are free to ask a question such as "What should I pay attention to today?" or keep your mind clear and simply wait to see what appears. Keeping the mind clear is a fun way to pull your daily card because it leaves your consciousness open to impressions. You can shuffle the deck any way you like.

Flip your card and scan the card completely, without making any value judgments. Note the first element, shape, or symbol that makes an impression on you. Create meaning out of this. For example, say you flip the Seven of Cups and your attention is drawn to the silhouette of the man. You may decide that today will feel like a dark day where you are absorbing the things around you without reacting to them, simply watching.

Once you have selected your card, you may keep it out and available to you, placing it in a frame on your desk or pulling the image as the screensaver of your phone. You may put the

. . . .

card to the side and forget about it. It is up to you. A single important action remains to complete the card-a-day practice: revisit the card at the end of your day.

Check out the card again during the evening or at bedtime. Did what you intuited seem to happen? Did it play out? Did something surprising happen in relation to the card? This is also a great time to look up the card in books, find some different meanings, and do a bit of research, comparing it all to the experience you had. You may want to journal your findings or record them in some way.

Don't be surprised if intuitive pops happen one day and a psychic flash comes another day. I recall in the early days of my card-a-day practice, the Knight of Swords appeared. I knew in a flash that the knight reflected an old friend whom I hadn't heard from in a while. I knew looking at the card he would call that day, though we had nothing scheduled. Indeed, he called me later in the afternoon. I was beside myself with excitement for seeing it in the card.

That was the only time the Knight of Swords reflected that particular friend. This brings me to a really important point. There is no right or wrong meaning for a tarot card. In fact, the cards hold infinite meanings. How can this be? Because they were created by the human mind, used by the human mind, and are infinite like the human mind. Does each card hold a traditional meaning? Absolutely. And a serious reader should learn what these meanings are, especially the major arcana cards, which are grounded in archetypes. These are essential for you to examine and explore. But the important work comes from applying your own personal experience to each of the cards. Plus, you don't know how psychic or intuitive you have the potential to become—or maybe you do. Stay open to all experiences.

The structure of tarot will teach you about the elements that make up your body and soul and the universe around you. Their repeating numerical patterns teach you to live in sync with life's cycles from sunrise to sunset, from season to season, and from one year to the next. The closer you listen and pay attention to tarot's structure, the more you'll learn about yourself and your life. Tarot teaches us that nothing is permanent. Life is a state of constant flux and change because the Fool keeps moving from card to card. Every morning is a new chance to pull a card. This newness resides in every second of our lives. This lesson is a true gift.

Working with tarot inadvertently fosters a meditative mindset. Whether you have attempted meditation or never tried it, the act of clearing the mind and pulling cards is the first step in a powerful tool to be used in any number of ways. Trust me when I tell you you'll see a difference in your life after pulling a card a day for about six months, especially if you are doing so in conjunction with a specific question, such as "What can I focus on to find contentment" or "What can I do to find the ideal career?" Answers will come to you, but the answers are not from the cards. They come from you. Tarot is an incredible tool to use to learn about yourself.

• • • • • •

Meditation into the cards is an excellent way to learn about the tarot. To meditate and explore a tarot card, calm the mind and body and focus on the image, committing it to memory as best you can. Once you firmly have the card in your mind's eye, close your eyes and see the card in your imagination. Move into the card. This can happen in any way you like: you may walk, fly, or hop into the card; it is your experience. Feel free to talk to the characters or creatures on the cards and investigate the environment. What advice does the Queen of Pentacles offer you? What does her voice sound like? Listen to any sounds or music playing. Do you hear the river's water in the Six of Swords? Does the Wheel of Fortune make noise as it spins? Are you haunted by the howling of the Moon's animals? Note anything you feel on your body. Does the Fool card's alpine wind chill your skin? Is the Ace of Wands hot to touch? Note any particular smell that greets you. Does the Empress card smell like a rich summer wheat field? Are the Magician's roses and lilies fragrant? You can ask these questions and make these investigations by simply looking at the actual card, but to bring in image inside of you will result in a richer and lasting experience.

. . . .

Tarot's Structure

The easiest way to begin reading the cards is to understand the tarot's basic structure and what the structure means when certain cards appear in a reading. As stated in the first chapter, it turns out that tarot's structure is a triad with three important variables: the major arcana, the minor arcana, and the court cards. It is important to distinguish the difference between these three sections and what they imply when they appear in a reading.

The major arcana is the twenty-two cards carrying major archetypes. An archetype is a recurring symbol or typical example of something that is cross-culturally recognizable. The Empress as a mother figure or the Lovers are easy-to-grasp examples. These archetypes mean something in each of our lives and either represent situations, people, or qualities within ourselves. When a major arcana card shows up, it reflects a major life moment. Only twenty-two of the seventy-eight cards are majors. The rest of the deck aligns with a regular pack of playing cards.

A minor arcana card reflects our daily lives. These are the ins and outs and ups and downs of regular day-to-day life. Typically they hold lesser weight than the trump cards, which is another name for the majors. Minor arcana cards run from ace to the number ten and often show where we are in the current life or emotional cycle.

Yoga Studio Example

A simple way to understand the difference among the major and minor arcana cards is to imagine yourself in a yoga studio. There you are on a purple mat in a zen studio, ready for class. The poses you perform as you move through the yoga sequence—mountain pose, down dog, and cobra—those poses are all like the major arcana. They are the ultimate form of yogic movement and reflect the archetypes of Mountain, Dog, and Snake. The instructor usually comes around and makes adjustments as students practice. These adjustments align with the minor arcana. The minor arcana are the small, daily things we do that may not mean much individually but when added up produce big results. And just like an adjustment, a minor arcana moment has a way of opening us up in a new way that has big impact down the line.

High School Example

A second easy way to understand the differences between majors and minors is to think of high school. The major cards are those really big events you look back and remember, like prom or graduation or what the first day of high school felt like. The minors are random days where stuff happened but they didn't really stick out in your memory. Still, collectively, those days made up your entire high school experience.

Court Cards

If majors are big events and minors are daily activities, then the court cards are the people who populate your big event and daily happenings. These are the students, teachers, and parents filling your school. Court cards are the instructors and fellow yogis filling up your favorite exercise studio. Since court cards can reflect other people and they also reflect aspects of your own personality, it is up to you, the reader, to figure out who and what the court cards represent. Identifying who court cards are talking about in a spread comes with practice. At first you might feel like you are guessing, but trust your instincts, and soon you'll be able to pinpoint exactly who they are.

Cheat Sheet for Your Court Cards

Pages: Youthful, innocent, playful energy

Knights: Teen male energy

Queens: Mature female energy

Kings: Mature male energy

. . . .
Hidden Gifts of Tarot

Tons, piles, oceans of hidden gifts are tucked away inside the tarot, especially when tarot becomes a lifelong practice. Like any practice you devote time to, it becomes deeper and more meaningful over time. The wonderful thing about tarot is that is doesn't take long to shuffle and pull a single card every day. It can begin with a simple daily five-minute practice.

Tarot takes issues, problems, and scenarios out of your mind and spreads the issues across the table. We can feel overwhelmed by the things we mull over in our head. Once we formulate a question and begin to pull cards, we can look at our issues from a bird's-eye view. This distance can bring a great deal of clarity to our issues and concerns.

Tarot will teach you about the difference between intuition and psychic ability, two distinctly separate things. Intuition is an innate knowing, like a voice inside you or a sense of where you should go or what decision to make. Intuition will guide you through all your tarot readings and acts like the subtle voice in your head telling you what symbol to focus on or what the card is trying to tell you. Psychic facilities are a different form of knowing and will happen when outside information enters the inside of the body. Psychic facilities occur in different ways for different people.

It is worth the time and energy it takes to understand how your body is psychically, intuitively, and sensorially built. Each one of us feels the world around us in different ways. Psychic and intuitive facilities are akin to our sexual and sensual nature. Each of us responds differently to stimuli. Learning how we operate intuitively means that we are getting to know who we really are. The exciting part comes when we identify an opening in our intuitive psychic body that we wish to explore and develop. Artists do this in studio art classes where they paint or draw a still life or model. Focusing on their subject, they develop their artist sense of "seeing" deeper. A musician does this through music rehearsal as they move deeper and deeper, forging a relationship between music and their chosen instrument. You can do this with your very own body, using tarot as a catalyst. The path of exploring yourself and your abilities never ends; the deeper and wider you go, the more it expands because you are an extraordinary universe in and of yourself. And you, like the universe, are infinite—as above, so below.

Determine and explore for yourself how you operate. Even if what you are experiencing makes no sense, it is important to explore it. Don't rush to put labels on what you experience, but move through them. Record your experiences in a journal or confide in a like-minded friend or colleague. Often, supernatural or psychic experiences are well expressed through poetry, as often the act of articulating the experience dumbs the experience down. Language can be a gift and a curse. Play with words to express and record your experiences.

. . . .

Clairvoyance is described as seeing an image or picture in the head. This includes premonitions. Clairaudience is the ability to hear messages but without actually using your ears. This may come in the form of your own inner voice or the voice of others. It may also come as a deeper form of hearing and intuiting sounds on other levels of reality. Clairalience is the ability to smell scent outside the natural world, such as detecting the scent of a relative or friend who has passed to the other side. Clairgustance relates to smelling a supernatural scent; however, it is the ability to taste a flavor, giving us information without actually eating or tasting anything. Claircognizance is the ability to know something without knowing why you know it. Of all psychic abilities, this one is linked closely with intuition, and it may be hard to separate the two.

Empathy and clairsentience are two of the most experienced psychic phenomena. They include the ability to feel what other people are feeling simply by being near them. Discovering you carry empathic abilities can be confusing because empaths often mistake other people's feelings and emotions for their own. To be alive is to participate in the act of giving and receiving energy. Feelings and emotions are part and parcel to energy give-and-take. Tarotists, especially when they read for others, directly confront how they give and receive the energy.

In addition to noting the difference between psychic and intuitive abilities, it is worth noting the difference between intuition and associative memory. Intuition and associative memory are often confused. Intuition is a deep and innate knowing while associative memory is mental conditioning. An associative memory example can be understood by thinking of a stop sign while driving. The associative memory links the visual of a stop sign to the braking of your car. Once learned, this behavior happens automatically. This is not intuitive knowing; it is associative learning. Associative memory is a helpful mental tool allowing us to perform a variety of tasks without having to stop and think about them. However, the associative memory also operates in our value judgments and independent projections. At the worst end of the associative memory spectrum, this is where racism and hatred or dangerous and reactive behavior is learned. On the lighter end of the spectrum, it can be where the individual decides what a situation, person, or thing is based on prior experience rather than taking the time to explore the situation, person, or thing in the moment. The tarotist should be aware of the difference between associative memory and intuition because intuition springs from deep within personal authenticity. The intuition should not be lumped in with value judgments. Learning to identify and separate these behaviors is a fascinating process and leads to a richer experience of life and its possibilities. Thank you, tarot!

· · · · · ·

. . . .
How to Form Good Tarot Questions

Humans possess the spectacular ability to imagine and dream. Once a vision, fantasy, or idea is experienced, thought, and felt, the next step always comes in question form: How do I make that happen? When it comes to forming an excellent question for tarot or for anything you want, there is a little-known secret. *The power lies in the question, not the answer.*

How can this be? It seems like the power lies in getting what you want, and everyone obviously wants what they want. However, it is basic human nature to move to the next question as soon as the immediate question is answered. The brain is given a question; its automatic reaction is to find the answer and move to the next question like a game of leap frog. Our needs may be satisfied but the brain is already looking to solve the next hurdle or puzzle. This is what keeps our lives evolving. Smart and thoughtful questions move us faster in the direction we'd like to go. This is why creating a thoughtful question is of paramount importance and fills life with extraordinary possibility and richness.

Avoid any question beginning with "why" or "when." Asking a question like "When will I fall in love?" is one of the worst sorts of questions because it causes your brain to cave in. It leaves no room for the brain to explore and discover a satisfying answer that will set you on the path for receiving or obtaining what you want.

Thoughtful questions acknowledge the personal power you possess over your future actions. They put your brain in the driver's seat. Powerful questions often begin with the words "what" or "how." They set you up for an answer you can take action on. They actually trick your brain into productivity. Instead of asking "When will I fall in love?" ask "How can I cultivate an amazing romantic relationship?" The answer you glean from a tarot card will tell you how you can cultivate it.

Thoughtful Question Construction

1. Acknowledge the role you play in your future.

2. State your desired outcome in the question.

3. Construct the question.

4. Ask the question every day until your desire, idea, or passion is satiated.

Example

Holly is a casting director who is generally happy in her life, love, and career. However, she feels creatively stymied. While she enjoys her job, loves the talented actors who walk through her door, and enjoys her success, she has risen as far as she can go in her profession. She feels something is lacking. She knows there is something else that will make her happy and deeply

. . . .

satisfy her in a creative way. Perhaps it is a new job or maybe a hobby. She considers moving to a new city. She honestly doesn't know what it is that is missing, but she is aware something is lacking. Holly's life is filled to the brim with a super busy schedule. She has little time to explore creative options. She decides to create a thoughtful question for her tarot cards. She makes it a point to ask her question every day over her morning tea. She knows once she creates a thoughtful question and spends a few minutes daily with her question that her deck will eventually reveal her path.

Holly understands she plays a direct role in her future. She deliberates over how to state her desired outcome by listing what she wants on a sheet of paper. Holly is aware of three specific things she desires: (1) she seeks creative fulfillment; (2) she desires a lifestyle affording plenty of time for her to enjoy her passions; and (3) Holly wants to give back to others through her work and make a real difference in people's lives.

Holly constructs her question: "How can I fulfill myself creatively while having more than enough money for an enjoyable lifestyle and, in the process, give back to others?" She is off and running, and she receives her answer faster than she ever imagines.

It is human nature to repeat patterns. Nature's patterns repeat, habits repeat, lessons repeat, and our questions repeat. A tarot practice teaches us the value of repetition as we greet cards again and again. Tarot's structure repeats as the Fool makes his run from the Magician to the World only to cycle through and begin again. He runs from the ace to the ten and back again for another loop. He never slows, never stops. He repeats and repeats ad infinitum.

If you want something new, if you want to change something, if you want to create a new possibility, repeat your questions until they are answered. Ask your questions every day at the same time because repetition is helpful. Ask your questions over coffee, in the shower, when you turn on your car. Ask your tarot deck every day. Ask these questions as if your life depends on it because, honestly, it does.

How you form your questions is the most important part of the practice. Why? Because the question is what organizes the mind. A good question tricks your mind into finding the best answer. Once a question is unrolled, it is the nature of the supercomputer brain inside our heads to figure out the answer.

· ·

Reversals

Reversals are the name for cards appearing upside down. Readers should develop the habit of flipping cards from the top of their deck as if flipping the pages of a book: from left to right. It doesn't matter how the reader shuffles. If and when they decide to read reversals, the reader will know for sure if the card is reversed.

· · · · · · ·

Reversals may be used in any number of ways:

Ignored: The reader should ignore a reversal when they are first learning to read the cards. The reader is never required to read a reversed card as a reversal. In fact, many readers ignore reversed cards altogether. This is especially advisable when a reader is first learning the cards, especially if they find reversals confusing.

Opposite Meaning: Traditional divination says to read a card's opposite meaning if it appears reversed. Waite's own divinatory reversals hold close to this idea. Oppositional meaning tends to become inadvertently moralistic. If the reader considers any card "good," they may be tempted to read its reversal as "bad." Life is simply not that cut-and-dried. Naming an experience good or bad before it is explored will shut down possibility, especially in a reading. Better to read reversals with subtle nuance or not at all.

Blocked Energy: Often a reversal can mean the essence of the card is blocked. In this case, decide on a course of action that will set the energy free.

Cards Requiring Extra Attention: Reversals, especially in spreads containing a large number of cards, can become part of the pattern of the spread. They can scream out to the reader, "Hey, look at me!"

. . . .
How to Become the Best Possible Reader

Practice, practice, practice!

. . . .
Pamela Colman Smith's Stage Cards

The Rider-Waite-Smith deck contains a beguiling mystery. Pamela created fifteen cards in the deck holding unique attributes. These thirteen cards stand out from the remaining sixty-five cards she designed because each card is drawn as if the characters are standing upon a stage. These are called "stage cards." The characters stand on smooth flooring, indicative of a stage. A flat, scrim-like backdrop appears with a painted scene. Each stage card bears a double horizontal line marking the spot where scrim meets stage.

Stage cards include:

- Two of Swords

- Five of Swords

- Seven of Swords

. . . .

- Four of Wands

- Nine of Wands

- Ten of Wands

- Two of Cups

- Five of Cups

- Eight of Cups

- Ten of Cups

- Page of Cups

- Two of Pentacles

- Four of Pentacles

- Six of Pentacles

- Eight of Pentacles

Pamela had a professional background and deep love for the theater. Her tarot cards clearly are inspired by the characters and sets of her prized miniature theater. Pamela's theater and costume design experience fostered a deck that could be as universally used and loved as Shake-speare's *Romeo and Juliet*. Each reader can place herself in the context of each card. Pamela's illustrations provide ample space for universality and personal projection.

It's not curious or surprising that Pamela crafted stage cards. The looming question is why only fifteen? Did Pamela begin with designing these cards and then switch midway? Why four pentacles, three wands, three cups, and three swords? Why a single court card? The numbers do not match. Numerologically they do not add up to any spectacular result.

It is conceivable that as Pamela began illustrating the minor arcana, she began to sketch each card as appearing on her miniature stage. Indeed, three of the stage cards are numbered two. She may have switched her style and wished to construct fluid cards in entire environments without the impediment of staging. The eloquent Six of Swords with boatman, river, and pas-sengers or quiet Eight of Cups would have suffered terribly had she been forced to adhere to perimeters of staging.

While we may never know why thirteen stage cards exist, we can use them to inform our readings. We can use their appearance for an additional twist and questions when they appear in a reading.

· · · · · ·

How to Interpret a Stage Card

Examine what the word *stage* means. A stage is a period of time we move through, like the stage of childhood. A stage is a horse-drawn carriage, a stage coach, and therefore a vehicle of movement similar to the Chariot card. Universally, a stage is a platform for entertainment, be it a play, musical, dance, concert, opera, award ceremony, political speech, or presentation. Using the latter definition, we can imbue the stage card's appearance with meaning and extra questions when it appears in a reading.

There are three ways to participate in a stage performance:

1. Audience member (observer)

2. Performer

3. Creative (creator/composer/playwright of the piece)

When a stage card appears in a reading, identify if you are:

1. The observer of the situation? (audience member)

2. Playing along in someone else's game/story? (performer)

3. The creator of the situation? (composer, writer, creative)

Once you determine what role you play in the situation at hand, ask yourself the following questions according to the role you chose:

1. If you are the observer:

   - What am I waiting for?
   - Is this amusing or damaging?
   - Is the price I'm paying worth it?
   - What am I learning?

2. If you are playing along in someone else's drama:

   - Am I trying to gain attention?
   - Is a catharsis coming?
   - Do I care too much about what others think?
   - Am I people pleasing and at what cost?
   - Am I expressing myself?

3. If you are the source of the situation/drama:

- Why am I creating this?

- Am I purposefully manipulating events?

- How does this match up to the internal story in my head?

- Is this what I want?

- What am I learning?

Feel free to examine what would happen if you were to switch roles.

. . . .

FAQs

I'm afraid to get the card wrong. What should I do?

Nothing shuts down a tarot reading like fear of "getting it wrong." Tarot is a tool. Tools are meant to be used. Feel your fear (if it pops up) and let it pass. Flip and read your cards with an open, curious mind. You'll be surprised at all the wisdom you glean!

What gives tarot its power?

You do. Tarot's power begins and ends with the person using it. The cards are useless alone. People who fear the cards or believe the cards hold mysterious power also funnel collective energy into tarot because ideas and attention contain power.

Do I need special powers to read tarot?

No.

Do I need to be psychic to read tarot?

Nope. However, tarot offers the practitioner an excellent way to hone their sensual, psychic, and sensorial skills. You see, everyone is born with different sensitivities. Each of us unique. Tarot opens up the space of exploration. Tarot tests us. What do we know? Why do we know it? Where is the information coming from? Just as yoga or dance teaches us what is physically possible, tarot opens the creative imagination to inner landscapes.

Does someone have to give me my first deck as a gift?

Nope. That's an old wives' tale that no longer serves its purpose.

. . . . . .

Chapter Nine

Is tarot evil?

Is a gun evil or is it the person who uses it? Tarot consists of seventy-eight paper cards printed with colorful images—nothing evil there.

Does the Death card mean physical death?

No. Tarot is meant to be read metaphorically.

Do I have to do what the tarot says?

You don't have to do anything you don't want to do. Tarot will never tell you to do anything. Tarot reflects possibilities, suggestions, and ideas you may not have thought of. It offers confirmation, clarity, and creative reaction to any situation encountered in life. Because tarot does not operate on a literal level, it will never tell you to do something.

How do I know what a card means?

Every tarot card holds a bottomless meaning of interpretation. Here's how you can cycle through it, in order of importance:

1. Your instinctual, intuitive reaction to a symbol.

2. A historical, spiritual, or scholarly definition.

3. You are a natural-born storyteller; we all are. Let the cards tell you a story, and discover where you identify with it.

What spread I should use if I am a beginner?

A single card is always effective, concise, and to the point. Pulling a single card will avoid confusion. The three-card spread can indicate past/present/future or hindsight/insight/foresight.

How should I shuffle?

You can shuffle any way you like. There is no right or wrong way to shuffle as long as your cards are good and mixed. You can shuffle Vegas-style or simply mix them around on a table like card soup.

Do I need to be psychic?

Not at all. However, do not be surprised if you discover hidden talents while reading the cards.

· · · · · · ·

CHAPTER TEN

Malkuth (Kingdom)

78 Spreads

The following tarot spreads have been created out of a simple formula:

1. The theme of each spread is inspired by a single RWS tarot card.

2. The questions of each spread are based on specific symbols found inside that particular card.

3. The shape of each spread is inspired by a graphic found on each card.

The major arcana spreads have quotes from Arthur Waite's *Pictorial Key* to accompany them.

Reader's Choice

You are free to remove the card each spread is based on and keep it in sight during your reading. This will help you gain entrance and knowledge of the card. Alternately, you may choose the card from a separate deck so you always shuffle with a full deck for these readings. If the card inspiring the spread appears in the spread, it will take on heightened meaning.

· · · · · · ·

· ·

The Fool "Optimism Through Adversity" Spread

With light step, as if earth and its trammels had little power to restrain him, a young man in gorgeous vestments pauses at the brink of a precipice among the great heights of the world; he surveys the blue distance before him-its expanse of sky rather than the prospect below. The edge which opens on the depth has no terror; it is as if angels were waiting to uphold him, if it came about that he leaped from the height. His countenance is full of intelligence and expectant dream.[60]

Cast your cards to invoke the Fool's optimism no matter what energy surrounds you.

1. Bag—What do I carry with me from the past?

2. White Rose—What has yet to blossom?

3. Dog—What do my animal instincts compel me to do?

4. Cliff—What am I risking?

5. Brink—What do I risk by not stepping forward?

6. Air—What helps me to think clearly?

7. Direction—Where should I head?

8. Posture—What simple message brings me forward?

60   Waite, *Pictorial Key.*

· · · · · · ·

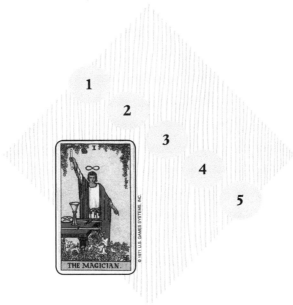

The Magician "Power Generation" Spread

In the Magician's right hand is a wand raised towards heaven, while the left hand is pointing to the earth. This dual sign is known in very high grades of the Instituted Mysteries; it shews the descent of grace, virtue and light, drawn from things above and derived to things below. The suggestion throughout is therefore the possession and communication of the Powers and Gifts of the Spirit.[61]

Cast your cards to invoke the Magician's magical ability. The cards follow the shape of his energetic flow.

1. Upward Hand—What is my purpose?

2. Downward Hand—Where do my talents lie?

3. Suits on Table—What tools are at my fingertips?

4. Snake Belt—How can I use myself as an instrument of the greatest good?

5. Posture—How do I allow divine energy/light/power to flow through me?

61   Waite, *Pictorial Key.*

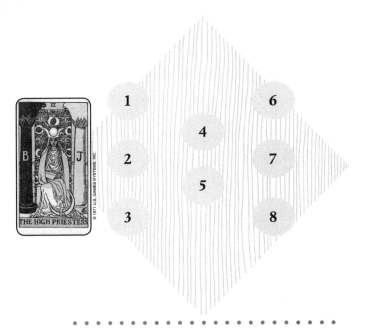

The High Priestess "Inner Knowledge" Spread

In a manner, she is also the Supernal Mother herself—that is to say, she is the bright reflection. It is in this sense of reflection that her truest and highest name in bolism is *Shekinah*—the co-habiting glory....Mystically speaking, the *Shekinah* is the Spiritual Bride of the just man, and when he reads the Law she gives the Divine meaning. There are some respects in which this card is the highest and holiest of the Greater Arcana.[62]

The High Priestess knows everything about you. Cast your cards to gain her inner knowledge. This spread imitates the High Priestess and her two outer pillars.

1. Triple Crown—What is evolving?

2. Book/Scroll—What do I know?

3. Dress—What covers me?

4. Cross—What is the nature of reality?

5. Veil—What is hidden?

6. Pomegranate—What is growing?

7. Water—What moves through me?

8. Moon—What is illusion?

62 Waite, *Pictorial Key.*

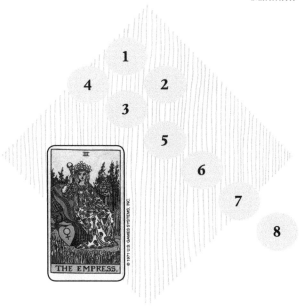

The Empress "Love and Evolution" Spread

The Empress signifies the door or gate by which an entrance is obtained into this life, as into the Garden of Venus; and then the way which leads out therefrom, into that which is beyond, is the secret known to the High Priestess: it is communicated by her to the elect.[63]

Cast your cards to experience and invoke love and evolution. The cards form the shape of her scepter.

1. Symbol of Venus—What do I love?

2. Wheat—How do I nurture others?

3. Waterfall—What emotion is flowing?

4. Zodiac Crown—Who am I?

5. Scepter—What power do I wield?

6. Throne—What stability do I maintain?

7. Hidden Pregnancy—What is being born?

8. Pomegranates—What fertile grounds await?

63   Waite, *Pictorial Key.*

. . . .
The Emperor "Stability" Spread

He is executive and realization, the power of this world, here clothed with the highest of its natural attributes… He is the virile power, to which the Empress responds, and in this sense is he who seeks to remove the Veil of Isis; yet she remains *virgo intacta*.[64]

Cast your cards to invoke the Emperor's stability in the shape of a square.

1. Throne—What is the stability I have created?

2. Bulls—What gives me strength?

3. Ankh—What is eternal?

4. Ball—What am I exuding that will come back around?

5. Crown—How to I connect with divinity?

6. River—How do I remain emotionally resilient?

7. Mountain Range—How can I lift my vision higher?

8. Armor—How can I protect myself while staying open?

64   Waite, *Pictorial Key.*

. . . .

The Hierophant "Grace" Spread

He is rather the *summa totius theologiæ*, when it has passed into the utmost rigidity of expression; but he symbolizes also all things that are righteous and sacred on the manifest side. As such, he is the channel of grace belonging to the world of institution as distinct from that of Nature, and he is the leader of salvation for the human race at large. He is the order and the head of the recognized hierarchy, which is the reflection of another and greater hierarchic order.[65]

How does Grace appear in your life? Cast your cards in the shape of the Hierophant and his two disciples to find out.

1. Hand Gesture—What blessings do I give to others?

2. Triple Cross Staff—How is my fate, fortune and destiny connected?

3. Triple Crown—Where does my authority lie?

4. Cloak—What protects me?

5. Dual Keys—What doors does my knowledge unlock?

6. Pillars—What is truth?

7. Double Clerics—Who can I count on for support?

8. Slippers—What keeps me grounded?

65   Waite, *Pictorial Key*.

• •

The Lovers "Mountain" Spread

This is in all simplicity the card of human love.[66]

Examine aspects of passionate love with a spread inspired by the Lovers card's mountain.

    1. Nudity—What makes me comfortable in my own skin?

    2. Sun—Is this relationship worth the effort?

    3. Angel—What does love teach me?

    4. Snake—What mistake can I avoid making?

    5. Apple—What do I have working in my favor?

    6. Fire—How can I keep our passion alive?

    7. Mountain—How high will we climb together?

66   Waite, *Pictorial Key.*

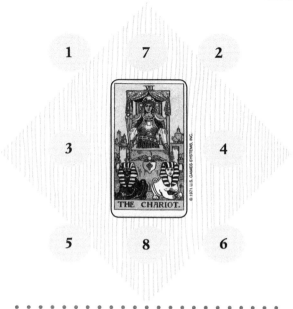

• • • • • • • • • • • • • • • • • • • •
The Chariot "Progression" Spread

He has led captivity captive; he is conquest on all planes—in the mind, in science, in progress, in certain trials of initiation.[67]

Cast your cards to move in the best direction possible. The spread is shaped like a stage or the Chariot's coach.

1. Lunar Breastplates—What is changing?

2. Crown—How do I remain above the fray?

3. Laurel—How will I be victorious?

4. Sphinxes—What are my choices?

5. Curtains—What should I keep close to the vest?

6. Carriage Column—Where is my stability?

7. Winged Symbol—How do I fly?

8. City—What will I build?

67   Waite, *Pictorial Key.*

• • • • • •

383

Strength "Fortitude" Spread

Fortitude, in one of its most exalted aspects, is connected with the Divine Mystery of Union; the virtue, of course, operates in all planes, and hence draws on all in its symbolism. It connects also with *innocentia inviolata*, and with the strength which resides in contemplation.[68]

Cultivate inner and outer fortitude by casting your cards in the shape of Strength's lemniscate.

1. Female—How can I be both vulnerable and strong?

2. Lion—What do my instincts tell me?

3. Lemniscate—How can I expand my thinking?

4. Hand Gesture—How can I be gentle with others?

5. Garland Belt—Where should I place a boundary?

6. White Gown—How can I bring peace to my inner world?

7. Mountain—What is the long term aspiration?

8. Yellow Background—How can I access creative
   solutions and responses at every turn?

68   Waite, *Pictorial Key.*

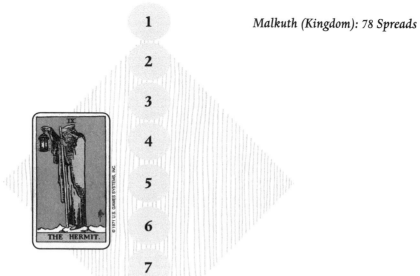

· ·

The Hermit "Wisdom" Spread

The Divine Mysteries secure their own protection from those who are unprepared.[69]

Gain Hermit-like wisdom by casting your cards in the shape of the Hermit's staff.

1. Cloak—How do I remain still?

2. Staff—What helps me move forward?

3. Lantern—How do I protect sacred knowledge?

4. Star—How can I spread inspiration?

5. Mountain Range—What challenge do I face?

6. Mountain Top—What challenge will I overcome?

7. Beard—What wisdom do I possess?

8. Age—What have I learned?

69   Waite, *Pictorial Key.*

· · · · · · ·

Wheel of Fortune "Destiny" Spread

The symbolic picture stands for the perpetual motion of a fluidic universe and for the flux of human life. The Sphinx is the equilibrium therein. The transliteration of Taro as Rota is inscribed on the wheel, counterchanged with the letters of the Divine Name—to show that Providence is implied through all.[70]

Cast your cards in the shape of a wheel to align with the winds of fate, fortune, and destiny.

1. Wheel—Where is natural energy moving me?

2. Sphinx—What is the riddle I must solve?

3. Serpent—What is exiting?

4. Jackal—What is rising?

5. Lion (Leo)—Where do I need to be strong?

6. Ox (Taurus)— Where should I be steadfast?

7. Person (Aquarius)—Where should I be compassionate?

8. Eagle (Scorpio)—What must take flight?

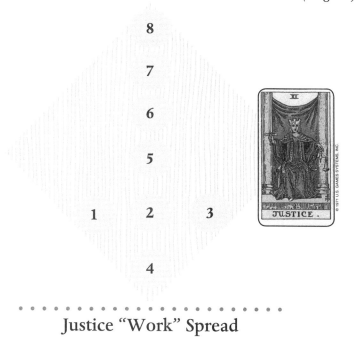

- -

Justice "Work" Spread

The operation of this is like the breathing of the Spirit where it wills, and we have no canon of criticism or ground of explanation concerning it. It is analogous to the possession of the fairy gifts and the high gifts and the gracious gifts of the poet: we have them or have not, and their presence is as much a mystery as their absence.[71]

Cast your cards in the shape of Justice's sword to gain insight on your work, career, and life path.

1. Double-Edged Sword—What duality must I embrace?

2. Scales—Are my actions balanced?

3. Hanging Veil—What is hidden?

4. Crown—What do I know beyond a shadow of a doubt?

5. Throne—What action can I take toward security?

6. Slipper Pointing Out—How can I move in the right direction?

7. Lack of Blindfold—What do I need to see that's right in front of me?

8. Yellow and Gold Colors—What specific action should I take next?

71   Waite, *Pictorial Key.*

- - - - - -

The Hanged Man "Mystic Vision" Spread

It should be noted (1) that the tree of sacrifice is living wood, with leaves thereon; (2) that the face expresses deep entrancement, not suffering; (3) that the figure, as a whole, suggests life in suspension, but life and not death. It is a card of profound significance, but all the significance is veiled.[72]

Invoke inner vision by casting your cards in the shape of the Hanged Man's tree.

1. Gallows/Cross—What are the boundaries of my state of existence?

2. Leg Position—What crossroad am I at?

3. Arms—Over what am I powerless?

4. Halo—How can I acknowledge divine nature in everything around me?

5. Foliage—What lessons does nature teach me?

6. Serene Face—What is my insight?

7. Ropes Binding Feet—How can I give up the struggle?

8. Upside Down—How can I embrace new visions?

72   Waite, *Pictorial Key.*

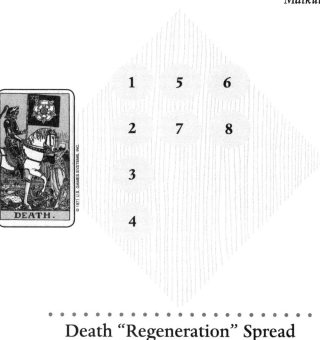

Death "Regeneration" Spread

The veil or mask of life is perpetuated in change, transformation and passage from lower to higher, and this is more fitly represented in the rectified Tarot by one of the apocalyptic visions than by the crude notion of the reaping skeleton. Behind it lies the whole world of ascent in the spirit.[73]

Cast your cards to reinvent your entire life in the shape of the Death card's flag.

1. Skeleton—What is temporal?

2. Armor—What protects me?

3. Horse—What moves me forward?

4. Dead King—What can I overthrow?

5. Praying Child—Who will listen?

6. Bishop—How to I find what clicks?

7. Twin Towers—What is before me?

8. Sunrise—How shall I ascend?

73   Waite, *Pictorial Key.*

Temperance "Integrate Power" Spread

It is called Temperance fantastically, because, when the rule of it obtains in our consciousness, it tempers, combines and harmonizes the psychic and material natures. Under that rule we know in our rational part something of whence we came and whither we are going.[74]

Cast your cards in the direction of Temperance's sacred fluid to unlock the power of integration into your life.

1. Wings—What is my true potential?

2. Lilies—What is my passion?

3. Crown—What do I know?

4. Path—What direction must I go in?

5. Mountain—What is my challenge?

6. Mixing fluid—How do I go with the flow?

7. Foot in water—How do I connect to my unconscious?

8. Foot on land—How can I ground myself?

9. Glowing crown—What is possible?

74   Waite, *Pictorial Key.*

The Devil "Unleashed Possibility" Spread

> What it (the Devil) does signify is the Dweller on the Threshold without the Mystical Garden when those are driven forth therefrom who have eaten the forbidden fruit.[75]

Eat forbidden fruit, encounter the world with unfiltered eyes, and throw the gates of possibility open as you cast your cards in the shape of the Devil's horns.

1. Inverted pentagram—How am I different?

2. Hand gesture—Where have I been mislead?

3. Lovers—Who do I dominate?

4. Nudity—Where am I most vulnerable?

5. Chains—What binds me?

6. Torch—What passion burns at my soul?

7. Bat wings—What has gone awry?

8. Horns—Where do my animalistic instincts lead me?

---

75   Waite, *Pictorial Key.*

The Tower "Shatter False Illusions" Spread

The Tower has been spoken of as the chastisement of pride and the intellect overwhelmed in the attempt to penetrate the Mystery of God; but in neither case do these explanations account for the two persons who are the living sufferers. The one is the literal word made void and the other its false interpretation. In yet a deeper sense, it may signify also the end of a dispensation...[76]

Shake up your life and cast your cards in the shape of the tower and lightning.

1. Crown—What is no longer true?

2. Lightning—What wakes me up?

3. Left Figure—What tricks does the material world play?

4. Right Figure—What belief must I release?

5. Clouds—What new possibility is forming?

6. Yod Fire Sparks—How can I open myself to divine inspiration?

7. Flaming Windows—What gets rid of what I don't need?

8. Cliff—What risk should I take?

The Star "Vulnerability and Inspiration" Spread

The figure will appear as the type of Truth unveiled, glorious in undying beauty, pouring on the waters of the soul some part and measure of her priceless possession. But she is in reality the Great Mother in the Kabbalistic Sephira Binah, which is supernal Understanding, who communicates to the Sephiroth that are below in the measure that they can receive her influx.[77]

Cast your cards to ignite the muse, cultivate tender vulnerability, and open yourself to inspiration by casting your card in the shape of the Star's eight-pointed star.

1. Posture—How can I remain open?

2. Nudity—How is vulnerability an asset?

3. Stars—How do I hone my focus on the highest possible source?

4. Jug—How can I collect wisdom?

5. Bird—What gives me wings for both worlds?

6. Tree—How do I stay grounded?

7. Mountain—What is possible?

8. Flowers—What is manifesting right now?

77   Waite, *Pictorial Key.*

The Moon "Lunar Reflection" Spread

The face of the mind directs a calm gaze upon the unrest below; the dew of thought falls; the message is: Peace, be still; and it may be that there shall come a calm upon the animal nature, while the abyss beneath shall cease from giving up a form.[78]

Stand between the Moon's white towers and bask in the lunar glow.

1. Dual Towers—What false towers have I built?

2. Dog—What is the loyal, responsible thing to do?

3. Wolf—What does my primal self want?

4. Moon—What does intuitive clarity tell me?

5. Sun—What harsh reality exists?

6. Pool—What is my subconscious showing me?

7. Lobster—What is emerging from the depths of my soul?

8. Path—Where will this new illumination lead me?

78   Waite, *Pictorial Key.*

The Sun "Illumination" Spread

The characteristic type of humanity has become a little child therein—a child in the sense of simplicity and innocence in the sense of wisdom. In that simplicity, he bears the seal of Nature and of Art; in that innocence, he signifies the restored world. When the self-knowing spirit has dawned in the consciousness above the natural mind, that mind in its renewal leads forth the animal nature in a state of perfect conformity.[79]

Cast your cards in the shape of a sunflower and allow the sun's energy to permeate every level of your being.

1. Sun—How do I let the highest, clearest energy flow through me?

2. Child—How do I retain innocence?

3. Nudity—How can I let down my guard?

4. Banner—What do I need to express to others?

5. White Horse—What is magical about my life?

6. Wall—What boundary do I need to create?

7. Sunflowers—How can I be creative?

8. Red Head Feather—Whose soul am I linked to?

79   Waite, *Pictorial Key.*

Judgement's "No Going Back" Spread

It is the card which registers the accomplishment of the great work of transformation in answer to the summons of the Supernal—which summons is heard and answered from within.[80]

Cast your cards in the shape of the red cross on Judgement's flag to encourage the card's life-changing properties.

1. Trumpet—What is my wakeup call?

2. Angel Gabriel—Where is divine intervention?

3. Red Cross—Who helps me?

4. Flag—What should I feel free to express on the outside?

5. Coffins—What is stagnant?

6. Open Arms—What do I embrace?

7. Dead Rising—What marks my second chance?

8. Water—What changes forever?

80   Waite, *Pictorial Key.*

The World's "Big Bang" Spread

It represents also the perfection and end of the Cosmos, the secret which is within it, the rapture of the universe when it understands itself in God. It is further the state of the soul in the consciousness of Divine Vision, reflected from the self-knowing spirit.[81]

Unleash the magic of the World card into every segment of your life by casting your cards in the shape of the infinity wreath.

1. Dancer—What can I celebrate?

2. Magic Wands—What can I conjure?

3. Wreath—What continues?

4. Androgyny—How do I find integration and expression?

5. Head (Aquarius)—What am I thinking?

6. Lion (Leo)—What is my passion?

7. Ox (Taurus)—How can I ground myself?

8. Eagle (Scorpio)—What helps me fly?

81   Waite, *Pictorial Key.*

Ace of Pentacles "Manifest Potential" Spread

Seasonal shifts pull the soul in new directions. Cast your cards when you feel the urge to create something new in your life. It may be a new job, new habit, new relationship, or new hobby. This spread helps you get your thoughts together and leads you toward the manifestation of something wonderful in the natural world.

Cast in the shape of the Ace of Pentacle's garden gate and create a threshold with your cards.

1. Pentacle—What do I have?

2. Palm—How do I support my desire?

3. Garden Gate—What threshold do I need to cross?

4. Flower—What is my natural talent?

5. Path—What should I focus on to stay true to my path?

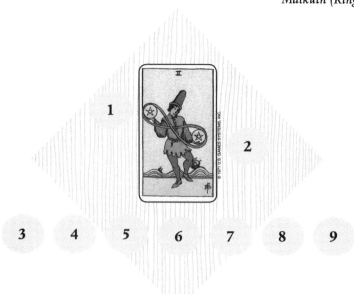

· ·
Two of Pentacles "Make the Best Choice" Spread

The Two of Pentacles reflects choices. Choices can be a luxury or they can be agony. Cast your cards to help figure out the best choice for your current situation. Nine cards are selected because nine is the number of wish fulfillment.

Select the first two cards intentionally. They should each represent the choices you are deciding between, like the two pentacles in the juggler's hands.

Intentional Choice 1   Intentional Choice 2

3. Number Two—What energy surrounds my options?

4. Lemniscate—What remains constant, no matter my choice?

5. Dance—What can I get excited about?

6. Stage Card—What am I being overly dramatic about?

7. Ship Moving Down Wave—What works in my favor?

8. Ship Moving Up Wave—What challenge must I face, no matter what?

9. Card's Advice—Which choice should I make?

· · · · · · ·

· ·
Three of Pentacles "Long-Term Project/Goal" Spread

Long-term goals and projects require dedication, collaboration, and effort. They echo the figures seen on the Three of Pentacles who work together to create a beautiful sacred space.

Support yourself and your big idea by casting your cards in the symbol of creative trinity, a triangle.

1. Church—How does my sense of spirituality support my work?

2. Bench—What continues to give me a leg up?

3. Apron—How can I best protect myself during the process?

4. Covered Head—What to I need to keep close to the vest?

5. Mason—What helps me work with clarity?

6. Two Figures—Who can I consult for help along the way?

7. Triad—What image or symbol should I focus on that encourages the final outcome?

· · · · · ·

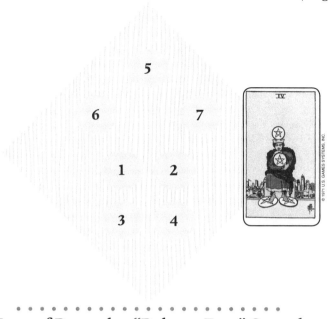

Four of Pentacles "Release Fear" Spread

Holding tightly to things, be they ideas, objects, people, or behavior, is a sure way to lose or suffocate them. Trusting the present moment is a sublime life tool. It allows you to release emotions and old habits. The knowledge that you will always be okay, that you'll always have what you need at your fingertips, is truly sacred knowledge.

The Four of Pentacles reflects stability through its number, but the figure looks to be holding on for dear life. Cast your cards to foster trust in letting go by making a square and a triangle.

1. Dark Cloak—What am I hiding from the world?

2. Stage Card—Who am I doing this for other than myself?

3. Grasping—What am I holding too tightly to that must be let go?

4. City—What have I built that I can be proud of?

5. Block—What security can I depend on, no matter what?

6. Eyes—How can I best stay in the present moment?

7. Crown—What is my highest ideal and greatest gift that occurs when I release fear?

Five of Pentacles "Through Thick and Thin" Spread

The Five of Pentacles often reflects the ups and downs and highs and lows of any relationship or marriage. The ability to survive tough times reveals the strength between people. Challenges often show us what we are made of. Tough times offer depth to any relationship. Cast your cards to help see yourself through tough times so when the snow stops falling, you'll be sitting pretty.

Cast your cards in the shape of two figures and the glimmer of hope above them.

1. Storm—What is our challenge?

2. Snow—How is my ego getting in the way?

3. Couple—What draws us together?

4. Crutches—What supports me?

5. Posture—What wounds me?

6. Stained Glass—How can I let more light into the relationship?

7. Church/Sanctuary—What action will save us?

Six of Pentacles "How to Open and Give More to Others" Spread

Each of us is a universe unto ourselves. When we open our hearts and perceptions, we find we can give more of ourselves to the world around us and to others. This engages a symbiotic relationship of energy, flow, and beauty. Our energy flows to others and reciprocal energy returns.

Cast your cards to engage in this heart-opening spread inspired by the Six of Pentacle's scales.

1. Scales—How am I too judgmental of myself and others?

2. Coins—What can I offer?

3. Beggars—What or who needs my attention?

4. Merchant—How can I give the best of myself?

5. Fortress—What single action helps me to become more successful?

6. Secret Red Tab—What is the secret to getting out of my own way?

. . . .
Seven of Pentacles "What Now?" Spread

The Seven of Pentacles reflects a moment where you've been working really hard and garnered results but are wondering what you should do next.

Cast your cards in the shape of the pentacles on the card.

1. Pastoral Landscape—What is the state of my current situation?

2. Vegetation —What gifts have I already manifested?

3. Tendrils—What is developing?

4. Hoe—What tool is at my disposal?

5. Boots—What supports me?

6. Figure's Gaze—What do I need to focus on?

7. Posture—What should I do next?

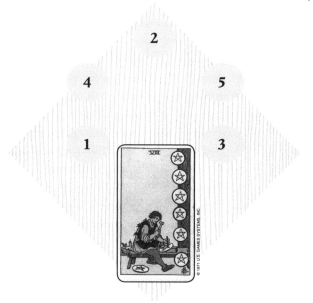

Eight of Pentacles "Work You Love" Spread

It is said that when you do work that you love, it ceases to feel like work and more like play or flow. Passionate individuals who love their work say they'd continue whether they are paid or not. Cast your cards to bring you closer to the work you were meant to do (unless you are already doing it—then *good for you!*).

Cast the cards in the shape of the five-pointed star.

1. Bench—How do I rise above the noise and distraction to find my inner purpose?

2. Apron—What is my advantage?

3. Tool—What tool do I need to get to work?

4. Distant City—Who desires what I offer?

5. Displayed Pentacles—How can I believe in myself in a deeper way?

Nine of Pentacles "Luxurious Life" Spread

True luxury is a state of mind. It has nothing to do with the objects surrounding you or the dollar amount they cost. Luxury isn't bought; it's experienced. Appreciation of anything comes from within you. Sunlight sliding over the body is a luxury. Buttered toast is a luxury. Hugging a child is a luxury. Cast your cards to engage and enjoy simple things. They contain the secret key of intense pleasure.

Cast your cards in the receptive shape of the Nine of Pentacles' neckline.

1. Dress—What makes me feel wonderful?

2. Falcon—What can I always depend on?

3. Grapes—What brings me immense sensual pleasure?

4. Vineyard—What beauty surrounds me?

5. Tree—What grounds me in the intricacies of life so I can reach higher?

6. Snail—How can I slow down to appreciate what is right in front of me?

7. Tendril—What will develop when I stay focused on the moment?

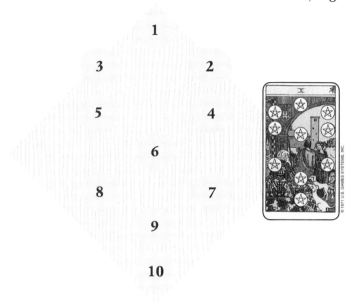

Ten of Pentacles "Threshold of Treasure" Spread

A specific magic occurs when tarot pentacles reveal the true nature of the material world. Pentacles are the only visible suit of tarot—the only suit we can hold, taste, and feel. All other suits are invisible. This knowledge allows us to interact and understand the interplay between the visible and invisible in new and evocative ways. The material world becomes an unfolding treasure responding to our thoughts, desires, actions, and imaginings. Cast your cards to pass through a threshold of magic and into unfolding possibility.

Cast your cards in the Ten of Pentacles' "secret in plain sight" shape of the Tree of Life.

1. Family—Who supports me?

2. Generations—What have I inherited?

3. Dogs—How can I connect with animal energies?

4. Tree of Life—How can I move toward divinity?

5. Old Man—How do I best cultivate wisdom?

6. Married Couple—What bonds me to others?

7. Child—What can I play with?

8. Threshold—How do I move through the profane and into the sacred every day?

9. Scale Tapestry—How do I integrate balance in all things?

10. Castle Tapestry—What is possible?

Page of Pentacles "Sharpen Focus" Spread

The gift of the Page of Pentacles lies in her ability to apply laser focus to any situation, task, or challenge. Cast your cards in this spread when you need to sharpen your focus and hone your powers of discipline to any task.

Cast your cards in a circle like the pentacle in the page's hand.

1. Gaze—What will keep my thoughts focused?

2. Pentacle—What happens when I focus on the task at hand?

3. Grove of Trees—What unseen troves of magic support me?

4. Mountain—How high is it possible to rise?

5. Pointed Foot—What step should I take in the near future?

6. Plowed Field—What is possible if I am disciplined?

Knight of Pentacles "Vow of Silence" Spread

Expression is always a healthy activity; however, sometimes we are asked to keep a sacred secret. Sometimes a secret is so delicious it can be excruciating to harbor. Alternatively, it is possible to weaken the sacred nature of a thing if we are quick to share it. Often, keeping things to ourselves will give it and ourselves power, especially if we share because we seek the approval of other people. If you have a habit of hanging everything out for the world to see, cast your cards in this spread to cultivate the power of silence and subtlety, just like the Knight of Pentacles.

Cast your cards in the shape of the five-pointed star on the knight's pentacle.

1. Pentacle—What is the nature of the silence needing to be held?

2. Armor—How am I protected?

3. Closed Lips—How do I keep my secret?

4. Horse—What power do I gain?

5. Plowed Field—What develops if I hold on to this energy?

Queen of Pentacles "Self-Care" Spread

The Queen of Pentacles cares for everyone around her with love, tenderness, and an eye for material comfort and sensuality. We can take care of others better when we take good care of ourselves.

Cast your cards in the shape of the queen's crown to consider how you can treat yourself like royalty.

1. Pentacle—What splurge should I indulge in?

2. Royal Clothing—How can I improve my wardrobe?

3. Roses—How can I exercise self-love?

4. Bunny—How can I change my inner dialogue and speak to myself as kindly as I'd speak to a child?

5. Goat—What gives me more energy?

6. Pan—How can I have a wickedly good time?

7. Abundance—What happens when I am kinder to myself?

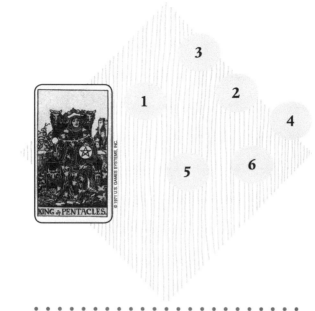

King of Pentacles "Financial Growth" Spread

The King of Pentacles, king of the material world, is a wealthy man whose money works for him in a multitude of ways.

Cast your cards in the shape of the king's kingdom to concentrate on financial growth and increase material stability.

1. Pentacle—How can I track my spending?

2. Garden—How can I reward myself for changing my habits?

3. Bull Horns—How can I change my mindset?

4. Armor—What helps me to protect my assets?

5. King's Head—How can I set realistic financial goals?

6. Castle—What will happen if I take proactive steps now?

Ace of Cups "Emotional Flow" Spread

The Ace of Cups reflects an open channel of love, emotion, and creativity. Allowing emotions to flow rather than stifling them to please others leads to personal happiness and expression.

Cast your cards in the shape of Waite's W initial seen on the card to discover what magic lies in cultivating emotional flow.

1. Clouds—What is my general situation?

2. Angelic Hand—What opportunity is being offered to me?

3. Cup—What is the true nature of my heart?

4. Dove—When I allow vulnerability, what gifts do I receive?

5. Sacramental Bread/Wafer—What do I need to accept?

6. Fountain—What happens when I give the love I crave?

7. Lotus Flower—What makes rebirth possible?

8. Pool of Water—What can I focus on to stay open?

Two of Cups "Ideal Partner" Spread

An ideal partner may be an actual person, a romantic entanglement, or something more abstract, like work that suits you or a house and home that feels like it was constructed just for you. Ultimately, we want to parter with the people and things that suit us best. But do we know and attract what is best for ourselves? This spread will help you. Often just stating your desire for an ideal possibility and releasing attachment to its form will bring it to you.

Cast your cards in the triangle shape of the card to discover and encourage a willing parter to reveal themselves and appear by your side.

1. Lion—What fierce action can I take to attract my ideal partner?

2. Wings—How can I encourage divine intervention?

3. Cups—How can I cultivate a sense of openness toward what is best for me?

4. Dual Snakes—How can I integrate what and who I love while maintaining autonomy?

5. Hand Gesture—What single, small action brings my partner closer to me?

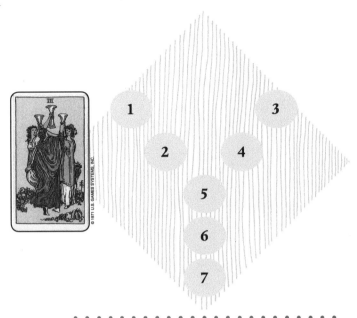

Three of Cups "Lighten Up" Spread

We all go through grouchy, intense periods of time when it feels like the weight of the world is on our shoulders. During these stretches, it is often hard to see the forest for the trees. This expression means we are too close to heaviness, sadness, or our personal blinders to see the big picture. During moments like these, it's helpful to take a breath, step back, and lighten up. Seeing friends and venting is often just the trick to release pent-up frustrations.

Cast your cards in the shape of the cup on the card to find ease and space for the present moment and allow stress and heaviness to float away.

1. Left Maiden/Air/Kether—What is a new way of understanding my life?

2, Center Maiden/Fire/Chokmah—How can I make my passions a reality?

3. Right Maiden/Water/Binah—How can I soften my resistance and become pliable to possibility?

4. Three Figures—Who supports me?

5. Grapes/Intoxication—How can I release stress permanently and sink into bliss?

6. Celebration—What can I celebrate in this moment?

7. Harvest—What will result if I lighten up?

Four of Cups "Embrace New Possibilities" Spread

The Four of Cups reflects a figure who is offered an opportunity in the form of a cup. Does he see it? Will he acknowledge it? Life is fast and confusing sometimes. We can't possibly see all opportunities and possibilities as they fly at us. We can make an effort to keep our awareness open to important and potentially life-changing opportunities when they come our way.

Cast your cards in the shape of the tree trunk to find the support you need and recognize a new possibility.

1. Hand with Cup—What small adjustment can I make to see new possibilities?

2. Three Cups—What excellent possibilities are already in my grasp?

3. Tree—What support can I count on through thick and thin?

4. Closed-Off Posture—What helps me loosen up?

5. Cloud—What magical attribute is working in my favor?

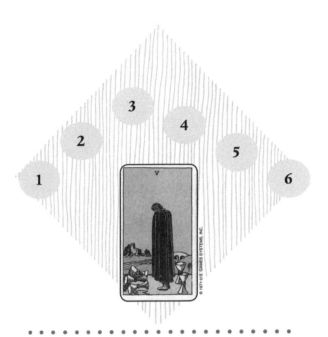

Five of Cups "Replace Bad Habits with Good Ones" Spread

Humans are habitual creatures. Our tendencies can be a help or a hindrance. Good habits support success, health, and happiness. Old habits stifle us and become obtrusive as we grow and evolve if we don't let them go.

Cast your cards in the shape of the bridge on the Five of Cups card. It will help you cross over and figure out how to swap a negative, destructive, or disruptive habit for an empowering one.

1. Black Cloak—Why does my habit need discarding?

2. Three Spilled Cups—What price do I pay for my bad habit?

3. Two Standing Cups—What positive habit can I replace it with?

4. Water—What is my challenge to dropping the habit?

5. Bridge—How can I cross once and for all?

6. Distant Castle—What is the result of my bravery?

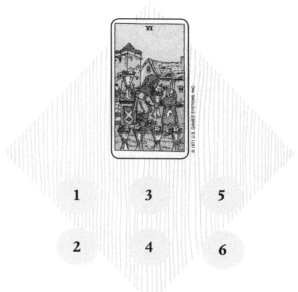

Six of Cups "Memory Lane" Spread

The Six of Cups is often described as the "walk down memory lane" card. It is fun to wander down memory lane when time and imagination afford it. Looking back on the past offers an opportunity to revisit old narratives through a fresh set of eyes. We are free to add, amend, or replace old stories with new insights. It is important, however, to not let the stories of your life define you. Instead, write your story fresh each day with actions, intentions, and energy that reflect the essence of who you truly are.

Cast your cards in the shape of the Six of Cups' three figures to discover new wisdom and heartfelt messages by taking a saunter down old familiar roads.

1. Town Square—Where have I felt most protected?

2. Flowering Cups—What is the great gift of past experience?

3. Boy—What great gift have I received from another?

4. Girl—How can I learn to accept love, tenderness, and kindness when it is offered?

5. Gloved Hand—How did I learn to protect myself?

6. Figure Walking Away—What old narrative can I release?

Seven of Cups "Castles in the Air" Spread

The Seven of Cups is often called the "castles floating in the air" card. This expresses the idea that dreams are illusions and nothing more, yet each invention, medicine, literature, theory, and breakthrough existing in the world was once an idea, a floating castle in the air, in the form of someone's imagination. Knowing this, you can work with the Seven of Cups to bring your flights of fancy, daydreams, and thoughtful meanderings to fruition.

Cast your cards in the shape of seven floating cups to dream far and wide—and then make those dreams a reality.

1. Female Head (Empress)—What springs from my creativity?

2. Glowing Figure (High Priestess)—What deep secret needs to emerge?

3. Snake (Magician)—How powerful am I?

4. Castle (Tower)—What shall I destroy to be reborn?

5. Jewels (Wheel)—What good would I do with all the money in the world?

6. Wreath (World)—What is eternal?

7. Dragon (Sun)—What passion burns inside of me?

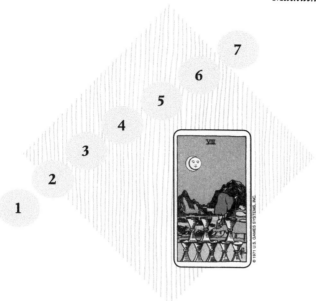

Eight of Cups "Moving On" Spread

There comes a time in everyone's life when it is time to move away from a pattern, behavior, or person. These moments are different for each of us, yet we are well aware of them, whether they creep up on us or hit us like a lightning bolt.

Cast your cards in the direction of the figure who moves upward when you are actively ready to head for higher ground.

1. Eight Cups—What is the situation/state/thing I will leave behind?

2. Boots—What supports me?

3. Boulders—What stands in my way?

4. Walking Stick—What helps me navigate the path?

5. Eclipse—What secret magic works in my favor?

6. Water—How do I keep my emotions in check?

7. Path—What can I trust to guide me?

Nine of Cups "Wish Come True" Spread

An old saying reminds you to be careful what you wish for; you just might get it. The Nine of Cups lets you know you'll indeed be getting your heart's desire. What do you want more than anything?

Cast your cards in the shape of the magic genie's cups to glean information about your deepest desire and highest thoughts.

1. Genie—What do I want more than anything?

2. Crossed Arms—What blocks me?

3. Cups—How will I feel when I get it?

4. Tablecloth—What is a hidden and unforeseen consequence?

5. Bench—What keeps me steady through it all?

Ten of Cups "Family Harmony" Spread

The Ten of Cups is often considered "the happily ever after" card. We know this fairytale ideal does not really exist. First, because we are always living in our present, and "ever after" implies the future. Second, because even well-adjusted, silly, and happy families, relationships, and situations will face challenging times. Good thing we can always look to the cards for solutions and suggestions.

Cast your cards in a rainbow shape to invoke familial harmony in any challenging situation.

1. Home—What is the current situation?

2. Stage Card—How can I face the obstacle/challenge?

3. Clasped Couple—What can I depend on?

4. Open Hands—How can I stay open to possibility?

5. Dancing Children—What small adjustment brings everyone together?

6. Rainbow—What is the silver lining and lesson of this challenge?

Page of Cups "Psychic Development" Spread

The Page of Cups is the most psychic card of the deck. Use her as inspiration when you want to improve your psychic and intuitive abilities. These abilities can be used to bring us closer to the life we desire.

Cast your cards in the shape of a receptive cup to hone your psychic skills.

1. Fish—How can I foster trust in my psychic and intuitive flashes?

2. Water—How can I keep my psychic channels open?

3. Youth—How can I look at the world through childlike eyes?

4. Stage Card—Should I share my gifts with others?

5. Cup—What helps me hone these skills and move deeper into personal alignment?

Knight of Cups "Romantic Seduction" Spread

The Knight of Cups is the gentle, poetic romancer of the deck. His appearance invokes sweet words, thoughtful gifts, and sensual notions.

Cast your cards in the shape of Hermes' wings, found on the knight's helmet, when you want a little help in seducing someone tasty.

1. Wings—How should I make my intentions known?

2. Horse's Gait—What's the best way to approach them?

3. Cup—What can I offer them?

4. Cliff—What do I risk?

5. Armor—What protects my heart?

6. Horse—What helps me become slow and steady?

7. River—Where is this taking me?

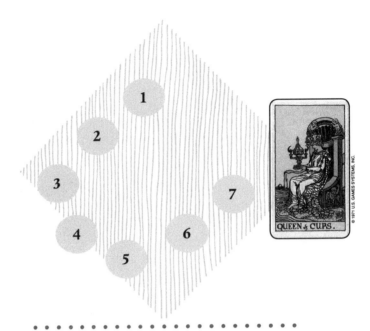

Queen of Cups "Cultivate Beauty" Spread

Cups are the suit of emotion, compassion, and love. Experiencing beauty is like falling in love. The beauty of a flower, a landscape, a person, or a poem offers an opportunity to transcend ourselves. Our heart beats a little bit faster, our ego slips away, and we open in appreciation for such a thing existing. The greatest gift we give ourselves is to expand and cultivate our sense of beauty, to let it unfold and recognize beauty in new forms.

Cast your cards in the shape of a shell with the help of the Queen of Cups. She is an expert at spying and cultivating compassion and beauty. She will help you to discover it in the most unlikely places.

1. Gown—How can I treat myself like the beautiful creature I am?

2. White Cliffs of Dover—What inspires my imagination to new heights?

3. Crown—How do I keep my crown chakra open?

4. Mermaids—How can I encourage magic to greet me?

5. Sand—How do I stay grounded when I'm flying?

6. Stone—What do earth elements teach me?

7. Surf—What messages are revealed in the waves?

8. Shell—What treasures await?

King of Cups "Emotional Strength" Spread

Emotions are like waves breaking upon the shore. They influence and form our behavior, attitudes, and lifestyle. Emotions can feel like tsunamis or gentle laps. The strength of the King of Cups lies in his ability to maintain an even course, no matter what emotion or feeling he encounters. This is why the King of Cups is the most successful artist of the deck and a visionary who is able to see his inspirations through to their finished product and completion.

Cast your cards like waves in the ocean to gain his wisdom.

1. Waves—How can I best sustain emotional highs and lows?

2. Ship—What message do I need to hear?

3. Sea Monster—How can I let what frightens me empower me?

4. Throne—How do I embrace my calling?

5. Fish—What should I bring to the surface after I dive deep?

6. Cup—How can I remain open and clear so I can be open to holding each new experience as it comes at me?

Ace of Wands "Embrace Your Passion" Spread

Everything existing in the world began with a spark: great love affairs, classic works of fiction, and everything containing consciousness. The Ace of Wands reflects a singular spark of passion. The spark contains the power to transform the individual; sometimes it can transform the world.

Cast your cards in the shape of an explosion with the Ace of Wands to embrace your passion. Discover where it might take you. Don't worry if you don't know what that passion is just yet. The more open and active you are, the quicker it will come.

1. Castle / Home—What is the state of my present situation?

2. Wand—What is the nature of my passion?

3. Angelic Hand—What divine influence works in my favor?

4. Clouds—What remains unseen?

5. River's Water—What challenge extinguishes my flames?

6. River Path—Where will my passions take me if I follow up on them?

7. Green Leaves—What will emerge as I remain in tune to the stirrings within me?

Two of Wands "Plotting and Planning Expansion" Spread

The Two of Wands is the combination of divine inspiration meeting duality, and it is this energetic process that ensues. This happens when an idea or insight hits you, you see how it will take form in the world, and you take action, sometimes before you even realize it.

Cast your cards in the shape of dual wands to help guide your inner sparks to fruition.

1. World—What do I envision?

2. Bay—What awaits my call?

3. Red Rose—How do I infuse beauty in my work?

4. White Lily—How do I infuse authenticity in my work?

5. Plowed Field—What is my next small step?

6. Distant Mountains—How do I remain open to divine inspiration?

Three of Wands "Patience" Spread

Wands rush us to action, feeling, and sensory overload. Waiting can feel excruciating when we want something with every fiber of our being. We must trust our action will bring us required results without rushing, pushing, or forcing things to happen just because we want them in the moment. The Three of Wands reflects following through on a passionate idea. You stand waiting for the response. During such times, turn your thoughts to other matters. Try your best to forget it altogether. A wise witch forgets about her spell as soon as she casts it. She clears her mind and allows the forces that be to take care of it for her. Her trust and faith is steadfast, as yours should be.

And for moments where, try as you might, you still find yourself obsessing, cast your cards in the shape of three wands and a wish to know that everything will be okay.

1. Wand One—What I felt.

2. Wand Two—What I did.

3. Wand Three—How results may appear.

4. Ships—What can I do to remain steady?

5. Sea—How can I foster support?

6. Distant Land—Who hears my intention?

7. Response—What response should I remain open to?

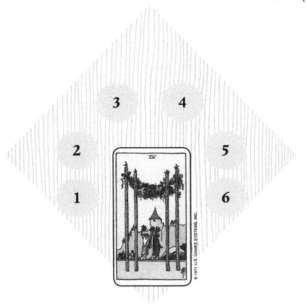

Four of Wands "Stability of Passion" Spread

Wands are explosive. Such is the nature of the suit of fire. Wands are exhausting when burning too brightly, yet they become elusive if blown out. The Four of Wands is an opportunity to stabilize passion in a steady, healthy, sustainable manner. It transforms into a self-infusing force in life.

Cast your cards in the shape of garland to access the wisdom of the Four of Wands. It will keep a steady keel for matters meaning the world to you.

1. Flowers—What is blooming?

2. Garland—What do I have the power to create?

3. Celebration—What reason do I have to celebrate?

4. Bridge—What challenge do I still need to confront?

5. Moat—What is my emotional state regarding the maintenance of my passion?

6. Walled Fortress—How do I protect my passion in a sustainable way?

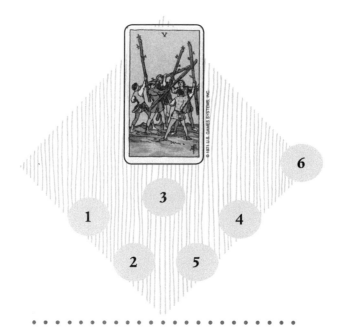

Five of Wands "Settle Down Now" Spread

The Five of Wands reflects a passionate skirmish. While this often reflects an exciting conflict of creative ideas, it can also be a sticky place, especially for people who are uncomfortable with confrontation or when tensions run super high.

Cast your cards, one for each figure and a single card for a last piece of advice, to calm yourself if you find yourself at your wit's end, at the mercy of another person's crazy energy, or to give yourself a moment's peace.

1. Anger—Why am I so worked up?

2. Wands—What is at stake?

3. Energy—How can I transform the energy into a healing force?

4. Solid Stance—How do I cultivate the strength I need to wrap this up?

5. Upward Face—What is the higher reason for all of it?

6. Horizon Line—Where should I aim my sights?

Six of Wands "Road to Success" Spread

We all dream of success while working toward the culmination of our heart's desire. The journey toward fruition is what really counts. The Six of Wands allows us to luxuriate in our success, encourage us to receive praise and recognition, and step with pride for the work we have accomplished thus far.

Cast your cards like an unfolding path to continue paving the road to your success.

1. Wand—What keeps me focused on my long-term goal?

2. Wreath—How do I stay in the moment?

3. Marchers—Where can I cultivate allies?

4. Horse—What can I always rely on?

5. Horse Covering—What is hidden that I should see?

6. Horse Looking Back—What great lesson am I learning?

7. Rider's Stance—What keeps me upright and steady through it all?

Seven of Wands "Perseverance" Spread

The Seven of Wands reflects a moment of extreme self-defense. Our attackers can come in the form of people, the begrudging or belittling voices in our head, or even patterns ingrained in the body.

Cast your cards in a fence of defense to find renewed strength and perseverance through moments like these.

1. Held Wand—What am I defending?

2. Six Wands—What am I up against?

3. High Ground—What is my advantage?

4. Unmatched Shoes—How can I hold two opposing thoughts confidently in my head?

5. Leaves—What will blossom if I stay the course and
   let no one, not even myself, dissuade me?

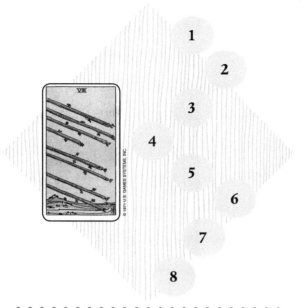

Eight of Wands "Ready, Aim, Fire" Spread

The Eight of Wands reflects pure energy moving across a field, as if an advancing army had catapulted it into the air. The card is intention in flight. To be sure all of your intentions hit their intended mark, cast your cards in this spread, one question for each wand.

1. Wand 1—What is the nature of my intention?

2. Wand 2—What helps me formulate it articulately?

3. Wand 3—How does my intention help others?

4. Wand 4—What does it add to the world?

5. Wand 5—Why is this important to me?

6. Wand 6—What obstacle stands in the way?

7. Wand 7—How can I steer clear and shoot over the obstacle?

8. Wand 8—What secret do I need to know?

Nine of Wands "Breaking Barriers" Spread

The fellow on the Nine of Wands is a true survivor. He's been through the ringer, yet he pushes ahead. The pulsing energy of fire can take its toll, but those who are persistent will find new and miraculous worlds appearing before them.

Cast your cards in the shape of a square to harness the energy of the Nine of Wands and break barriers as they appear to challenge you.

1. Bandage—What is the wound that lets in the light?

2. Fence—What stands before me?

3. Wand—What do I have at my disposal as I move forward?

4. Sideways Glance—What should I be wary of?

Ten of Wands "Regeneration" Spread

The Ten of Wands reflects the culmination of energy, passion, and tireless work. It is the end of a cycle, as all tens are. We all need to honor the cycles of our lives. We can't move full speed ahead all the time. Rest is as important as work; in fact, renewal makes for more effective work. The Ten of Wands reminds you to put down your wands—effort and extended energy—and rest.

Cast your cards with five cards in a row to remind you to regenerate your mind, body, and spirit.

1. Posture—What will help my body repair itself?

2. Load—How can I put down my burdens?

3. Manor—Where can I go to rest and rejuvenate?

4. Fields—What will appear as a result of my work?

5. Stage Card—How can I quiet my mental chatter
   and learn to focus on my inner self?

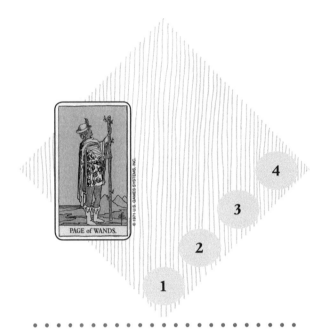

Page of Wands "Adventurous Soul" Spread

Where do you want to go? What adventures do you seek? Access the page's energy. The Page of Wands is the intrepid traveler of the deck. She journeys far and wide. She lets her wild curiosity chart her course.

Cast your cards in the upward slope of the pyramids to discover where your adventurous soul is leading you.

1. Red Flame Feather—What stokes my passion?

2. Page's Gaze—Where do I need to go?

3. Pyramids—What sacred knowledge is learned when I am adventuring?

4. Red Desert Sands—How do I stay grounded and centered
   while circumstances and places change around me?

Knight of Wands "Make Your Move" Spread

Is there something in your life—a project, a relationship, or a goal—that needs one final boost of energy to move it toward completion? Are you feeling shy and need the power of extroversion for a task? The Knight of Wands' energy is explosive and combustible. Utilize the Knight of Wands' fiery energy for anything you need to push over the finish line, from romance to work to family.

Cast your cards in the shape of distant pyramids and enjoy the Knight of Wands' power boost.

1. Wand—How do I best harness my passion?

2. Armor—What protects the vulnerable parts of myself?

3. Flaming Elements—How does the energy affect my aura?

4. Horse—What aids me in my quest?

5. Distant Pyramids—What is my ultimate prize?

Queen of Wands "Own Your Passion" Spread

What do you love more than anything? What is the greatest passion of your life? Do you need soul clarification? Are you looking to stoke your internal fire? The Queen of Wands is the shining flame of the tarot deck because she knows what thrills her and saturates herself in it. Every moment of every day, she immerses herself in passion's fire and garners personal evolution. She owns who she is and what she loves.

Activate the Queen of Wands inside you by casting your cards in the shape of her sunflower.

1. Throne—What is my birthright?

2. Lion—How am I fierce?

3. Sunflower—How can I best harness my energy?

4. Black Cat—How do I focus energy and attention toward elements that satisfy me?

5. Pyramids—How can I store my energy and access it at any time?

6. Leg-Parted Posture—How do I maintain ownership over my physical body?

King of Wands "Visionary" Spread

How can you make a difference in the world? Can you focus on your gifts, do what you love, and make the world a better place? I know you can. Visionaries see the big picture. They use failure as an engine. They remain focused. They obtain their goals.

Access the King of Wands' energy inside you, let nothing deter you, and cast your cards in the shape of his wands to make your vision a reality.

1. Wand—What is my vision?

2. Salamander—How does passion inspire direct action?

3. Throne—What natural gifts do I already possess?

4. Lion—What challenges me in obtaining my goal?

5. Desert—What simple, singular action helps me to achieve it?

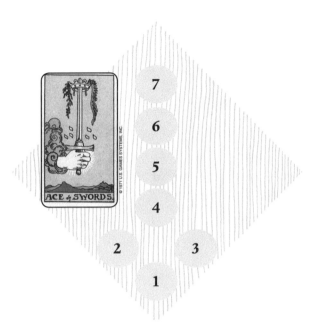

Ace of Swords "Choose Your Thoughts" Spread

Are you distracted? Do you need to focus? Do you let self-doubt and random emotions cloud how you act in the world? Control your thoughts and control your experience of the world. Become the active observer of yourself. Allow negative or painful thoughts and feelings to slip away. Take action on the good ideas fostering pleasure, satisfaction, and growth. Allow darkness and negativity to perish by removing their power over you. Your mind is a powerhouse. Use it wisely.

Cast your cards in the shape of the all-powerful sword to cultivate and hone the power of the mind.

1. Clouds—What is manifesting right now?

2. Angelic Hand—What are my gifts?

3. Grip—What ideas do I cling to that must slip away?

4. Sword—What thought/idea/decision should I live by?

5. Olive Branch—What mental symbol brings me peace?

6. Palm Branch—What helps me rise above dark thoughts and feelings?

7. Mountaintops—What can I attain with the power of the mind?

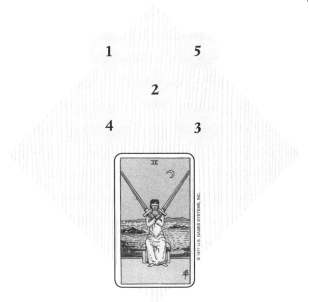

Two of Swords "Reset the Mind" Spread

Do you seek inner peace? Do you yearn for the power of contemplation? Do you need to make an important decision? Restore inner peace, calm, and zen when you need it most.

Cast your cards in the *X* shape the figure makes with her arms.

1. Blindfold—What is the best way to block out chaos and confusion?

2. Swords—How am I my own worst enemy?

3. Stage Card—How do I drop concern for what other people think?

4. Water—How do I find inner peace?

5. Distant Shore—What possibilities await?

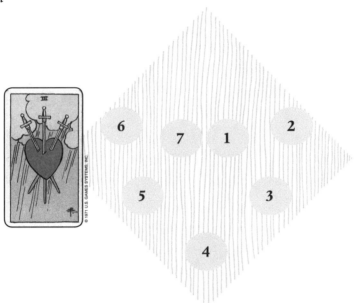

• •
Three of Swords "Embrace Heartbreak" Spread

Is your heart torn apart? Are you experiencing a breakup, betrayal, or the deep emotional pain of loss? There's no way around heartache during the course of our life. It is a pain we all must bear. Ease pain by embracing it. Reject and repress nothing. Be kind to yourself in the process. Feel every feeling. Be kind and loving toward yourself until it passes.

Cast your cards in the shape of your tender heart to remind you these feelings won't last forever.

1. Heart—How can I stay present and experience the discomfort so it moves through me?

2. Rain—What eases my suffering?

3. Sword 1—Past pain.

4. Sword 2—Present pain.

5. Sword 3—Future pain.

6. Clouds—What changes?

7. Wind—What is the lesson?

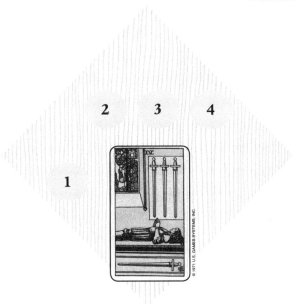

Four of Swords "Restful Night's Sleep" Spread

Are you struggling with sleep? Does night find you awake, tossing and turning? Daytime is excruciating without enough sleep. Peace and quiet pervades the Four of Swords. Activate the restful, restorative qualities of this card to help you back into an excellent sleep schedule.

Cast your cards like the swords in this card for helpful solutions to get you sleeping soundly. Keep the Four of Swords visible during the reading. Meditate on the card before going to sleep.

1. Sword 1—What energy is keeping me awake?

2. Sword 2—What can I replace this energy with?

3. Sword 3—How can I become present in the moment and allow myself to drift to sleep?

4. Sword 4—How do I set up the most comfortable sleeping situation ever?

Five of Swords "Banish Passive-Aggressive Behavior Once and for All" Spread

Is a passive-aggressive person or situation making you crazy right now? Passive-aggressive situations are stressful, harmful, and soul sucking. The Five of Swords reflects unkind actions, fights, and mental abuse. Cast your cards to release yourself from unkind behavior. Create boundaries. Passive-aggressive behavior only works if you play into it. Learn from the experience, change your energy, and banish passive-aggressiveness from your life forever.

Cast your cards in the shape of the swords on the card.

1. Sword 1—What is the root of the issue?

2. Sword 2—How do I stay calm and focused in the situation?

3. Sword 3—How do I change my energy and reaction to this situation?

4. Sword 4—What limits do I need to set?

5. Sword 5—How do I stay mindful and never repeat this situation ever again?

Six of Swords "Better Times Lie Ahead" Spread

Are you ready for a new outcome? Looking to move toward greener pastures and happier experiences? The Six of Swords is often called the "better times lie ahead card." It is a transitional card reflecting figures escaping a situation or moving ahead to distant shores. Bouncing off that interpretation, cast your cards when you want to look toward a positive future.

Cast your cards in the shape of a boat to begin your journey.

1. Swords—What is the root of the issue? (choose this card intentionally or randomly)

2. Boat—What will help me get over it?

3. Boatman—Who helps me to move ahead?

4. Water—How can I remain emotionally open and deep?

5. Child—How can I protect myself?

6. Cloaked Figure—What hidden element do I not yet see?

7. Distant Shore—What can I look forward to?

Seven of Swords "Clean Getaway" Spread

Are you looking for a clean break and a quick getaway? The Seven of Swords reflects a creeping figure who slips away unnoticed by others. There are times when we need to leave a situation and only take the good with us. Doing so, we leave past habits and negative behaviors behind.

Cast your cards in the shape of a tent top to make your break.

1. Swords in Hand—What valuable lesson will I take from this situation?

2. Swords Left Behind—What do I no longer need?

3. People in Background—What permanent boundaries must I erect?

4. Posture—How can I be integrated in my approach?

5. Stage Card—How can I be more authentic to myself in the future?

Eight of Swords "Release Ties of Bondage" Spread

Do you feel tied down? Are you being stifled and suppressed by a person, situation, or even yourself? Free yourself from the ties that bind by understanding why you are here to begin with. The Eight of Swords can reflect an imprisonment leading to great freedom. When the blindfold comes off, you will see the world with a new set of eyes and never return to this place again.

Cast your cards in a straight line to evolve into who you were always meant to be.

1. Swords—What thoughts imprison me?

2. Castle—How do I release old behavior?

3. Binds—How can I save myself?

4. Shore—How do I safely land on two feet?

5. Distant Cliffs—What direction shall I head in?

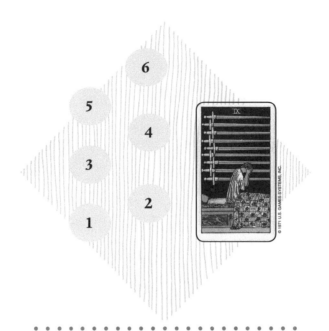

Nine of Swords "Change Thought Patterns" Spread

Do you feel like you are driving yourself crazy? Are you being held hostage by thoughts continuously running through your mind? Thought habits can lodge in the mind just like physical habits in the body.

Cast your cards like the wall of swords to break free of old thoughts when they have outlived their purpose and need to be set free.

1. Swords—How do I let negative thoughts go and replace them with new, empowering ones?

2. Quilt—What protection can I count on?

3. Bed—What fills me when I release angst and pain?

4. White Nightgown—How do I wipe the slate clean?

5. Hands on Face—How can I rejuvenate myself?

6. Etching Carved in Bed Frame—What single action can I take to stop wounding myself and start healing?

Ten of Swords "Break the Cycle" Spread

Are you ready to break a cycle? Are you noticing how situations and events return to you again and again? It's not always easy to break cycles. If it was, we wouldn't struggle with it and history wouldn't repeat itself. Perhaps the Ten of Swords looks like the scene of a bloody murder because deep, true, irrevocable change is frightening. It sets us off into unknown territories. It reflects a cycle reaching its complete and utter conclusion.

Cast your cards in the line of a spine and end the situation forever.

1. Body—What is finished?

2. Hand Gesture—What secret will I uncover?

3. Swords in Spine—How can I integrate a new reality?

4. Water—What will wash away past pain?

5. Red Fabric—What do I need to sacrifice?

6. Dark Night—What is the darkness part of this situation?

7. Rising Dawn—What new reality unfolds?

Page of Swords "Get to the Bottom of the Situation" Spread

Is there a mystery you need to solve? The Page is Swords is the plucky detective, the Nancy Drew, of the tarot deck. Use her enterprising, clever energy to get to the bottom of any mystery, unravel secrets, and cultivate truth.

Cast your cards in the shape of the birds rising high in the sky.

1. Posture—Where do I stand?

2. Rugged Terrain—What is my challenge?

3. Sword—How can I keep the highest thoughts and clearest thinking?

4. Birds—How can I better interpret messages?

5. Wind—How can I adapt to shifting winds and changing situations?

6. Clouds—What helps me see the truth?

7. Trees—What is revealed?

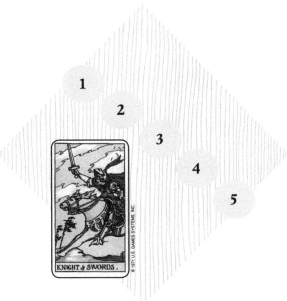

Knight of Swords "Do the Right Thing" Spread

Are you ready to take a stand? Knight energy is decisive and swift. Once an idea takes hold or a decision is made, it should be executed promptly and swiftly. Often, the universe or the world unfolds in a manner in which swift response is required and extraordinary results are garnered. Open yourself to these opportunities so doubt, fear, and timidness do not hold you back from doing the right thing.

Cast your cards in the shape of the knight's sword.

1. Gait—What needs my attention?

2. Sword—How do I stand up for truth?

3. Speed—How do I trust the energy surrounding me?

4. Butterflies—How do I stay connected to the highest ideal?

5. Knight—What action is required?

Queen of Swords "Articulate Thoughts with Ease" Spread

Invoke the power of language through the clear and concise articulation of thoughts. Articulation and the way we put words together affects how we think about ourselves on the inside and how we organize our life on the outside. It carries a transformative power whose butterfly effects work outwardly and inwardly.

Cast your cards to articulate creatively, precisely, and with the utmost ease.

1. Crown—How can I open to high-level wisdom?

2. Bird—What message is the animal world sending me?

3. Butterfly—How can I invoke beauty through words?

4. Tree—How can I remain grounded in all three worlds?

5. Blooming Clouds—How do I gather support in all places?

6. Cloud Cape—How do I keep my highest self with me during regular life?

7. Hand Gesture—How do I stay open and available to new inspiration?

King of Swords "Make it Happen" Spread

King energy is mature and masculine. Access this energy to become effective and produce results. The King of Swords sees clearly into the heart of the situation and takes direct action.

Cast your cards in a stable and powerful square.

1. Gaze—What helps me focus on the end goal?

2. Sword—How can I best express my truth?

3. Clouds—What helps me rise to the challenge?

4. Blue Sky—How can I move past previous limitations?

Symbol Dictionary

WE HAVE TO recognize, in a word, that there is no public cannon of authority
in the interpretation of Tarot Symbolism. The field is open therefore; it
is indeed so open that anyone of my readers is free to produce an entirely
new explanation, making no appeal to past experiments; but the adventure
will be at his or her own risk and peril as to whether they can make it
work and thus produce a harmony of interpretation throughout.

Arthur Waite, *Shadows of Life and Thought*

This section provides meanings and interpretations for myriad visual language and symbolic images found across the Rider-Waite-Smith cards. Tarot, magic, and ritual are highly symbolic in nature because a symbol speaks directly to the subconscious. A symbol is like shorthand to the human psyche, and like a shot of whiskey, its effect is immediately felt. Words and sentences must be deciphered and understood, even if the process takes only a millisecond. The symbol, in contrast, offers immediate understanding.

It is supremely important to understand that symbol dictionaries (any symbolic dictionary) are a mere starting point. No symbol can be entirely defined by another person or group of people. It is personal, cultural, and experiential associations that give a symbol its power. Your own unique eyes, sensitivities, and personal breadth of experience are the power generator behind any symbolic system. Claim the world of symbols as your own. Anything you look at suddenly becomes like a tarot card, easily decipherable and read. When the world around you becomes a landscape for contemplation, richness, and meaning, your world will transform before you and inside of you. Your experience of life will be deepened. You will never be bored because everything before you offers a message and meaning to be unraveled. Why is symbolic reading so transformative? Because the closer you look at something, the more you will discover, the deeper you will be drawn into the experience of that thing, and mystery upon unraveling mystery will unfold before your eyes.

You could create an individual symbol dictionary in your tarot journal or grimoire. Assign at least one page (if not more) for each symbol. List all the associations, feelings, intuitions, and meanings you have experienced for that symbol. Don't limit yourself to traditional symbols like suns, moons, and stars. If curling muscular biceps are an image that fills you with excitement, list it. If rosy red summer tomatoes fill you with the heat of summer, list it. If items like books, vinyl records, and watercolor paint sets fill you with cozy feelings, list them. List terrifying, creepy, and uneasy symbols too. Find inspiration in tarot decks, items in your house, and your waking and sleeping dreams.

Symbolic reading is an excellent tool for unlocking the tarot. Symbolic reading is helpful if you are a professional reader and must perform quick party readings for large groups of people. Additionally, you can take the symbolic reading technique out of the tarot and use it to find richness in your life and find signs and meanings in the landscape all around you at any moment.

How to Do a Symbolic Reading

You can create an entire reading, construct a narrative, and derive meaning from a single symbol. The process is simple:

Symbolic Reading Technique

1. Clear your mind.

2. Shuffle the cards.

3. Flip a card.

4. First image that catches your eye? That's your symbol.

5. Interpret.

Angel—A group of spiritual creatures and heavenly guardians and messengers. The Rider-Waite-Smith features four Christian archangels: Raphael, Gabriel, Uriel, and Michael.

Ankh—Egyptian symbol of life and death.

Apple—A mythological symbol serving many functions across cultures, from immortality to love charms, from magic to sexual bliss. The apple appears in the tarot as a symbol of the temptation of Eve in the Garden of Eden.

Apron—Important Masonic symbol typically depicting heritage, degree, and the practice of speculative Masonry. In the Rider-Waite-Smith deck, the apron is a symbol of operative Masonry.

Armor—Protection, experience in battle.

Bag—What you carry with you; past lessons.

Bandage—Healing properties, mending wounds, recent strife.

Banner—Proclamation.

Beach—Threshold and boundary space where the elements converge, particularly earth, air, and water.

Beard—The wisdom acquired by a long and rich life.

Bed—Sacred respite and sleep space.

Bench—Masonic symbol that also indicates an elevated plane and place on which to perform work.

Bind—To harness and contain.

Bird—Symbol of the human and cosmic spirit due to its ability to move between earth (human) and sky (spirit).

Blindfold—Occult initiation. Inner sight. Interior worlds.

Blood—Life force.

Boat—Passage from one reality to another. Also see "ship."

Book—Emblem of destiny, wisdom, and scholarship.

Bridge—Place of passage and space linking two worlds or realities.

Bunny—Fertility and life cycles.

• • • • • •

Butterfly—Ancient symbol of the life cycle and elemental symbol of air.

Castle—Home, dwelling, safety, family, protection, familiarity.

Cat—Power of transformation and sensual beauty.

Chain—Heavy oppression.

Child—Purity and innocence. Mystic wisdom and openness.

City—Commerce and the urban environment.

Cliff—No going back, potential danger, landmark.

Cloak—Transformation, protection and devotion; a garment often infused with the magical qualities of a magician or with the power to conceal a true identity.

Clouds—Unseen and mysterious forces. Additionally, clouds, like water surfaces, often reflect the nature of the wind, which can be interpreted as the energy of the situation at hand.

Coffin—Death.

Coins—Commerce, money, and wealth.

Communion Wafer—According to the Christian faith, the communion wafer represents the body, or flesh, of Jesus.

Courtyard—Safety and childhood protection.

Crawfish—Subconscious urges.

Cross—Religion and spirituality, the four elements, axis mundi and celestial pole containing the tension of oppositional polarities and intersection.

Crown—The Hebrew name for the first Sephira on the Tree of Life. Reflects human connection to the Divine.

Crutches—Support and healing.

Cup—Feminine receptivity and the element of water.

Dawn—New beginning. Awakening.

Desert—Landscape used to evoke the element of fire in the wands court cards and reflects all qualities of fire, passion, willpower, courage, spirituality, energy.

Dog—To ancient and primitive religions, dogs were guides and guardians of the underworld. Modern thought assigns loyalty and companionship to the dog.

· · · · · · ·

Dove—Peace, love, compassion. Symbol of Christian Holy Spirit/Holy Ghost. See also "bird."

Dragon—Primordial power. Mythological symbol of ancient and modern people combining multiple elemental creatures usually embodying snake or crocodile scales, forelegs and the head of a lion, eagle, or hawk. Often winged and in various animal combinations.

Eclipse—Unique and transitory moment in time.

Family—Home and the people you are related to, including marriage and adoption.

Field, Plowed—The fecund potential of elemental earth.

Fish—Conveys the suit of cups and element of water.

Flames—Fire and all elements associated with passion, instinct, and consummation.

Flowers—Manifestation of elemental earth and quantifiable growth.

Garden Tool—Object used to make work easier and encourage growth.

Garden—A perfected world of cosmic harmony, design, and manifestation.

Gate—Threshold and place of passage from one reality to another.

Globe—The world as seen from a wide point of view. The big picture.

Grape (Vine)—Fruit of earth and one of the oldest symbols of natural fecundity.

Halo (Nimbus)—Symbol of divinity in the form of glowing radiance. Used in Christian iconography dating back to the fifth century and adapted from ancient sun gods.

Hammer—Helpful or hurtful tool.

Hand Gesture—Imparts hidden language and directs the flow of energy.

Heart—The human-life-sustaining organ of tenderness and love.

Horn (Instrument)—A wake-up call.

Horns (Animal)—Symbol of strength, vitality, and masculinity based in ancient religions and cattle herding and hunting societies. Double symbolism revealed when the horn becomes the container and thus imbues the masculine symbol with feminine power, i.e., the sword transforms in the cup. Classic symbol of the Devil in Christian belief.

· · · · · · ·

Horse—Universal symbol of power and mastery, associated with all elements. Death is usually reflected as a black horse, while white horses assume solar power, as seen in the Death and Sun cards. A horse's gait reflects the energy of a situation at the heart of a tarot reading.

House—Domesticity, comfort, and home.

Iris—Flower connected to the Greek goddess Iris, intermediary of the gods.

Jewels—Riches, treasure, and wealth.

Key—Answers, locking and unlocking.

King—Mature masculinity.

Knight—Adventure, teen energy.

Lantern—Protector of light.

Lemniscate—Symbol of infinity.

Lightning—Illumination, weapon of spiritual transformation.

Lily—Rebirth, motherhood, purity, virtue.

Lily Pads/Lotus Flowers—Regenerative symbol of the soul.

Lion—Symbol of gold, royalty, the sun, strength, and Leo.

Mermaid—Elusive, mercurial water creature carrying the power and potency of the sea. Symbol of the unconscious. Associated with water gods and goddesses.

Monk—Organized religion.

Moon—Occult power, femininity, intuition, and emotion.

Mountain—Meeting place of heaven and earth. The highest any individual can reach toward the infinite; sometimes marks barrier or obstacle.

Nudity—Openness, vulnerability, and freedom. Depicted on Adam and Eve, it reflects the state of primal innocence before their fall.

Ocean—Adventure, emotion, unknown.

Olive Branch—Peace.

Ouroboros—Symbol of a snake or salamander eating its own tail as a symbol of infinity and eternity. The phrase "one is all" often accompanies the image.

· · · · · ·

Page—Childlike youth, innocence, and curiosity.

Palm Branch—Suffering when in conjunction with the Virgin Mary but also victory and longevity.

Parents—Family.

Path—The road that appears before you.

Pentacle (Pentagram)—Five-pointed star and geometric symbol signifying the four elements and the human soul. It was used as the seal of Jerusalem from 300 to 150 BCE. Masons call the symbol a "flaming star," and it enjoys a long history of magical and protective use. When one point is up and two points are down, the pentacle is a sign of white magic. Reversed, with one down and two up, it is considered a sign of the Devil, with the two upward points reflecting Devil horns.

Pentagram (Inverted)—A reversed pentacle, with one point down and two up, is considered the sign of the Devil and an inversion of natural things.

Pillar—Support and structure. Used to symbolize the Kabbalistic Tree of Life. Two pillars usually reflect the left and right side of the tree, with a human in the middle as the center pillar.

Pitcher—Feminine symbol for the womb and liquid vessel similar to a cup.

Pomegranate—Fertility.

Pool—The wellspring of psychic life and symbol of human consciousness.

Pumpkin—Manifestation and harvest.

Pyramids—Suggests the immortality of the Egyptian pharaohs who lie within, also temples to the sun.

Queen—Mature feminine energy.

Rainbow—A celestial bridge linking spirit and earth.

Ram—Solar, hot-headed, bullish energy. Symbol of Aries.

Red Feather—Red is the energy of the spirit, and a feather is the link between world and spirit, therefore the red feather is soaring spiritual energy.

River—Rivers reflect the natural state of energetic flow. Passage of time. High Priestess energy running through the deck.

Salamander—An emblem of the element of fire and all that fire represents. The fire association is likely due to the ancient Roman naturalist Pliny the Elder, who claimed that a salamander could quench a fire with its body, and by the fact that salamanders often took refuge under logs and wood. The wood was brought in for a fire, and the salamanders would appear from the flames.

Scale—Divine judgment, law and order, and the sign of Libra. It represents the point when the sun crosses the equator southward.

Scepter—An ornate symbol of power and authority often taking on spiritual connotations.

Scroll—Secret information, prophecy, and ancient wisdom.

Sea Monster—Adversary, myth, deep-seated fears in the unconscious.

Shell—Feminine symbol of water, beauty, and eroticism.

Ship—Feminine symbol of security, as the ship's interior acts as a womb. Messages, commerce, quest, adventure, passage. Intentions set forth into the world.

Skeleton—Death of the flesh.

Skull—Symbol of mortality but also spirit and energy because the skull is the most resistant part of the human body to decay.

Snail—A typical symbol of slowness and ease. Ancient cultures associated the snail with the moon because it shows and hides its horns like the moon slowly reveals itself. The spiral shell evokes the Golden Spiral and infinity.

Snake—Ancient and complex animal symbol associated with fertility, the penis, the umbilical cord, gyration of birth, and the primeval life force. The snake suggests earth, water, darkness, and the underworld. Regenerative and self-sustaining properties are reflected in the shedding of its own skin. Duality of strength and danger as seen in the latent spiritual power suggested in the coiled yogic Kundalini snake said to reside at the base of the spine.

Snow—Crystalline form of water suggesting moments of intense transformation.

Soldier—Authority and law.

Sphinx—An eternal enigma who is the source of ancient wisdom containing the power to unlock the future. Guardians of the mystery. Originally a human-headed lion in Egypt offering sun god qualities, the symbol was romanticized by occultists.

• • • • • •

Staff (Crook)—A male symbol of supreme power and authority often held by wizards, kings, and wise men.

Stained Glass Window—Christian spirituality and parables are depicted inside the glass.

Star—Stars in the sky, embedded on royal crowns or on fabric reflect heavenly bodies and the celestial realm.

Sun—A universal symbol of life force and creative energy as the center of our solar system and the source of all life and manifestation.

Sunflower—All solar qualities, radiance, joy, and expansion can be applied to the sunflower, who echoes the sun in its bright yellow petals and warm face.

Sword—Symbolizing element of air.

Tav—Hebrew letter meaning "mark."

Tent—Temporality because the tent is portable and usually assembled and disassembled.

Tetramorph—Tarot's tetramorph is based on the four biblical tetramorphs found in the first chapter of Ezekiel who have the heads of a man, lion, ox, and eagle.

Threshold—Space marking the boundary between realities.

Throne—Seat marking power, authority, and stability.

Tower—Ambition, aspiration, watchfulness, and strength. Link between sky and earth.

Tree—Universal symbol of life, interconnectedness, and bridge to other realms.

Veil—Separation and protection. The skein or caul marking the division between the unseen metaphysical world and the seen manifest world. What separates the material from the spiritual world.

Wall—Boundary line and a symbol of separation.

Wand (Ceremonial or Magic Wand)—Wand held in hand to be used in a ceremony, not the organic wand used to symbolize the suit of wands. Connection to the Divine. An object used to direct will and intention.

Wand—Symbol of the suit of wands, representing fire.

· · · · · ·

Water—Element represented by the suit of cups. Universal symbol of life suggesting the fluidity of emotion, dreams, creativity, and love.

Waterfall—Space of energy, creativity, and positive ions.

Waves—Symbol reflecting quality of air in a tarot card but also a sign of tides, lunar power, and forces of fate and the ups and downs of life.

Wheat—Fertility, sustainability, and new life as the regular cultivation of grain in a grain-based culture represented continued life and assured sustenance for all.

Wheel—Symbol of cosmic, karmic, and ceaseless momentum. Time, cycles, life and death.

Wings—Speed, ascension, and inspiration. Linked with the element of air and often found on intermediaries between human and gods. Angels depicted with wings began in sixth century CE art.

Wolf—Humanity's animal nature and fear of letting it show.

Wreath—Celestial symbol of perfection. In life, a symbol of domination and victory; in death, it is a symbol of resurrection.

GLOSSARY

Alchemy, Alchemical—A seemingly magic transformation or a medieval practice that predated chemistry which attempted to transmute elements, specifically items into gold. The work was often expressed via art, symbols, and metaphors and carried a spiritual allegory.

Arcana (Major, Minor)—Secret or mystery, usually used in reference to the tarot deck's cards.

Archangel—An angel of the highest rank, archangels are "higher" angels and considered more powerful than traditional angels.

Archetype—A fundamental concept or universal ideal.

Associative Memory—Spontaneous mental conditioning occurring in all humans where emotional and physical links are made between two separate things. Associative memory is not intuition but learned conditioning.

Astrology—Divination via celestial events.

Attribution—The qualities or features attributed to or given to something. Tarot cards carry multiple attributions, often magical or astrological.

Benediction—Hand blessing given during holy services (Hierophant, Devil, Ten of Swords).

Binah—Third Sephira on the Tree of Life, meaning "understanding." Associated with all tarot threes.

Bodhi (Bo) Tree—Worshiped by Buddhists and Hindus, the sacred tree under which Buddha gained enlightenment.

Card-a-Day—A daily tarot practice where a tarotist pulls a single card every day for guidance, inspiration, education, or divination.

· · · · · · ·

Cardinal Virtues—Four essential values identified by ancient philosophers Plato and Aristotle, which were later adapted by forerunners of the Christian church as desirable characteristics: Justice, Prudence, Temperance, and Fortitude. Three of the four virtues appear in the major arcana. The virtues were a popular topic of Renaissance art.

Cartomancer—An individual who divines using tarot, oracle, or playing cards.

Cartomancy—Divination by cards.

Chakra(s)—Wheels of spiritual energy located inside the human body.

Chesed—The fourth Sephira on the Tree of Life, meaning "mercy." Associated with all tarot fours.

Chokmah—The second Sephira of the Tree of Life, meaning "wisdom." Associated with all tarot twos.

Cipher Alphabet—An alphabet used to conceal secrets; a secret code. In relation to the RWS deck, Mathers decoded the cipher alphabet in the Cipher Manuscripts, which were the foundational documents of the Golden Dawn.

Clairalience—The ability to smell scent outside the natural world.

Clairaudience—The ability to hear messages but without actually using your ears.

Claircognizance—The ability to know something without knowing why you know it.

Clairvoyance—The ability to "see" an image or picture in your head.

Consciousness—Awareness or individual perception.

Cups—The tarot suit reflecting the element of water, also signifying emotion, feelings, and love.

Dee, John—Queen Elizabeth's astrologer and occult philosopher.

Deity—Divine god or goddess.

Direction—Refers to the traditional four directions, north, south, east, or west.

Divination—The act of foretelling a future event via supernatural means.

Divine/Divinity—The state of being divine; refers to godlike qualities.

Dweller at the Threshold—Guardian of the subconscious.

Ego—Part of the mind containing personal identity.

• • • • • • •

Element, Elemental—Referring to the four classical elements, earth, air, fire, and water.

Empathy/Empath—The ability to feel the emotional state of others by being near them. Empaths actively experience this ability on an ongoing basis.

Empowerment—Becoming stronger and more confidant in the self.

Esoteric—A thing intended to be understood by a small or select group. Confidential. Private. Secret.

Eucharist—Christian rite where consecrated bread and wine are consumed in honor of Jesus and his Last Supper. Seen on the Ace of Cups in the symbol of dove, wafer, and cup.

Exoteric—Information that is intended for public consumption. In relation to the RWS deck, exoteric is the oppositional reference to the secret canon of tarot in the Golden Dawn's *Book T*.

Fecundity—Fertility.

Geburah—The fifth Sephira on the Tree of Life, meaning "strength." Associated with all tarot fives.

Golden Dawn—Influential magical group springing from the nineteenth century who contributed to modern occultism. Arthur Waite and Pamela Colman Smith were both members.

Hero's Journey—A term coined by Joseph Campbell referring to the cross-cultural pattern of mythology and storytelling sharing common elements worldwide.

Hod—The eighth Sephira on the Tree of Life, meaning "splendor." Associated with all tarot eights.

Holy Table—An altar.

Initiation—A ritual created to bring individuals into a secret group.

Kabbalah (also Qabalah)—Ancient Jewish mystical system describing the operation of the universe in relation to divine manifestation. The Tree of Life is used to express divine nature. Tarot scholars associate the tarot with the tree as a way of understanding both.

Kabbalistic Attribution—The Hebrew letter assigned to each major arcana.

· · · · · · ·

Kether—The first Sephira on the Tree of Life, meaning "crown," and associated with all tarot aces.

Key—Cards. In relation to the Rider-Waite-Smith deck, the individual cards are often referred to as keys.

Lemniscate—Sideways eight reflecting the yin and yang of never ending life; also the Martinistic symbol of Christ.

Lotus Flowers—Symbol used by Golden Dawn and a myriad of cultures; in a broad sense they symbolize rebirth.

Major Arcana—The first twenty-two cards of the tarot deck, numbered 0–21. Also called trump cards.

Malkuth—The tenth and final Sephira on the Tree of Life, meaning "kingdom." Associated with all tarot tens.

Metaphysical—Related to a reality beyond what is perceptible to the senses.

Middle Pillar—The integrating pillar on the Tree of Life, composed of Sephiroth 1, 6, 9, and 10.

Minor Arcana—Aces through tens and all court cards of the tarot deck. Often called pip cards or minors.

Narrative—The arc or events in a story. As related to tarot, the cards reflect a narrative for the reader.

Netzach—The seventh Sephira on the Tree of Life, meaning "victory." Associated with all tarot sevens.

Numerology—Knowledge of the occult significance of numbers. Relating to tarot, each card carries a number that can be used for further interpretation.

Nymphs—Feminine spirits of the natural world. These mini goddesses and minor deities sprang from lakes, springs, seas, rivers, and waterfalls.

Occult—Secret. Relating to or dealing with supernatural phenomena. Something hidden from view.

Operative Masonry—Freemasons who are active, working, professional Masonic builders.

Ouroboros—Symbol of a snake or salamander eating its own tail as a symbol of infinity and the never-ending circle of life.

· · · · · · ·

Pentacles—Tarot suit relating to the element of earth and reflecting material items, people, and money.

Pillar of Mercy—The right pillar of the Tree of Life; comprised of Sephiroth 2, 4, and 7.

Pillar of Severity—The left pillar of the Tree of Life; comprised of Sephiroth 3, 5, and 8.

Prana—The Sanskrit word describing the vital universal life force of all things. The term is used often in yoga, Hindu philosophy, and martial arts.

Pranayama Breath—Intentional breathing focused on controlling and extending the yogi's breath, which is considered the universal life force. The practice is believed to open energetic pathways, purify the mind, and contain numerous holistic, emotional, and physical benefits.

Profane—Of the normal world and secular rather than spiritual.

Psychic—Manner of gaining knowledge through something other than direct communication.

Querent—An old-fashioned term for a person who visits and receives a reading from a tarot reader.

Reversals—Tarot cards that appear in a spread upside down. It is up to the reader to assign additional meaning to a reversal if they choose.

Rota—Latin word meaning "wheel." Found on the Wheel of Fortune card.

Sacred—Defined space that is holy or supernatural.

Scrim—Piece of gauze or fabric used in theater as a painted backdrop. Each of Pamela's stage cards reflects a scrim.

Sepher Yetzirah—Ancient text explaining the Kabbalistic Tree of Life.

Sephiroth—The ten circles of Divinity on the Tree of Life.

Serpent-Cincture—The symbol of a serpent or snake devouring its own tail, as in the belt of the Magician card. Conventional symbol of eternity. See also "ouroboros."

Shadow Self—Phrase and idea created by Jung, meaning the part of the human psyche where we bury our deepest desires, fears, talents, and issues we are unable to bring to the surface, acknowledge, and accept. Often associated with the Moon card and what lingers beneath the surface of the water pools inside the tarot.

• • • • • • •

Significator—Card purposefully chosen to represent the person the reading is for or the situation the reading pertains to.

Speculative Masonry—Freemasonry for men who are not professional Masonic builders.

Stage Card—Thirteen tarot cards designed by Pamela Colman Smith that are drawn on a stage.

Subconscious—The part of consciousness that the individual is not aware of.

Supernal Triad—The top triad of the Tree of Life, the first three Sephiroth forming a trinity and locking in the godhead.

Supernatural—An occurrence or things relating to an order of existence beyond the visible universe.

Swords—Tarot suit relating to the element of air and reflecting the qualities of the mind, thoughts, and calculation.

Synchronicity—The experience of two or more events appearing to be meaningfully related.

Tattva Tradition—The Golden Dawn used tattva symbols and invocations to work with as they rose through initiatory grades.

Tetragrammaton—The fourfold expression of the Hebrew deity and God, containing the Hebrew letters Yod Heh Vau Heh.

Tetramorph—Four creatures found in the four corners of the Wheel of Fortune and World cards. This is a cross-cultural symbol reflecting four directions in space and divine dominion. Tarot's tetramorph is based on the four biblical tetramorphs found in the first chapter of Ezekiel who have the heads of a man, lion, ox, and eagle.

Timing—Using the tarot cards to predict the date or time of a future event.

Tiphareth—The sixth Sephira on the Tree of Life, meaning "beauty." Associated with all tarot sixes.

Tora—Scroll on the High Priestess's lap. Also appears on the Wheel of Fortune card.

Tree of Life—Representation of the nature of divinity and reality via ten circles and pathways looking like a tree.

Trump Card—Slang for a major arcana card numbered 0 to 21. Each ascending card carries a higher or greater power over the last.

Undine—From the Latin word *under*, meaning wave or water. A European tradition of the spirits who inhabit the element of water.

Visualization—Using a tarot card or other image in the mind's eye and exploring it through the creative imagination.

Wand—The tarot symbol depicting the element of fire. In other, earlier decks, called a staff or stick.

Yesod—The ninth Sephira on the Tree of Life, meaning "foundation." Associates with all tarot nines.

Yoga—A broad group of physical, mental, and spiritual practices developed in India.

Yogi—One who practices yoga.

THANK YOU

Deep gratitude to the following:

To the librarians of the Berg Collection of English and American Literature, the New York Public Library, Astor, Lenox and Tilden Foundations, thank you for the peace and quiet of your sequestered wooden rooms and allowing me to convene with Stoker, Yeats, Waite, and Pamela.

To Rebecca Zins, my editor, thank you from the bottom of my heart. You are amazing. I love working with you. To Mary Greer, thank you for your enthusiasm and for your lifetime pursuit of the tarot that profoundly touches each and every one of us. Barbara Moore, you are the reason this book came to light—for the lessons and eloquence, spoken and unspoken, you continue to shower upon all of us; and thank you for believing in me. Stuart Kaplan, for sharing your story, wisdom, and collection; it was a true honor. Thank you. Lynn Sparrow, a true delight, for your support and enthusiasm, thank you. Susan Wands, beguiling, beautiful creature and steadfast friend whose kindness, giving, and care knows no bounds. Thank you for holding Pamela up for all the world to see. Forever your "Ducks." Wald and Ruth Ann Amberstone. I could not have written this book without the foundational understanding of the Tree of Life you gave me at the Tarot School. After all these years, I still look to the cards and hear your voices in my head. Thank you for being my teachers.

Deep gratitude for sub rosa undercurrents who thread silken strands of meaning through a person's life. These connective threads, like spider's silk, thin and invisible, often lie unseen until a roving path of sunlight illuminates it. They become dazzling strings of possibility if only for a few moments. Time is oppositional. It doesn't erase; it enriches. For this wellspring of creativity, healing, and possibility, I am eternally grateful. Thank you.

Thank you to my supernatural woodland muse, Autumn Marie, who keeps a golden toe dipped in each world. Thank you for the tarot of the body and showing me how movement speaks, heals, and often communicates on a deeper level than words. Bill and Isabella, my two pillars, a boyishly handsome husband and a gorgeous, beautiful girl. I love our trinity of a family and each of you so much. Endless thank yous for bearing with me while writing this book. I promise you both: fiction next.

· · · · · · ·

IMAGE CREDITS

PAGE	CREDIT INFORMATION
	Rider-Waite Tarot Deck®, also known as the Rider Tarot and the Waite Tarot, reproduced by permission of U.S. Games Systems, Inc., Stamford, CT 06902 USA. Copyright ©1971 by U.S. Games Systems, Inc. Further reproduction prohibited. The Rider-Waite Tarot Deck® is a registered trademark of U.S. Games Systems, Inc.
4	Marseille Tarot used by permission of Lo Scarabeo.
4	Shadowscapes Tarot by Barbara Moore and Stephanie Pui-Mun Law used by permission of Llewellyn.
4	Steampunk Tarot by Barbara Moore and Aly Fell used by permission of Llewellyn.
6	Photo of Arthur Edward Waite, London, January 13, 1921, from the Miriam and Ira D. Wallach Division of Art, Prints and Photographs: Photography Collection, The New York Public Library. New York Public Library Digital Collections. Accessed May 29, 2018. http://digitalcollections.nypl.org/items/510d47db-b7b1-a3d9-e040-e00a18064a99
6	Photo of Arthur E. Waite from *Strange Houses of Sleep*, 1906. The Internet Archive. Accessed May 30, 2018. https://archive.org/details/strangehousesofs00waitrich
6	Photo of Pamela Colman Smith from Babel Hathitrust Digital Library. "The Delineator, Vol 80, Pamela Colman Smith, She Believes in Fairies, November 1912." Accessed May 30, 2018. https://babel.hathitrust.org/cgi/pt?id=iau.31858046092171;view=1up;seq=308
6	Photo of Stuart R. Kaplan courtesy of Stuart R. Kaplan. Image is not for reproduction.
9	From *Book of Friendly Giants* by Pamela Colman Smith. Reproduced from the library of Stuart R. Kaplan.
23	Reading Room of the British Library. Wood Engraving, 1859. Library of Congress Prints and Photographs Online Catalogue. Accessed May 30, 2018. http://www.loc.gov/pictures/item/2007682650/
25	W. B. Yeats drawing by Pamela Colman Smith from Miriam and Ira D. Wallach Division of Art, Prints and Photographs: Print Collection, The New York Public Library Digital Collections. http://digitalcollections.nypl.org/items/33ee7390-45ca-0133-a62c-00505686a51c
27	Toy theater photograph from The University of Michigan. "Brush and Pencil: An Illustrated Magazine of the Arts of Today, Volume 6, Issue 3, P. 135, 1900." Google Digitized. Accessed May 30, 2018. https://books.google.com/books?id=2ge1PI33O9cC&pg =PA143&source=gbs_toc_r&cad=3#v=onepage&q&f=false

• • • • • • •

90	Fool image from Eunice Fuller, *The Book of Friendly Giants*, illustrated by Pamela Colman Smith. New York: The Century Company, 1914. Courtesy of Stuart R. Kaplan.
	Ellen Terry and her dog photo courtesy of the private collection of Geraldine Beskin, owner of Atlantis Bookshop in Bloomsbury, London.
	Tarot of Marseille image used by permission of Lo Scarabeo.
94	Visconti Tarot image used by permission of Lo Scarabeo.
100	Visconti Tarot image used by permission of Lo Scarabeo.
104	Tarot of Marseille image used by permission of Lo Scarabeo.
108	Emperor image from Eunice Fuller, *The Book of Friendly Giants*, illustrated by Pamela Colman Smith. New York: The Century Company, 1914. Courtesy of Stuart R. Kaplan.
	Visconti Tarot image used by permission of Lo Scarabeo.
112	Tarot of Marseille image used by permission of Lo Scarabeo.
116	Tarot of Marseille image used by permission of Lo Scarabeo.
120	Chariot image from Eunice Fuller, *The Book of Friendly Giants*, illustrated by Pamela Colman Smith. New York: The Century Company, 1914. Courtesy of Stuart R. Kaplan.
	Tarot of Marseille image used by permission of Lo Scarabeo.
124	Tarot of Marseille image used by permission of Lo Scarabeo.
128	Hermit image from Eunice Fuller, *The Book of Friendly Giants*, illustrated by Pamela Colman Smith. New York: The Century Company, 1914. Courtesy of Stuart R. Kaplan.
	Visconti Tarot image used by permission of Lo Scarabeo.
132	Visconti Tarot image used by permission of Lo Scarabeo.
138	Tarot of Marseille image used by permission of Lo Scarabeo.
142	Visconti Tarot image used by permission of Lo Scarabeo.
146	Death image from Eunice Fuller, *The Book of Friendly Giants*, illustrated by Pamela Colman Smith. New York: The Century Company, 1914. Courtesy of Stuart R. Kaplan.
	Visconti Tarot image used by permission of Lo Scarabeo.
150	Tarot of Marseille image used by permission of Lo Scarabeo.
156	Lévi's Devil from the Internet Archive, "Transcendental Magic, its Doctrine and Ritual." Éliphas, Lévi. 1896. Accessed May 30, 2018. https://archive.org/details/transcendentalma00leviuoft
160	Tarot of Marseille image used by permission of Lo Scarabeo.
164	Tarot of Marseille image used by permission of Lo Scarabeo.
168	Moon tower illustration from the Miriam and Ira D. Wallach Division of Art, Prints and Photographs: Art & Architecture Collection, The New York Public Library. "From a drawing by Pamela Colman Smith." New York Public Library Digital Collections. Accessed June 6, 2018. http://digitalcollections.nypl.org/items/6666c040-6a6d-0135-0fd6-0b924b53236c
	Tarot of Marseille image used by permission of Lo Scarabeo.
174	Tarot of Marseille image used by permission of Lo Scarabeo.
178	Tarot of Marseille image used by permission of Lo Scarabeo.
182	Tarot of Marseille image used by permission of Lo Scarabeo.

· · · · · ·

192   Ellen Terry photo from Billy Rose Theatre Division, The New York Public Library. "Ellen Terry in *The Merchant of Venice* by William Shakespeare." New York Public Library Digital Collections. Accessed June 13, 2018.
http://digitalcollections.nypl.org/items/510d47de-963d-a3d9-e040-e00a18064a99

Ellen Terry illustration from Library of Congress Prints and Photographs Division, Washington. "The reappearance of Ellen Terry in the October *McClure's* 15¢" 1907. Accessed May 30, 2018.
http://hdl.loc.gov/loc.pnp/pp.print

204   Sola Busca Tarot image used by permission of Lo Scarabeo.

216   Sola Busca Tarot image used by permission of Lo Scarabeo.

218   Ace of Cups images from Eunice Fuller, *The Book of Friendly Giants*, illustrated by Pamela Colman Smith. New York: The Century Company, 1914. Courtesy of Stuart R. Kaplan.

224   Photo of Ellen Terry in a flowy costume from Billy Rose Theatre Division, The New York Public Library. "The Amber Heart." New York Public Library Digital Collections. Accessed June 13, 2018.
http://digitalcollections.nypl.org/items/510d47d9-d29d-a3d9-e040-e00a18064a99

234   Giant feet image from Eunice Fuller, *The Book of Friendly Giants*, illustrated by Pamela Colman Smith. New York: The Century Company, 1914. Courtesy of Stuart R. Kaplan.

256   Sola Busca Tarot image used by permission of Lo Scarabeo.

268   Creeper image from Eunice Fuller, *The Book of Friendly Giants*, illustrated by Pamela Colman Smith. New York: The Century Company, 1914. Courtesy of Stuart R. Kaplan.

Sola Busca Tarot image used by permission of Lo Scarabeo.

272   Background castle and cliffs illustration from Eunice Fuller, *The Book of Friendly Giants*, illustrated by Pamela Colman Smith. New York: The Century Company, 1914. Courtesy of Stuart R. Kaplan.

298   Tarocchi of Mantegna (E-series) image used by permission of Lo Scarabeo.

302   Tarocchi of Mantegna (E-series) image used by permission of Lo Scarabeo.

304   Tarocchi of Mantegna (E-series) image used by permission of Lo Scarabeo.

318   Photo of Ellen Terry from Billy Rose Theatre Division, The New York Public Library. "Ellen Terry." New York Public Library Digital Collections. Accessed June 13, 2018.
http://digitalcollections.nypl.org/items/510d47df-4f11-a3d9-e040-e00a18064a99

320   Sola Busca Tarot image used by permission of Lo Scarabeo.

330   Dover cliffs image from Eunice Fuller, *The Book of Friendly Giants*, illustrated by Pamela Colman Smith. New York: The Century Company, 1914. Courtesy of Stuart R. Kaplan.

Sola Busca Tarot image used by permission of Lo Scarabeo.

340   Sola Busca Tarot image used by permission of Lo Scarabeo.

342   Sola Busca Tarot image used by permission of Lo Scarabeo.

356   Sola Busca Tarot image used by permission of Lo Scarabeo.

· · · · · ·

XIV

TEMPERANCE

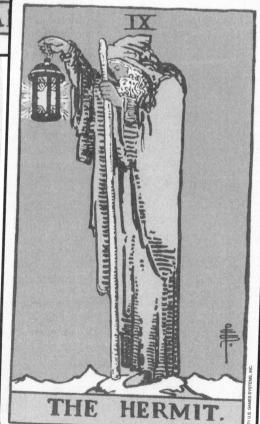

IX

PAGE of SWORDS.

THE HERMIT.

BIBLIOGRAPHY

Baroni, Helen Josephine. *The Illustrated Encyclopedia of Zen Buddhism.* New York: The Rosen Group, 2002.

Barrabbas, Frater. *Magical Qabalah for Beginners.* Woodbury, MN: Llewellyn, 2013.

Carr-Gomm, Phillip, and Richard Heygate. *Book of English Magic.* New York: The Overlook Press, 2010.

Decker, Ronald, and Michael Dummett. *History of the Occult Tarot.* New York: The Overlook Press, 2013.

Dell, Christopher. *The Occult, Witchcraft and Magic: An Illustrated History.* London: Thames & Hudson, 2016.

DuQuette, Lon Milo. *The Chicken Qabalah.* York Beach, ME: Weiser, 2001.

Eliot, T. S. *Collected Poems, 1909–1935.* London: Faber & Faber Limited.

Fiebig, Johannes, and Evelin Burger. *The Ultimate Guide to the Rider Waite Tarot.* Woodbury, MN: Llewellyn, 2014.

Gilbert, R. A. *A. E. Waite: A Magician of Many Parts.* Wellingborough, Northamptonshire: Crucible, 1987.

Greer, Mary. *Women of the Golden Dawn: Rebels and Priestesses.* Rochester, VT: Park Street Press, 1998.

Greer, Mary, and Tom Little. *Understanding the Tarot Court.* Woodbury, MN: Llewellyn, 2006.

Hulse, David Allen. *The Key of It All: An Encyclopedic Guide to all the Sacred Languages and Magickal Systems of the World.* St. Paul, MN: Llewellyn, 1994.

Kaplan, Stuart, and Jean Huets. *Encyclopedia of Tarot.* New York: U.S. Games Systems, 1990.

Katz, Marcus, and Tali Goodwin. *Secrets of the Waite-Smith Tarot: The True Story of the World's Most Popular Tarot.* Woodbury, MN: Llewellyn, 2015.

Kenner, Corrine. *Tarot and Astrology.* Woodbury, MN: Llewellyn, 2011.

Leach, Maria, and Jerome Fried, eds. *Funk and Wagnalls Standard Dictionary of Folklore and Legend.* New York: Funk and Wagnalls, 1949.

MacDonald, Irwin M. "The Fairy Faith and Pictured Music of Pamela Colman Smith," *The Craftsman* (October 1912).

"Made Veteran Humorist Laugh," *The Evening Statesman* (February 27, 1907).

Owen, Alex. *Places of Enchantment: British Occultism and the Culture of the Modern.* Chicago: University of Chicago Press, 2004.

Parsons, Melinda Boyd. *To All Believers—The Art of Pamela Colman Smith.* Delaware Art Museum, 1975.

Ransome, Arthur. *Bohemia in London.* Chapman and Hall, 1907.

"Representative Women Illustrators," *The Critic*, volume 36 (1900), 527.

Ronnberg, Ami, and Kathleen Martin, eds. *The Book of Symbols: Reflections on Archetypal Images.* Taschen, 2010.

R. R. G. "Pamela Colman Smith, She Believes in Fairies," *The Delineator* (November 1912), 320.

Shakespeare, William. *The Merchant of Venice.* New York: Signet Classic, 1998.

Smith, Pamela Colman, "Alone," *The Green Sheath*, no. 3 (1903), 9.

———, *Annancy Stories* (R. H. Russell, 1899), 51.

———. Handwritten letter to Arthur Stieglitz, November 19, 1909.

———. "Pictures in Music," *The Strand Magazine: An Illustrated Monthly*, vol. XXXV, January–June 1908.

———. "Should the Art Student Think?" *The Craftsman*, vol. XIV, no. 4 (July 1908).

Tell, Gardner. "Cleverness, Art and an Artist," *Brush and Pencil: An Illustrated Magazine of the Arts*, volume 6, issue 3, 1900.

Tolle, Eckhart. *The Power of Now.* Canada: New World Library, 1999.

Tresidder, Jack. *Watkins Dictionary of Symbols.* London: Watkins Publishing, 2008.

Waite, Arthur Edward. *Collected Poems.* London: Rider Publishing, 1914.

———. *The Doctrine and Literature of the Kabalah.* London: The Theosophical Publishing Society, 1902.

———. *The Holy Kabalah.* Secaucus, NJ: Citadel Press, 1929.

———. *Shadows of Life and Thought: A Retrospective Review in the Form of Memoirs.* London: Selwyn and Blount, 1938.

Williamson, Marianne. *A Return to Love: Reflections on the Principles of A Course in Miracles.* New York: Harper Collins, 1992.

"Witchery in London Drawing Rooms," *Brooklyn Eagle*, November 1, 1904.

INDEX

• • • • • •

• • • • • • •

· · · · · ·

• • • • • •